INDIA'S FOREIGN POLICY

CONTEMPORARY TRENDS

Edited by

R.S. Yadav
Suresh Dhanda

SHIPRA

(First Published in India in 2009)

Price Rs. 350; US$ 17.50

ISBN: 978-81-7541-475-4

2012 Impression

India's Foreign Policy: Contemporary Trends

Published by:

SHIPRA PUBLICATIONS
LG 18-19, Pankaj Central Market
I.P. Ext., Patparganj, Delhi 110092
Ph. 22235152, 22236152
Br. Off.: 4617/18, Ansari Road, Daryaganj,
New Delhi 110002; Ph. 6594 6453, 9810522367

Email: info@shiprapublications.com
Website: www.shiprapublications.com

In Honour of
Professor Devendra Kaushik

Preface

Changes in Post-cold war era in domestic as well as external milieu of India, have not only posed new opportunities and challenges for its domestic politics, but have also led to dynamic changes in its orientation and outlook towards outside world for the pursuit of its national interests. In the domestic sphere, India's projection of 8-10 percent of growth of GDP, acquisition of nuclear status, performance in soft infrastructure (with exceptional growth in IT sector) etc. have not only changed India's perception of itself, but also the world's perception towards it. The changes in the global environment such as, the demise of socialist system, initiation of process of globalization, declining position of international organization and reduction in importance of forums like NAM have made it imperative for India to review its old foreign policy nuances. As a result, despite hesitation to make a departure from continuity, India has been gradually moving towards a new phase in its global outlook. This change has been, drastic and significant, to the extent that a paradigm shift is evident in India's foreign policy.

Taking full cognition of tremendous shift in the global strategic and economic scenario it becomes imperative for India to take new initiatives to fine tune its foreign policy to reap maximum dividends. This shift is manifest in India's departure from its policy of non-alignment to alignment with powers, joining of new regional economic groupings, and linking it from proximate neighbours to extended neighbourhood. India is also exhibiting consciousness about non-conventional concerns and issues, as well as, orienting itself towards changed context of security threats of both traditional and contemporary nature. Simultaneously, it is equipping itself with new capabilities and strategies through acquisition of nuclear status, strategic partnerships with major centers of power, assertion for UN Security Council membership and enhanced bilateral and multilateral economic cooperation.

However, in this changed context, it is not going to be smooth sailing for India. If, at the domestic level, there is a need for India to develop requisite consensus for its foreign policy goals, then, at the external level, it has to acquire acceptability as a power center among community of nations. Along with this, concerted efforts are to be evolved, with the help of like minded powers, to deal with multiple and complex threats in the wake of prevailing international terrorism and proliferation of weapons of mass destructions (WMDs). Simultaneously, multilateral cooperation needs to be generated to handle the recessionary trends in global economic system. For this, need is not only to have a sound policy capable of dealing with contemporary challenges, but also to develop a long term vision for India's foreign policy. Present volume aims at tracing the emerging trends, as well as, suggesting some measures for the policy planners for shaping India's long-term foreign policy perspectives.

In the accomplishment of this task we have received help from number of individuals and institutions, we are indebted to them. We are also grateful to all the contributors who promptly responded to our request and send their papers. However, Professor Devendra Kaushik deserves special mention as he has not only always been perennial source of academic inspiration to us, but also guided us throughout this project. We are also thankful to Principal Y.P. Mehta, Prof. Leela Yadava, Sh. Anil Gautam and Mr. Vivek Rattan for their unstinted support and encouragements. Mr. D. Kumar also deserves appreciation in bringing out this volume with meticulous care and efficiency.

R.S. Yadav
Suresh Dhanda

Contents

V. Security Challenges

VI. Non-Conventional Affairs

Introduction

I

Developments in the global system in the last two decades have been of a very significant nature which has affected not only the very characteristic of it, but rather had serious bearing on India as well. They provided numerous challenges and opportunities for the policy makers in the country. Changed context has not only transformed the very structure and geo-political setting of the global system, but also influenced the operational dynamics in a significant manner. The degree of departure made from geo-politics to geo-economics has made the global milieu qualitatively different from the one which used to be witnessed during the cold war era. Consequently, foreign policies of states are bound to reorient and readjust themselves to these new realities. India is no exception to such a phenomenon. It not only has to respond to the new changes, but also has to achieve its foreign policy goals by skillful handling of the global milieu.

Three important factors have influenced the making of India's foreign policy in the post–1991 era. First, in the changed character of the world order in the post-cold war era India no longer has to constrain itself to South Asia. It has to interact with new actors who have acquired importance in the transformed world order. Second, the introduction of structural reforms and steadily performing economy has not only changed India's perception of itself but the world perception towards India. Its performance in soft infrastructure, with its exceptional growth in information technology sector, has changed the status of Indian economy to a large extent. It has been rightly observed that, "India, with its good legal structure, corporate governance, banking system, financial sector, property rights security, its skilled manpower and young work force, has become the new economic icon of the emerging power...."[1] Finally, its nuclear test in May 1998 has further enhanced its status as a major power. It has boosted its image from a developing state to that of a power to be reckoned with. Thus, the over all image of India in strategic, economic and political terms has led to a qualitative transformation of its status in the world.

India's foreign policy today demonstrates an increasing tempering of Nehruvian idealism and movement towards pragmatism in a multilateral and rule based global system.[2] It is a departure of its earlier power of idea to that of augmentation of economic and political power. Its new thrust of non-alignment also seems to be engaging many to meet out its new security and economic requirements. Consequently, it is building strategic, political and economic alliances at the bilateral, regional and global levels. For playing a larger role it is inevitable for India that engagement with neighbours be its top priority. Consequently, it is not only wooing both Pakistan and China on the one hand, and strengthening economic cooperation with all the states in South Asia through SAARC, on the other hand. Pursuit of CBMs with Pakistan as part of contemporary peace process and enhancing trade and initiating border talks through special political representatives with China are proofs of such policy. Even involvement of outside powers at this juncture has been welcomed. This is manifest from the grant of observer status to USA, China and Japan during the last SAARC conference.

At regional level, India's involvement and interests are clearly manifested in its extended neighbourhood policy. Under this policy engagements in the Central Asian republics (CARs) and Southeast Asia are envisaged. India's long term energy security and economic interests are being pursued through the building of warm relations with CARs. Efforts are also made to expand its influence in this region by participating in the activities of the Shanghai Cooperation Organization (SCO) as observer and acquisition of first ever military base by India outside its sovereign jurisdiction. Through its 'Look East' policy, India is enhancing its influence among Southeast Asian states by actively participating in the activities of ASEAN and ARF. This regional role is further extended by enthusiastically initiating the process of cooperation through East Asia Summit (EAS). These moves have strengthened India's strategic understanding and economic cooperation in this region. India is also looking to Malacca straits through its strategic vision and it is sought to be accomplished by forming the Indian Ocean Rim – Association for Regional Cooperation (IOR-ARC) in 1997. However, the momentum of cooperation could not achieve the desired pace through the activities of the association.

India's foreign policy pursuit is not limited to neighbours or extended neighbours only, rather its engagement at international level is to enhance its power and influence with all the major powers of the day. Most dramatic outcome has been in its relations with the USA as the two states have moved from the position of 'estranged democracies'[3] to 'engaged democracies'.[4] Beginning with 'military-to-military cooperation' with the Kickleighter proposal, both have committed themselves to reach the stage of "natural ally"[5] and 'objective convergence in the areas of *values* as well as *interests*.'[6] Signing of Indo-US civil nuclear deal has further strengthened their ties as it has accorded special status to India as sixth nuclear power state, outside the nuclear regime. Besides, India is also pursuing strategic partnership with other major global powers like EU, Japan and Russia and 'strategic cooperation' with China. In addition, it is also making efforts to get a permanent seat in UNSC.

India's efforts at this juncture have been evaluated differently by the analysts. Some have viewed this projection of India towards a global role as bandwagoning with the hegemonic power, while others are of the view that India is more concerned with the accommodation of its national interest in a multilateral world order based on global governance by existing institutional arrangements. The second assessment seems nearer to reality as India is not much concerned with the change in system; rather it seeks to make adjustment to existing order where India's national interest could be attained. It seeks to expand its power and influence by enhancing bilateral cooperation with the USA, EU, Russia, China and Japan as well as by involving itself in the regional and global arrangements by skillful use of its soft power.

However, every thing is not going to be smooth for India, as long term consequences of such policy need reconciliation of numerous sorts. C. Raja Mohan is right in his observation that India's imperative of idealism and moralism has not completely disappeared. Its change from traditional emphasis on the "power of the argument" to a new stress on the "argument of power" will result into tension between "power and principle" and is bound to be difficult to reconcile.[7] Besides, it has to find ways to limit the pursuit of 'national interest' in order to contribute to 'collective interests' of the global system. Further, it will be hard for India to make choices in favour of one power or the other in future balance of power in the world. Moreover, its contribution for peace and stability in the neighbourhood and extended neighbourhood would dramatically increase India's burden.[8] To what extent it is going to be successful in such endeavour, only time can tell.

For clarity and understanding of the new moorings of India's foreign policy, the book, containing nineteen essays, has been divided into six parts. First part presents the theoretical and operational dynamics of the contemporary world order to evaluate and find out how India is adjusting itself to the changing international environment. The second part focuses on India's relations with major power centres, as new realities of post-cold war era have transformed the underpinnings of the global order in a significant way. Here, an effort has been made to know that why there has been a paradigm shift in Indo-US relations. India's relations with Russia have also been examined in a new framework to find out not only the continuity and change but also how strategic partnership between them has evolved and is working. Thrust of both these have been to discern the likely implication for such relationship on the future role of India in a global scenario. The relations with neighbours have been the area of core concern for the third section. This becomes all the more significant in the light of development of India's ties with most of its neighbours. In the changed context, it is pertinent to have a fresh look on these relations. India's relations with two major countries like China and Pakistan, along with Myanmar and two small neighbours, affecting South and Southeast Asian polity in a significant way, have also been evaluated. Selection of these neighbours, however, in no way reduces the importance of other states for the understanding of changing contours of India's foreign policy towards them. The fourth part encompasses the essays related to India's regional approach towards its extended neighbourhood. Its understanding with West Asia, Southeast Asia and Central Asia has been evaluated to discern the impact of regional milieu of India. Its relations with the European Union and SAARC have been incorporated to understand the impact of emerging thrust of economic regions in global politics and how India is responding to this dimension with the introduction of structural reforms in its economic orientation in the post-cold war era. Security concern of the country can not be ignored by the experts of country's foreign policy as the latter works as one of the core objectives of its foreign affairs. Consequently, the fifth part is concentrated on India's response towards these security challenges. Old security concerns regarding Kashmir and new challenges emanating from Post-Pokhran-II and Post–9/11 are taken into account. The last segment comprises various non-conventional issues affecting India's foreign policy in the changing times. These new areas are energy security, economic policy, environment protection and refugee problems. These are not mere domestic issues, but are closely linked with global happenings and are likely to have spill over impact on India's foreign policy. Though some more areas could have been incorporated in the present work, yet due to scarcity of time and limitation on the part of contributors such additions have not been possible. However, this has in no way impinged on the understanding of the changing contours of India's foreign policy in the new global context.

II

The study begins with a discussion on theoretical framework for the post-cold war global order. Shifting paradigm of the world order has been evaluated by Devendra Kaushik with his deep insight and authentic facts at his command. This has been done to present a categorical view of global milieu in which India's policy makers can realize their objectives in a most appropriate manner. He evaluated the emerging challenges and opportunities for India's foreign policy in the shifting global paradigm. Kaushik is critical of the process of globalization and emerging unipolarity which are strengthening the hegemony of USA. But more importantly the rising power of Asia and declining economic position of USA in the contemporary global power structure are highlighted by him. In his view the disturbing trend has been the thinking of Indian policy makers, who are visualizing an important role for India by enhancing its power capabilities supported by the Americans. He comes out with the deepening tripartite Eurasian cooperation among India-Russia-China as the only solution to save the mankind from disastrous course of endless struggle against unipolarity under US hegemony. Simultaneously, he argues in favour of the need for theoretical re-orientation of non-alignment to fight against the subversive and exploitative tendencies of the present global order. Hence, there is need to evolve a new national consensus regarding theoretical basis of India's foreign policy, along with the support from major Asian and Latin American states, to create a countervailing force against the negative consequences of present world order.

R.S. Yadav traces the changing contours of India's foreign policy in the context of new international milieu as the latter works as major determinant in the making of any country's foreign policy. He analyses India's foreign policy in the context of structural and operational dynamics of the changing world. Structurally, he is of the view that world situation is still in a flux and is full of uncertainties. This has been established from the interpretation of various scholars, who have concluded that present world order is of a hybrid nature, mixing realist, idealist and constructive explanations. Hence multi-level interdependence exists where all states are connected to various permutations and combinations. Operationally, the world is neither unipolar nor multi-polar, but a slight edge has been towards USA and the latter is maintaining the position with the collaboration of one or the other centre of power. Most of the developing countries, including India, are managing their interests in a very difficult manner in an undemocratic order. Thus to fulfill its foreign policy goals, India is managing through the three fold strategies: shifting alignments; consolidating economic cooperation; and, confronting strategic challenges. Despite these it is going to be very arduous for India to attain its objectives without skillful maneouvering of its diplomacy at global, regional and bilateral levels. Thus vast changes in India's foreign policy orientation are inevitable to handle the emanating crises arising from the changed global milieu. It has to save its autonomy in the era of globalization and to build new kind of domestic consensus and economic power to save itself from the negative onslaughts of the prevailing realities of contemporary world.

Chintamani Mahapatra has analyzed the problems and prospects of 'paradigm shift' in India-America relations in the context of changing global milieu, along with the prerequisite of national interests of both the states. The author believes that despite the opportunities available to India for a new beginning, successive governments could not make use of the situation during the cold war period to develop friendly relations with USA. The issues like India's stand on NPT and USA's policies on arms supply to Pakistan and support for the latter on Kashmir issue worked as major irritants in their bilateral relations during that period. However, this scenario has undergone transformation during the post-cold war era. The disintegration of regimes in Eastern Europe and Soviet Union made Pakistan and China less important for the US security concerns. Simultaneously, introduction of economic reforms process by India attracted the attention of US business groups. This compelled the US government to alter its traditional dominant paradigm to make use of opportunities available in the former. Though Indian nuclear tests of 1998 raised some doubts about the continuation of such momentum, yet economic boom in India removed such apprehensions. A new nuclear India with emerging economic clout and long democratic tradition created a new and positive image in the minds of American policy makers. In this context visit of US president Bill Clinton to India in March 2000 worked as the beginning of consolidation of strong foundation for India-US relations. This policy of cooperation continues to remain with more vigorousness during the regime of President Bush as well. The 9/11 incident once again brought back Pakistan as a frontline strategic ally of USA in its global war against terrorism. Consequently, questions are being raised again about the durability of new US initiatives towards India and the viability of a paradigm shift in America's South Asia policy. But with the course of time, this perception has also proved wrong. It is because Bush administration engaged India with more robustness in its war on terror. The new administration also carried forward the idea of strategic partnership initiated by both Clinton and Vajpayee. It led to the establishment of New Steps in Strategic Partnership (NSSP) between the two states. As a result, bilateral collaborations in civilian nuclear technology, civilian space programme, transfer of dual use technology and superior military-to-military cooperation were worked out between them. The agreement on Indo-US civil nuclear deal is working as a cementing force in their bilateral relations. Author is also aware about various irritants in the way of finalizing this deal, yet he is hopeful that this deal is likely to provide a new direction to their bilateral ties. However, the changed global geo-politics and geo-economics, the failure of American unilateralism, rising anti-Americanism in the Islamic world, common conventional threats to international community, unprecedented growth in the Chinese power and influence and rapid rise of Indian economy are likely to determine the nature of Indo-US relations in the years to come.

R.S. Yadav has discussed the issue of emerging strategic partnership between India and Russia. He has discussed how in the post-cold war era, the past legacies of Soviet era , along with multiple developments at global and regional levels, have transformed Indo-Russian relations from bilateral 'strategic cooperation' to 'strategic partnership' which is more comprehensive and is based on mutually agreed areas of economic, military, political and technological cooperation, with similar if not identical, security threats and perceptions of the emerging world order. Consequently, defense cooperation, political understanding and economic cooperation between the two are encouraged not only to strengthen their bilateral ties but also to make efforts for the global peace and security. Both are aware of their limitations in fulfilling this gigantic task. Hence, to achieve their target they are making efforts to involve like minded countries and regions, particularly China and Central Asian Republics, in their pursuit of building a multi-polar world order to attain global peace and security for the smooth conduct of their bilateral ties.

Relations with neighbours have always attracted more attention in any country's foreign policy. India is no exception to this. In the case of India both China and Pakistan have figured as core countries in its foreign policy orientation, whereas other small neighbours have received comparatively lesser attention. Changed developments in India-China relations had affected India's foreign policy outlook in a greater degree in the past, and are likely to do so in future as well. Roop Singh Bareth has evaluated the changing contours of their bilateral ties in the context of India's security concerns. He begins his analysis in the form of changing concept of security from military to human. However, his emphasis continues to remain on military security. He links up South Asian security problems with the cold war politics. He visualizes that major determinants of security environment in the South Asian region have been India, China and Pakistan. This conventional security problem has been altered in a significant way with the introduction of nuclear dimension in May 1998. He is of the view that Chinese behaviour has been primarily responsible for development like Pokhran-II. Consequently, he warns Indian foreign policy makers about threat from Chinese nuclear and missile capabilities, and suggests a "Sino-centric" and expansionist foreign policy strategy to cope with such threat. He favours a prudent approach based on realities rather than "rhetoric". Simultaneously, he emphasizes bilateral collaborations based on mutual respect and reciprocity. Bareth also thinks that the issue of Tibet has remained and is likely to remain the most volatile cause of misperceptions and misunderstandings between India and China. Hence, the Tibetan card should be realistically re-assessed in the context of the new developments that have taken place in the 1990s and in view of the emerging attitudinal changes in Chinese foreign policy on the issue of Sikkim. Therefore, India should settle territorial issues with China through diplomacy. Simultaneously, economic and technological collaboration should be used to strengthen such a process.

Savita Pande discusses the situation of prevailing imbroglio between India and Pakistan. She opines that both the states are involved in the twin categories of disputes – major and minor. Kashmir issue, proxy war, Kargil war and nuclear rivalry are major disputes prevalent between them, while problem of Siachen, Sir Creek and Wullar Barrage issues are minor areas of conflict between the two states. She thinks that problem of terrorism, nuclear weapons and ballistic missiles also pose serious threats to the security of the region. The volatile nature of such disputes may trigger full-scale war at any moment. Resolution of such issues lies in the establishment of confidence-building-measures (CBMs), through the process of dialogue and encouragement of people- to- people contacts between the two countries.

Udai Bhanu Singh discusses India-Myanmar relations in the context of the former's border management strategy. He is of the view that Western border of India has drawn sufficient attention of security experts, while the eastern border has not received the requisite focus. As a result, vulnerabilities of India's eastern borders, particularly its border with Myanmar, have often been ignored. This problem becomes all the more serious in the light of continued intrusion and ethnic insurgencies in the eastern states of India. Author is of the view that Myanmar can work as an important component of India's 'look-east policy', being the only Southeast Asian nation with which India shares a land border. He lists various common interests of both the countries. He also examines the issues like drug trafficking, HIV, immigration and insurgency, etc. which can work as negative factors for India's security. To authenticate his point of view ample statistical support in the form of different tables has been provided. Periodic meetings between the surveyor generals of the two countries are suggested to avoid the possibility of conflict between the two states. According to him mutual problems of encroachment can be resolved by holding periodic survey and inspection of boundary pillars. Various steps can be taken by both of them to consolidate their bilateral ties and to remove the prevailing irritants. Besides, Myanmar can also facilitate India's growing energy requirements. There is need to streamline trade, set up composite check posts to prevent drug trafficking and conduct joint operations to track down insurgents from each other's territory. These measures may form the basis of a mature relationship between the two countries.

Contemporary changes have not only influenced India's relations with neighbours, but also affected its ties in the extended neighbourhood of West, Southeast and Central Asia. Baljit Singh in his article has evaluated such relationship in an indepth manner. In the contemporary world, India's growing relations with Israel and USA are causing doubts in the Arab world, despite India's clarification that its improvement of relations with Israel is in no way going to be at the cost of Arab countries. However, this was not sufficient to completely remove misperceptions in the Arab world. Rather Arabs started perceiving India as the junior partner to implement goals of the US foreign policy in the Persian Gulf. It is opined that pragmatism with neo-liberal ideology seems to be the defining code of India's policy towards West Asia. Similarly Southeast Asia, attracted India's attention not only for economic reasons, but also from the perspective of security. Given the great business opportunity available, it is advised that India should follow the economic diplomacy in a more careful manner. Central Asia is also looked at by India not only as a potential target for its energy requirement, but also due to convergence of interests on issues like terrorism/fundamentalism, regional peace and security concerns. However, India's policy responses toward this region remain lukewarm. Consequently, India needs to follow a cohesive and holistic foreign policy approach with regard to these areas, so that its long term interests may be achieved.

Rajendra K. Jain highlights the relations between India and the European Union in the form of former's emerging economic cooperation with this new region. He visualizes EU as India's largest trading partner and a major source of FDI inflows since the initiation of economic reforms by it in 1991. The progress between India and EU in addressing their economic, political and security concerns have been analyzed in terms of their summit meetings. Recognition of India's growing regional stature and influence, along with its global economic clout, has attracted EU's attention towards the former. Growing economy of a billion plus people with an annual GDP growth rate of over six per cent for over a decade, the world's fourth largest economy, acquisition of nuclear weapons, steadily improving relations with USA and the acceptance of India as a potential global player in international politics and world trade organization – all these factors have contributed to India's admission into the elite club of nations with which EU has an annual summit. Simultaneously, India's perception of EU has changed considerably in recent years. It no longer regards EU as a mere trading bloc, but increasingly considers it as an emerging actor with a growing political profile in world politics. In case of security cooperation, however, it does not regard this region of much use due to its divergent security moorings. India continues to face traditional security threats like problem of territorial integrity, border control, insurgencies and separatist tendencies, while EU is mainly concerned with non-traditional security threats in the form of organized crime, terrorism, etc. Therefore, due to divergent security needs and priorities most EU member states do not share the same urgency and interest towards India as they have with European states or USA. But the author opines that initially there may be cooperation with India in terms of soft areas such as money laundering, technical cooperation and exchange of information, but gradually hard security issues are likely to form the part of agenda between them. At present Beijing seems to be more central to European interests than India. This creates panic in the mind of common man in India as he tends to feel that EU is obsessed with China and considers it a matter of a sort of political discrimination in EU's treatment of a democratic India, favouring China, with which EU has few common political values.

Ashok Kumar has tried to evaluate India's emerging concerns towards the states of Central Asian Republics (CARs). For him, Central Asia is not only a geographically proximate region of India, rather it has wider implications for its foreign policy. In the changed context of global order, CARs are becoming a very vital area of interest for outside powers and neighbours due to geo-economic, strategic, demographic and political factors. Prevailing conditions of influence building in this volatile region did not allow India to remain a mere spectator to the happenings in this proximate area, because developments in CARs are going to have spill over impact on this country. Economically Indian interests are there due to availability of raw materials, minerals, oil, natural gas, vast trade and FDI opportunities. At present bilateral trade between India and these states is not very significant, but there are huge possibilities for further growth and diversification. Strategically, interests of both of them converge around security and stability in this region. Besides both are equally concerned about the problems of terrorism and drug trafficking. Politically, historical understanding of Soviet era and commonality of approach on numerous global issues have provided a sound framework for their warm bilateral ties. However, future of their relations will be dependent upon how the global scenario unfolds and also on the pace of economic development in India and CARs.

Suman Sharma in her paper examines the role of India in SAARC to consolidate the regional co-operation. She traces the historical roots of regionalism in India's foreign policy and examines India's response and approach to the SAARC in this context. However, initial efforts to unite Asia failed primarily due to politics of cold-war, Sino-Indian rivalry, and victory of communist movement in China. Ultimately SAARC was founded and India enthusiastically participated in it. It was aimed to do away with contentious bilateral issues from regional co-operation. India also wishes to soften the political and strategic divergence in South Asia by inculcating greater economic and cultural cooperation. Due to its size and power potential, India is also the most significant actor in this forum. Later on, post-cold war imperatives of economic liberalization and globalization and end of cold war provided a greater opportunity for India to give a desired shape to SAARC. However, bilateral disputes between India and Pakistan continue to impede and torment the processes of development of SAARC, but the author is optimistic that in the long run India will be able to promote peace, harmony and economic progress through SAARC.

The essay by Kulwant Kaur is focused on the issue of cross-border terrorism especially in the post-9/11 phase. She is of the view that now the issue of terrorism has been redefined in term of "global terrorism" and a categorical distinction has been made by not linking it with either religion, nationality, civilization, or ethnic group. The author considers India as the biggest victim of terrorist activities in the world, which is manifest from increasing number of terrorist attacks in India. It also exposes determination of Islamabad to destabilize India despite its commitment to work for elimination of global counter-terrorism. But post-9/11 provided more strategic leverage to Pakistan than India in counter-terrorist strategy of USA. She blames the US policies towards Islamic fundamentalism in Pakistan. Developments in Pakistan like legitimization and consolidation of military rule, upsurge of radical Islam, strengthening of mullah-military alliance and continuation of terrorist infrastructure in the state have serious implications for India. On the other hand, Pakistan failed to freeze the assets of terrorist groups or individual terrorist involved in destabilizing the region. As a result, activities of *Jihad* in Kashmir, growth of fundamentalism and sectarian forces have consolidated their hold in the region. Their activities pose not only a threat to the on-going peace process, but also endanger communal harmony, national integrity and unity in the region.

Therefore, the author is in favour of adoption of concerted and coordinated policies at national, regional and international levels. A national strategy based on a broader consensus among different strata of society and political groups can help fight the threat posed by terrorism. Therefore, the need is to have a coordinated approach to work in unison with other states who are busy in fighting the global war against terrorism, along with its own battle of terrorism. Care must also be given to address the basic factors like environment of discontentment, exclusion, poverty, political oppression, human rights abuses, regional conflicts etc., so that root cause of terrorism can be eliminated. Beside these, improvement in the intelligence system, spread of education and awareness, encouragement of religious tolerance, building of active civil society, delivering socio-economic justice, solution of regional conflicts, encouragement to the role of regional, international and specialized agencies to counter terrorism, need to be encouraged simultaneously.

Rajpal Budania, in his essay, has undertaken an in-depth analysis of problem of security of India. After defining various dimensions of security, the author tries to differentiate between the problem of security faced by Western countries and developing countries like India in terms of both the military and non-military dimensions. Non-military dimensions include security concerns related to economic, diplomatic, environmental and socio-political nature. In this context, Indian security concerns could be limited to external and internal levels. India's external security concerns and policies are shaped by its disputes and conflicts with the neighbouring states. Armed aggression by neighbours, cross border terrorism, regional and sub-regional crises, border disputes, etc. form the part of its external problem. Narrow nationalism, population explosion, poverty, deteriorating ethos, secessionist movements, cultural, religious and language diversities, demands for regional autonomy, collapse of administration etc. are the major domestic threats affecting its security. Hence a sound linkage is found between external and internal threats. For instance, its internal vulnerabilities in the form of communalism, regionalism and linguism, etc. provide opportunities for external intervention. To meet these threats, India needs not only a secure and effective system of governance, rapid economic progress and social justice, but also strong military capabilities and sound foreign policy.

Suresh Dhanda, in his paper, analyzes the nuclear policy of India since its inception. He elaborates the pace of India's nuclear policy during various political regimes. He considers the Pokharn-II test as a turning point in its nuclear policy, as it manifested India's status as a nuclear weapon state. Since then, India is seriously engaged in revising its plans and enhancing weapons capabilities to build a credible minimum deterrence. This sudden shift in nuclear policy has been attributed to changing nature of threats to its national security. China's nuclear capabilities along with Sino-Pak nexus on the issue have changed the context of the post-cold war global strategic environment. Adverse non-proliferation regime against India seems to have acted as a major factor determining India's new orientation. However, the sense of prestige or status that nuclear weapons bring can not be ruled out completely. Now with the changed status as NWS, the issues like nuclear force structure, custody, command and control of nuclear weapons, nuclear doctrine, etc. also became essential. The author opined that though India has an effective nuclear force structure as compared to that of Pakistan, yet it still lacks the nuclear triad necessary for second strike capability leading to credible minimum nuclear deterrence. India has a declared no-first use nuclear doctrine, along with its satisfactory safety and security track record of handling nuclear arsenals. Simultaneously, it is still in favour of comprehensive and foolproof disarmament and non-proliferation regime provided these are non-discriminatory in nature.

Ajay Singh Manhas, in his essay views the Kashmir problem as the bone of contention between India and Pakistan. According to him the rigid stand by both the countries on the issue had made the resolution of this conflict difficult. Investigating the genesis of the problem, he considers Nehru responsible for internationalization of the problem. By accepting the option of plebiscite, Government of India has itself put a question mark on the validity of accession. Further, India-Pakistan wars of 1965 and 1971 have complicated the matter. Through the war of 1971 India succeeded in making the Kashmir issue a bilateral one, yet it failed to take the leverage of its winning position. After failure to capture Kashmir through wars Pakistan shifted its technique and adopted a policy of cross-border terrorism to attain its objectives. But India also failed to develop a coherent approach in this regard. The author is of the view that a consensual view to handle the Kashmir problem is still missing. However, with the initiation of contemporary peace process in the form of CBMs may bring a ray of hope for them to resolve this problem.

R.S. Yadav views that post-cold war era and globalization have not only changed the meaning of the term security, but also made energy security an important component of India's foreign policy concern. Though India obtains its energy from numerous sources, yet oil, natural gas and nuclear are three important constituents which have direct foreign policy bearings. India produces nearly 32 to 33 million tonnes of oil but its consumption is nearly five times of its production. It is the fifth largest consumer in the world. At present its import of oil is to the tune of 70 percent which is likely to touch 91 percent by 2020. Despite its huge and active engagements abroad, it is likely to remain a serious problem for its policy makers in the times to come. India also produces a large quantity of natural gas, but experts are afraid that its demand will outstrip its production soon. Nuclear energy is an area where India has developed huge infrastructure for its peaceful uses. It is also one of the very less utilized resources by India. But the availability of nuclear fuel and global politics of such supply by NSG countries are the major problems. Though India has been successful in the acquisition of nuclear fuel for its civilian use by signing agreement with the USA, France and Russia, yet domestic political consensus on the issue is still missing. Objectively speaking the necessity for deal is not only beneficial for Indo-US ties, but is likely to strengthen India's position in world politics as it is going to open its gates for the availability of nuclear fuel from NSG countries. The increase in crude prices and non-availability of such fuel in the long run are other positive factors in going for such a deal. Now India has two fold policy options: one, cooperating with Russia, China, CARs and other oil reserve states to get requisite oil and natural gas; and two, to open its gates for the supply of nuclear fuel from NSG countries to augment its nuclear energy output. Though all this is not going to be problem-free, India, on the one hand, has to follow an integrated approach towards energy security and on the other, to streamline its domestic road blocs in this process. Thus its foreign policy needs to be geared up for the skillful handling of these global and domestic challenges.

Anand P. Mavalankar, in his essay touches upon a crucial aspect, i.e. economic dimension of India's foreign policy. The end of the cold war and simultaneous introduction of liberalization, privatization and globalization (LPG) by the Government has brought about the importance of this dimension in India's foreign policy. With the introduction of structural reforms India is making a genuine beginning towards integrating its economy with the world. Author is of the view that international pressure, weak performance by public sector, lack of growth opportunities, decline in political institutions, processes and norms, industrialization, etc. have been the main factors responsible for the introduction of this process in the country. Besides globalization, the world economy from 1970s onwards has led to changes in the whole global environment. The information revolution has demolished the information barriers between markets and suppliers in different countries. Consequently, India's foreign trade policy underwent significant transformation and new orientations in foreign economic policies are bound to be noticed.

Anand Mathur, in her paper, highlights a serious non-conventional issue affecting India's global outlook. The author opines that on environmental issues perceptions of both the developed and developing countries are bound to be different. Besides, the developed countries are imposing their values on less developed countries, which can be termed as the problem of 'eco-imperialism'. Developed countries are using the developing states as their dumping grounds for their toxic and other waste materials. India is no exception to this phenomenon. But time has come for India to involve itself in collaborative measures taken by world community for environmental sustainability as well as protection of its national interests concerning this issue. India's response to global environmental concerns is reflected in a three-fold manner: (i) protection of environment; (ii) preservation of natural resources; and, (iii) to meet out its own energy needs. To meet these responses India has adopted a multi-pronge strategy: (a) concerted efforts and joint strategy against developed world; (b) preservation and sustenance of resources; and (c) coherent energy security policy. Hence, India should not only acknowledge the importance of environment for its foreign policy but also make efforts in realizing the desired goals.

Ram Niwas Beniwal, in his essay, deals with the problem of refugees and India's policy concerning that group. He considers that anti-colonial wars, self-determination movements, international conflicts, revolutions, coups, regime changes, ethnic and communal conflicts, restructuring of state boundaries, population transfers, etc. are the main causes of refugee problem in this region. But India's track record regarding global response to refugee problem seems to be one of apathy. It is evident from the fact that so far India has neither signed the international obligations for the treatment of refugees, nor it has passed any comprehensive legislation on the issue. However, in practice India has provided a 'safe haven' to the refugees in need. Since its inception, it has accommodated large number of refugees from Pakistan, Myanmar, Bangladesh, Afghanistan, Sri Lanka, Tibet, Iran, Somalia, Sudan, etc. It also encouraged the role of UNHCR and NGOs working towards the resolution of problems of refugees. But due to lack of constitutional provisions and acts passed by legislation, judiciary has failed to protect the rights of refugees. Thus, it is in India's interest to sign the 1951 convention and 1967 protocol, because signing of these are going to improve its relations with neighbours. Recognition and adaptation of such norms by India is bound to facilitate its long term foreign policy objective in South Asia.

Notes and References

1. Ummu Salma Bava, "India's Role in the emerging Global Order", *Friedrich Ebert Srifting Briefing Paper*, no. 4, March 2007, New Delhi, in www.fes.de/globliazation
2. For details see, C. Uday Bhaskar, "Indian Foreign Policy Orientation in the Twenty First Century: Continuity and Change", in www.surztosuva.org.ak/south-asia/2006/bhaskar.pdf.

3. Dennis Kux, *India and the United States: Estranged Democracies, 1941–1991*, National Defense University Press, Washington DC 1993.
4. Strobe Talbort, *Engaging India: Diplomacy, Democracy and the Bomb*, Brookings Institutions, New York, 2002, (rvd edn 2006)
5. For detail see, C. Raja Mohan and Parag Khanna, "Mutual Interests and Democratic Affinity," *Policy Review*, February/March 2006.
6. Pranab Mukherjee, "India's Strategic Perspectives," Carnegie Endowment For International Peace, Washington DC, 27 June 2005 in www.carnegieeddowment.org/files/ Mukherjee_Transcript_06-27-051.pdf (emphasis in original)
7. C. Raja Mohan, "India's New Foreign Policy Strategy", in www.carnegieendowment.org/ files/ mohan.org.
8. *Ibid.*

1

Indian Foreign Policy: Challenges and Opportunities in the New Millenium

Devendra Kaushik

India's size, population and potential have marked it out for a larger dynamic role in the world. One-fifth of humankind cannot afford to adopt an ad-hoc and reactive approach in its foreign policy. It has to construct an "ideal vision" of its own and strive to attain it with the cooperation of other members of the international community. Jawaharlal Nehru, the first Prime Minister of India, who was otherwise generally averse to India claiming a leadership role, had stated that the country with its vast resources and population "will always make a difference in the world.... Fate has marked it for big things".

Needless to say there is a vital linkage between the internal and external policy of every country. India always looked upon its struggle for independence as an integral part of the world-wide struggle against colonialism. Hence it was natural for her to forge together with Indonesia and Egypt a policy of non-alignment in the middle of the last century. This policy which was neither a policy of neutrality nor of "non-involvement" in world affairs was the only sensible course open to the foremost newly independent country that India was, to respond to the numerous threats posed to its freedom by the cold war rivalries in a bipolar world. The politics of military blocs was a serious threat to the independence of the newly free Afro-Asian countries.

Non-alignment also greatly helped in strengthening the country's democratic political system through building a broad national consensus in the domain of foreign policy. Non-alignment meant that the newly independent countries judged all international issues on merit, staying away from the rival military blocs, the membership of which could compromise their independence.

Thanks to this policy, India managed to play a larger role in world affairs than what its actual power warranted. A number of conditions that prevailed at that time, including elements such as India's own image as a country emerging peacefully from colonialism, its leadership role in a group of similarly situated countries, and of course Nehru's own image and personality, made this larger Indian role possible.

However, it could not last long. The global order did not recognize moral values and authority; without many real allies and with major regional issues unresolved and in the absence of adequate military might moral authority of India proved of little consequence. The India-China border conflict in 1962 virtually destroyed the moral authority-based foreign policy course of non-alignment and the influence that India had acquired in world affairs since independence through its pursuit. India somewhat recovered from this setback in the early 1970s but things were not quite the same again.

The demise of the Soviet Union in 1991, the end of the cold war bipolar era and the beginning of a new unipolar era of globalization under the US hegemony brought India face to face with new challenges in the domain of its foreign policy. It is not surprising that due to an atmosphere of political instability prevailing in the country during the nineties of the last century and ideological confusion which has continued all through the first decade of the 21st century, Indian foreign policy has remained hamstrung with a certain ambiguity. It is certainly not an easy task to reconcile neo-liberalism with traditional ambitions and reflexes as also with lingering impulses of solidarity with the third world, a legacy of the non-alignment

Based on a new political realism and a pragmatic approach, Indian foreign policy is currently faced with the task of evolving its response to the new challenges of the post-cold war world and the era of globalization in a unipolar international system. An important development in the global power structure is the rapid rise of Asia as an economic power against the backdrop of decline of the United States as an economic power. Although as the sole surviving super power the USA still militarily continues to dominate the present unipolar world order, it remains to be seen how long it can sustain its political and military domination of the world in the face of its rapid decline as the pre-eminent global economic power.

More than the foreign policy making community in the countries of the developing world spanning the three continents of Asia, Africa and Latin America, it is perhaps its Indian counterpart which needs to correct its perceptions of the US power and its beneficent effects on the world order. Indian Prime Minister Manmohan Singh's speech at the India Today conclave offering unreserved support to the efforts of the industrially advanced nations of the world to promote liberal democracy of their type among the less advanced nations and the statement of Pranab Mukherjee (then Defence Minister) during his address at the Carnegie Foundation in New York about the total convergence of "values and interests" of India with the United Sates have been rightly hailed in certain circles in India as "paradigm shift" from the days of non-alignment policy under Jawaharlal Nehru. The new power elite in India has thus finally taken a stand which does not take into account the need to counter the negative political and security consequences of US-led unipolar international order by maximizing foreign policy options as an emerging economic power.

Overawed by transient US military supremacy and dreaming to achieve a world power status by riding Washington piggyback, the Indian foreign policy making elite seems to be blissfully ignorant of the fast changing realities of the world and the new opportunities for ushering in a multi-polar or polycentric world order following collapse of the biopolar global power structure. Nehru had the distinction of being the first Asian to have visualized the emergence of Asia as a powerful force on the world stage. It is relevant to recall Nehru's forecast contained in his address to the First Asian Relations Conference in 1947 in Delhi about the emergence of Asia as an important factor in world politics. At this conference Nehru had stressed the need for Asian unity and announced the arrival of Asia on the world stage. Later, addressing the UN General Assembly special session in Paris in 1948, Nehru declared: "The World is something bigger than Europe. Asia counts in world affairs. Tomorrow it will count much more than today". That "tomorrow" has now finally arrived.

Asia, comprising China, India and a large part of Eurasian Russia, and containing more than half of the world population had not been the primary focus of international politics until recently. It is only during the last decade and a half that this continent has emerged as a region whose economic, military and diplomatic power has surpassed that of the West. China's GDP grew fastest at an average rate of 10.3 per cent during 1980–1990, while India's grew at 5.6 per cent. Subsequently, during 1990–2000 and 2000–2004 period, China's GDP again grew fastest at the rate of 10.6 per cent and 9.4 per cent respectively on an average annually while India's grew at 6 per cent and 6.2 per cent per year. In 2003–2004 India's GDP growth rose to 8.5 per cent.

In 2004 in terms of absolute level of Gross National Income (GNI) at Purchasing Power Parity (PPP) exchange rates, China's share was the second largest in the world at 7.6 trillion dollars, second only to the United States at 11.7 trillion dollars. India with 3.4 trillion dollars in GNI was fourth after the US, China and Japan (3.8 trillion dollars). By 2007 India was estimated to replace Japan as the country with the third largest GNI. China's economy is expected to overtake the USA in absolute terms in GDP/PPP computations by 2015 or 2020.

By 2005 Russia witnessed a steady economic growth over a period of seven years at a stretch with the country's GDP increasing by 50 per cent during the 1999–2005 period with 6.4 per cent growth in 2005 alone. Russia's foreign exchange reserves, the fourth largest in the world, increased from 12 billion dollars in 2000 to 217 billion dollars in April 2006. The stabilization fund set up to park oil revenues over 27 dollars per barrel of oil exceeded 66 billion dollars in April 2006. India and China too have accumulated large foreign exchange reserves. China has surpassed Japan to become the world's largest holder of foreign exchange reserves. China's State Administration of Foreign Exchange manages the bulk of China's 1.65 trillion dollars in foreign exchange. China holds nearly 500 billion dollars worth of US Treasury Bonds. India is next to Russia in its foreign exchange reserves of 190 billion dollars. China with its nearly 2 trillion dollar foreign exchange reserves was, as one western expert described it, "the largest lake of money in the world". By comparison the United States is a "vast sink-hole of debt that get bigger everyday". The cost of war in Iraq is 8 million dollars per hour. While China adds 30 million dollars to its foreign exchange reserves every hour, the United States loses 80 million dollars also by the hour. According to the 2007 edition of the BRIC Report China and India – "Chindia" – will be at the very top of the Super League by 2050, ahead of even the United States.

In 1820, before the advent of the industrial age, Asia accounted for 60 per cent of the world output. By 1940 its share had declined to 20 per cent. At its present rate of growth it is soon going to claim 60 per cent of the world output. At present, Asia with 60 per cent of the world population accounts for two-third of the world's hydrocarbon reserves and 40 per cent of the world GDP. With its larger share of younger and educated global workforce, Asia has the potential of filling the gap in the world's human resource requirement against the backdrop of ageing population of the world.

In May 2003 in his meeting with President Hu Jintao of China, Prime Minister Atal Bihari Vajpayee declared that with the increasing cooperation and dialogue between India and China an "Asian Century" was going to be ushered in. The Asian century will promote the interests of world peace and prosperity. It will not be a challenge to world stability but the bedrock of a new equitable world order.

The deepening of tripartite Eurasian cooperation among India, Russia and China is the only concrete path for saving the mankind from a disastrous course of endless conflicts towards which the unipolar international order under US hegemony is pushing the world. As the communiqué issued after the New Delhi Conference of the Foreign Ministers of the three countries rightly emphasized, "democratization of international relations is the key to building an increasingly multipolar world order that would be based on principles of equality of nations, respect for sovereignty and territorial integrity of countries, international law and mutual respect".

It is time, India sheds once and for all its flippant approach to a multipolar world order which is the only desirable replacement for a unipolar global system running counter to the healthy interests of the international community. By working actively for tripartite cooperation among India, Russia and China, New Delhi will only help the United States to better serve its natural interests by becoming a normal law-abiding member of the world community and gaining economically through its mutually beneficial cooperation with the three important Eurasian powers. Development of cooperation among the three countries forming the Eurasian triangle and cooperation between them and the United States, West European States, Japan and South Korea, through construction of mega projects of infrastructural development has the potential of extricating the global economy from its current recession turning into economic depression.

The challenge confronting Indian foreign policy in the 21st century emanates mainly from globalization under a US-led unipolar world order. The collapse of the Soviet Union and socialism was hailed by Western ideologues Francis Fukuyama (*End of History,* 1992) and Samuel Huntington (*Clash of Civilizations,* 1994) as the final triumph of universal liberal democratic capitalist values. Following the 11 September 2001 terrorist attack on America, the fight against Islamist terrorism has been equated with fight against tyranny, for western style democracy. President Bush has come out with the doctrine of 'pre-emptive wars' against 'enemy' countries to be named by the United States. All these American-led military actions are legitimate activities in defence of democracy.

The Indian foreign policy makers have to fine tune and adapt the old policy of non-alignment to this new international situation of a US-led unipolar world sustained by ideology driven doctrine of 'pre-emptive wars' in the name of advancing liberal democratic values ensconced in the unhindered flow of the process of globalization. The need of the hour is to build a new national consensus for updating the theoretical basis of the policy of non-alignment to meet the new challenges. It is heartening to find that US-led policy of unipolarity is meeting strong opposition from several important countries in Asia and Latin America which are realizing the growing need for creating countervailing forces to checkmate the negative features of the unipolar world order and globalization. Globalization has not uniformly benefited all countries and all sections of their population. It has resulted in greater disparities both among nations as well as inside nations. According to the latest World Bank estimates of 2008 the rate of decline of poverty in India was faster between 1981 and 1990 than between 1990 and 2005. India according to new estimates had 456 million people or about 42 per cent of the populations living below the new international poverty line of 1.25 dollar per day. The number of Indian poor constitutes 33 per cent of the global poor. India also had 828 million or 75.6 per cent of its population living below 2 dollars a day which is worse than the sub-Saharan Africa, the poorest region of the world accounting for 72.2 per cent of its population living below 2 dollars a day level. This situation calls for Indian foreign policy to address itself more seriously to the problems of regulating foreign trade between the developing and developed countries at the WTO. Indian foreign policy has to take new initiatives to reach out to the various regional economic groupings for mutually beneficial economic cooperation. India needs to reach out to powers other than the USA and West Europe through a more pro-active foreign policy. The growing global momentum towards a polycentric world order opens up a new vista of opportunities which if properly harnessed by countries like India, China and Russia can help the international community to cope with the serious challenges to world peace and prosperity posed by a unipolar system, faltering by an already ailing American power.

2

Changing Dynamics of India's Foreign Policy

R.S. Yadav

Foreign policy of a country is determined by both domestic and external factors of that state. Consequently, international milieu represents one of the major components in the making of any country's foreign policy. This becomes all the more important when external environment undergoes significant transformations. The end of cold war and simultaneous growth of globalization are indicative of such a change, as they have changed the political and economic structures and processes of the world in a substantial manner. Politically the world is no more bipolar as it used to be during cold war, rather a peculiar situation having edge towards unipolarity and hegemonism is being witnessed. Even the nuclear club of P-5 has been extended to P-8 (though not recognized) with the addition of India, Pakistan and North Korea. New permutation and combinations are being framed in the form of regional groupings. Existing global institutional organization is being marginalized to the extent of facing crisis of its relevance. Third worldism has also become insignificant with the reduced status of the forum like NAM. Consequently, these developments have influenced the study of foreign polices of states in a significant way. India's foreign policy is no exception to this phenomenon. Hence it becomes pertinent to know how India's foreign Policy has been able to adjust with the new international milieu. To understand the changing dynamics of India's foreign policy, this paper has been divided into five segments. In the first part theoretical understanding of changed world system has been attempted. In the next part operating dynamics of international order is examined to find out its basic features. In the third part operational dynamics of India's foreign policy has been studied. In the fourth part problems and prospects for India are debated and analyzed. Finally a conclusion is drawn to suggest future direction of its foreign policy.

I

Not going into the typologies of world order in the post-cold war era, it is certain that international milieu has undergone huge transformations both in its structural, as well as, in its operational dynamics.[1] It is also true that though nearly two decades have passed, yet world is still surrounded by ambiguity and instability. Hence scholars have interpreted this changed globalized order in different ways. Due to the amorphous nature of complex changes a theorization of this transition is not only very difficult but also intractable.[2] It is being realized that in the new context politically segmenting the globe into "three worlds" is obsolete and economically the division of the world into "two worlds" (i.e. North and South) is also no longer possible to sustain. Even earlier characterization in the form of "Centre-periphery" will also not be applicable in the present context.[3] Rather in the process of analyzing globalization of the world in terms of "post-coloniality" and "post-socialism" will be more appropriate. But here also due to lack of convergence of interests between them, the two are not likely to be able to oppose the onslaught of globalization.[4] Thus, understanding the international system in the age of globalization is full of uncertainties.

In another context, when international relations are being evaluated in the post-globalization era, it is found that conceptually it is a period of marked transition to challenge the hegemony of statist notion of the national interest. New agenda recast in the era includes issues like-global political economy, the environment, social movements, non-governmental organizations (NGOs), civil society, global governance, transnationalized forms of violence, etc.[5] Consequently, two simultaneous gestures, that would recast the disciplinary parameters of international relations, are required. In this context, on the one hand, it is necessary to think beyond the motifs of the post-cold war era and globalization. On the other, it is necessary to re-think the morphology, governance and violence of global order in a way that acknowledges the transnational and inter connected nature of forces that shape the contemporary era.[6] Despite all this, Matin Coward thinks that basic assumption of statism has not undergone much change. Therefore, he concludes by observing that "recasting of the discipline beyond the confines of statism represents a revivification of the tradition of IR and, hence, deserves to retain this term as a signal of fidelity to a certain set of common problematics."[7] Here he seems to be in complete agreement with J. Rosenberg who remarked that "like it or no ... realism ... is setting on the intellectual foundations... which we ... need to make sense of international relations".[8] Thus, in the contemporary world of realism, the only hyper power is going to remain one pole and rest of the world is to face the brunt of *realpolitk* in terms of hegemony and dominance of economic, political and military nature.

In another interpretation, the post-cold war world has been defined as – major, middle and minor Powers[9]. This order has given the USA "the status of sole superpower in a semi-uniploar international system".[10] This super power is not only autonomous in its economic, political and military affairs but also acquires pre-dominant position, system or global-influence, mostly based on power-projection capabilities. It is considered as 'subject' or system determining state in the global order. Minor-powers are 'objects' or 'system-ineffectual' not having any autonomy in their foreign policies or security concern. To alternate the sharpness of the distinction between *major* power and *minor* powers, "one can posit an in-between category of *independent centers of power* (or system-influencing states) in respect of states that do not have the leverage to influence the course of international system as a whole, but which posses enough capabilities to have a considerable degree of foreign policy autonomy and the capacity to resist the application of unwelcome decisions, especially in the realm of security, in their own region".[11] According to Nayar, India falls in this category of *middle-powers* or *great regional powers* and is aspiring to acquire the status of a major power. Though India seems to have the credentials for such status, yet the powers are reticent to support its case.

Fukuyama argued the case in favour of a unipolar world as he linked the phenomenon of end of cold war to "end of history" and "triumph of democracy".[12] He conceived that the demise of communism has led to the end point of ideological evolution and the emergence of Western liberal democracy as the final form of human government. In the ideological conflict between the then two superpowers liberal capitalism proved more successful and ultimately established its supremacy. In one sense of the term Fukuyama is right as there is no longer one single competitor to liberal capitalism as an over arching ideology. Besides, powers are no more interested to settle the issues of conflict through the instrumentality of war. But this is not the correct picture of the global scenario. Liberal capitalism has many competitors, albeit fragmented ones. For instance, China and Russia are in capitalism and global market, yet neither is liberal nor fully capitalist. Besides, fundamentalism taking the shape of global terrorism is another challenge to emerging liberal capitalism. Moreover, ethnic, religious and 'national' communalism do work as important irritants in this new process. Therefore, to interpret the current change as end of history or triumph of liberal democracy does not present a true picture of the present global order.

Rejection of the above thesis has been done by a new kind of interpretation by Huntington, who believed that instead of ideological or economic divisions, now the world would be divided on the basis of cultural fault lines among states.[13] He classified the world into eight important civilizations (Western and Latin American, African, Islamic, Sinic, Hindu, Orthodox, Buddhist and Japanese) and averred that the future course of conflicts will be witnessed on the fault times of these civilizations. But realistically speaking, neither his division nor his categorization is correct, as nations continue to give serious consideration to national boundaries which are more explicit than these vague partitions. Besides, divergences continue to exist within these civilizations themselves, and as a result, conflicts within the same civilization can be witnessed. Thus one thing is certain that chaotic world order seems to be the story of the day and India has to interact its foreign policy goals not in a well knit and defined world order, but in an uncertain world. And ultimately lots of difficulties are bound to be there to cope up with the current global scenario.

Joseph S. Nye, Jr. is of the view that on the basis of current distribution of power, world order can be termed as one based on "*multilevel interdependence*". Current global pattern resembles complex 'three-dimensional chess game'.[14] In this complex system, in terms of military power, the world is largely unipolar with the United States as the sole superpower. But at the second level, in terms of economic issues, the United Sates is not a hegemonic power or an empire, rather it has to bargain on equal terms with European Union, if the latter acts in a unified way. At the bottom level are the transnational relations that cut across and cross borders outside the control of governments and include actors as diverse as bankers and terrorists. Here power is chaotically dispersed. Besides, in this kind of world order, which is already economically multipolar and there will be a diffusion of power as the information revolution progresses, interdependence is going to enhance and transnational actors will be more important. Therefore, India has to interact with a world which is very complex and can not be comprehended with the terminology like unipolarity, hegemony or multipolar world order.

Although suggested as policy measure for the USA to "manage the transition" in its favour, Richard N. Haass presented an altogether different picture of world order which is more akin to prevailing realities.[15] He is of the view that present world order is in an "age of non-polarity" wherein the world is dominated not by one or two or even several states but rather by dozens of actors possessing and exercising various kinds of power. This represents a tectonic shift from the cold war era. In this context, six major and numerous regional powers play important role. The six major powers representing current global scenario are: China, European Union (EU), India, Japan, Russia and the USA. Main regional powers are: Brazil, Argentina, Chile, Mexico and Venezuela in Latin America; Nigeria and South Africa in Africa; Egypt, Iran, Israel and Saudi Arabia in the Middle East; Pakistan in South Asia; Australia, Indonesia and South Korea in East Asia and Oceania. Besides, a good many global, regional and functional organizations will form important segments of the current global order. Even large number of global companies, militia, political parties, religious institutions, drug cartels, NGOs, etc. will form part of such world order. Thus, today's world is "increasingly one of distributed, rather than concentrated power." Hence, India has to develop its foreign policy in a hybrid kind of world which is evolving and where diffused and multi-layered power structure is present, and in this process it also has a significant position of its own as part of major powers who are going to determine the future direction of the world.

Thus, end of cold war and globalization process have theoretically changed the structural and operational dimensions of global politics. On the one hand, a situation of non-polarity is witnessed with hegemony and dominance of the only hyper-power (i.e. USA). It has created a situation of uncertainty and fluidity in international relations. On the other hand, India's multifarious engagements with the USA, and its efforts towards alternative strategic partnerships along with forging of new economic groupings, have denied it of a certain status in the global system. As a result, an exact outcome of its new foreign policy orientation has become very unpredictable.

II

Theoretical changes at the global level have far reaching implications on the practice of international relations. Consequently, India is bound to respond to these operational dynamics to achieve its foreign policy goals in the changed global milieu. Before analyzing India's new foreign policy outlook, it becomes essential to have a glimpse of these global changes and to assess how these have been responded to by different states. Besides, it is equally important to know that how these changes have transformed the bilateral and multilateral responses among states.

If a broad look at the working of international relations in the changed times is taken it becomes manifest that the present world is neither completely unipolar nor it has moved to multipolarity, rather a very precarious situation has emerged inducting fluidity to the practice of international relations. The emergence of so-called 'democratic order' and 'triumph of capitalism' have given birth to hegemony and dominance of the only superpower, i.e. USA. This factor became evident during the recent gulf wars and the role played by the US-NATO combine during these crises. These developments have not only put a question-mark on the relevance of the United Nations, but even reduced its stature as international organization established to save the succeeding generations from the scourge of war. It is, however, equally true that complete *pax-Americana* has not been evolved as a result of its increased status. The forces of fundamentalism and terrorism continue to provide a big challenge to the superiority of the USA. Incident of 9/11 and continuous attacks of *Al-Queda* and its leader Osama Bin Laden against US interests, despite the latter's stringent action including war, is a proof of such resistance. But in the over all bilateral and multilateral ties with the outside world American dominance and hegemony can be noticed.

Simultaneously, other centres of powers like European Union, Russia, Britain, France, Germany, Japan, China, India, etc. are also, making efforts for their autonomy. However, they are not doing it in defiance of dictates of the USA, rather they are busy in enhancing their closer ties with the USA. They seem to be enjoying relatively better autonomous positions, as compared to rest of the developing states, not because of their better economic and political clout, but because of their non-conflictual attitude towards the USA. Despite this understanding, however, a complete convergence of interests between the USA and these states is missing. Rather both of them are having hate-love relationship which has neither polarized them into a complete divergent position, nor it provided space for independent working for these countries.

Rest of the developing countries are neither secure, nor autonomous in their working in international relations. They are completely peripheral and are being marginalized to the extent of being neglected. They are swaying between both the USA and other centres of powers. They don't form any political group to drive leverage from either of them. Due to the changed context of globalization even their economic bargaining position has been reduced and they don't have any role in the decision-making process in the new global economic order. Even their membership of different third world groupings (e.g. NAM) is of no consequence as the latter are too weak to assert any confrontationist/concerted stand with any powerful group.

India's position is also being sandwiched in the middle group. On the one hand, it is strengthening its position through various new permutation and combinations with the United States, and on the other, it is hobnobbing its position among other centres of power and developing states. However, through its signing up of 'agreed minutes on defence relations' (1995), 'General Security and Military Information Agreement (GOSMIA)' (2002), 'High Technology Cooperation Group' (2002), 'Next Steps in Strategic Partnership' (2004), 'New Framework for the US-India Defence Relationship' (2005), India has consolidated its military-to-military relations with the USA.[16] Through the agreement on civil nuclear energy deal and joint strategies on international terrorism it is busy in enhancing its relations with the USA. This kind of India's tilt towards the USA is evident from its efforts toward the promotion of process of globalization and engaging, even sometimes following, dictates on the issue of nuclear counter proliferation, global terrorism and nuclear civil energy agreement.[17] Yet, India is also aware of its limitations in going along with the interests of the only hyper power. Consequently, it is simultaneously making efforts to forge India-Russia-China triangle and bilateral strategic partnerships with Russia and China. Besides, it is part of the new combinations, like G-4, BIMSTEC, ASEAN, ARF, IOR-ARC, India-Brazil-South Africa, SCO (as observer), etc. to enhance its credibility in the developing world. Besides, efforts are being made to revitalize NAM and the UN, alongwith democratization of the latter, accommodating India's demand for permanent membership due to its post-Pokhran II status. Thus, at this juncture India is facing an uncertain and undemocratic global order which require serious efforts on its part to get security guarantee and autonomy in the decision-making process. Hence, in this complex and ambiguous international order it has to choose its options with extra care.

III

The above scenario has not only provided India ample opportunities, but also thrown manifold challenges. In short, it has to reorient its foreign policy. Changing contours of India's foreign policy can be well discerned at three levels:

Shifting Alignments

Visualizing the recent global changes and enhanced role of the USA, India has opted to be closer to the only superpower in the post-cold war global system. India-America relations are no more constrained with the differences of the cold war era, rather they are moving in the direction of enhancing all round cooperation in the areas of economic, strategic and even nuclear. During the last 15 years, despite divergences of approach on numerous foreign policy issues, both have shown a level of maturity in their bilateral ties. Their relations are now no more constrained by the developments in a third country. The path of their bilateral cooperation, however, is not smooth enough due to their divergent worldview and foreign policy orientations. But the compulsions between them are equally strong so as to bind them for fruitful cooperation. Simultaneous with the building of closer ties with the USA, India is also maintaining close relationship with Russia and China in the form of 'strategic partnership'. This collaboration is based on cooperation in all areas of activities. Besides the strengthening of economic, strategic, and political ties, the three have given expression to forming a triangular relationship to withstand emerging hegemony and dominance of the USA and are in favour of establishment of multi-polar world order in the post-cold war era.[18] Though they may not be making open proclamation of such intentions, yet their activities do reflect this lurching fear in their mind. Some scholars do feel that there are numerous irritants to such thinking, yet given complementarities between these three states, possibilities of such triangular relationship are very strong. Though policy makers in India may not be always upbeat on this idea, yet they are doing every thing possible to strengthen individual ties with both Russia and China.

To avoid any negative fallout of global developments India is more in favour of a multi polar world order through the strengthening of international institutional framework. It is evident to India that in the present times in the name of pre-emptive attacks, role and relevance of the UN system have been questioned and is being hijacked by the combined forces of the USA and NATO. Consequently, democratization of this institution is a dire necessity not only for the nations of the third world but also for all other members of the global community. In the context of changed geo-strategic, economic and demographic realities, India also aspires for a permanent seat in this structure along with countries of Europe, Africa and Latin America. This quest of India is manifest from its efforts towards manoeuvring the veto power along with its concerted efforts through other aspirants of the G–4. This effort is being made without a confrontationist approach, rather through conviction and friendly ties with the concerned countries of the world. In the given scenario though it seems quite difficult for India to attain this position, yet an initiation of the process might result in fulfilment of its objective in the long term.

Relations with the Central Asian Republics (CARs) have also emerged as an important area in Indian foreign policy outlook in the post-cold war era because of this region's geo-strategic location and proximity to India.[19] The developments in this region are bound to have spillover impact on Indian foreign policy. India had deep linkages with these states during the time of erstwhile Soviet Union. In the present context, due to economic, strategic, political and energy constraints, along with the convergence of interests between the two, India is bound to be attracted towards this region. Common threat of Islamic fundamentalism and terrorism are also likely to work as cementing force in their relations.

Changed global milieu has influenced the regional environment of South Asia. As a result, India's policy towards its neighbours has witnessed multiple changes and is faced with new kind of challenges as well. India's policy towards China has seen qualitative changes with the establishment of JWG on borders and with the recognition of LAC as *de facto* border by the two. Both powers also decided to enhance mutual cooperation by keeping aside the border problem. India's nuclear explosion in 1998 created some misunderstanding between them, but it was soon overcome by the political visit of Indian leaders to China. Later by signing the agreement on principles to resolve border issue, appointment of political representatives to look into the working of JWG and recognition of Tibet and Sikkim as part of Chinese and Indian territories respectively, both came closer to each other. Convergence of their views on the changing nature of international power structure and declining role of international organization have provided them further opportunities for coming closer to each other.

Relations with Pakistan have neither followed the general rule of emerging relaxation in the post-cold war period, nor has there been any constructive improvement in their bilateral ties. In the post-Geneva accord period, it appears that Indo-Pak relations are going to be cordial in future. Substantiated by "Bus Diplomacy" by Vajpayee during his visit to Lahore in February 1999 no one expected the 'u' turn in their ties in the aftermath of Kargil war. Later, attack on Indian Parliament in December 2001 brought them to the brink of war as India mobilized its forces on the Pakistani border. Similarly, Musharraf's Agra visit also turned out to be a fiasco. Hence, their relations again reached a nadir. However, later the Srinagar initiative by India in 2003 again brought about a ray of hope. The reciprocal posture by Pakistan and initiation of foreign secretary level dialogues during 2003–2008 led to the enhancement of CBMs of both military and non-military nature between the two countries. The growth of bilateral cooperation in the form of rail-road linkages, initiative of soft-border and cooperation in disaster management both the countries are enhancing people-to-people contacts. If other imponderables continue to remain favourable then both these nuclear powers are likely to have smooth ties between them.

Consolidating Economic Cooperation

Recognizing the global shift from geo-politics to geo-economics India introduced structural reforms in the country. As a result, it adopted the policy of "Look East" to forge deeper economic ties with the countries of East and Southeast Asia. In this process, it joined the ASEAN first as its "sectoral" dialogue partner and finally as "full dialogue partner". Besides economic cooperation, it also joined ASEAN as a founding member of ARF (ASEAN Regional Forum) to cooperate with the states of this region in security matters. This, along with its military-to-military cooperation with the USA, made it a prominent actor in the security arrangements in the Asia-Pacific. This emerging thrust of India is evident from the bilateral economic cooperation and the establishment of joint ventures by India with the major countries of this area. Simultaneously, efforts are being made to develop all round cooperation with the countries of Southeast Asia and to meet out the emerging challenges of the new world order cropping up in the form of terrorism, drug trafficking and other such problems.[20]

The demise of one global power also led to the rise of a phenomenon of economic regional groupings. Hence, India is busy in developing cooperation with ASEAN, SAARC and IOR-ARC. Besides, efforts are also being made to cultivate inter-group and intra-group cooperation. Consequently, to enhance economic ties between countries of SAARC and ASEAN, a new initiative in the form of BIMSTEC has been taken.[21] In a larger context, India is also associated with the formation of a larger group of East and Southeast Asia, along with New Zealand and Australia, in the form of East Asian Summit (EAS) of 16 countries. Thus, in the light of an emerging new economic order India is consciously making efforts to make itself an economic power to reckon with.[22]

India's quest to be an economic power of substance demands the availability of huge resources at its command so that it can sustain its projected annual growth rate of 8 to 10 per cent. Presently India produces 30 per cent of its energy resources indigenously and is dependent on imports to the tune of 70 per cent. As a result it is busy in compensating the same through numerous collaborations with countries like Vietnam, Sudan, Syria, Russia, CARs, and traditional Gulf states. In 1995 it also concluded a tripartite agreement with

Turkmenistan and Iran to import oil through pipelines. India is also engaged in joint investments in oil exploration activities abroad with a number of countries. In this context, its ONGC Videsh Ltd. (OVL) concluded agreements with Vietnam and Russia. The first such joint venture in Vietnam became operational in December 2002. Second joint venture in Sakhalin-I in Russia became functional in October 2005 in which India has 20 per cent of its share. In January 2006 Exim Bank of India also provided a huge loan of US$ 392 millions for such investments in Sudan. It is the second largest investment by the OVL after Sakhalin-I. In January 2006 again during his visit to Beijing Indian minister for energy signed an agreement with China's National Petroleum Cooperation (CNPC) for their joint bids with India's OVL for oil exploration projects abroad. In future this joint partnership may facilitate the growth of foundation for Asian Energy Union. Russian leadership also seems to be inclined towards such proposals. Besides, India is making efforts to acquire more and more oil and natural gas through pipelines from Iran, CARs, Myanmar and Bangladesh. Though supply through these pipelines may not be smooth, yet India is making serious efforts for their earliest construction.[23]

Confronting Strategic Challenges

Nuclear issue has always been sensitive to India's foreign policy. It has acquired added importance in the post-Pokhran II era. India's track record in terms of nuclear non-proliferation has been very transparent and perfect. This is also evident from its nuclear policy of 'no first use' and 'unilateral moratorium' on explosions. However, it continues to pursue the policy of development of 'minimum nuclear deterrence' for its security. But how the nuclear powers in its neighbourhood and nuclear suppliers' group are going to react to this development is a matter of concern. Its July 18, 2005 agreement with the USA on civilian nuclear energy cooperation has raised a lot of hue and cry in the country. Experts seemed to be divided on the question of separation of civil military weapon oriented nuclear programme, as well as, the long-term consequences of such agreement for India's foreign policy. Now questions arise: can India remain independent in term of pressures from the USA? Does opening of all its clear facilities (including fast breeder reactors and other research facilities) for the inspection of IAEA compromise its security? These and other related questions are of great concern for the foreign policy makers today.

Terrorism is a serious problem affecting India's domestic stability and security. This problem is not new as it has been existing in Punjab and Jammu & Kashmir in the 1980s. Even the role of outside powers used to be there as was evident from many incidents during that period. But after the event of 11 September in the USA it has acquired a new dimension. Later on, the developments in Afghanistan and America's response have brought international terrorism at the doorstep of India. As a result, India gave an open offer of cooperation to the USA to crush the Taliban and suppress terrorism but the latter continues to rely on Pakistan. This has raised numerous questions about the similarity of approach on this issue between India and America. Though it seems that terrorism has acquired a global dimension, yet it must be admitted that the problem continues to be different in terms of its definition, methodology and consequences from country to country. Time and pace of development of terrorism in the two countries are not only different in nature but also require different prognosis. Hence, in the changed context international terrorism and terrorism prevailing in India are two different situations. India has thus to understand these basic differences while making friendly gestures to the outside world for the resolution of this problem. Besides, it has to be careful in selecting the options for the resolution of the problem of terrorism in its country and global terrorism.

IV

However, the realization of these new goals is not going to be a smooth process for India's foreign policy makers. They have to comprehend various challenges and devise multi-pronged strategies for skillful handing of issues at global, regional and bilateral levels.

(a) Most arduous task at global level is to understand the complexities of the issues confronting them by contemporary international relations. As explained earlier, the emerging unipolarity has caused a serious threat to nation-states in the name of 'pre-emption' and 'export of democracy' by the only superpower, i.e. the USA. This has been further complicated by a weak United Nations. Even the available forums of concerted efforts by the countries of 'South' are no more resilient to withstand these dominant assertions of the only hyper power. Even India's support base in the erstwhile socialist world is not in a position to confront such hegemony and dominance in the new context.

Besides, process of globalization has emerged as a significant force in the post-cold war world. This change has created a paradoxical situation. This development has been creating a 'closed polity' by way of hegemony and dominance of the only superpower in the international system, whereas in the economic sphere it has introduced an 'open economy' through the process of liberalization and privatization. Hence, political accommodation in terms of 'democratization of international system' is not available to a developing country like India. Simultaneously, its opening up of market is not going to provide it economic opportunities through the international economic institutions like, IMF, World Bank and WTO. Thus, it has been rightly observed that "If on the one hand, undemocratic reality of global distribution of power has to be negotiated by foreign policy makers, on the other, constraints and opportunities have to be dealt with by every nation-state including India."[24]

Presently, India is also facing a daunting task to create a balance between different prevailing centres of power. In this changed scenario apart from the only superpower, certain other power centres in the form of European Union, Japan, Russia, China, Germany, India, etc. are emerging. Though these centres are not homogenous in their fight against emerging unipolarity, yet they are making efforts for their autonomy and space in the global decision making process. The challenge before India is how to create a niche for itself by evolving a balance between the USA, on the one hand, and these emerging power centres, on the other hand. The latter are fighting against the American hegemony and dominance by establishing a multipolar world order. India seems to have made efforts in both the directions during last two decades. If, on the one hand, by making effort to create military-to-military cooperation through 'Next steps in Strategic Partnership' (NSSP) (2004) and 'New Framework for the US-India Defence Relationship' (2005), India is coming closer to the United States, then on the other hand, efforts are being made to enter 'India-Russia-China Strategic Triangle' to withstand the pressures of the USA. However, theory and practice of Indo-US cooperation reveals that India is coming closer and sometimes even working as an ally of the USA. Bilateral strategic partnership and trilateral collaborations are yet to be consolidated. Thus, to create a delicate balance between these forces will be a difficult task for India in the near future.

Moreover, by the acquisition of nuclear status in May 1998 India has not been able to resolve its security problems. Besides, security threats from the neighbours, India has to confront the global politics of nuclear proliferation. Since late 1970s India has been consistently pressurized to sign the NPT and later CTBT, so that its nuclear capabilities can be 'capped, reduced and eliminated.' But now the situation has changed after the utilization of nuclear option by India. Now it is being denied the status of nuclear weapon state, as well as, it is engaged in the 'counter proliferation' strategies by the USA. Besides, energy security is emerging as a new area of challenges for the states interested in enhancing their economic development. Here India has been denied its energy security due to Caspian Sea and Central Asian oil politics. Pipeline politics of 'Central Asia-Iran-Pakistan-India' and 'India-Myanmar Oil Pipeline' are designed to devoid accesses of oil to India. Even Nuclear Civil energy deal under 123 agreement is not free from constraints like Hyde Act (2006). Consequently, this deal has created negative fallouts in the domestic milieu of the host country. Hence, new paradigms of security are being witnessed in the changed context, which are more complex and ambiguous than the earlier threats of cold war era.

(b) The regional environment encompassing India is not only volatile but also faced with numerous challenges influencing its foreign policy options. The situation in Central Asian Republics (CARs) and West Asia is tense due to prevailing power rivalry for influence building and control over the precious resources. All the five states of CARs, along with states surrounding the Caspian Sea, have to withstand the pressure of MNCs of the USA, UK, Italy, etc., as well as, the Russian, Chinese and Indian thrust for getting oil. Domestically all are passing through the process of state and nation-building in a region bereft of democratic norms. They are also witnessing ethnic and religious strife in their multi-cultural and multi-racial systems. Two gulf wars in West Asia, along with continued differences among Israel and Palestine, have created a difficult condition not only for peace and tranquillity in the region but also for oil price and its supply to large parts of the world, including India. The transportation of oil through pipelines from these regions has also been disrupted due to politics and outside powers' interests in this area. India, though it has good relations with both these regions, has not been able to manoeuver its position in a direction favourable to its foreign policy goals.

As is evident in the post-cold war era, economic factors have acquired significance in the relations among the states. Consequently, growth of regional economic groupings has been inevitable. But despite the urgency and necessity of such collaborations among the states of this region, they have not been able to forge closer economic ties. Though some economic regional groupings such as – IOR-ARC, BIMSTEC, SAFTA (under SAARC), etc. have been established, yet for one or the other reason they have failed to deliver the requisite result. CARs have also formed SCO, along with Russian and Chinese participation, but India's role remains limited to an 'observer'. These efforts could not become a reality due to 'trust deficit' among the major states in the region. Due to this trend SAFTA can not become viable and IOR-ARC and BIMSTEC are yet to take off. All these groupings could not flourish due to lack of institutionalization and absence of strategies capable of handling the emerging challenges of the new global system.

Moreover, the region is also facing some non-conventional security threats with spillover impact on India's foreign policy. The incident of 9/11 and America's attack on Al Qaeda's activities in Afghanistan have brought out international terrorism on the door steps of India. It has not only aggravated the already prevailing proxy war scenario between India and Pakistan but has enhanced the risk of such terrorist activities in surrounding regions of West, Central and Southeast Asian States. This has further provided momentum to the already existing activities of small arms exports among ethnic and terrorist groups in the area.[25] Financing such activities for a longer period is a big challenge for them. So to sustain such activities these groups are involved in the process of drug trafficking in the region. Consequently, smuggling along 'triangle of crescent' and 'golden triangle' became a routine activity. As a result, India became sandwiched as it forms the central area linking these two regions. Thus, these activities have encouraged several non-conventional threats for India, which foreign policy makers have to deal with utmost seriousness and promptness.

(c) Bilaterally India is mending fences with both of its major neighbours–Pakistan and China. In the 21st century India and Pakistan started a composite dialogue to enhance confidence-building-measures (CBMs) between them. Under this process troops reduction; dialogue on Sir Creak, Wullar Barrage, Siachen, Baghliher dam, etc. were initiated; running of Thar Express (in addition to Samjhauta Express); running of bus; opening of consulates; agreed mechanism on terrorism; opening transportation of goods through trucks from Wagha, etc. have improved their relations. However neither the end of acts of terrorism nor SAFTA (because of non-grant of MFN status by Pakistan) have become a reality. Non-establishment of a stable regime in Pakistan is proving another irritant between the two countries.

In the post-Pokhran II phase a slight irritant was noticed between India-China relations. However, things were brought under control through the mutual visits of leaders of both the states. Visits of Indian leaders Jaswant Singh (1999 and 2002), K.R. Narayanan (2000), George Fernandes (2003) and Atal Bihari Vajpayee (2003) restored the earlier warmth in their ties. These were reciprocated by China in the form of visits by Tang Jiaxuan (1999), Li Peng (2001), Zu Rongji (2002), Wen Jiabao (2005) and Hu Jintao (2006). Both also agreed to appoint 'special political representatives' in 2003 not only to boost their ties but also to take some bold initiatives which the Joint Working Group (JWG) cannot take. Sincerity of their efforts is witnessed from their dialogue process, as up to October 2007 both had been able to conduct 33 rounds of talks (1981–1987 = 8 rounds; 1988–2003 = 14 Rounds by JWG; and 2003–2007 = 7 Rounds by Special Political Representatives) to resolve their border problem.[26] Even both agreed in 2003 on the 'Declaration on Principles for Relations and Comprehensive Cooperation' and in 2005 on the 'Agreement on the Parameters and Principles for Settlement of Boundary Question'.[27] However, these CBMs and goodwill have not served the purpose and the border problem still remains unresolved.

Despite the above efforts of CBMs, India has not been able to improve its relations with neighbours. Trust deficit state of affair continues to work as a major irritant between them. In case of Pakistan, until the problem of terrorism and proxy war is resolved India can't be tension free from its side. Similarly, India has extended a number of concessions to China, and now it is latter's turn to show the grace in making adjustments on the border. It has also to refrain itself from staking its claim over Arunachal Pradesh which has been not an area of dispute between them since long. Therefore, without building genuine confidence with its neighbours India can't remain in peace with them. Without the cooperation between India, Pakistan and China neither peace can prevail in South Asia, nor these states can contribute to the cause of global peace. In the case of South Asia, all of them have not been able to acquire sufficient strength to work as a countervailing force against unipolar hegemony and dominance at global level. If India and Pakistan are balancing US position in South Asia, then India and China have also not adopted a position of direct opposition to the only superpower. Even the India-Russia-China strategic triangle has remained in its infancy, unable to manifest its direct opposition to the USA.

Thus, at all the three levels – global, regional and bilateral – India is witnessing grave challenges for its foreign policy not only in terms of mending its fences with its neighbours but also to withstand the threat of unipolar global order. Despite its goodwill in the region and acquisition of nuclear weapons status it is not in a position to work as an independent centre of power in global arena.

V

From the above analysis it can be discerned that in the light of contemporary transformations in the global milieu, changes in India's foreign policy are inevitable. Since the nature of these changes has been of a vast magnitude, an all-round and multi-dimensional changes in Indian foreign policy can not be ruled out. However, all this has not been very smooth and without long term consequences. Now multiple challenges at all three levels are being witnessed by foreign policy decision makers. Indian policy makers have not only to deal with the problems inherited from the past, but also to resolve new crises emanating from contemporary developments. Simultaneously, they have to carve autonomy for India in the prevailing global order. Hence, there is need for its policy makers to have a holistic view of current changes, along with the process of globalization. India has to make efforts to reap the benefits arising out of this process without compromising its sovereignty. Besides, there is need for an evolution of a new consensus on foreign policy in the light of bizarre changes. Earlier consensus has become redundant due to new kind of ideological moorings being witnessed at the domestic level. Moreover, despite its enhanced capabilities, it has to think beyond 'bilateralism' to confront the new challenges in the form of 'doctrine of pre-emptive attack' and 'export of democracy' in an era where institutions like NAM and UN are also facing the crisis of their oblivion. Finally, without the development of its economic strength it may not be possible for it to face the challenges of the world market.

Simultaneously, strengthening of its socio-economic fabric with an egalitarian order is also the need of the hour so that domestic factors may not constrain its foreign policy outlook. Thus, new orientation and consensus on foreign policy goals are the pre-requisite to meet out the challenges of the contemporary world.

Notes and References

1. Generally on the basis of Units and characteristics orders have been classified as follows:

Typologies of Order

Sl. No.	*Type*	*Unit*	*Characteristics*
1.	Globalized	Global System	End of national politics, societies and economics
2.	International	State	Concern with Agenda of Sovereignty and Stability
3.	World	Humanity	Concern with agenda of rights needs and justice
4.	Globalized International	Globalized States	Agenda of managing relations between states penetrated by global system but still distinguishable within it.

Source: John Baylis & Steve Smith, *The Globalization of World Politics: An Introduction of International Relations*, New Delhi, Oxford University Press, 2007, p. 731.

2. For details see, Bhupinder Brar, "Theorizing Transition: Post-Coloniality, Post-Socialism and Coming Age of Globalization", *International Studies*, 39(4), Oct.-Dec. 2002, pp. 323–334.
3. *Ibid.*, pp. 325–326.
4. *Ibid.*, p. 334.
5. Martin Coward, "International Relations in the Post-Globalization Era", *Politics*, 26(1), 2006, p. 59.
6. *Ibid.*
7. *Ibid.*, p. 60.
8. J. Rosenberg, *The Follies of Globalization Theory: Polemical Essays*, London, Verso, 2000, p. 81.
9. For details see, Baldev Raj Nayar, *India in the World Order: Searching for Major-Power States*, Foundation Book, New Delhi, 2004.
10. *Ibid.*, p. 247.
11. *Ibid.*, p. 4.
12. Francis Fukuyama, "The End of History," *National Interest*, no. 16, Summer 1989, pp. 3–18.
13. S.P. Huntington, "The Clash of Civilization," *Foreign Affairs*, 72(3), Summer 1993, pp. 22–49.
14. Joseph, S Nye, Jr., *Understanding International Conflicts*, Pearson Education, New Delhi, 2008, p. 277.

15. Richard N. Hass, "The Age of Non-polarity: What Will Follow US Dominance," *Foreign Affairs*, March/June 2008.
16. For critical evaluation of these agreements see, Kanti Bajpai, "Where are India and the US Heading?", *Economic & Political Weekly*, 6 August 2005, pp. 3577–3781; Achin Vanaik, "Significance of Framework Agreement on Defence", *Economic & Political Weekly*, 6 August 2005, pp. 3581–3585, Varghese Kotthara, "India-US Defence Cooperation: Expectations and Prospects", *Economic & Political Weekly*, 6 August 2006, pp. 3585–3589, and Sukumar Murlidharan, "Partnership and its Discontents", *Economic & Political Weekly*, 6 August 2006, pp. 3589–3591.
17. For text of Civil Nuclear Energy agreement see, http://meaindia.nic.in/pressrelease/2007/08/03pr01.pdf
18. For details see, R.S. Yadav, "India-Russia Strategic Partnership: Implications for Common Security of Asian" in Mahavir Singh, ed., *Building A New Asia*, New Delhi, 2005, pp. 173-174. Also see Zhou Vuyun, "Strategic Triangle of China, India and Russia: Ideal and Reality", R.R. Subramanian, "Russia-India-China: Strategic Cooperation and A Pan-Asian Order", and Hari Vasudevan, "Russia-India-China Cooperation: The Shaping of a Nation in Russian Foreign Policy", in the same volume. Also see, Mahavir Singh and Victor Krasilch Tchikov, eds., *Eurasian Vision*, New Delhi, 2003; Devendra Kaushik, "The Triangle for Peace and Prosperity", *World Focus*, 24 (10-11-12), October-November-December, 2003; Chintamani Mahaparta, "India, China and Russia: Strategic Triangle is Possible", *Strategic Analysis*, 22(II), February 1999, pp. 1793–1796, "India-Russia-China: A Strategic Troika", (Series of Articles), *World Focus*, 26(4), April 2005.
19. For details see, R.S. Yadav, "India and Central Asian Republics: Challenges and Opportunities", in *B.G. Gafurov: Dialogue of Cultures and Civilizations*, Moscow, 2000, Also see, Surendra Gopal, ed., *India and Central Asia: Cultural, Economic and Political Links*, New Delhi, 2001.
20. For details see, Hoshiar Singh and R.S. Yadav, "India and Asia-Pacific in the Changing World Order" in M.L. Sondhi and K.G. Tyagi, eds., *Asia-Pacific: Security, Globalization and Development,* New Delhi, Manas, 2001, pp. 230-258.
21. Ibrokhim R. Mavlonov, "Central Asia and South Asia: Potential of India's Multilateral Economic Diplomacy in Inter-Regional Cooperation", *Strategic Analysis*, 30(2), April-June 2006.
22. V.P. Dutt, *India's Foreign Policy: Since Independence*, New Delhi, 2007, pp. 213–214.
23. *Ibid*, pp. 237–241.
24. C.P. Bhambri, "Indian Foreign Policy: A More Varied Menu", *India Quarterly*, 62(4), October-December 2006, pp. 82–83.
25. R. Hariharan, "Militancy and Small Arms Proliferation", *The Hindu*, 20 April 2007.
26. Pallavi Aiyar, "Another Round of Talks Begins", *The Hindu*, 24 September 2007.
27. For full text of declarations see, *Strategic Digest*, 33(7), July 2003, pp. 543–546; *The Hindu*, 25 June 2003; "India-China Relations", *World Focus*, July 2003, pp. 16-20, http://meadev. nic.in/ind-chn-decla.htm; and *Strategic Digest*, 35(5), May 2007, pp. 500–504; http://meaindia.nic.in/treatiesagreement/2005/11ta1104200510.htm.

3

Paradigm Shift in Indo-US Relations: Problems and Prospects

Chintamani Mahapatra

The dominant paradigm of Indo-US relations from the very birth of India as an independent country and through more than four decades of the Cold War was marked by a love-hate relationship, particularly in the realm of political and security issues. The paradigm included co-operative economic and cultural relations between the two within thc framework of a socialistic pattern of economic policy adopted by India and the dynamic capitalism of the United States.

It was thus difficult to discover any fixed pattern of bilateral relationship between the US and India. US-India relations actually seemed shapeless and grotesque. India was non-aligned, but did not completely stay away from building cooperative ties with the US. New Delhi more often than not sought to persuade Washington to refrain from contributing to military build-up in Pakistan. Indian diplomacy was partly responsible for US policy of not directly siding with its ally Pakistan during Indo-Pakistani wars in the 1960s and the 1970s. India adopted a slightly modified approach when it requested Washington for assistance in the wake of Chinese invasion of India in 1962. Prime Minister Jawaharlal Nehru going against the spirit and principle of non-alignment wrote to President John F. Kennedy for help and received assurances of support to meet the challenge from Communist China.[1] Both during the 1965 and 1971 wars between India and Pakistan, an American strategic ally and non-aligned India, the US Administrations imposed arms embargo against both the warring parties. Consequently, the US received a volley of criticism from Islamabad for not fulfilling the treaty commitment and from India for equating the victim of aggression with the actual aggressor. Thus, economic, cultural and educational cooperation; and political differences and strategic divergences together constituted the dominant paradigm of Indo-US relations. This paradigm continued to be the hallmark of relationship even after India moved closer to the Soviet Union – the principal adversary of the United States – since 1971.[2]

India's strategic proximity with the Soviet Union unquestionably was a bilateral irritant and infuriated the United States at times, but it failed to rip apart cooperative ties in non-security areas between India and the United States.[3] Notwithstanding American discontent and disapproval of India's qualified non-alignment policy, Washington continued to uphold a functional relationship with India in social, cultural, educational and even economic areas. It was primarily on the politico-security issues that the two countries did not see eye to eye, especially on a series of cold war events, including the Korean War, Vietnam War, Hungarian and Czech crises, wars in the Middle East, Arab-Israeli disputes, Vietnamese military intervention in Cambodia, the Soviet invasion of Afghanistan, racial and political conflicts in the African Continent and many others. It is noteworthy that the US was the single largest foreign investor in India and was the largest trading partner of India during much of the Cold war years.

On matter of principle, the non-aligned India went against the establishment of foreign (Western) military bases in the Afro-Asian world. It was at odds with the US strategy of forward defence, which necessitated establishment of military bases and facilities in the third world countries. Moreover, India carried on a propaganda offensive against Big Power (read America) presence in the Indian Ocean and contested any interference by external actors in South Asian affairs. Some analysts christened this as Indian "Monroe Doctrine".

Besides serious areas of divergences on international issues, the two countries confronted each other on some of crucial issues of critical importance to bilateral interactions. To begin with, the subject of nuclear proliferation gravely hunted this bilateral relationship for an extensive period of time. The differences arose since the days of negotiations for a universal nuclear non-proliferation treaty close on the heels of the Chinese first nuclear test in 1964. It turned more acute when India refused to sign the NPT and conducted its first nuclear test in 1974. The United States had come forward with a civilian cooperation agreement with India in support of Nehru's vision of promoting nuclear research and nuclear power generation as part of his initiatives to build up the science and technology infrastructure of newly independent India. The Indo-US civilian nuclear collaboration had led to setting up of the Tarapur nuclear power plant with American assistance. But India's stand during negotiations for the NPT upset the Americans and the latter's design to put in place a discriminatory non-proliferation regime frustrated India's proposal for a nuclear free world. When India opposed the NPT that came into operation in 1970 and four years later tested a nuclear device as PNE, hell let loose. The US erected a string of barriers in the form of non-proliferation regimes and domestic legislations to target India's nuclear programme.[4] Since then India has remained a prime target of the US non-proliferation legislations, such as the NNPA and the US backed international regimes, such as the Nuclear Suppliers' Group. No other single issue generated as intense mutual hostility between the two countries as the nuclear issue. The two sides unleashed divergent proposals in the field of nuclear diplomacy leading their respective camps and targeting each other's nuclear programmes. The US consistently promoted regional nuclear free zones and India advocated a nuclear free world. India found the US policy unacceptable and discriminatory. The US saw in the Indian proposal an impossible demand because that would negate all nuclear strategy and war fighting doctrines of its military.

The second most significant bilateral irritant was the issue of US arms transfer to Pakistan during the Cold War period. Initially, the US defended its supply of sophisticated weapons to Pakistan on the ground that it was an anti-Communist rather than an anti-Indian move.[5] When Pakistan actually used those weapons against India during wars, the US had no answer. But the US justifications remained the same. Massive amount of US arms supply to Pakistan during the Afghanistan crisis of the 1980s threatened to alter the military balance in the region, but Washington's priority was clear. It intended to bleed the Soviets white at any cost. India was a friend of the Soviet Union, but Pakistan was an ally against the Soviet military presence in Afghanistan and thus the US cared little about the military equation in South Asia. More significantly, it was during this time that the US disregarded its non-proliferation norms and policies and allowed Pakistan to proliferate in exchange of Islamabad's vital support to US strategy of evicting the Soviet soldiers from Afghanistan. Pakistan's so-called "Islamic bomb" was made in the midst of an American-backed jihad against the Soviet-supported Godless Communist forces in Afghanistan.

Soon after the Soviet withdrawal from Afghanistan and on the eve of the disintegration of the Soviet Union, Islamabad announced loud and clear that it had gone nuclear. Pakistan's Foreign Secretary made this declaration on the US soil. Ironically, the US imposed the Pressler Amendment within a year after the end of the Soviet occupation of Afghanistan cutting off all military and economic assistance to Pakistan. Since Pakistan had little to lose, announcing its nuclear weapons status had little adverse effect on it. But this nuclear move was made by Pakistan in the wake of its new Kashmir offensive against India.

Thirdly, the US tilt towards Pakistan on the Kashmir issue was yet another core issue that unfavourably affected New Delhi's relations with Washington. The US always equated India, the victim, with Pakistan The aggressor, and did not maintain silence on this issue until Pakistan's crushing defeat in 1971 war. However, by recognizing Bangladesh and accepting the principle of bilateralism enshrined in the Shimla Agreement as an appropriate means to resolve the outstanding issues between India and Pakistan, the US continued to profess an equidistance policy in South Asia. The Kashmir issue once again popped up as an irritant when a State Department official, Assistant Secretary of State Robin Raphel, challenged the legal validity of the Instrument of Accession only to be countered by her senior to appease Indian critics.

In the new context of the post-Cold War dynamics, Kashmir issue got further complicated when Pakistan linked the Kashmir issue with the nuclear question and launched a proxy war by funding, training and equipping the anti-Indian militant groups in Kashmir. Islamabad sought direct American intervention in resolving the Kashmir issue arguing that its nuclear weapons programme could be abandoned if only the Kashmir issue could be resolved satisfactorily. According to some reports, Pakistan was about to launch nuclear weapons against India in 1990 as part of its attempt to end the Kashmir dispute with India once and for all. Robert Gates, the current US Defense Secretary, then a high CIA official, reportedly dashed to New Delhi and Islamabad to prevent a probable nuclear exchange. There are others who refute such reports, but it was clear that by linking the Kashmir issue with the nuclear issue, Pakistan sought to draw the attention of international community, particularly the US, in its effort to internationalize an issue that needed to be resolved bilaterally under the Shimla Agreement. Pakistan and the US together had just won the Afghan War by compelling the withdrawal of the Soviet forces and thus Pakistan's efforts to draw the US into the Kashmir question raised suspicion in India about the US motivation.

The Clinton Administration, that had put forward nuclear proliferation as one of the priority foreign policy issues, and declared a policy of "cap, freeze and roll back" of South Asian nuclear programmes, found the Pakistani effort to link Kashmir with the nuclear issue quite useful. Thus, when Pakistan proposed a South Asian Nuclear Weapon Free Zone, the US promptly endorsed it much to the chagrin of India.[6]

In the mean time, Pakistan-sponsored terrorist activities in Kashmir went on causing human disasters. The US was neither prepared to declare Pakistan as a state-sponsor of terrorism nor to accept Kashmiri terrorism as an international security threat. Terrorism in Kashmir was a local affair for the State Department and Indian complaints about the transnational connections of Kashmiri terrorists fell on deaf ears in Washington. Indian leaders and commentators put lots of hopes on the US to restrain the hazardous Pakistani policies and in the face of American inaction or lack of attention held Washington partly responsible for instability and bloodshed in Kashmir.

Post-Cold War Era

In the post-Cold war era, the collapse of the Soviet Union led to strategic unimportance of Pakistan and China to US security planners, and Indian economic reforms attracted US business attention and by implication altered the traditional dominant paradigm of US engagement with India.[7] The evolution of the new paradigm was nonetheless a slow process due to a variety of reasons. The US indifference to Pakistan-sponsored spread of violence and terrorist activities in Kashmir, its apathy towards the emergence of the Pakistan-backed

Taliban force in Afghanistan, the disproportionate attention focused on China, inaction or ineffective response to Sino-Pakistan WMD cooperation and articulation of a policy of "cap, freeze and roll back" of South Asian nuclear programme threatened to perpetuate the old paradigm of US-India relations. While prospects of Indo-US economic cooperation brightened due to growing Indian economic openness, the new political and strategic variances between New Delhi and Washington temporarily sustained the traditional paradigm.

The Indian nuclear tests of 1998 in the backdrop of an expanding Sino-Pakistani collaboration in Pakistan's efforts at WMD capacity building, and the Clinton Administration's apparent appeasement policy augmented the trust deficit in Indo-US relations. Imposition of US sanctions on India endangered the mounting economic and socio-cultural ties between the two countries. However, in less than two years, India watchers in Washington witnessed the Indian economy grow at about five per cent in a milieu of Asian financial meltdown, in the midst of a global recession and despite US sanctions. A new nuclear India with emerging economic clout and long democratic tradition recreated the American image of India. US President Bill Clinton visited India in March 2000 to lay the foundation of an innovative structure of US-Indian relations.

The traditional paradigm of Indo-US relations thus began to change since the early months of the 21st century. Spending five days in India and five hours in Pakistan, President Clinton adopted a new American approach to South Asia. He signed several agreements on trade, investment, environment and other issues with his Indian counterpart to restructure the bilateral relationship. In Pakistan he refused even to shake hands with the military ruler Pervez Musharraf who had come to power by staging a coup in October 1999. He preferred to address the Pakistani people on television from his hotel room. In his speech, Clinton listed out his various pieces of advice for the Pakistani military ruler and emphasized the need to restore democracy in that country. Months before his arrival in India, President Clinton had already won the hearts and minds of Indian people by taking a just position on the Kargil Conflict and exerting pressure on Islamabad to call back the "intruders." His role in resolution of the Kargil Conflict set a new trend in US approach to South Asian conflict. During his stay in India President Clinton signed a 'Vision Statement" with Indian Prime Minister Atal Bihari Vajpayee outlining a brand new strategy to enhance and uplift US-Indian relations.

Defeat of the Democratic Party candidate in 2000 US presidential elections and victory of Republican candidate George Bush raised questions about the durability of Clinton approach and implementation of the "Vision Statement." But doubt was soon dispelled when it came to be known that President Bush already had a "new big idea" about India. When he delivered a speech at the National Defense University outlining his missile defense plan, India sprang a surprise by endorsing Bush's plan which raised eyebrows around the world. Indian response to Bush's missile defence policy signified that the new American Republican President will carry forward his democratic predecessor's new initiatives towards nuclear India. That would in turn symbolize a bipartisan support to emerging US-India relations under a new paradigm.

The terrorist attacks on the US on 11 September 2001 sprung back Pakistan as a frontline strategic ally of the US in the so-called global war against terrorism. It also renewed questions about the durability of new US initiative towards India and the viability of a paradigm shift in America's South Asia policy. The lacklustre US response to India's offer of "unconditional support" to its fight against terrorism and the Bush Administration's determination to enroll Pakistan as an important ally in the global anti-terror war strengthened the view that Indo-US relations would return to square one.

However, as events unfolded, skeptics were proven wrong. The Bush administration more robustly engaged India in the midst of its war on terror. Pakistan's re-emergence as a close US strategic ally was not allowed by the Bush administration to derail the emerging relations with India. By carrying forward a joint initiative by President Bill Clinton and Prime Minister Atal Bihari Vajpayee to forge strategic partnership between the two countries, the Bush declared from White House his decision to take additional measures in this direction and called it the Next Steps in Strategic Partnership or NSSP. This initiative included bilateral collaboration in civilian nuclear technology, civilian space programme, transfer of dual use technology and superior military-to-military teamwork.

The most momentous outcome of the fresh directions in Indo-US relations are marked by unprecedented cooperation in the field of defence and security, indicated by qualitative and quantitative expansion of military exercises, arms transfer and military doctrines. A brand new initiative, known as the Indo-US nuclear deal, launched by US President George Bush and Indian Prime Minister Manmohan Singh in July 2005 has had the potential to cement the emerging strategic partnership between India and the US.[8] But the long debate over this deal in the US as well as in India indicated that several members of the foreign policy community in both the countries were not prepared to accept such a deal. The American opponents feared that this deal would hit a sharp nail into the non-proliferation regime, make US non-proliferation policy appear dubious, encourage other countries to proliferate, isolate the Pakistanis, annoy the Chinese and reward the Indians with civilian nuclear technology despite the nuclear tests of 1998 and Indian decision to develop and deploy nuclear weapons. The Indian opposition to the nuclear deal was based on the perceptions that it would compromise Indian sovereignty, enhance US influence over strategic decision making, make India more vulnerable to US arm twisting diplomacy and prevent India from conducting further nuclear tests in the future.

The opposition in the US to cooperation with India in civilian nuclear technology practically ended with the passage of the Henry J. Hyde US-India Peaceful Atomic Energy Cooperation Act in the US Congress and signing of the Act by President George Bush on 18 December 2006. One does not find any edit-page articles in the American media since then. Nor have important think-tanks like the Brookings Institution and Council of Foreign Relations devoted their attention to this issue. The Congressional concerns over this deal were deftly handled by the Bush administration officials. The antagonists of this initiative in the US appeared to have been contented with the provisions of the Henry Hyde Act, which allowed the Bush Administration to go ahead and conclude the necessary 123 agreement with India along the lines delineated in the Act.[9]

The impact of the Henry Hyde Act was quite different in India. It raised suspicions, generated political heat over the linguistic imperfections that seemed insulting to India; and became a reference point for the opposition parties to criticize the nuclear deal. The Manmohan Singh Government in India did come up with clarifications and justifications, but was certainly not able to give "acceptable" answers to questions and doubts raised by the Left Parties, Right Wing BJP or even strategic experts or scientists. Significantly, the Indian political left and political right got united in opposing the deal. The CPI (M), a significant supporter of the ruling coalition government, found serious objectionable provisions in the Act and took the position that the US legislation on the nuclear deal was "not acceptable," and asked the Government to discontinue talks with the Bush Administration, as the law contradicted most significant assurances given by the Prime Minister to Parliament. External Affairs Minister Pranab Mukherjee argued that India did not have to worry about the legislation passed by the US Congress as it was meant for the US lawmakers. According to him, India was obliged only to the bilateral agreement (123 Agreement) and that "the US Administration had categorically assured India that this legislation enabled the United States to fulfill all of the commitments it made to India in the July 18 and March 2 Joint Statements and that this legislation explicitly authorized civil nuclear cooperation with India in a manner fully consistent with those two Statements." The CPI (M) fired back saying that the US administration was bound by the provisions of its Act while negotiating this agreement. This could not be accepted by India, as it negated the most significant, if not all, assurances given by the Prime Minister to Parliament. Thus, further negotiations on this score must not proceed. The Bharatiya Janata Party too demanded that the Government reject the Henry J. Hyde Act, which contained "humiliating conditionalities" and imposed "conditionalities, which were worse than those in the NPT (Nuclear Non-Proliferation Treaty) and the CTBT (Comprehensive Test Ban Treaty).

Some nuclear scientists too raised objections to the Act on its requirement related to conduct of future nuclear tests by India. It was argued that once India conducted any future tests, the US would ipso facto cancel the civilian nuclear cooperation with India. Former Atomic Energy Commission Chairman, P.K. Iyengar, went on to say that it was impossible to have a minimum credible deterrent without conducting nuclear tests. But the bill, according to him, indicated that the cooperation would be terminated if this was done.

India's main concerns continue to be the following: Firstly, the nuclear agreement with the US would force India to team up with the US on certain foreign policy issues. Secondly, it would make it difficult for India to conduct nuclear tests in the future without compromising its foreign, particularly US, collaborative nuclear programmes. Thirdly, the deal does not guarantee equal treatment of India with other nuclear weapon powers, since enrichment and reprocessing technology would continue to be denied to India. Fourthly, US supply of nuclear fuel will have limited duration rather than perpetual, as expected. Fifthly, the US is likely to have intrusive inspection over India's civilian nuclear programmes and close watch on the military programmes. Sixthly, the initiative is hailed by the US as a non-proliferation initiative and ultimately aims at circumscribing India's nuclear weapon capability. Restriction on enrichment and reprocessing technology, future nuclear tests and limiting or stopping the production of fissile material are actually measures to limit India's nuclear deterrent. Seventhly, even the argument on energy security is weak in the sense that nuclear technology by 2020 will constitute only 5 per cent of electricity generation and less than 4 per cent of total energy sources of India. For a small gain, India cannot afford to sacrifice a great deal on its freedom of action in national security front.

The Government of India has the duty and the responsibility to satisfy the Indian public and mainstream political parties by convincingly addressing the questions and concerns raised throughout the debate over the nuclear deal with the United States. Majority of the members of the Indian Parliament do not accept the deal in its current form. However, Indian Constitution has no provision for ratification of international agreements and treaties. The Government has the legal authority to carry forward its foreign policy decisions. The current Government appears confident that its decision to forge civilian nuclear cooperation is a good decision and is in the national interest of India. It thus seems to be moving ahead with the remaining procedures to implement the 123 agreement that would facilitate concrete civilian nuclear cooperation between India and the US and between India and other nuclear technology suppliers. The step in this direction will not be complete until India is able to successfully negotiate an India-specific safeguards agreement with the IAEA, the Nuclear suppliers' group gives the green signal to its member countries to conduct civilian nuclear trade with India and the US Congress gives its final approval to the 123 agreement by an up and down vote.

There is little doubt that civilian nuclear cooperation between the United States and India would solidify the emerging paradigm of bilateral relations with India. But the uncertainty that prevails is whether this new emerging paradigm can survive the failure of the nuclear deal to materialize. Can the government of India succeed in its efforts before facing the Indian electorate in 2009? Can the Bush Administration get the final approval of the Congress to the 123 agreement before the November 2008 elections? The delay and procedural hurdles have already begun to impact upon Indian diplomacy and foreign policy. Today, there is a bipartisan consensus in the US over the need for promoting multidimensional ties with India. But the current political commotion in India over the 123 agreement has indicated that India is a divided house on the issue of establishing better and closer relations with the United States. This is already sending a damaging message across the United States.

One can discern smiles on the faces of the Pakistanis, the Chinese and probably the Russians. Pakistan has demanded the similar treatment offered to India on the civilian nuclear sector by the US. The Bush administration's refusal to concede Islamabad's request has been taken lightly in India in view of its wishes fulfilled with minimum or no effort. Now Pakistan has a chance to heartily laugh at Indian indecision and squabbling over the nuclear deal. The degree of the Pakistani happiness will be proportionate to the intensity of the domestic political conflict over the nuclear issue.

The Chinese ruling elite as usual have refrained from overtly expressing their delight over the indecisiveness of the Indian democracy over an issue of vital national interest. But their quiet satisfaction is clearly visible to the observant eyes. Failure on the part of India would be welcome in China, since Beijing would not have to show its hesitation or haggle for economic or political gains at the Nuclear Suppliers' Group in exchange for its quiet acquiescence to alter the guidelines to enable India to enter the international nuclear market. More significantly, Beijing will consider any delay or bumps in improving US-Indian relations idyllic, since it would spare it from brooding over the ramifications of Indo-US strategic partnership.

Russia, the dominant inheritor of the former Soviet Union, has begun to flex its muscle in international politics. A rapidly growing economy with rising oil and gas revenue has enabled Russia, a military giant, to demand more space in world political and strategic affairs. Russians continue to view India as a strategic partner and are trying to increase their involvement in India's military market as well as in the energy sector. As Indian demand for energy will exponentially rise along with its galloping industrial expansion, all major powers with various sources of energy are keeping a watchful eye on the Indian energy market. Russians view an American effort to enter the Indian market through the nuclear deal as a challenge to their ambitions.

While India's traditional friend and erstwhile enemies have cause for delight in the current domestic tug of war over the Indo-US nuclear deal, the new partners of India too have begun to exhibit their shifting political posturing. Australia, for instance, has been blowing hot and cold over its intention to sell or not to sell uranium to India. Statements from Australian political leaders and officials are timed and shaped by indications of growing closeness or distance between India and the US, particularly in the field of nuclear trade. Whenever there is an event that indicates successful move towards a nuclear deal between India and the US, a statement or two is reported from Australia dangling hopes of uranium trade with India. Any event or issue that signals difficulty in signing and sealing the Indo-US nuclear deal, someone or the other from Australia puts a new spin and talks tough on uranium trade with India. The latest example is a report that suggests that if the Labour Party wins the next election in Australia, it would oppose any sale of uranium to India.

Whether one appreciates or not, most of the American allies in Asia and Europe continue to watch the signal from Washington before making economic or strategic ventures into non-traditional areas. There is little doubt that improvement in India's relations with Australia, Japan and South Korea and ASEAN countries has been partly facilitated by comprehensive expansion in Indo-US relations. But for the Clinton initiative in March 2000 and the Bush administration's determination to upgrade relations with India, India's growing economic and political links with these countries and many others would have been far from soft and shiny, as they appear to be.

One can venture a prediction that any clamminess in India's relations with the US will have cascading effect on India's over-all foreign relations with a host of countries, which share a common economic and strategic outlook with the United States. It is also likely that failure on the part of India to prevent delay or abandonment of the nuclear deal will bring considerable negative consequences for the bilateral relationship with the US. There will be, for sure, no rupture in the relationship. Even during the Indo-US duel over alliance politics versus non-alignment and a long era of India's strategic closeness with America's main adversary, the Soviet Union, the two countries experienced fruitful cooperation in very many areas. But this kind of relationship reflected the traditional paradigm. The new and emerging paradigm of Indo-US relations is very unlikely to survive the failure of the nuclear deal to take off.

Simultaneously, there is little possibility of the old paradigm returning to dominate Indo-US relations. The shifts in the global geo-politics and geo-economics, the failure of American unilateralism, rising anti-Americanism in the Islamic World, common unconventional threats to international community, unprecedented growth in the Chinese power and influence and rapid rise of Indian economy all will determine the nature of Indo-US relations in years to come. The failure of the nuclear deal will thwart the projected strategic partnership between India and the US. India will certainly witness erection of new and stronger barriers to acquiring advanced technologies in all dual use areas, including nuclear and space sciences. But the US will not be able to sideline India in global politics and economics. It would be premature at the moment to visualize the nature of a future paradigm of Indo-US relations.

Notes and References

1. For a good account of Kennedy Administration's approach towards India, see Jane S. Wilson, "The Kennedy administration and India," in Harold Gould and Sumit Ganguly, ed., *The Hope and the Reality: US-Indian Relations from Roosevelt to Reagan* (Boulder, Westview Press, 1992).
2. The present author has extensively dealt with Indo-US relations since the end of Second World War. For details, see Chintamani Mahapatra, *Indo-US Relations into the 21st Century* (New Delhi, Knowledge World, 1998).
3. Considerable frustration and exasperation of some US policy makers over India's closer ties with the former Soviet Union is revealed in Henry Kissinger, *The White House Years* (Boston, Little Brown and Co., 1979) and William Burr, ed., *Henry Kissinger Transcripts: The Top Secret Talks with Beijing and Moscow* (New York, The New Press, 1999).
4. For a detailed account of Indo-US nuclear tension see George Perkovich, *India's Nuclear Bomb: The Impact on Global Proliferation* (Berkeley, California University Press, 1999). For an Indian perspective, see Brahma Chellaney, *Nuclear Proliferation: The US-Indian Conflict* (London, Sangam Books, 1983).
5. For a balanced account of this see Dennis Kux, *United States and India: Estranged Democracies* (Washington, DC, National Defense University Press, 1992).
6. For details, see Chintamani Mahapatra, "American Approaches to Nuclear Proliferation in Asia," in Jasjit Singh, ed., *Asian Strategic Review,* 1993-94 (New Delhi, IDSA, 1993)
7. A few reports released by think tanks in the US clearly indicate a paradigm shift in US perception of India . See, for instance, Selig S. Harrison and Geoffrey Kemp, *India and America After the Cold War* (Washington, DC, Carnegie Endowment for International Peace, 1993); "South Asia and the United States After the Cold War," Asia Society Study Mission, New York, 1994; and *A New US Policy Towards India and Pakistan*, Report of an Independent Task Force, Sponsored by the Council on Foreign Relations, 1997.
8. Fact Sheet, US-India Civil Nuclear Cooperation Initiative—Bilateral Agreement on Peaceful Nuclear Cooperation, Office of the Spokesman, Department of State, Washington, DC, 27 July 2007. http://www.state.gov/r/pa/prs/ps/2007
9. The US official point of view has been very well articulated in R. Nicholas Burns, "America's Strategic Opportunity with India: The New US-India Partnership," *Foreign Affairs*, November-December 2007. Various dimensions of the US debate can also be found in Karl F. Inderfurth and Bruce Riedel, "Breaking More Naan with Delhi: The Next Stage in US-India Relations," *National Interest*, November-December 2007.

4

India–Russia Strategic Partnership

R.S. Yadav

The end of cold war has led to the transformation and restructuring of international system in substantial form. Two developments in the form of emerging unilateralism in global politics and globalization in economic sphere have emerged as outstanding features of the post-1990s world order. These changes are not only related to the relations among the major actors, but have also affected the foreign relations of numerous states. Being no exception, India-Russia relations are also affected in a significant way by these developments. Both are coping with the emerging strategic and economic situations owing to the fallouts of these catastrophic events. Both have started on a hesitant note due to their new engagements and reorientations of their foreign relations, in general, and building new bridges with the only superpower, in particular. At bilateral levels, relations between them in a substantial way must have economic bearings as both are passing through the process of structural reforms in their domestic affairs. However, the legacy of past relations between the two, alongwith multiple developments of global and regional levels, circumscribed them to engage with each other in mutual cooperation and has ultimately led to strategic partnership. This strategic partnership is not confined to their bilateral interests only but has regional and global ramifications too. Before analyzing the development and implications of strategic partnership between India and Russia, it is necessary at the outset to spell out the concept of 'strategic partnership'.

What is Strategic Partnership?

Indo-Russian relations in the post-cold war era started in the form of 'strategic cooperation' and are moving in the direction of 'strategic partnership'. If these two terms are to be understood it becomes clear that 'strategic partnership' concept is wider and comprehensive than strategic cooperation. In case of the latter, it would "imply a more proximate exchange and cooperation of views by both countries to the common challenges posed in the economic, political and security spheres."[1] Strategic partnership, on the other hand, would "imply a relationship which would not only incorporate strategic cooperation but also an added emphasis on converting the strategic convergences between the two nations into more meaningful defence and security cooperation.... In other words, an evolving alliance relationship, but short of it"[2]. Thus, the countries involved in a strategic partnership have to be "mutually interested in long-term economic, military, technological cooperation with similar, if not identical, security threats and perceptions of the coming world order."[3] India-Russia emerging ties to a great extent are not only interested in developing their bilateral economic, political and military relationships, but are also based on their common perceptions about the future of Asia and the world. To a great extent Moscow-New Delhi relationships meet the requirements of the above definition due to following reasons:

(i) India-Russia economic and political relations are on an upward swing.
(ii) Defence cooperation between the two is gaining strength day by day.
(iii) There is a broad identity of views-between the two countries on the basic regional and global issues.
(iv) The gap between the views of India and Russia on the issue of nuclear non-proliferation is not so wide and can be bridged or at least appreciably narrowed down.
(v) There are obvious parallels in the security challenges faced by the two countries.
(vi) Emerging convergence on security matters between the two is more akin to the idea of common security in Asia.
(vii) In the context of globalization, liberalization and privatization both are not only facing similar problems but are sharing common perceptions to get rid of the adversial impacts of these phenomena.

Thus, the emerging strategic partnership between India and Russia is not limited to defence cooperation between the two, but is rather involved in a more comprehensive outlook of cooperation among these states. Besides, it is based on the convergence of their perceptions about the future of Asia and emerging world order. Finally, this partnership is not against any third state, rather it is devised as a means to regulate the bilateral, regional and global emerging partnership affairs so as to preserve peace and stability in their region and the world.

Evolving Strategic Cooperation

In the post-cold war era, Indo-Russian relations started on a low profile as Russia was busy in developing a balanced approach in South Asia. Besides, due to continued pragmatism of Gorbachev era, Indian sub-continent still occupies one of the last places in the list of Russian foreign policy priorities. This was very much evident from the "Concept of Russian Federation's Foreign Policy" released at the end of 1992. Visits of Burbulis (Secretary of State) and Yevgany Primakov (Head of Russian Intelligence Service) brought out some sort of reconsiderations on the part of Russia. However, a "new beginning" of the process of change started only after the visit of President Yeltsin to India in January 1993. Signing of 10 agreements, including the Treaty of Friendship and Cooperation, and resolving the long pending issue of debt repayment between the two, normalized their ties and tilted Russia's balance in South Asia in favour of India.

The period from 1993 to 96 could be considered as a turning point for emerging strategic cooperation between the two as it laid down the trajectory for Indo-Russian strategic partnership. This change has been caused by the exchange of visits by the important dignitaries of both the countries during this period – President Boris Yeltsin (1993), Prime Minister Viktor Chernomyrdin (1994), Foreign Minister Yevgeny Primakov (1996 March and December) from the Russian side; and Prime Minister P.V. Narasimha Rao (1994), External Affairs Minister Pranab Mukherjee (1995 May and August) from the Indian side. Besides this, numerous parliamentary delegations paid mutual visits during this period. Moreover, the period of 1993-1995 can be regarded as a turning point in Russia's national development. Russia was disenchanted with its pro-Western approach in its foreign policy. "The hasty and thoughtless westernization of the country led to the political crisis of Spring-Autumn 1993, resulting in an attempt to stage a Coup d' etat in the beginning of October. The elections to the Duma showed that nationalist feelings and disenchantment with the West was gathering momentum among the political elites."[4] Finally, the Yeltsin-Kozyrev tilt towards West was also partly due to the impending fear of the eastward expansion of NATO.[5] The changes in Russian foreign policy towards India became more significant with the take over of Yevgeny Parimakov as Foreign Minister in January 1996.

The above changed context, along with the treaty of Friendship and Cooperation (28 January 1993); Declaration of Further Development and Enhancement of Cooperation (30 June 1994); and the Moscow Declaration on the Protection of Interests of Pluralistic States (30 June 1994) worked as important factors in building strategic relationship between the two countries.[6] However, Russian Prime Minister Yevgeny Primakov's visit to India, after the Pokhran II, on 20–22 December 1998, strengthened their cooperation further because during this visit, besides signing of seven agreements between them, both agreed on long term strategic cooperation, recognizing India's position on Kashmir and endorsement of its claim for the permanent seat in the UN Security Council.[7]

'Strategic Cooperation' to 'Strategic Partnership'

The formal 'Strategic partnership' agreement between India and Russia was signed during the visit of Russian President Putin to India in 2000.[8] This has taken India-Russian ties to new heights. It has significantly contributed to the further deepening of the strategic dimensions of relations between the two countries by conclusion of 10 agreements, including defence deals worth 3 billion dollars. The declaration proclaims the "establishment of relations of strategic partnership between them based on mutual understanding and long term confidence in each other" and envisages the "elevation of their multifaceted ties to an even higher and a qualitatively new level" by imparting them a "specially close and dynamic character both in the bilateral field and in the international arena".[9] The preamble of the declaration refers to the "conviction that it is necessary to build a multi-polar global structure based on sovereign equality of all states and peoples" and "desire to jointly contribute to the strengthening of international peace and security as well as to the promotion of the establishment of a new, just and stable world order...."[10] This development of partnership has not only enhanced the multi-faceted cooperation between them, but has also influenced the prospects for common security in Asia. The improvement or strengthening of their bilateral ties is manifested through their changing relations in following areas.

(a) Defence Cooperation

Despite the disintegration of erstwhile USSR, India and Russia are still major partners in defence deals. Three levels of defence cooperation continue to prevail between the two countries – (a) supply of arms by Russia; (b) helping India in the production of nuclear energy; and, (c) institutionalization of defence deals. In 1991, India was dependent in a big way on Soviet arms – 65 per cent for its army; 80 per cent for its air force; and 85 per cent for its navy. This is still continuing, either in the form of supply of spares for the old Soviet arms or purchase of new technologically advanced weapons.[11] For the supply of weapons India and Russia signed numerous MOUs during the visits of Primakov (I998), Putin (2000), Vajpayee (2001), George Fernandes (2003), etc. for building long term strategic partnership up to 2010. Russia is the main supplier of MIG-AT Jet Traver; SU-30, MIG-27, MIG-29 Fighter aircrafts; Kamov-31 and Kamov-28 helicopters; 300-T Tanks; 4TU-22M3 Backfire Strategic bombers; Akula class nuclear submarines; and, finally Gorshkov aircraft carrier to India.

India-Russia defence relations were strengthened with their cooperation in the nuclear field. Earlier Soviet Union had supplied nuclear fuel for Tarapur nuclear plant despite the protests from the United States. Later, Rajiv Gandhi and Gorbachev agreed to set up two nuclear power plants of 1,000 megawatt capacity each at Kudankulam in 1988. But it was actually implemented only after the signing of agreement with Russia in 1998 during Primakov's visit to New Delhi. Experts have estimated that the Indian nuclear power engineering market is at $30 billion, for which Russia is competing with the French and American companies to acquire a major share. Besides, India is planning to raise its level of production of nuclear power from 2,000 to 6,000 megawatt by 2010 and subsequently to 20,000 megawatt by 2020.[12] In this scenario, possibility of large share of Russia can not be ruled out at present.

For long term defence cooperation mere supply of arms will not be sufficient, rather an institutional framework between the two is needed. Both countries are aware of this fact. Consequently, Russia is not only selling arms to India but is also providing technology for its reproduction, either independently or through joint ventures. Both the countries are also engaged in the setting up of such joint ventures in Third countries as well. The protocol signed in Moscow by Defence Minister George Fernandes on 17 January 2003 is a significant landmark in the Indo-Russian Military-Technical Cooperation. Now, India is involved in the Russian programme for development of a fifth generation combat aircraft and plans to set up joint ventures in defence industry patterned after Indo-Russian Brahmos Company for production and marketing of supersonic cruise missiles. These joint ventures will yield benefit for both the defence and civilian sectors in both India and Russia.[13] Thus Russia has not only cooperated in meeting India's need for arms and supply of spares, but both have also well adapted themselves to the changing needs of globalization and privatization. Besides, both have not looked at their cooperation from the narrow perspective of mutual security, but are very much orienting themselves to the changed context of regional and global milieu.

(b) Political Understanding

The above partnership is the product of emerging political understanding among them on numerous bilateral, regional and global issues. This is evident from the fact that in recent past important leaders of both countries visited each other, e.g. President Vladmir Putin (2000 and 2002), Defence Minister Igor Ivanov (2002), and Prime Minister Vajpayee (2001 and 2003) and Defence Minister George Fernandes (2003). These visits signify the emerging commonalities between India and Russia on issues of vital interests. In this changed context both are sharing their perceptions on the problems of strengthening the United Nations, new world order, democratization of the international organizations, improvement in global financial institutions, security and stability in Central Asian Republics, nuclear non-proliferation, etc. Besides, India and Russia are making common efforts to do away with the problem of international terrorism. This has become all the more important in the wake of crisis in Afghanistan and 9/11 event in the United States. The terrorist activities in Kashmir and Chechnya provided a sound bond for common approach toward this menace. Indian and Russian initiatives in 2000 in the United Nation's Security Council are a proof of such thinking. This fact has been reiterated in the strategic partnership document where both have agreed on their concerted efforts to "fight against international terrorism, separatism, organized crime and illegal trafficking in narcotics."[14]

India and Russia are building their partnership through improvement of their relations with China. And both acknowledge that a 'strategic triangle' among India-Russia-China is required to promote peace and stability in Asia. Prime Minister Primakov's remarks on this issue during his visit to New Delhi in 1998 could be visualized in this context. Though India did not accept this idea in an explicit manner, yet both are individually making efforts to improve their bilateral ties with China. The simultaneous visits of President Putin to China and India in December 2002 have been viewed as a step forward in the direction of consolidation of ties between the three. To some extent this could also be inferred from the similarities found between the declarations of Beijing and New Delhi, issued after the visit of President Putin. All the three hold similar views on various international issues including terrorism, Iraq, West Asia, Afghanistan, developments in Central Asian Republics, role of United Nations and the regional security.[15]

India and Russia also share common perception regarding the peace, stability and developments in Central Asian Republics (CARs). If Russia is worried about this region because of its close neighbourhood, India is also very much concerned due to likely spill over impact it is going to have on this country. On the issue of terrorism, Islamic fundamentalism and political instability, in this region, both India and Russia are equally worried. Both are keenly watching the competitive influence building attempts by the outside powers in this geo-strategically volatile region. The availability of oil around Caspian Sea,[16] terrorist activities in Afghanistan with linkages in Tajikistan, Islamic fundamentalist resurgence and its support from the neighbouring states, etc. have brought both India and Russia closer to each others' foreign policy initiatives in this region. Though, a regional cooperation organization – Shanghai Cooperation Organization (SCO) – with the support of Russia and China has been formed, Putin is continuously making efforts to induct India into this organization. Thus, strategic partnership has enhanced and strengthened sound political understanding between the two countries.

(c) Economic Cooperation

Although economic factor has acquired primacy in the post-cold war global politics, the Indo-Russian partnership could not grow to the level of their cooperation in defence and political areas. This is evident from Indo-Russian trade and joint ventures run by both the countries. A look at the Indo-Russian trade statistics given below reveals this factor in a more explicit manner.

A close look of the Table 4.1 reveals that the volume of India-Russia trade is not significant. Their bilateral trade is approximately 1.5 per cent of the total trade of India. India's share of import and export is nearly 1 per cent

Table 4.1[17]: India-Russia Trade, 1993–94 to 2001–02

(*Million US $*)

Year	*Indian Exports*	*%of Indian Exports*	*Indian Imports*	*% of Indian Imports*	*Total Trade*	*%of Indian Trade*
1993–94	648.60	2.92	256.89	1.10	945.49	1.98
1994–95	807.38	3.07	504.54	1.76	1311.92	2.39
1995–96	1046.55	3.29	857.53	2.33	1904.09	2.78
1996–97	811.84	2.42	628.96	I.I6	1440.80	1.98
1997–98	954.12	2.72	679.02	1.63	1633.14	2.13
1998–99	706.26	2.14	545.42	1.29	1254.68	1.66
1999–2K	948.99	2.58	623.94	1.25	1572.93	1.82
2000–01	869.93	1.97	517.19	1.03	1387.12	1.47
200I–02	796.83	1.82	538.36	1.05	1332.19	1.41

and 2 per cent, respectively. This has become all the more difficult due to non-existence of proper banking, financial institutions, convertible currency, etc. between them. Moreover, the demand for hard currency for their mutual export-import is another serious problem between the two. Additionally, India had to pay 1 billion US $ annually to Russia as a part of its payment for debt up to 2005, followed by a smaller amount till next 33 years. The economic situation became more critical due to a weekly auction of rupee debt fund by the Vnesheconombank (Bank of Foreign Economic Affairs).

However, things are on an upward swing now as the governmental level Indo-Russian Inter-Governmental Commission on Trade, Economic, Scientific, Technological and Cultural Cooperation has been working towards promoting bilateral cooperation. It covers cooperation through eleven working groups, which ultimately are bound to influence their bilateral trade. Moreover, the recent agreement on Indo-Russian transport corridor may also help in enhancing bilateral trade by reducing transport costs. Present route, which passes through Suez Canal and enters into the Russian port of St. Petersburg via Kotka (Finland) and Rotterdam (Netherlands), is long and time consuming. The new route will be Mumbai-Bandar Abbas (Iran) – Astrakhan (Russia). Work is underway for construction of a 250 kilometer long railway line linking Bakdash on the Korobogozgol Bay on the Caspian Sea in Turkmenistan to Yeralievo in Kazakhstan. From Yeralievo to Russia the railway line is already functional, ships will carry the railway goods across the Arabian Sea from the Persian Gulf port of Bandar Abbas.[18] However, by which time and to which extent this will boost their bilateral trade is difficult to infer at the moment.

Despite some problems in trade, numerous Indian public sector companies are actively working with the Russian companies. State Bank of India, Canara Bank, India Trade Promotion Organization (ITPO), Tea Board of India and ONGC (Videsh) are actively collaborating with Russian Companies and government enterprises. ONGC (Videsh) is not only collaborating with the Russian oil company, but is also competing with the Japanese and American companies in Sakhalin oil exploration project. India has already invested approximately US $1.7 billion in this project and is likely to get oil to the tune of 2 to 4 million metric tons and 5 to 8 million cubic meters of gas annually. The only apprehension lies in the fact that this project is in the hands of the public sector companies in both the states, which are progressively moving towards privatization. As such the fate of this project is very difficult to predict. Despite availability of different trade avenues, attempt towards diversification of trade and successful working of some joint ventures in different areas, the certainty about strengthening of economic cooperation between the two is moving at a much lower pace than expected and a situation of uncertainty still looms large.

Global and Regional Implications

The strategic partnership between India and Russia has not only enhanced multi-faceted cooperation between them, but has also significant implications for emerging new world order, in general, and building up of a new Asia, in particular. It will have deep bearings for the adjoining regions, as well as, development of pan-Asian security in following ways:

(i) The end of cold war has led to the emergence of uni-polarity in the world order through the assertive foreign policy followed by the United States. It has not only destabilized the regions adjoining India and Russia, but has also violated the very dictates of international organization. Happenings in Afghanistan and Iraq have questioned marked the very functioning, and even existence of the United Nations. Thus, a concern for multi-polarity in international system has been one of the considerations in building relations between India and Russia. The recent decision of Washington to designate Pakistan as a "major non-NATO ally" (MNNA) further justifies the need for reviving their earlier ties.

While signing the strategic partnership agreement in 2000 both proceeded with the "conviction that it is necessary to build a multi-polar global structure based on sovereign equality of all states and peoples, democratic values and justice confirming their adherence to the common ideals of peace, democracy, rule of law, human rights and fundamental freedoms, non-violence and secularism....[19] and wish to "contribute to the strengthening of international peace and security, the democratization of international relations, as well as to the promotion of the establishment of a new, just and stable world order...."[20] This was reaffirmed by Prime Minister Atal Bihari Vajpayee in his address to the Russian Science Academy (12 November 2003) when he observed that the Indo-Russian relations have helped us to "evolve a comprehensive vision" in "promoting peace, security and stability both in Asia and the world."[21] Consequently, both have advocated the establishment of a multi-polar world as it is an unavoidable trend for the benefit of world peace. They are opposed to any country seeking any kind of unilateralism and hegemonism in the post-cold war era.

Hence, it is noteworthy that while highlighting 'Global Challenges and Threats to World Security and Stability' (13 November 2003) both stressed that "United Nations Organization has a vital role in tackling major international issues. The United Nation should be scanned and reformed to reflect the current realities, with a view to preserve and enhance its efficacy and efficiency."[22] Its reform, however, must presuppose respect for and observance of the UN Charter, instead of discarding or bypassing it. Though the above assertions are similar to the earlier idea of 'common security' opposing unilateralism, yet this assertiveness is not in explicit opposition of the United States of America. Rather, this time opposition was through 'engagement and containment' of the USA as well as considering the USA as their cooperative partner in the world by both the states. In their relationship with the United States, though both proceed from their respective divergent national interests and different ways, yet they hold the similar constructive standpoints of avoiding confrontation.

(ii) Another, similar but related interest to be achieved through this partnership is the evolution of 'triangle for peace and prosperity' by involving China as their third partner.[23] Though it was not explicit, but some experts are of the view that indirectly that thinking was prevailing during Prime Minister Deve Gowda's visit to Moscow, in March 1997.[24] During that visit, despite NATO's meeting at Helsinki, Yeltsin had shown much warmth than expected and Russia devoted due attention to that visit. Besides, the simultaneous presence of Chinese Foreign Minister Quan Quichen in Moscow gave birth to the speculation about the emerging triangular cooperation between India, China and Russia. During Primakov's visit to New Delhi in 1998 this idea was formally put forward by Russia. This idea of "strategic triangle" was based on the commonality of approach followed by three sides on a number of issues, such as:

(a) India-China relations in the changed context not only acknowledging but also reaffirming their firm conviction on the continuation of Panchsheel (five principles of peaceful coexistence). The broad similarity of it is found in Indo-Russian strategic partnership document as well, where it has been stated that this partnership is "based upon the principles of sovereignty, equality and territorial integrity of states, non-interference in their internal affairs, mutual respect and mutual benefit."[25]

(b) The three are making bilateral or concerted efforts towards the establishment of a multi-polar world order.

(c) They are opposed to any kind of hegemonism and unilateralism and are not in favour of any kind of interference in domestic affairs in the name of human rights, democracy or any other such pretext.

(d) Despite the difference of approach on the issue of nuclear non-proliferation in the context of NPT and CTBT, all three are in favour of nuclear disarmament as the ultimate goal for the world.

(e) They are in favour of strengthening of the United Nations as a mechanism for resolving international conflicts.

(f) They are also in favour of the growth of new international economic order to cope with the adverse impact of globalization on the developing countries.

These shared interests and identical approaches, are likely to serve the three countries in achieving a successful breakthrough in the direction of triangular cooperation. During the last few years some attempts in this direction have also been made by them. Modest beginning by India-Russia-China in the form of informal meetings of foreign ministers of three countries during the UN session in 2002 is a clear manifestation of this initiative. Moreover, establishment of military bases in Central Asian Republics and Pakistan by USA, during Afghanistan crisis, were looked upon with serious concern by all the three states. The apprehensions regarding destablization in the adjoining region are bringing out a common response from these states. Finally, the recent economic situation prevailing at global level is also a favourable development for the growth of a strategic triangle between them.

(iii) Establishment of peace and stability in the Central Asian region has been an important factor in the foreign policies of India and Russia due to convergence of geo-political interests.[26] In the post-cold war period, the growing Islamic factor increasingly assuming aggressive fundamentalist overtones in some of the Central Asian Republics and fueling secessionist movement in the Chechen Autonomous Republic of Russia, also impinges on the situation in India where a secessionist movement in Kashmir is being sustained through trans-border terrorism. Talibanisation of Afghanistan, Tajikistan and Pakistan has given birth to warlord culture or "Kalashnikov culture" which has emerged as a serious danger for the fragile ethnic mosaic of this region. The developments could create problems of instability and disorder in this proximate region of India and Russia.

Due to emerging globalization and liberalization, this region has also attracted attention of India and Russia. Availability of vast resources of oil and natural gas reserves has attracted the influence-building activities of advanced nations. Three states of Central Asian Republics (Kazakhistan,

Turkmenistan and Uzbekistan) possess the large oil fields and natural gas. Caspian Sea region is perceived as the third largest area of oil after Persian Gulf and Siberia. Kazakhstan is also described as being on the way to becoming another Kuwait. Besides, different republics possess a significant quantity of resources of uranium, gold, silver, aluminium, cotton, etc., which have implications beyond this region. Moreover, various MNCs are engaged in competition for the exploration of oil from the area. Important companies involved in this competition are Chevron (USA), British Gas (UK), Agip (Italy), Elf-Flaine (France), Lukoil (Russia), Gazprim (Russia), ONGC (Videsh) (India) etc.[27]

Existing multi-religious, multi-cultural, multi-lingual and multi-racial set up in India and pluralistic composition of Russian society brought about a convergence of interests between the two in the Central Asian Republics. Both the states favoured the continuation of plurality and multi-cultural system of governance in these republics. This conviction for plurality is well explicit in the 1994 "Moscow Declaration on the Protection of the Interests of Plural States" signed by Boris Yeltsin and P.V. Narasimha Rao during the latter's visit to Russia. It criticized and condemned the "forces of aggressive nationalism, religious and political extremism, terrorism and separatism, which strike at the unity of pluralistic states" and urged the world community to respect and strengthen their territorial integrity.[28]

Thus, Central Asian Republics, due to their geo-strategic, geo-political and geo-economic linkages provide convergence of interests between India and Russia. The latter is interested in the development of cooperation between India and the Central Asian states as a means of counterbalancing the influence on Central Asia of neighbouring Islamic countries as well as of the USA and other Western countries. India, for its part, is concerned in countering the influence of its arch-rival, Pakistan, in Central Asia, believing that Islamabad's close links with Central Asia would enable Pakistan to acquire strategic depth in any future war against India.[29]

(iv) Finally, threat of international terrorism in Asia has been another factor bringing the two countries closer and simultaneously affecting this region due to their emerging partnership. India and Russia affirmed their belief in "cooperation in the fight against international terrorism." The developments in Chechnya and Kashmir, along with the happenings in Afghanistan have created a convergence of interests of the two. Both India and Russia also submitted their proposals to the UN on how to deal with this problem. Visualizing the gravity of the situation in their "Joint Declaration between India and Russia on Global Challenges and Threats to World Security and Stability" (13 November 2003) both have evolved "essential steps in effectively and comprehensively dealing with the threat of international terrorism"[30] as under:

- creation of environment for total rejection of terrorism and absolute unacceptability of any of its forms;
- consistent and uncompromising approach to terrorism and giving up "double standards";
- preventing the flow of funds for terrorist activities;
- effective implementation of the UNSC Resolution 1373 aimed against those who support, fund or abet terrorists or provide them shelter or asylum to engage in cross-border terrorism;
- promotion of confidence between members of the anti-terrorist coalition by, inter alia, due consideration of interests of each one of them and ensuring that the fight against terrorism is strictly based on rules of international law and principles of the UN Charter;
- reinforcing national and international legal instruments for countering terrorism, making the existing anti-terrorist conventions genuinely universal, and earliest completion of negotiations on the draft conventions in the UN, including the comprehensive convention against international terrorism submitted by India and the international convention on suppression of the acts of nuclear terrorism submitted by the Russian Federation;
- steadfast cooperation to prevent terrorists from acquiring weapons of mass destruction, their means of delivery and materials and technology related to their manufacture;
- improvement of mechanism of legal assistance and extradition in order to ensure the inevitability of punishment for terrorist crimes;
- efforts to promote coexistence of different religions, cultures and civilizations by stressing greater mutual understanding and respect amongst them, especially the idea that terrorism can not be identified with any particular religion or ethnic group.[31]

It is evident that the emerging strategic partnership between the two is closely linked to their global and regional outlook apart from their bilateral compulsions. But the changes in their external milieu are difficult to be handled by them. It is constrained by numerous theoretical and operational understandings. Theoretically, establishment of multi-polar global order can not be visualized with the concurrence of the hyper power, i.e. USA. Whereas through this partnership both India and Russia are engaging the USA in an accommodative role, yet it will be largely dependent upon the American response to this thinking. Similarly, some scholars are skeptical about the establishment of strategic triangle between India, Russia and China.[32] But some experts rule out such apprehensions.[33] However, it is certain that at this moment a consensus has been missing among the three countries on building of such partnership. Until and unless differences on major issues between them are resolved such a development is ruled out for the present. Thus, Asian security will be dependent upon the development of common perception between India, China and Russia; and simultaneous accommodation of their interests by the USA.

Practically, there are certain problems which are of a global nature, hence cannot be resolved by either the concerted efforts of India and Russia, or by the developing commonalities with other states of Asia. For instance, terrorism is a world wide phenomenon, having global roots and repercussions. Hence, India-Russia partnership alone can not resolve such issues without the support of world community. Similarly, peace and stability in the region of Central Asia can not be strengthened without the support of all the concerned powers. Besides, until and unless India and Russia are successful in their economic reforms and are able to strengthen their economies, building of a new Asia will continue to be adversely effected. Moreover, despite development of sound understanding between the two on some critical issues (i.e. nuclear non-proliferation), complete convergence between all the powers and major Asian states is required.

At global level, despite some constraints, India and Russia are significantly moving towards strategic partnership between them encompassing multi-dimensional interests. Their relations in turn are bound to have positive implications for the development and security of Asia. Both India and Russia are opposed to unilateralism and hegemonism. They agree on the necessity of building a multi-polar global structure and are accordingly reorienting their relations in the context of the changed world order, by agreeing on common strategies to combat global and regional problems. They are adopting policies of accommodation in the region and are making efforts to reinforce the importance of national and international institutions.

At bilateral level, despite beginning on a hesitant note, India and Russia evolved a strong bond between them in the form of strategic cooperation. Through numerous politico-strategic initiatives in the form of 'Treaty of Friendship and Cooperation' and bilateral agreements of varied nature both were successful in developing political, social, cultural and defense cooperation between the two states. However, economic cooperation between them could not proceed with the desired momentum. In the post-Pokhran II phase their 'strategic cooperation' got transformed into 'strategic partnership' with the strengthening of their defence cooperation, political understanding and economic cooperation. Their convergence of views on the developments in Asia and at global level brought them closer to each other. But every thing has not been smooth and fine both at the bilateral and regional/global levels. However, the prevailing situation of non-polarity at global level; emerging economic strength and stability in Russia during Putin era; financial crisis in the USA, in particular, and in global capitalism in general, and evolving strategic cooperation between India and China are positive developments favouring the growth of warm relations between India and Russia. Besides, India's acquisition of nuclear status through Pokhran II, and, its recognition with the waiver agreement by Nuclear Suppliers Group (NSG) and, its entering into civil nuclear energy cooperation with France and USA are important. Besides, it has entered into similar agreement with the Russia which may further enhance their partnership. However, all this will depend upon how Indian policy makers perceive this changed global order and try to attain their national interests by reorienting their foreign policy in this new internal milieu.

Notes and References

1. Subash Kapila, "China's Quest for Strategic Cooperation with India: Perspectives", *South Asia Analysis Group*, Noida, Paper No. 936, 2004.
2. *Ibid.*
3. Artem Rudnitsky, "Russia and India: In Search of a New Strategy", *World Affairs*, Vol. 3, No. 2, April–June 1999, p. 82.
4. *Ibid.* p. 84.
5. For details regarding early foreign policy orientations of Russia see, Devendra Kaushik, "Commonwealth of Independent States and India.," *International Studies*, Vol. 30, No. 2, April–June 1993.
6. For details see, Devendra Kaushik, "India and Russia in the Post-Cold War Period: Imperatives for Building a Strategic Relationship" in Lalit Manshingh, et al., *eds., Indian Foreign Policy: Agenda for the 21st Century*, New Delhi, 1998, Vol. 2, pp. 291–298.
7. John Cherian, "Primakov's Visit", *Frontline*, 15 January 1999; and Baidya Bikash Basu, "Primakov's Visit", *Strategic Analysis*, Vol. 22, No. II, February 1999. Also see, Jyotsana Bakshi, "Russia's Post-Pokhran Dilemma", *Strategic Analysis*, Vol. 22, No. 5, August 1998, pp. 721–736.
8. For the text of documents and critical appraisal see, "Indo-Russian Strategic Partnership for Enhanced Cooperation", *Strategic Digest*, Vol. 30, No. 11, November 2000, pp. 1154–1156; "Visits of Mr. Vladimir Putin, President of Russia, to India: Statements and Speeches", *Strategic Digest*, Vol. 30, No. 10, October 2000, pp. 1453–1459; Devendra Kaushik, "India-Russia Relations New Prospects", *World Focus*, Vol. 24, No. I January 2003; Jyotsna Bakshi, "India-Russia: Strategic Partnership: President Putin's Visit", *Strategic Analysis*, Vol. 24. No. 3, November 2000, pp. 1539–1544; and Baidya Bikash Basu, "Putin's Visit and Future of India-Russia Defence Cooperation", *Strategic Analysis*, Vol. 24, No. 9, September 200, pp. 1763–1769.
9. *The Hindu*, 4 October 2000.
10. "Indo-Russian Strategic Partnership for Enhanced Cooperation", *Strategic Digest*, Vol. 30, No. 11, November 2000, p. 1554.
11. Rudnitsky, n.3, p. 86. Also see, Basu, n.7; and John Cherian, "Clinging the T-90 deal", *Frontline*, 16 March 2001.
12. Kaushik, n.8, p. 54.
13. *Ibid*, p. 5.
14. "Indo-Russian Strategic Partnership for Enhanced Cooperation", n.13, p. 1556.
15. Kaushik, n.8, p. 5.

16. For details see, R.S. Yadav and Suresh Dhanda, "Òil Politics of Caspian Sea and Central Asia: Policy Options for India," *Contemporary Central Asia*, Vol. 10, No. 2, August 2006.
17. R.S. Yadav, *Bharat ki Videsh Niti: Ek Vishleshan*, Allahabad, Kitab Mahal, 2005, p. 181.
18. Kaushik, n.8, p. 6.
19. "Indo-Russian Strategic Partnership for Enhanced Cooperation", n.10, p. 1554.
20. *Ibid.*
21. http://meaindia.nic.in/speech/2003/11/12ss01.htm.
22. http://meaindia.nic.in/declarest3.tement/2003/1l/13jd01.htm.
23. For details see, Devendra Kaushik, "The Triangle for Peace and Prosperity", *World Focus*, Vol. 24, Nos. (10-11-12), Oct-Nov-Dec. 2003.
24. M.L. Madhu, "For Multi-polar World: Role of Russia, China and India", *The Tribune*, 22 May 1997; V.P. Dutt, "India's Options: Russia's Slow Emergence", *The Tribune*, 19 April 1997; Alexai Almanov and Sergai Strokov, "Moscow Looks East Ward", *Outlook*, 9 April 1997; and *Times of India*, 26 March 1997.
25. "Indo-Russian Strategic Partnership for Enhanced Cooperation", n.10, p. 1554.
26. For Indian interests in this region see, R.S. Yadav, "India and the Central Asian Republic.," *World Focus*, Vol. 20, Nos. 10-11-12, Oct-Nov-Dec. 1999.
27. *Ibid.* p. 63.
28. For text of the declaration see, Jyotsna Bakshi, *Russia and India: From Ideology to Geopolitics*, New Delhi, 1999, Appendix I, pp. 291–293. Also see, "A New Entente: Narasimha Rao's Moscow visit", *Frontline*, 29 July 1994.
29. Anita Inder Singh, "India's Relations with Russia and Central Asia", *International Affairs*, Vol. 71, No. 1, January 1995, p. 80.
30. http://meaindia.nic.in/declarestatement/2003/11113jd01.htm.
31. *Ibid.*
32. Rudnitsky, n.3, p. 96. For comments by Alexander Salitsky and Sham Lal see Kaushik, n.23, p. 46.
33. Kaushik, n.23, pp. 44–48. Also see, Chintamani Mahapatra, "India, China and Russia: Strategic Triangle is Possible", *Strategic Analysis*, Vol. XXII, No. 11, February 1999, pp. 1793–1796.

5

Changing Security Paradigm and India-China Relations

Roop Singh Bareth

I

The national security has remained the foremost endeavour of all the states at all times irrespective of their geo-political locations and power profiles. Though the nature of challenges primarily determines the threat perceptions and security concerns of the states, discipline of strategic studies has remained, by and large, 'state-centric' in its nature. The problem of national security and its perceptions differ from state to state, therefore, the nature of challenges together with state and its capabilities, which are mainly responsible for dealing with the security threats, may be external or internal and military or non-military they are important variables in the theorization of the conceptual frame-works of security.

In the classical sense, national security is understood and defined as protection from external aggression, i.e. military defence against military threats or attacks. In other words, security was placed as the top-most national interest – 'non negotiable' national interest[1], to be promoted and protected by national power defined mainly in terms of military power. This viewpoint was based on the assumption that the best guarantee to one's security is to boost one's military power and thus 'national power' remained the 'supreme virtue' in the security strategies and defence policies and as such 'peace' and 'development' were relegated to secondary positions in such calculations.

The 'military' component still holds the key-position in all strategic calculations and defense strategies, but in the modern times 'security', in the true sense, involves something more than this. A broad definition of national security is needed which involves non-military threats and internal threats which are posed to the national security and are certainly, in some circumstances, no less dangerous than the external military threats. The non-military threats emanating from economic, political, socio-cultural, environmental sectors constitute severe challenges to the national security and deserve serious consideration in the study of security problems and perceptions. Now a days, the non-military threats to security have emerged as of prime concern for the global community. Underdevelopment and declining prospects for development, mismanagement and waste of resources, degradation of the environment and threats to sustainable development constitute prime challenges to security. Not only this, gross and systematic violations of human rights, malnutrition afflicting a large proportion of the world's population and mass-poverty along with centralization of wealth and monopoly over global resources all lead to inter-state rivalries resulting in insecurities. According to Arnold Wolfers, in a broader definition, "security, in an objective sense, measures the absence of threats to acquired values, in a subjective sense, the absence of fear that such values will be attacked"[2]. Hence, the conception of security need not be restricted merely to the condition of 'the absence of war' or 'preparation for war'. In a holistic view, 'security' is a multi-dimensional phenomenon in which domestic, regional and global components of a varied nature loom large and "the military aspect of security is seen to be merely a part of a bigger picture"[3]. So, in a broader sense, security means the capability of a state to protect its 'core values' both from internal as well as external threats.

Building a sound theory of 'national security' has always been a problematic proposition. The concept suffers from vagueness and as such has often been used for rhetorical purposes rather for sound analytical value. Security does not end up with the ability to protect one's core values, it involves a sense of security as well and, hence, it is also a psychological phenomenon. Dietrich Fischer has pointed out that security has two aspects. First, the absence of objective dangers, and second, the absence of subjective fears[4]. Therefore, security is not merely a condition of being protected; it is also a feeling of safety and a sense of freedom from fear or apprehensions. This is the reason that in the analytical realm of security, the problem of security is as important, some times more than the perception of threats. The crux of the matter is what are the threats? They may be external or internal; and how they are perceived? Sometimes the exposed dangers or threats are deliberately exaggerated to justify the military preparedness and resultant military expenditures and some times they may be overlooked. In the sound strategic analysis, the states should possess a 'sense of security' as well as 'be secured' actually if attacked. Hence, in the theoretical domain of security the perception of threats as well as the preparedness for threats both are important indices. Furthermore, security is also not an absolute phenomenon. It is not possible to measure security of a state on absolute yardsticks. It could be understood in relative conditions and hence, it comes out to be a 'relational phenomenon' in practice. The ability of a state to defend its core values is judged in relative positions in a given strategic environment. Not only the threats are perceived, in order to give full security against those threats, the sources of threats, its magnitude etc. are equally important in defense strategies and logistics. If security includes 'perceptions of threats' and 'preparedness for threats' through military measures, it also encompasses the creation of 'conditions for peace' through non-military measures in its domain. But in the theoretical formulations, Barry Buzan has rightly pointed out that both the Realists as well as the Idealists have weakened the conceptual analysis as "the former have subsumed security under their preferred idea of power and the latter have subsumed it under the notion of peace". Thus, the concept of security is a complex proposition which need to be understood and analysed with a broader view in which all aspects be taken care of both through military and non-military measures.

II

It is a strange fact of history that the advent of democracy in India in 1947 coincided with the emergence of cold-war politics which clouded the Afro-Asian scene at such a critical juncture when these states were yet to establish their independent identities in the comity of nations. India's independence, thus, not only ushered a new era in Asia and the third world but also coincided with the dawn of a new epoch in the world history. Inaugurating the Asian Relations Conference (ARC) in New Delhi on March 23, 1947 Pandit Nehru, visualizing the dawn of a new epoch, called upon the delegates that there was a widespread urge and awareness that the time had come for "peoples of Asia to meet together, hold together and advance together"[6]. It was not a vague desire but the compulsion of events which forced the newly independent states to think and act along these lines. The old order of imperialism and colonialism was fast receding into the oblivion and a new international system, dominated by two rival hegemonistic super-powers as "prime movers of the world" had emerged on the horizons. Equipped with the most deadly weapons of the time, the two super-powers plunged into the politics of bi-polarization along with the formation of military blocs and political groupings in which the 'independence' – in the true sense of the term, and 'security' of the newly independent states were put to severe threats. These states were forced to make undesirable compromises with their sovereign identities and unwilling concessions in the realm of security.

Nearer home in the regional milieu several significant developments took place which re-oriented and re-focused the problem of India's security into a new and altogether different rather difficult context. Notable among them were, first, the emergence of a hostile state — Pakistan in 1947 and second, the establishment of People's Republic of China (PRC) after the communist revolution in 1949. The formation of Pakistan as a separate sovereign state after the partition would not have had as grave consequences as emergence of Pakistan as a "hostile neighbour" did[7]. Similarly, any political change across the Himalayas would not have mattered much to New Delhi as did China's emergence as a communist giant more so at the time when the global environment was fully charged, in the most bitter form, with the politics of bi-polarization and the resultant cold-war euphoria. The defence policy enunciated and very well implemented by the British India was neither functional nor desirable in the changed circumstances and therefore it was, indeed, a herculean task to prepare and practice a policy to seek solutions for the security problems in the context of deteriorating domestic conditions, on the one hand, and the outside uncomfortable regional milieu over-shadowed with the cold-war politics, on the other hand.

Political Solutions to the Security Problems

It was under the background of this emerging strategic scenario in the sub-continent that independent India had to reformulate its political perceptions and priorities and accordingly had to recast its strategies for security. The principle of non-alignment, above all, was a political strategy to keep the cold-war politics and military rivalries away from Asia so as to ensure "Asia for Asians". On the one hand, it was a strategy to keep off super-powers rivalries and active involvement so that India could naturally attain and establish its dominant position in the region, while on the other hand it was a long-range pursuit to attain international prestige through newly created Afro-Asian non-aligned bloc in the bi-polarised world. Forging Sino-Indian friendship expressed as "Sino-Indian axis" at Bandung was no less a collective endeavour to seek political solutions of the security problems not only in the sub-continent but in Asia at large. Similarly, the diplomatic efforts through ARC's for forging Afro-Asian solidarity, the initiation of solving J&K problem through the good offices of the UN or resolving the Tibetan issue through the Panchsheel, irrespective of their final outcomes, were enough to prove that in the initial phase serious efforts were made by New Delhi to diffuse and dissolve the security-problems through political solutions and conversely, it appears that no well thought out defense policy based on sound military preparedness and strategic calculations was formulated. All the political arrangements made through ARC's or through the Panchsheel were found incapacitated and the strategies of non-alignment also got exposed when Pakistan joined SEATO in 1954 dragging down the cold-war politics to the doors of India, and the Chinese aggression in 1962 totally exposed India's defense policy, if there was any, and defense preparedness.

After 1962, Nehru was a 'broken man' and India was an exposed and humiliated nation, yet it is true that the 'widespread urge' for resolving security problems through political and not through military measures continues to remain relevant even today and therefore, it provides a vantage point at the dawn of the new millennium for the academics to re-examine and re-establish its relevance and hard necessity in the conflict-riddled world equipped with the deadly weapons of mass destruction.

III

The last decade of the 20th century witnessed one of the most rapid pace of changes in the global environment in the recent human history. Beginning with the fall of Berlin wall in 1989 a number of developments have occurred, most notably, the disintegration of the USSR in 1991, which has substantially altered the power equilibrium in the international system causing serious consequences for the regional and the sub-regional systems in the world. The end of the Soviet Union is not merely the demise of a state, rather it is the break-down of the super-powers dominated 'international bi-polar system' and hence a "systemic collapse" with far-reaching consequences. The new "poly-centric system" is still to establish itself in the true sense and this seems to be one of the reason that the post-cold-war international scenario is severely infected with the voices of 'unilateral interventionism', 'unstability' and 'insecurity'.

The logical conclusion of the above mentioned trends is that the 'phenomenon of intervention' has become a fact of international life. On the pretext of self-defense, or in the name of human rights, or on account of LPG reforms, the developed and powerful states of the 'North' are seeking clues shamelessly to make interventions to aggrandize their selfish interests in the developing nations of the 'South'. Sanctions are imposed arbitrarily and interferences are made in the domestic affairs of the states in the name of self-defense, human rights, arms control, non-proliferation of nuclear and missile technologies and intellectual property rights. Recently, the then UN Secretary General Kofi Annan expressed his deep concern against the "doctrine of pre-emptive military intervention" and observed that "if it were to be adopted, it could set precedents that would result in the proliferation of the unilateral and lawless use of force with or without credible justifications"[8]. It is a paradoxical situation that the US is no longer worried of any super-power rivalry, yet it is deeply shocked and frightened by the "rogue states" and other well-armed bands of highly motivated groups and this has resulted in a major 'paradigm shift' in the US foreign policy as well as in its defense strategies.

The beginning of the nineties coincided with the dawn of a new era of globalization, liberalization and privatization in the international economics and trade. The state economies, particularly in the developing countries, so far protected and confined within the state boundaries, have been forced to globalize their markets and resources. The state control over its economic enterprises was forced to be liquidated gradually and the MNCs and the TNCs were allowed to enter the domestic markets and thus 'non-state actors' and the 'supra-state structures' started to redefine and redesign the emerging international economic and trade system in the world. In the field of science and technology, the 'technetronic' and the 'cybernetic' advancements have almost revolutionized the means and patterns of communication in the world rendering physical distances and detachments of national boundaries almost ineffective and immaterial. Thus, the international scenario, emerging at the dawn of the new millennium, seems to the qualitatively different and challenging in terms of security syndrome and strategic environments.

IV

The end of the 20th century witnessed a significant change in the security environment of South Asia. After a 'self-induced restraint of about twenty-four years, India, on May 11 and 13, 1998 redemonstrated its will and capability for the nuclear option through *Pokhran*-II in the deserts of western Rajasthan. Nothing that has happened in India and Pakistan in the last fifty years or so has potentially graver consequences for the future of the people than the nuclear weapons tests of May 1998. Whatever may be the pros and cons of the *Pokhran*-II in the wider realms of the international peace and security, it is a truism to say that it has substantially affected and altered the security environment in South Asia. In the regional context, India, China and Pakistan have been the major internal actors who had determined and designed the security environment in the region. Unfortunately, India's relations with either had remained far from cordial and this had resulted into not only mutual distrust and hostility but into open blood baths which had considerably deteriorated the security environment in this region. *Pokhran*-II, therefore, makes a land-mark in this regard with far reaching consequences and complications in their bi-lateral and tri-lateral relationships and, hence, deserves to be probed in depth in order to analyze and assess the emerging security scenario in the region.

Pokhran-II and the PRC

In fact, the nuclear rivalry in the region was first triggered on by China when it exploded its first nuclear test at Lop Nor in the plateau of Shanghai on October 16, 1964[9]. The ostensible reasons or compulsions behind China going nuclear may be lying elsewhere and not be necessarily rooted in the regional politics, yet it had tremendous impact on Sino-Indian relations as a natural fall out. Sisir Gupta, a noted academician and one of India's ablest diplomats, had rightly pointed out India's perception with his observation that: "without using its nuclear weapons and without unleashing the kind of war which would be regarded in the West as the crossing of the provocative threshold, China may subject a non-nuclear India to periodic blackmail, weaken its people's spirit of resistance and self-confidence and thus achieve without a war its main political and military objectives in Asia"[10]. India's apprehensions were not totally unfounded. In the following years, China's attitude, particularly the Sino-Pak collusion to create hostile political environment and insecure security scenario in the region, compelled India to review its nuclear policy of non-proliferation. The India-China conflict of 1962 – the severest blow to the India's foreign policy, left Nehru 'broken' and totally incapacitated to review or reformulate India's security policy and only few months quietly passed away before the Chinese re-appeared with the nuclear teeth. Lal Bahadur Shastri did absolve the humiliated nation by winning 1965 war against Pakistan and also made some efforts to obtain a nuclear guarantee from the nuclear weapon states[11] but his tenure was too short to permit any significant change at the policy formulation level and as such the task was left to his successor, Mrs. Gandhi[12]. Due to deteriorating security scenario in the sub-continent, 'flexibility' crept into the basic postulates of the doctrine of non-alignment and the Indo-Soviet Treaty of Peace and Friendship was signed in August, 1971. Though, it was viewed as a 'major compromise' with the principle of non-alignment, Mrs. Gandhi boldly defended this flexibility in India's policy and stated, "We will shift as and when our national interests compel us to do so"[13]. Finally, in May 1974 *Pokhran*-I, called as a 'peaceful nuclear explosion', witnessed the complete change in India's nuclear policy, and India reluctantly crossed the conventional threshold to join the nuclear club in the comity of nations[14].

Pokhran-II, though, carried out after a lapse of twenty-four years, struck a 'balance of terror' in the true sense by imposing the "power-parity" between the two states across the Himalayas. China remained no less behind in condemning the *Pokhran*-II along with some other western powers but at the bottom of its heart it accepted India's power profile to reckon with. It proved to be a positive factor in stabilizing their bilateral relationship and thus rather than retarding it allowed the accelerated pace of positive development in their cordial relationship irrespective of many other irritants and obstacles. Looking in the past, it appears quite true that inspite of many reasons, mainly political, responsible for the steep deterioration in Sino-Indian relations in the end of the fifties, the Chinese brute military aggression would not have humiliated India had the power-parity been maintained. This is one of the reasons that in the new millennium both the countries have willingly down played and pushed 'the border dispute' – which once caused a bloody war, under the carpet and are embarking, very confidently, upon the path of economic co-operation and technological collaboration. Thus, it appears that 'power-parity' seems to be a precondition for "controlled peace" if not "complete peace" for the future co-operation between the two Asian giants and wisdom lies in maintaining it.

The Chinese foreign policy has always remained 'Sino-centric' and proved to be the most 'prudent policy' in promoting and protecting its national interests. Commenting on the character of the Chinese foreign policy, J.N. Dixit rightly pointed out that "the Chinese do not believe in pulling other people's chestnuts out of the fire".[15] Chinese, in the past, have proved beyond doubt that they hardly hesitate in resorting to military measures in order to 'teach a lesson' whenever their national interests so warrant. Therefore, India should involve and implement a prudent policy based on 'realities' rather than 'rhetorics' and allow the fullest co-operation and collaboration in their bi-lateral relationship on the basis of mutual respect and reciprocity.

Tibet has remained and is likely to remain the most volatile cause of misperceptions and misunderstandings. Through the Panchsheel agreement the issue of Tibet has been resolved and India accepted 'Chinese suzerainty' over it and the Chinese also showed patience in not demanding India's 'erstwhile British rights' unilateral withdrawal till *Panchsheel* was signed. But in the following years, Tibet emerged as the major cause of rival perceptions leading to Dalai Lama's flight to India in 1959 and the consequent Chinese military assault in 1962. Even today, Tibet constitutes the main cause of suspicion and distrust. The issue is enough internationalized in the past but now it appears that the new leadership in China under Hu Jintao is sincere enough to resolve it and in this pursuit India's willing co-operation is considered as a precondition in Beijing. First, on the issue of Tibet, China's international image is much maligned and the world forces continue to keep the issue too hot to dance upon for China. In other words, Tibet is considered as a 'safe leverage' to pressurize China to counterpoise in International politics. Second, China itself is constrained due to its own limitations within Tibet. Third, the Beijing leadership is conscious of the fact that, in the final resolution of the problem of Taiwan, the peaceful solution of the problem of Tibet, if not a pre-condition, is at least a desirable one for the long range national interests. Last, as China is preparing hard for Olympics in 2008 to exploit it as an occasion to project its 'global image' particularly in the western world, Beijing seems to be serious enough in preparing a road-map to stage a successful come back for Dalai Lama to finally resolve the issue.

Keeping the pace of economic co-operation and technological collaboration at full swing, New Delhi has to play its diplomatic cards very carefully at least in this regard. The importance of Tibetan card be realistically re-assessed in the context of the new developments that have taken place in the nineties and in view of the emerging attitudinal changes taking place in the Chinese foreign policy towards India, particularly on Sikkim very recently[16]. Time has come when India should stop looking at Tibet through the eyes of the West, rather it should independently evaluate the issue in view of its own national interests. In this regard, if at all an occasion arises when Tibetan issue seems to be nearer to resolution, India should have little hesitation in accommodating Chinese sensitivities and in offering its good offices[17]. In such negotiations, India should firmly stand for resolving the border dispute and a sound strategy be prepared in which both the issues be resolved amicably. The territorial imperative has created a deadlock in the Sino-Indian relations for almost more than four decades. Now time seems to be ripe for serious deliberations. Tang Jiaxuan, the Chinese State Councilor has said that Russia and China have recently sorted out their border dispute once and for all. He made an optimistic observation that "being personally involved in the settlement of this question, I know very clearly that the boundary question between China and Russia was far more complicated than that between our two countries[18]. The territorial issue be, therefore, amicably resolved through political dialogue and diplomacy within the ambience of national interests.

It is crystal clear that initial momentum in China's relations with the South Asian countries came from its hostility towards India. China continuously played 'anti-Indian card' for a fairly long period of time through India's neighbours – Pakistan, Nepal and Bangladesh and under the same strategy to mount pressure on India, the Sino-Pak collusion appeared and was strengthened to the extent that Beijing made available all possible help to provide 'nuclear teeth' to Islamabad. However, as an instant reaction to *Pokhran*-II, Pakistan has also carried out successful nuclear explosion projecting its nuclear power profile. The nuclear proliferation in South-Asia has led to certain objective conditions: First, India and Pakistan both had been compelled not to resort to military measures in order to resolve their disputes. In other words, a condition of 'controlled peace' is imposed in which India should take initiative and advantage too, to restrain and if possible resolve the bilateral problems through non-military measures, i.e., through diplomatic dialogue and political solution. Second, Pakistan is a 'garrison-state' surviving on its military power but its internal conditions are alarmingly pushing it towards a chaotic and 'civil-war' like conditions. India must evolve a contingency plan and prepare for pre-emptive strategies to deal with 'dis-uniting Pakistan' especially in view of its nuclear weapons and religious militancy. Third, in the context of improved and still improving Sino-Indian relationship, India may take advantage, if diplomatic cards are played carefully, to wean China away from the Sino-Pak collusion aimed against India so as to forge a conducive security environment in the region to realize legitimate Indian interests. The Chinese Vice-Foreign Minister Wu Dawei, who was recently in New Delhi for the detailed discussion of Chinese Premier, Wen Jiabao's proposed Indian visit this year had said that "India and China have agreed at their 'first-ever strategic dialogue' and both the countries shared the view that terrorism, particularly, the possibility of weapons of mass destruction and sensitive technologies falling in the hands of terrorists, presented a grave threat which could not be tackled unitaterally"[19]. Thus, India can initiate and involve China in making a conducive strategic environment in the region.

Foreign policy is always a paramount necessity of a sovereign state. Independent India had devised new conceptual paradigms in its foreign policy to negotiate the bipolar world in the cold war milieu. In the post-cold war scenario, it is true that the strategy of non-alignment has been to a great extent rendered, 'non-functional' and *Panchsheel* has lost its appeal. India should evolve new theoretical formulations and paradigms in its foreign policy to restore its international prestige in the new global age.

Notes and References

1. Security is considered as 'non-negotiable' national interest. For detailed analysis, see, F.S. Northedge, *The International Political System* (Faber and Faber, London, 1976).
2. Arnold Wolfers, *Discord and collaboration: Essays on International Politics* (John Hopkins University Press, Baltimore, 1962): 150.
3. Barry Buzan, *People, States and Fear: The National Security Problem in International Relations* (Wheatsheaf Books Ltd., Sussex, 1983): 253.
4. Dietrich Fischer, *Nonmilitary Aspects of Security: A systems Approach* (UNIDIR, Dartmouth, 1995): 10.
5. Buzan, n.3, 173.
6. Jawaharlal Nehru, 'Changing India', *Foreign Affairs*, XLI (3), April 1963: 455.
7. See, Sisir Gupta, *India and Regional Integration in Asia* (Asia Publishing House, Bombay, 1964) and his, *India's Relations with Pakistan 1954-57.*
8. Kofi Annan, while addressing the UN General Assembly on 23rd September, 2003 expressed his deep concern against the doctrine of 'pre-emptive military intervention', B.M. Sharma and Roop Singh Bareth, *Good Governance, Globalization and Civil Society* (Rawat Publication, New Delhi, 2004): 106.
9. For details see, John Wilson Lewis and Xue Litai, *China Builds the Bomb* (Stanford University Press, Stanford, 1988).
10. Sisir Gupta, 'The Indian Dilemma' in Alastair Buchan (ed.) *A World of Nuclear Powers* ? (Prentice-Hall, Englewood Cliffs, 1966): 55–67.
11. In December, 1964 at a press conference in London, Prime Minister Lal Bahadur Shastri revealed India's efforts to obtain a nuclear guarantee from the nuclear weapons states. See, A.G. Noorani, 'India's quest for a Nuclear Guarantee' *Asian Survey*, Vol. 7, No. 7, July, 1967: 490–502.
12. For details regarding Mrs. Gandhi's decision for nuclearisation, See, K. Subrahmanyam, 'Nuclear India in Global Politics', *World Affairs*, Vol. 2, No. 3, July-Sept., 1998: 30.
13. Surjit Man Singh, *India's Search for Power* (Sage Publications, New Delhi): 180.
14. For the nature of the nuclear test, see, Adirupa Sengupta, 'Scientist says Bomb was Tested in' 74' *India Abroad* (New York), October 17, 1997: 14.
15. J.N. Dixit, *India's Foreign Policy* (Picus Books, New Delhi, 2003): 83.
16. C. Raja Hohan, 'Sikkim and the road to Lhasa', *The Hindu*, May 10, 2004.
17. Amit Baruah, 'A Reality Check on Tibet', *The Hindu*, August 21, 2004.
18. Quoted in, Amit Baruah, 'China backs India's Dialogue Policy on Kashmir' *The Hindu*, October, 20, 2004.
19. *The Hindu*, January 25, 2005.

6

India–Pakistan Imbroglio

Savita Pande

Regional security in South Asia has been well analysed by Barry Buzan whose regional security systems operate in "security complexes". In the South Asian region, a bipolar rivalry security complex prevails in which India and Pakistan are the main protagonists. To quote him, "The South Asian complex centers on the interlocked insecurities of its two major actors, India and Pakistan. Its structure is consequently quite straightforward, and the minor states are caught up in it, mostly for reasons of geography – Nepal, Bhutan, Bangladesh and Sri Lanka – make little impact. Afghanistan and Burma reside on its periphery. The core rivalry between India and Pakistan, which defines South Asian complex, has existed since both the states became independent in 1947. The two states have fought three wars (1947–48, 1965, 1971), and throughout the period each has been at the center of the other's local source of insecurity. Their rivalry has adopted most of the conventions that mark the relations between the competing states. They have unresolved territorial disputes in Kashmir and in Rann of Kutch, which give their hostility a tangible and enduring touchstone. Less tangibly, there is a long standing power struggle between them that reflects Pakistan's unwillingness to allow the naturally greater weight of India in de facto Indian hegemony over the subcontinent. This struggle has manifested itself in continuous arms race between the two that now seems close to spilling over into the great equalizer of nuclear weapons."[1]

In fact, the centrality of "Indo-Pak equation in the regional security domain is now an accepted norm." To quote Iffteqar Zaman, "Critical to peace in South Asia is the evolving political and strategic order in the region, in which a key determinant is Indo-Pakistan relations."[2] Interestingly, within this dominant discourse is the subset of two predominant security issues, believed to be impinging on global security: the Kashmir issue and the nuclear issue, interlinked by the west, topping the agenda. The Kashmir issue, in particular, became interchangeable with cross border terrorism for India and "self determination", "freedom struggle" or *Jihad* (holy war) for the Pakistanis in the 1990s. Climax was reached when Kargil war took place in the nuclearised region, dealing a severe blow to the bonhomie of Lahore Peace process started by Atal Bihari Vajpayee as he met his counterpart Nawaz Sharif in Lahore. Then came the Agra Summit in July 2001 when "cautious optimism" rose once again as "bold initiatives" were envisaged, all that happened was discussion on the Kashmir issue, cross-border terrorism, nuclear risk reduction, release of prisoners of war, and commercial ties which led to nothing, making the summit a failure, for all practical purposes.

As this paper goes to press, there is an uncomfortable thaw in the latest round of India–Pakistan Peace Process launched in 2004 as Prime Minister Vajpayee and General Musharraf met on the sidelines of the 12th South Asian Association for Regional Cooperation in the form of the composite dialogue which began in February 2004 which has almost become clichéd, General (now retired) Musharraf's bid to solve the disputes "out of the box" notwithstanding. The Joint Statements of 6 January 2004, 24 September 2004, 18 April, 14 September and 4 October 2005 speak of the movement made in the peace process on various issues, serve as examples. The peace process suspended again by India in July 2006 after the terrorist attacks on a train in Mumbai in which over 50 people were killed, however, was resumed in September when Indian Prime Minister Manmohan Singh met General Musharraf in Havana, Cuba, during the Non-Aligned Summit where came the proposal of 'joint anti-terrorism mechanism' a non-starter and produced nothing substantial for India. Even this clichéd process is standstill as Pakistan undergoes a tragic moment in its life as former Prime minister Benazir Bhutto died in the election rally in a terrorist attack.

The composite dialogue covers Kashmir, Siachen, Wullar Barrage/Tulbul Navigation Project, Sir Creek, terrorism and drug trafficking; economic and commercial cooperation, and promotion of friendly exchanges in various fields. While the major issues almost stand where they were, much has been said about the positive (small) steps. These include: the November 2003 ceasefire along the LOC, which ended armed hostilities after thirteen years, still holds. On April 7, 2005, a bus line between Srinagar, the capital of Jammu and Kashmir (J&K), and Muzaffarabad, the capital of Azad Jammu and Kashmir (AJK) part of Pakistan Occupied Kashmir was re-established, allowing divided families to meet for the first time since 1956. After the October 8,2005 earthquake in AJK region of Pakistan Occupied Kashmir, India and Pakistan agreed to open the LOC at five points to facilitate the provision of humanitarian assistance as well as meetings between divided families. In May 2006, agreement was reached to open the LOC to trade by launching a truck service on the Srinagar-Muzaffarabad route, as well as a second cross-Kashmir bus service, linking Poonch in J&K with Rawalakot in AJK region of Pakistan Occupied Kashmir.

Additional rail and road links have been reopened across the international border between the two countries. These include a bus service linking, Amritsar, holy city particularly for Sikhs, in India, with Nankana Sahib, the birthplace of Guru Nanak Dev in Pakistan. The immediate steps to stabilise ceasefire including a commitment to refrain from developing new posts and defence work along the LOC; monthly meetings between local commanders; and the speedy return of inadvertent line crossers, upgradation of the dial-up hotline between the DGMOs (Directors General Military Operations) has been made secured and dedicated; agreements on the pre-notification of ballistic missile flight tests; and operationalisation of the hotline between foreign secretaries lying in disuse since 1990s.

Post 9/11 Scenario

Pakistan once again came to the forefront of the US security calculation in the aftermath of the September 11 terrorist attacks in the United States masterminded by Osama bin Laden, the doyen of Islamic militancy supposedly living in Afghanistan at the time of the attacks and absconding since. Pakistan's strategic location, being the neighbour of Afghanistan, its economic needs, the domestic political fluidity all combined together in getting it the United States attention of an unprecedented sort as it agreed to play the ball. Not only did Musharraf reverse the agenda within, taking the Jihadis head on, attacking the *madaris and initiating* talks of reforming them.

Kanti Bajpai has listed four factors that contributed to the change in Pakistan after the 9/11 attacks when overnight, Islamabad was free to focus all its attention and resources on the great satan, India. First was its transformation from almost "pariah" state to an internationally respectable entity. Second was financial assistance to an economically wrought state. Third was the consolidation of Musharraf's rule. Fourth, the US war in Afghanistan because of which at one stroke got rid of three strategic liabilities for Pakistan – Al Qaeda, the Taliban, and indeed Afghanistan itself.[3] The US led campaign against terrorism of 9/11 saw no let up in the terrorist activities. Apart from the above listed attack on the Kashmir Assembly in October 2002 or the Indian Parliament two months later, attack on the Indian Army camp in May 2002, the massacre of the Amarnath pilgrims, the attack on the Akshardham temple in Gujarat in August 2002; and on the temples in Jammu in November 2002 are some of the cases that substantiate the point. The build up of troops on the border by India discussed above was in response to spurt in the activities ostensibly supported by Pakistan, particularly the attack on the Indian Parliament.

According to Stephen Cohen, Washington made seven demands of Islamabad, which the latter readily acceded to. These were (i) stopping Al Qaeda operatives at the Pakistan border and ending all logistic support for Osama bin Laden; (ii) providing blanket over flight and landing rights to the United States; (iii) access to Pakistani naval and air bases and along the border;

(iv) immediate intelligence and immigration information; (v) condemnation of the September 11 attacks and the curb of all domestic expressions of support for terrorism against [the United States], its friends or allies; (vi) termination of fuel shipments to the Taliban and the flow of Pakistani volunteers going to join the Taliban in Afghanistan; and (vii) breaking diplomatic relations with Afghanistan and providing assistance to the United States in bringing down the Taliban and Al Qaeda if the evidence strongly implicated Al Qaeda and the Taliban continued to harbour it and Osama bin Laden.[4]

A major non-NATO status was accorded to Pakistan in the beginning of 2004, the announcement for which was made by Colin Powell during his visit to Pakistan in 2004, formally designated so on June 16, 2004. India resented and regretted that the United States "kept it in dark" on the issue. Many also suspect that the origin to current peace process is also rooted in what is popularly called in this part of the world "American Pressure". Thus ensued, there are three strands of regular interaction taking place between India and Pakistan. The Aziz-Dixit popularly known as 'back channel', the Kasuri-Natwar interaction and the bureaucrats, led by the foreign office in both the countries belonging to various ministries related to the disputes being discussed through the "composite dialogue" moves for which were set rolling at the SAARC meeting in Islamabad by the then Prime Minister Atal Bihari Vajpayee. As usual the dialogue has been described as: "If the momentum of the meetings is kept and each time some agreement, however small it may be, is produced at the end of the meeting, the chances of desired resolution of all issues and disputes would certainly appear to be rather brighter".[5]

The Kashmir Dispute

Tracking a long journey, as a colonial legacy and unsettled issues of partition, from the throes of accession, 1947 aggression, UN mediation, plebiscite, 1954 elections and then the 1965 war, the issue finally came into the gambit of "bilateralism" in the Shimla Agreement in 1972, India's strongest defence against third party or international mediation. From then on till 1989 the issue remained buried under the claims and counter claims, the year being significant in this context because of Soviet withdrawal from Afghanistan and Pakistan's diversion of mercenaries trained to fight the Soviet supported regime in Afghanistan. As things stand now India claims, rooted in its declared secular framework, the entire state of Jammu and Kashmir, as its integral part and Pakistan, focusing on Islamic identity, harps on settling the issue according to the UN security council resolutions seeking to settle the issue according to the wishes of the people of Kashmir, meaning plebiscite, the announcement by Musharraf of keeping this resolution aside notwithstanding.

The issue is more complicated than this, rooted in Pakistan's changed military strategy. A serving Pakistani army officer, Brigadier Malik's book

The Quranic Concept of War is significant in this context, more so because the preface to the book was written by Gen Zia, then Chief Martial Law Administrator, himself. Two basic concepts that it underlines is, that terror should be struck in the heart of the enemy and any means are justified for that purpose including nuclear weapons. Secondly, war should be fought in the territory of the enemy. To quote relevant portions, "whatever the form or type of strategy directed against the enemy, it must in order to be effective, be capable of striking terror into the heart of the enemy. A strategy that fails to attain this condition suffers from inherent drawbacks and weaknesses: and should be reviewed and modified. *This rule is fully applicable to nuclear as well as conventional wars* and the aggressor was always met and destroyed in his own territory".[6] Significantly, a military assessment undertaken in Pakistan also stressed the point – that Pakistan lost the two wars because the war was fought on the Indian Territory. Then came Pakistan's Doctrine of Offensive Defence under which the warfare was to be conducted in the enemy territory – its changed mode – Low intensity Conflict or the more popularly known as proxy war or still more popularly known as cross border terrorism in India and "Jihad" or holy war in support to the "freedom struggle of Kashmir" in Pakistan. To quote Gen Beg, "In the past we were pursuing a defensive policy: now there is a big change since we are shifting to a policy of offensive defence. Should there be a war, the Pakistan army plans to take war into India, launching a sizeable offensive into the Indian Territory".[7]

Proxy War

The post-1989 South Asian security saga thus became almost synonymous with the Pakistan perpetrated insurgency first in Kashmir and then in the other parts of the country, reaching the Indian Parliament in December 2001. This has been aptly traced by an expert as large portions of the multibillion-dollar military aid given to the anti-Soviet Afghan rebels by the US Central Intelligence Agency (CIA) was siphoned off by the conduit–the ISI–to ignite a bloody insurgency in Indian Kashmir after the ISI failed to trigger an uprising in India's Punjab state despite arming Sikh dissidents beginning in the early 1980s'.[8] Part of the explanation lies in India's own soft response to this terrorism which further emboldened the Pakistani nexus in years that followed, continuing till date. Both the Afghan war veterans or *mujahideen*, as they were called and its own trained terrorists to bleed India as part of what it calls a war of "a thousand cuts."[9]

The policy started by Gen. Zia by exploiting religious sentiments in his Islamization drive inside Pakistan was carried to Kashmir with the help of the ISI in the name of Jihad, subsequently continued by his successors, including civilians from 1988–99. The rise of ISI in the 80s was phenomenal, apart from a massive spurt in its budget; the agency headed by a senior army officer was accountable only to Gen. Zia.

Indo-Pak tensions heightened once again in the wake of military exercises conducted by India under codename *Brasstacks,* ostensibly to test (India's) military readiness on a large scale, under the Chief of staff General Sundarji.[10] Pakistan moved its armoured forces to the border resulting in the tensions. However this crisis was dissipated eventually after direct meeting between the Prime ministers of the two countries and withdrawal of forces.[11] Tension returned to the region when soon after Pakistan conducted its exercises codenamed *Zarb-e-Momin,* placing its troops along the border and F-16s on red alert. India reacted by moving its forces – "three divisions of its troops from eastern to western sector", partly as reinforcements and partly to counter a marked increase in the cross border activity in Punjab and Kashmir.[12] The crisis this time was defused after the visit of the Deputy Director of the Central Intelligence Agency, Mr. Robert Gates, to the two countries, more commonly called the "Gates Mission".

Of course, the silver lining to the dark clouds hovering over the region over the relationship between the two countries were a number of confidence building measures, including non-attack on each others' nuclear installation; advance notification of military movement; joint military operation; exchange of defence personnel and of boundary maps; cooperation for controlling drug trafficking and smuggling, limited border trade, etc.[13]

Pakistan's post-1990 Kashmir strategy rested on promoting the Jamaat-e-Islami,[14] the use of Islamic extremists and its militant wing Hizbul Mujahidin at the cost of undercutting the more secular JKLF. Other offshoots of Gen Zia's Islamic adventurisms *a la* Afghanistan crises, were the militant organizations like Lashkar-e-Toiba and the Jaish-e-Mohammad, trained in the madrassas, the religious schools which mushroomed in Pakistan, especially in areas bordering Afghanistan which now were designed to impart training to the jihadis.

The 1990s, specifically 1993, saw the rise of the All Party Hurriyat Conference (APHC) backed by Pakistan, another actor in the process was a conglomerate, which is split along pro-Pakistan and Pro-Independents, moderate and extremists, continued negotiations or violence. The rise of religious right, MMA in the 2002 elections once again raised the issue of support to Kashmir cause in the name of Islam.

The rise of such religious extremism has brought in a sense of frustration amongst the innumerable amount of bereaved masses that reside in the underdeveloped areas of the South Asian region. This has led to the rise of violence in the civil society itself. India's attempts to deal with the problem, both military and otherwise, have brought little respite. This includes holding elections in the state of Jammu and Kashmir both in 1995–96 and in 2000; Sheikh Abdullah's autonomy plan seeking to abolish Article 370 (disagreed to by the Center), etc. There is no respite to the Kashmiri refugees numbering more than 20,000 and the institutions from schools, to sports and recreational facilities, to the business like tourism remaining devastated.[15]

High Mark of Insurgency: Kargil and After

The insurgency in Kashmir saw its high mark in the spring of 1999; India discovered a large number of insurgents, as per one estimate, "800–1000 officers and men of Pakistan's Northern Light Infantry and the Special Service Group (SSG) crossed the Line of Control into the Kargil Sector and occupied strategic heights," thus intruding several miles inside the Line of Control.[16] The war, which thus ensued, was localized in operation but global in terms of effect. Part of the reason lies in the fact that it came in the aftermath of the famous Lahore summit between the Indian Prime Minister Atal Bihari Vajpayee and his Pakistani counterpart Nawaz Sharif. This was the meeting which had resulted in the Lahore Declaration on February 21,1991. Besides, a joint statement was issued by the two countries and a Memorandum of understanding was signed by the foreign secretaries of the two countries. All these together talked of mutual understanding, non interference in each other's affairs, nuclear risk reduction, respecting the unilateral moratorium on nuclear testing by each, advance warning of missile test, cooperation in information technology and what all, resulting in an unprecedented euphoria and also complacency on the part of Indian security and intelligence apparatus.[17]

Pakistan is well aware of the strategic importance of the Kargil height, and the tactic of intrusion in disguise a la 1947 and 1965 wars fought in the region. Thus, it was from and on these forbidden heights that Kargil war was fought through May and July 1999, from Mushkoh, Kaksar, Batalik, Yaldar, Turtuk and then the Saltoro Ridge, marking the western flank Siachen Glacier... of the majestic snowfields of High Karakoram.[18] The Indian Army launched *Operation Vijay* on May 26, 1999 in Dras and Kargil sectors and eventually in a planned operation of air war involving Migs, Jaguars, and Mirages, peaks after peaks were sought to be vacated.

The crisis eventually was sorted out by Prime Minister Sharif's visit to the Whitehouse on July 4, 1999, following the Clinton-Sharif meeting that day Pakistan was forced to withdraw the mercenaries (it was disowning in the beginning of the conflict). Thus Indians would anyway have won the war but not without losing some precious lives of the young soldiers. The fallout of the war for the Indians was clear. It made them aware of their war preparedness and the status of their military capability.

Kargil clearly drove home points of precarious condition of intelligence in the country, considering the infiltration bore similarities of Pakistan's 1947 and 1965 misadventures in the region. The crisis having taken place in the aftermath of nuclearisation of the subcontinent also opened the debate specifically on the deterrence value of nuclear weapons, pointing that nuclear weapons deter only nuclear weapons, and generally on the nature of warfare. A Rand report, for instance, on the subject said, "The Kargil crisis represents a watershed in India-Pakistan security relations. It demonstrated that even the presence of nuclear weapons might not appreciably dampen security competition between the region's largest states. However, it remains an empirical question whether or not the Kargil war represents a foretaste of future episodes of attempted nuclear coercion if India and Pakistan believe that their nuclear capabilities provide them the immunity required to prosecute a range of military operations short of all-out war. Whether one side or both will act upon this belief depends in part on the particular conclusions and lessons they drew from the Kargil conflict."[19]

In terms of fallout, the report says, "Kargil (has) seriously compromised the legitimacy of Pakistan's claims on Kashmir. Further, while India has been reasonably successful in casting itself as a responsible nuclear-weapons state, Pakistan remains a suspect nation as far as the diffusion of strategic technologies is concerned."[20]

The fallout of the crisis was louder in Pakistan where blame and counter blame for the crisis between the civilian and the military authorities led to events, which culminated in the ouster of civilian elected Prime Minister Nawaz Sharif in a coup staged by General Musharraf in October 1999. The plane hijack in Kandahar exposed an even wider nexus, the spread of the ISI nexus in India's neighbourhood. The hijackers had boarded the plane at Kathmandu.

Even before talks of impact of 9/11 could be assessed on Pakistan's ventures in Kashmir, the state Assembly and then the Indian Parliament witnessed attacks by Jaish-e-Mohammad and Lashkar-e-Toiba militants, of the 14-member United Jihad Council based at Muzaffarabad in the Pakistan Occupied Kashmir, ostensibly at the behest of Pakistan's Inter-Services Intelligence (ISI) agency. This led to adoption of proactive stand by India in suspending diplomatic links, closing communication links and deploying troops across borders eventually by both the countries. Northern borders saw heightened tensions again as the armies of the two rivals were deployed following the attack by Islamabad-backed militant groups on Indian parliament on 13 December 2001. While dismissing India's allegation as baseless and inflammatory, Pakistan amassed and moved, "around four divisions, or over 80,000 Pakistani troops" on the border, in "anticipation of an Indian attack", the denials notwithstanding.[21] The then Indian Prime Minister Atal Bihari Vajpayee said in the Parliament that India was keeping its options open in response to the attack on parliament. The troops were later withdrawn.

The peace process which began subsequently had Kashmir as one of the eight issues. While nothing concrete emerged in the dialogues, it was in this background that Musharraf has made his several "out of the box" proposals. These include., his October 2004 proposal made at an Iftaar party, where he had suggested demilitarization of Kashmir, its division into seven zones that could be administered by India, Pakistan or the UN.'[22] He said, "Take Kashmir in its entirety. It has seven regions. Two of the regions are in Pakistan and five are in India. In my view, identify a region, whether it is the whole or seven or part, I do not know. Identify the region, demilitarise the region for ever and change its status', adding "status can be independence, condominium where there can be a joint control or there can be UN mandate" which has to be defined by "legal people."[23] Although he did not expand on the seven regions, they were understood to be the plains, including Jammu, foothills up to 7000 ft, Pir Panjal, the valley, the great Himalayan Zone, the upper Indus valley and the Karakoram. Out of these seven regions, five are within India, namely, Ladakh (Ismaili part), Kargil/Dras (Muslim), Poonch (contiguous to 'Azad Kashmir'), Jammu (Muslim-majority districts) and the Valley. the remaining two regions are PoK, and the Northern areas (minus Baltistan)[24] He made a four-pronged proposal: First, Kashmir would have the same borders but people will be allowed to move freely back and forth in the region; second, the region would have self governance or autonomy, but not independence; third, troops will be withdrawn from the region in a staggered manner; and fourth, a joint supervision mechanism would be set up, comprising Indian, Pakistani and Kashmiri representatives. He stressed that Pakistan is prepared to give up the independence or UN resolution option if this proposal can be worked out.[25] Again in December 2006, in an interview to an Indian television channel General Musharraf repeated a proposal of a phased plan to solve the decades-old Kashmir dispute, in which he said Pakistan would abandon its claim to the region if India agreed to give the territory autonomy under joint supervision by both countries.[26] Although a clarification was issued subsequently that the president at no point said that Pakistan is unilaterally ready to give up its stance on Kashmir.[27]

The proposal, described as "most viable and effective solution to the long-standing" issue, by Pakistan's former foreign minister Khurshid Mehmood Kasuri said in December 2007 invoked interests in New Delhi, inside and outside the government.[28] The proposal evoked little interest in New Delhi primarily because it sought to isolate the 'Muslim majority' areas on a religious basis, which in principle for New Delhi was a non-starter. Prime Minister Manmohan Singh, first in September 2004 in New York and then in November in Srinagar responded saying, I have made it quite clear that any redrawing of international border is something which is not going to be acceptable to us. Any proposal which smacks of a further division of our country on the basis of religion is not going to be acceptable to us. Within these two limits we are ready to look into any proposal are still not clear to us. I do not know what his plan is.[29] He repeated it later also, for instance he said at Amritsar in April 2006 that, "borders cannot be redrawn, but we can work towards making them irrelevant... just lines on a map". Given increased movement and trade across the border (LoC), the Prime Minister envisaged a situation "where the two parts of J&K can, with the active encouragement of the governments of India and Pakistan, work out cooperative, consultative mechanisms so as to maximise the gains of cooperation in solving problems of social and economic development in the region".[30]

India consistently maintained and reiterated on numerous occasions that "boundaries cannot be re-drawn" and the need was to make borders meaningless.[31] In September 2005, General Musharraf sought removal of Indian troops from Kupuwara, Baramula and Srinagar to boost the peace process.[32] Indian proposal is guarded and consistent. Prime Minister Manmohan Singh seemed to have taken the proposals positively, saying any effort in the direction of normalisation of Indo-Pak relations is welcome, adding, "We are also committed to a purposeful dialogue with Pakistan to resolve all outstanding issues. The only condition is that territory under control of Pakistan should not be used to promote cross-border terrorism directed against us." India has also repeatedly reminded Pakistan that addressing terrorism and improving the ground situation was a necessary condition to make any progress in Kashmir possible. While India has always raised cross border terrorism related issues in talks, Pakistan sticks to the so-called "human rights violations" and troops' reduction in the state.

Cross border terrorist attacks, in fact have not remained confined to Kashmir, but have spread to other areas also. Some of the more prominent ones include Ayodhya (July 2005), in Sarojini Nagar, Paharganj and Govindpuri in New Delhi (October 2005), in Malegaon in Mumbai (July 2006), at the Indian Institute of Science (IISc) in Bangalore (December 2005) and on the Delhi-Lahore Samjhauta Express (February 2007). These, in effect, make the issue of joint anti-terror mechanism a debatable issue.

The Nuclear Issue

Equally challenging, if not more, is the issue of nuclearisation of the subcontinent. The lid was off in 1998 with the *Pokhran* and *Chagai* tests of India and Pakistan, but it is an open secret that the two had attained the capability much earlier, in 1987. The issue is more complex than it would be, partly because of the inherent secrecy associated with the issues and partly because of the mindsets trained in the intentional and unintentional literature propounded by the threat. The difference in the rationale of the two countries for acquiring nuclear weapons is seminal to understand the nuclear scenario in the region. It has been aptly put by Jed Snyder, "The rationales for Indian and Pakistani acquisition of nuclear weapons (or other mass destruction arms) are distinct although not dissimilar. India's initial venture into nuclear arms attempted to convey regional and global prestige and influence, but was more immediately an answer to India's defeat in the 1962 Sino-Indian conflict and the subsequent 1964 Chinese nuclear test. Pakistan's nuclear weapons effort is a political-military instrument directed principally against India, whose larger conventional force can never hope to be matched by Pakistan. The Pakistani nuclear effort has reportedly been aided by China, with nuclear weapons design information, materials, and reactors. Islamabad's interest in nuclear capability was initially sparked by the 1971 war with India and over time became a symbol of prestige and influence, like its rival India. Most Pakistani strategists and military leaders regard the nuclear choice as a prudent strategic bargain. As Pakistan's former Army Chief of Staff, General Mirza Aslam Beg, noted that a nuclear deterrent for Pakistan represents "the cheapest option for peace," balancing India's other advantages. Apart from the consuming bilateral rivalry, both Indians and Pakistanis see nuclear weapons as an instrument of independence from the United States and other outside powers."[33]

Even those who claim that nuclear weapons have made the region more unstable or do not agree with the security argument do point out the basic doctrinaire difference in the nuclear posture of India and Pakistan. To quote Iffteqar Zaman, "It is notable that the Indian nuclear doctrine is silent on identifying specific sources of nuclear threat. The strategy is targeted at all nuclear powers, not just Pakistan and China. It clearly states that India's weapons will be deployed against 'any state or entity' that may threaten India, and hence the ambit of 'minimum' and 'credible' deterrence it talks about is inclusive of all states that possess nuclear weapons. Hardly anyone in a responsible position in India would condone the actual use of these weapons against any of these powers; it is basically the urge to achieve the status of being equal to them that motivates the Indian policy. In the case of Pakistan, India-focused as it is, the strategy is to acquire the 'requisite' number of warheads that will not only deter India, but also be effective in the event that it exercises the first-use option. This means that the magic number will always be subject to change"[34]

As for nuclear capabilities, one estimate puts Pakistan's weapons-grade material enough "to produce between 30–55 nuclear weapons and possesses the components and material to assemble a small number of nuclear weapons in a matter of hours or days", believed to be having "produced between 585–800 kilograms of highly enriched uranium" and "much smaller but unknown quantity of weapons-grade plutonium., estimated to be "enough to produce between 3–5 nuclear weapons".[35] It puts Indian nuclear capabilities at approximately 30–35 nuclear warheads', having produced 225–370 kilograms weapons-grade plutonium enough to produce 50–90 nuclear weapons and "a smaller but unknown quantity of weapons-grade uranium."[36]

For Pakistan, the nuclear weapons serve as an equalizer in upsetting the conventional superiority of India, the reason why it has refused a no-first use of nuclear weapons pledge. The Indian nuclear deterrent has officially been explained in terms of "deteriorating security environment" considerations from both China as well as Pakistan, two of India's neighbours with which it had fought wars and has unsettled boundary claims, including in Kashmir, coupled with the fact that the two have overt and covert military alliance involving transfer of nuclear and missile materials and technology.[37] The region in fact is unique in containing three nuclear powers placed in this configuration. The issue, thus, needs to be seen in the larger context than the immediate region because nuclearisation of the subcontinent is inherently directly linked with the Asian power, China.

The linking of two intangibles that is the Kashmir issue with the nuclear is also not new. Rooted in prescriptions of the "Route to Kashmir lies Through NPT" the buzz words now are "nuclear flashpoint" as also "nuclear arms race in South Asia". This was also the case in the so-called 1990 eyeball-to-eyeball confrontation between the two South Asian neighbours and the subcontinent saw the Gates Mission, to settle a crisis whose existence has been denied by the then army chiefs of both the countries.

Nowhere, is it counter questioned that if nuclear weapons could maintain peace in Europe for 50 years why not in this part of the world. Equally underplayed is the fact that China, whose nuclear weapons served as a deterrent to both the American and Soviet nuclear weapons, entered a maddening "nuclear arms race" a la superpowers in the cold war mindset. Equally underplayed are India's "no-first use" pledges, and the role of external factors in supporting and legitimizing the clandestine nuclear programme of Pakistan. So long as the Soviets were in Afghanistan, year after year the American President certified to the Congress that the country does not have nuclear weapons programme, despite evidence to the contrary by its own intelligence.

Besides, it is still early to comment on the nuclear scenario with issue like delivery capabilities, the nuclear doctrines and command and control authorities still evolving, their declaration from time-to-time notwithstanding. Pakistan in 2000 and India in 2003 set up their respective nuclear command structures, National Command authority and Nuclear Command Authority respectively.[38] As for their being made use of by India, one can quote Subramanyam in saying, "Nuclear weapons have one legitimate purpose – to deter intimation by another nuclear weapons power and retaliate if the nation has been struck with a nuclear weapon. India's sole justification for acquiring nuclear weapons is to deter Pakistan and China if ever they resort to nuclear blackmail. There is no other purpose of a nuclear weapon".[39]

Pakistan has the short-range, liquid-fuel Hatf I and Hatf II missiles having a range of 80 km and 180 kilometers, respectively, and the short-range Chinese-built and supplied M-11 (also known as Hatf III or Ghaznavi) with a range of 280–300 km; and the Ghauri series medium range missile (ranges and payload capacity of Ghauri I 1300 km 700 kg and of Ghauri II 2000 km and a 850 kg). It also has medium-range Shaheen series of missile with a Shaheen I having a range of 700 km and Shaheen II, of 2,000 kilometers but has not been flight-tested. Pakistan has three nuclear-capable types of aircraft: the F-16, the Mirage III, and the A-5 Fantan. F-16, primary nuclear-capable aircraft, can carry a 1,000 kg bomb to approximately 1,400 kilometers.[40]

India currently has three models of the short-range Prithvi missile with ranges and payload capacities of 150 km and a payload of 500 kilograms (Army version); 250 km and 500–750 kg (Air force version) and 350 km and 500 kg (Navy version). The naval version is also known as the Dhanush. It also has medium-range Agni missiles. India tested a short-range, single-stage version of the Agni missile in January of this year. It is road-mobile and has a range of 700 kilometers. The Agni I "technology demonstrator" has been tested to a range of 1500 km. The rail-mobile Agni II has a range of 2000–2500 km. India's nuclear capable aircraft include: the MiG-27, the Jaguar, the Mirage 2000, the MIG-29, the Su-30, the T-22, and the TU-95.[41]

Pakistan faces serious challenge today both internally and externally in the nuclear smuggling of components as well as nuclear technology to countries like Iran, North Korea and Libya. While the father of the Pakistan Nuclear bomb, A.Q. Khan has himself confessed to having committed the act and has since been granted pardon by General Musharraf, the latter is under serious challenge internally as well as externally. While the Islamists and other opposition parties are critical of him for different reasons, the world community at large is demanding more transparency, Musharraf's refusal to open up for IAEA or other probes, notwithstanding. Analysts generally, inside as well as outside Pakistan, find the explanation difficult to gulp down, since Kahuta is one place where even top leadership is denied access.[42]

The "Lesser Disputes"

Indo-Pak security imbroglio is also underlined by what some people have described as the "lesser disputes".[43] These include primarily the issues of Siachen, Sir Creek, and Wullar Barrage. The Siachen dispute is about the Glacier by that name over which both lay their claim. It owes its origin to the Shimla Agreement when the boundary is marked till the point NJ 9842, relying on the UN demarcated ceasefire line in 1949, beyond which glaciers were mentioned generally because of inaccessibility. In 1983, Indian Intelligence detected a column of Pakistani troops moving towards "Saltoro range," the only viable route to Siachen from POK.[44] Pakistan wanted to establish a permanent picket there: the Indians reacted, moved troops by helicopter.[45] There have been eight rounds of talks on the issue, which now seems permanent.[46] In 1985, Rajiv Gandhi and Gen Zia decided to resolve the dispute through talks; two years later in 1987, it saw worst ever clashes. The August

2004 talks between the defence secretaries also have nothing to report except decision to hold more talks. As per media reports, Pakistan referred to an understanding reached between the two countries in 1989, and sought redeployment of forces in Siachen prior to Shimla position, while Indian side said that the existing position in Siachen should be authenticated, a position unacceptable to Pakistan.[47]

The talks on Siachen resumed at the Defence Secretary level in August 2004 followed by Foreign Secretary level talks which were essentially symbolic. So were the talks at the summit level between Prime Minister Manmohan Singh and General Musharraf and at the levels of Foreign Secretaries, Foreign Ministers and Defence Secretaries at periodic intervals in 2005 and 2006. Basically disputes remained over authentication of troop positions, with media reports about Pakistan proposal to "acknowledge" the current position of the Indian troops rather than "authenticate" it notwithstanding.[48]

The Sir Creek is a 60-mile Estuary in the marshes of the Runn of Kutch forming the southern border between the two countries. The issue relates to the demarcation of boundary from (i) the mouth of the Sir Creek to the top of the Sir Creek and (ii) from the top of the Sir Creek eastwards to a point designated as the Western Terminus. The boundary thereafter has been demarcated. Pakistan claims on the Creek are based on its assertion that the boundary lies on the eastern side whereas India says that the boundary lies in the middle of the creek. The determination of the boundary in the Creek impinges on the Exclusive Economic Zone (EEZ) of either side by 250 sq. miles and therefore is not merely territorial but also making it a territorial-cum-resource dispute, and hence the deadlock. The issue has assumed particular importance because of the continental shelf claims that are to be submitted to the UN by 2009 and the beginning of the boundary will decide the maritime boundary of the two countries. India has also proposed that "pending formalisation of the boundary in the Sir Creek, the two sides could consider the delimitation of the India-Pakistan maritime boundary from seawards, by commencing at EEZ limit and proceeding landwards up to a mutually acceptable limit as per provisions under Technical Aspects of Law of Sea (TALOS).[49] Pakistan, however, maintains that they would consider maritime boundary only after the determination of land boundary in Sir Creek Area and that both these issues should not be de-linked but treated as a package[50] The region was tense in 1999 when Indian jets shot down a Pakistani patrol plane, the Atlantique, and Pakistan retaliated by firing missiles at Indian helicopters. Talks were initiated on the issue as part of peace process in August 2004 led by Indian Surveyor General Prithvish Nag and Pakistan's Additional Secretary of Defence Admiral Ahsan ul Haq Chaudhary to apprise each other with the ground situation and respective views on how to resolve the dispute which failed to make any meaningful headway, except agreeing "to continue the discussions."[51]

Technical level talks on the issue in December 2006 in Rawalpindi led to plans to hold a joint survey of the Sir Creek and adjoining areas by the hydrographers to be followed by determination of the maritime zones of both countries. The joint survey was complete by mid–March 2007 to verify outermost points of coastlines using the equidistance method. The consequent talks in Rawalpindi in May 2007 nevertheless remained inconclusive.[52]

The Wullar Barrage issue arose in 1985 after India started work on the Barrage on the Jhelum River at the mouth of the Wullar Lake near Srinagar. According to India the dam was meant to regulate navigation on certain months when the flow is low. Pakistan considers it violation of the Indus Water Treaty obligation by India. The halting of work at Wullar in the earlier agreement actually encouraged Pakistan to raise another dispute – the 450 MW Baghliar Dam on River Chenab. The hydropower project, after years of unsuccessful bilateral negotiations, was referred to the World Bank. Raising objections on the grounds that it adversely affected water flow in Pakistan, the latter took the issue to World Bank which is the guarantor of the Indo-Pak Indus Waters Treaty of 1960. Later the World Bank appointed neutral expert, Raymond Lafitte. Contrary to Pakistan's expectations, the expert in his report in February did not order halting of the project but asked for some modifications. Pakistan's subsequent objections to Kishenganga project also did not gain momentum.

Then, there are other issues on which talks have been held like one to curb drug trafficking. Talks between the Indian Narcotics Control Bureau (NCB) and the Pakistani Anti Narcotic Force (ANF) or the one on release of prisoners of war (POW) which entailed keeping each other informed or notified about any arrests made, provide consular access within three months of the arrest and expedite release as soon as the term of imprisonment was complete; following this fishermen on both sides were released.

Khaled Ahmed writes that the "importance and seriousness" of the three "non-core" issues lies in the fact that "they threaten to become core issues" if the two countries do not make up their mind about the post-nuclear status quo in the region.[53] An argument which seems far fetched, primarily because of the magnitude of the other problems. For instance, if the major disputes like Kashmir and a stable nuclear regime is ever resolved, sure these disputes will hardly have the potential of escalating into full scale wars. This, of course, is a hypothetical assertion.

Notes and References

1. Buzan, Barry: "Regional Security as a Policy Objective: The Case of South and Southwest Asia", in A.Z. Rubinstein (ed.), *The Great Game: Rivalry in the Persian Gulf and South Asia*, (New York: Praeger, 1983). pp. 247–248.
2. Iftekhar Zaman, "Living with a nuclearized South Asia: Re-thinking disarmament and security" http://www.unidir.org/pdf/articles/pdf-art2119.pdf
3. Kanti Bajpai, "South Asia After September 11, 2001" Talking points for the

RIETI symposium"http://www.rieti.go.jp/en/events/02121801/pdf/Bajpai.pdf. He also says, contrary to some Pakistani claims, Afghanistan was never an added strategic depth for Pakistan.

4. Stephen Cohen, "South Asia", *Strategic Asia, 2002-03*, p. 270.
5. Parvez Iqbal Cheema, "The Initial round", *The News*, July 11, 2004.
6. Brigadier S.K. Malik, *The Quranic Concept of War* (Himalayan Books, Delhi, reprinted in India, 1986), p. 60.
7. Interview of General Beg by Mushahid Hussain, "Pakistan Responding to Change", *Janes Defence Weekly,* October 14, 1989, p. 779.
8. Brahma Chellaney, "Fighting Terrorism in Southern Asia: The Lessons of History" *International Security,* Vol. 26, No. 3 (Winter 2001/02), p. 97.
9. Celia W. Dugger and Barry Bearak, "Falling Out: You've Got the Bomb. So Do I. Now I Dare You to Fight," *New York Times,* January 16, 2000, *Week in Review section*, cited in *Ibid*, p. 98.
10. Kanti Bajpai, et al., *Brasstacks and Beyond: Perception and Management of Crisis* (Manohar Publishers and Distributors, New Delhi), p. 2.
11. *Ibid.*
12. *Ibid.,* p. 11.
13. Hasan Askari Rizvi, "Pakistan and the Cold War Environment", in Craig Baxter and Charles Kennedy (eds.) *Pakistan 1997*, p. 42.
14. Seyyed Vali Reza Nasr, *The Vanguard of the Islamic Revolutiin: The Jamaat-I Islami of Pakistan* (Berkley, 1994).
15. Special report on Kashmir, National Commission Reports on Human Rights 1997–98 (New Delhi, 1999).
16. Waheguru Pal Singh Sidhu," Of Myths and Realities: The Kargil Experience", in Kanti Bajpai et al. ed. *Kargil and after: Challenges for the Indian Policy* (Har Anand, New Delhi, 2001), p. 109.
17. For text of Lahore declaration, see *The Hindu,* February 22, 1999.
18. *From Surprise to Rreckoning: The Kargil Committee Report,* (Sage Publications, New Delhi), p. 16.
19. Ashley J. Tellis, C. Christine Fair, Jamison Jo Medby, *Limited Conflicts under The Nuclear Umbrella: Indian and Pakistani Lessons from the Kargil Crisis,* (Rand Corporation, St Monica, California,) p. 1.
20. *Ibid.*, p. 67.
21. Thirteen people, including the five attackers, had died in the attack, Rahul Bedi, "India and Pakistan 'Reposition' Their Troops as Tension mounts Over Parliament Attack" *Janes Defence Weekly,* 19 December 2001.
22. Indo-Asian News Service November 16, 'No formal submission of Musharraf's Kashmir proposals' *http://in.news.yahoo.com/041116/43/2hwm5.html* K.J.M., Verma. 'Mark and Area, Disarm it, Decide on Freedom or Joint Control', *Indian Express*, October 26, 2004 *http://www.indianexpress.com/archive/StoryO-57711—*Mark-an-area-disarm-it-decide-on-Freedom-or-joint-control-.html
23. K.J.M. Verma, 'Mark and Area, Disarm it, Decide on Freedom or Joint Control', *Indian Express*, October 26, 2004. *http://www.indianexpress.com/archive/StoryO-57711*—Mark-an-area-disarm-it-decide-on-freedom-or-joint-control-.html
24. Khaled Ahmed, 'Musharraf's 'Seven-Regions' Options in Kashmir' *Friday Times*, November 30, 2004, *http://www.thefridaytimes.com/page8.shtml*

25. Jawed, Naqvi, 2005. 'New measures to boost Pakistan, India trade', *at http://www.dawn.com/2005/08/11/top1.htm*
26. Reuters Alertnet Indian PM welcomes Musharraf proposal on Kashmir 16 Dec 2006 16:09:06 GMT *http://www.alertnet.org/thenews/newsdesk/DEL83435.htm*
27. Musharraf's Kashmir Proposal: Analysis Husain Haqqani, 'Talking Without Thinking' Friday, December 15, 2006 *http://watandost.blogspot.com/2006/12/musharrafs-kashmir-proposal-analysis.html*
28. Mush's proposal best to resolve Kashmir issue: Kasuri 26 December 2007 *http://timesofindia.indiatimes.com/Pakistan/Mushs_proposal_best_to_resolve_Kashmir_issue_Kasuri/articleshow/2652286.cms*
29. 'No redrawing of boundaries: Manmohan', *The Hindu*, 22 December 2004.
30. B.G. Verghese, "Cooperative common future There is a role for both Kashmirs" *The Tribune*, online edition, April 10, 2006, *http://www.tribuneindia.com/2006/20060410/edit.htm#4*
31. Amit Kotwal, 'Let LoC be Line of Peace', *The Times of India*, 16 July, 2007.
32. Hussain, Fahd, 2005. 'Kashmir Troops Cut to Boost Peace, Musharraf tells Bush', at *http:// www.jang.com.pk/thenews/sep2006-daily/15-09-2005/main/ main4.htm*
33. Jed Snyder, "After the Cold War: South Asian Security" *www./ndu/inss/staff/snyder.html*
34. Iftekhar Zaman, "Living with a nuclearized South Asia: Re-thinking disarmament and security" *http://www.unidir.org/pdf/articles/pdf-art2119.pdf*
35. "India and Pakistan's Nuclear Capabilities: Derived From: Deadly Arsenals-Tracking Weapons of Mass Destruction" *http://www.ceip.org/files/projects/npp/resources/DeadlyArsenals/web%20pages/capabilitiesinsasia1.htm.*
36. *Ibid.*
37. See for instance Prime Minister's Atal Bihari Vajpayee's letter to the then US President, Bill Clinton, *http:www.indianembassy.org/indusrel/pmletter.htm.*
38. M.V. Rammana, "Zia Mian "The Nuclear confrontation in South Asia" *Sipri Yearbook*, 2003, Chapter 5, *http://editors.sipri.se/pubs/yb03/ch05.html*
39. K. Subramanyam, "Pokharan II and After", *The Times of India*, May 14, 1998.
40. "India and Pakistan's Nuclear Capabilities: Derived From: Deadly Arsenals-Tracking Weapons of Mass Destruction". *http://www.ceip.org/files/projects/npp/resources/DeadlyArsenals/web%20 pages/capabilitiesinsasia1.htm*

For a detailed analysis of Pakistans missile programme, including strategy, modis operandi, foreign collaboration etc. see Gaurav Kampani, "*Missile Programme*" *http://www.nti.org/e_ research/ profiles/Pakistan/Missile/—>*

41. "India and Pakistan's Nuclear Capabilities: Derived From: Deadly Arsenals-Tracking Weapons of Mass Destruction". *http://www.ceip.org/files/projects/npp/resources/DeadlyArsenals/web% 20pages/capabilitiesinsasia1.htm*
42. Zahid Hussain, "Confession or Cover Up", *Newsline,* February 2004, *http://www.newsline.com.pk*
43. See for instance Kahled Ahmed," "South Asia's Unresolved Disputes", Paper Presented in the Regional conference, *South Asian Free Media Association*, October 9-10, 2004, New Delhi.

44. A.G. Noorani, "Confidence-Building Measures on the Siachen Glacier, Sir Creek, and Wular Barrage: Easing the Indo-Pakistani Dialogue on Kashmir", Occassional Paper 16, Henry L Stimson Centre, 1994.
45. S.K. Lambah, "Sir Creek and Siachen Issues", Paper Presented in the Regional conference," South Asian Free media Association, October 9-10, 2004, New Delhi. Lamba cites the Pakistani writer Zulfikar Ali Khan in his paper.
46. Lt Gen. V.R. Raghavan, *Siachen: Conflict without End* (Viking, India, 2000)
47. "Pakistan, India To hold More talks on Siachen", *The News,* August 7, 2004
48. Iftikhar Gilani, 'India Considering Siachen Proposal' *Daily Times* January 18, 2007, at *http://www.dailytimes.com.pk/default.asp?page2007%5CO1%5C18%5Cstory_18-1-2007_pg7_1*
49. "India-Pakistan talks: Sir Creek "*http://www.indianembassy.org/South_Asia/Pakistan/ indpak(sircreek).htm*
50. "India-Pakistan talks: Sir Creek "*http://www.indianembassy.org/South_Asia/Pakistan /indpak(sircreek).htm*
51. Faizul Haque, "Sir Creek Talks Flop", *The Nation,* August 8, 2004.
52. Khan, Iftikhar A., 2007. 'Sir Creek Differences Remain', *The Dawn* (online edition), May 19, 2007 *http:/ /www.dawn.com/2007/05/19/ top13.htm*
53. Kahled Ahmed, "South Asia's Unresolved Disputes", Paper Presented in the Regional conference," *South Asian Free media Association*, October 9-10, 2004, New Delhi.

7

Border Management and India's Relations with Myanmar

Udai Bhanu Singh

Border management has come to acquire a new significance and connotation in the post Cold War scenario. The issues relating to border management can be negotiated relatively amicably when political goodwill exists between the concerned parties. In the case of India and Myanmar, this understanding acquires increased salience not simply because each would like to preserve its national interests, but that their geostrategic location makes it a wise decision in the regional and larger global context[1] The Group of Ministers report in dealing with the issue of border management interpreting the term 'Border Management' in its widest sense said that it "should imply co-ordination and concerted action by political leadership and administrative, diplomatic, security, intelligence, legal, regulatory and economic agencies of the country to secure our frontiers and subserve the best interests of the country." The concept of border security has changed. It is no longer viewed in conventional terms – it is more meaningful to view it in holistic terms. As such security and economics have become inextricably intertwined. While the western border of India has drawn the attention of security experts, the eastern border has not received sufficient attention. As a result, the vulnerabilities of India's eastern borders have often been ignored, in particular, the border with Myanmar. This paper provides the background to the Indo-Myanmar border development and seeks to delve into the factors which render the border volatile and attempts to list India's objectives and the possible steps India could take to secure this border.

Many factors have worked to highlight the geopolitical significance of India's border with Myanmar. This includes among other things the domestic political developments in Myanmar, the rise of China in both economic and military sense, and the salience of the Indian Ocean. A look at the background of the Indo-Myanmar border reveals its geo-strategic significance. Myanmar is situated at the tri-junction of East Asia, Southeast Asia and South Asia between 10 and 28 degrees North latitude. India has a 1643 km long border with Myanmar and a long maritime boundary. Four north-eastern states bordering Myanmar north to south are: Arunachal Pradesh, Nagaland, Manipur and Mizoram.

Table 7.1: Myanmar's Border with Indian States

Sl. No.	State	Kms
1.	Arunachal Pradesh	520
2.	Nagaland	215
3.	Manipur	398
4.	Mizoram	510
	Total	**1643**

The Myanmarese territory bordering India includes Kachin state, Sagaing division, and Chin state. Myanmar has a population of about 50 million and a rich ethnic mix.

Table 7.2: Language Based Ethnicity/Religious Population in Myanmar

Group	Percentage	Religious Identity
Bamar	69.0	Mainly Buddhist
Shan	8.5	Mainly Buddhist
Kayin	6.2	15/20% Christian
Rakhine	4.5	Mainly Buddhist
Mon	2.4	Mainly Buddhist
Chin	2.2	80% Christian
Kachin	1.4	80% Christian
Kayah (Karenni)	0.4	Mixed
Other indigenous	0.1	Mixed
Mixed Burmese and foreign	5.3	Muslims/mixed

Source: R.H. Taylor, "Do states make nations?: The politics of identity in Myanmar revisited", *South East Asia Research*, 13(3) pp 261–286.

It may be recalled that the British colonial policy of 'divide and rule' had drawn a distinction between "Burma Proper" inhabited by the majority Burman community and "Outer Burma" inhabited mainly by the minorities. While "Burma Proper" was directly administered under British India, the minorities were allowed greater autonomy. The map of modern Myanmar shows seven Burman dominated divisions, and seven ethnic minority states of the Chin, Kachin, Karen, Kayah, Rakhine (Arakan) and Shan. These political divisions are not an accurate reflection of the immensely complex ethnic structure of Myanmar which has over 100 languages and each ethnic group is further divided into several subgroups.

Table 7.3: India-Myanmar: Background Developments

I. Year	*II. Treaty*	*III. Features*
1826 Feb 24	Yandabo Treaty	1. Burma renounces claim upon Assam and its dependencies and on Manipur. 2. It cedes provinces of Arakan and Tenasserim to the British. 3. It agrees to pay a war indemnity of one million pound sterling to the British. 4. The British are now acknowledged as a Burmese power.
1886	Third Anglo-Burmese War	1. End of Burmese Kingdom with King Thibaw overthrown. 2. Burma becomes part of British Indian Empire.
1937 April 1	Government of Burma Act	1. Provided de-jure separation of Burma from India. 2. Granted Burma limited self-government (autonomy..
1937	Limited self government	1. Separation of Burma from Indian Constitution. Granted its own Constitution and limited self government under British rule.
1948 Jan 4	Independence	Burma attains independence
1951 July 7	India-Burma Treaty of Friendship, Rangoon	1. To remain in force forever unless either side wanted to terminate it. 2. Regular meetings between their representatives to exchange views on matters of common interest, and for mutual cooperation.
1956 Sept 5	India-Burma Trade and Commerce agreement	1. Provides necessary facilities for the import/export of commodities. 2. Facilitates the export of commodities which are in short supply in one country 3. Attempts a balance in their trade as possible 4. Accords each other's commerce treatment no less favourable than that given to any third country. 5. Promotes shipping 6. Agreement valid for five years.

(Contd.)

(*Contd.*)

I.	II.	III.
1960 Jan 28	1. Sino-Burmese border agreement 2. Sino-Burmese Treaty of Friendship and Non-Aggression	
1962 Dec 24	Agreement for promotion of trade	1. The two Governments agree to accord MFN status to their mutual trade 2. Payment in any convertible currency
1967 March 10	Land boundary treaty	Demarcated and delimited the boundary. Ratified on May 30 1967
1970 May 27	India Burma Trade Agreement`	To expand economic and trade relations on the basis of equality of rights and mutual benefit
1986	Maritime delimitation treaty	Delimitation of the Andaman Sea in the Coco Channel and in the Bay of Bengal.
1993	Maritime agreement	Established the tri-junction point in Andaman Sea between Thailand, India and Indonesia.
1994 Jan 21	India-Myanmar Border Trade Treaty	1. Border trade to be conducted through Moreh-Tamu and Champai-Hri 2. Exchange of locally produced commodities to continue as before including barter mechanism. 3. Trade may be conducted through freely convertible currencies or through counter trade arrangements.
2000 Nov 21	India-Myanmar Joint Statement	During Gen Maung Aye's visit to India from Nov 14–21 an agreement to extend a US $15 million credit to Myanmar was signed for sourcing industrial and electrical equipment from India.
2004 Oct 29	India-Myanmar Joint Statement	During Sr Gen Than Shwe's visit to India from Oct 25–29 the two sides agreed to expand bilateral interaction to the health, higher education and energy sectors. Agreements signed on cooperation in the field of non-traditional security, the Tamanthi Hydro-electric project, extending a line of credit of US $7 million for two telecom projects and a grant of $3 million for IT related projects.

The significance of Myanmar to India also lies in the fact that it has a common border with two important states China and Bangladesh. China, which has no opening to the Indian Ocean seeks to gain access through Myanmar. In a similar way, Bangladesh (not just Myanmar) holds significance for India in that it could provide an opening for India's Northeast to the Indian Ocean. Myanmar's territory is washed by the Bay of Bengal waters and the Andaman Sea. Myanmar's Coco Islands are cheek by jowl with India's Andaman and Nicobar Islands, and they are in close proximity to India's maritime trade routes. As such both India and China value the maritime importance of Myanmar. India and Myanmar signed a boundary agreement in 1967. A maritime delimitation agreement in 1986 defined maritime boundary between the two countries.

The four Indian states bordering Myanmar share many common linkages with Myanmar. Many of the ethnic groups in Arunachal Pradesh spill over in Myanmar. The Nagas lay claim to the districts of Lohit, Tirap and Changlang for their Greater Nagaland. The NSN(I-M) and the NSCN(K) as also the ULFA, arc all active here and the insurgents exploit the insecurities of minorities in an economically underdeveloped state. The NSCN had links with the Kachin Independent Organisation. (KIO). The vision of the Nagas of Greater Nagaland or Nagalim includes parts of Assam, Arunachal Pradesh, Manipur as also part of Northern Myanmar. NSCN(I-M) are considered the mother of all insurgent groups in the Northeast while the NSCN(K) which is headquartered in Myanmar is relatively weak The NSCN (I-M) with which the Centre engaged in talks has only a minority (about 10–15 per cent only) of Nagas who belong to Nagaland. The rest are all from other Northeastern states. NSCN(K) made Myanmar their headquarters. The Manipuri Nagas feel they have been neglected at the expense of the Meitis and the Kuki-Chin tribals.

Mizoram, formerly known as the Lushai Hills, has the advantage of a homogenous population. The Kuki-Chin-Mizo are the dominant tribal group constituting roughly 75 per cent of the population, and having common ethnicity in the adjoining Chin Hills of Manipur. A relatively peaceful state but for occasional demands for Greater Mizoram which obtains support from the Kuki-Chin Mizo ethnicity in adjoining Chin Hills of Myanmar. Mizoram falls on the drug route. NSCN (I-M) finds its supporters here.

On the other side in Myanmar, the three ethnic groups which are important to India are the Chins, Rakhins, and the Kachins. The three groups belong to the Tibeto Burman group. The Chins are to be found on the western part of Burma. The Chins of Myanmar have affinity to the Mizos of India and the demand for a greater 'Zomi-Mizo' have often arisen. But Mizoram has been among the quieter NE Indian States.

India's Objectives

The main objective is to devise the best means to base Indo-Myanmar relations on a stable basis. India's objective is to ensure that the area west of Chindwin river (a tributary of the lrrawaddy river) remains free of Chinese or Pakistani influence. India's broad objectives in Myanmar are as follows; First, Myanmar is an important component of India's Look East policy being the only Southeast Asian nation with which India shares a land border. This makes ensuring smooth trade an important objective. The centre seeks stability on the north-eastern border by ensuring economic prosperity of the region especially in view of the fact that it is a land-bridge to the South East Asian region. Viewed from Myanmar's perspective, its objective is clearly to get greater integration with the international community and greater manoeuvrability in its foreign relations (which would in a sense be an extension of its earlier emphasis on non-alignment).

Second, both India and Myanmar need to control insurgency in their bordering states.

Third, India is located between the 'Golden Crescent' in the west and the 'Golden Triangle' in the east. It is confronted with arms-drug nexus and faces a "silent emergency". Myanmar still has the dubious distinction of being the second largest producer of opium (after Afghanistan) and for having a high HIV rate. Though opium poppy cultivation has shown a decline from 163,000 hectares to 32,800 hectares between 1996 and 2005 or that poppy production declined by 26 per cent in 2005 (to 312 metric tonnes valued at $58 million) more needs to be done. This is because the traditional opium based drugs have been replaced by designer drugs like amphetamine-type-stimulants (ATS) ("speed", "ice" and "ecstasy"). An estimated 965,000 persons depend on opium poppy cultivation for their livelihood while the addicts (that includes intravenous drug users, where the imminence of an AIDS epidemic is real) number an estimated 500,000.[2]

Fourth, the two governments need to take steps with a holistic view of security in mind. This entails greater cooperation between the two governments to prevent outbreak of epidemics across borders especially considering the threat of HIV/AIDS, and recent outbreaks like the bird flu. This is the danger from 'the silent emergency'.

Fifth, and flowing all the factors above, is the need to ensure the development of the Northeastern states.

Sixth, is something that has not been explicitly stated but has perhaps always been at the back of Indian strategic thinking. This is the need to respond appropriately and in the right measure to the rise of China, especially its growing economic, political and military influence in Myanmar.

Table 7.4: India-Myanmar Drug Routes

Sl. No.	*Origin – Destination*	*Area covered*
1.	Sagaing area (NW Myanmar) to Mizoram	Tamu (Myanmar)–Moreh (Manipur) – Kaley and Tiddim–Mizoram
2.	North Myanmar to Imphal (Manipur)	Hampat and Tamu (Myanmar)–Moreh–Imphal (Manipur)
3.	West Myanmar to Aizawl (Mizoram)	Rikhandar–Champhai–Aizawl (Mizoram)
4.	South-West Myanmar to Aizawl (Mizoram)	Myanmar–Lungleh (Mizoram)–Aizawl (Mizoram)
5.	Myanmar to Guwahati and beyond	
6.	Somra (Myanmar) to Jessami (Manipur)	Somra (Myanmar) –Jessami in Ukhrul district (Manipur)
7.	Khamti (Myanmar) to Dimapur (Nagaland)	Khamti (Myanmar)–Noklak area of Tuensang–Mokokchung (Nagaland) or directly to Dimapur (also in Nagaland)
8.	Paletwa to Cox Bazaar in Bangladesh	Paletwa (Chin state in Myanmar)–Mizoram or Manipur–Alikadam (in CHT in Bangladesh) –Cox Bazaar (Bangladesh)
9.	North Myanmar to Dibrugarh (Assam)	North Myanmar–Arunachal Pradesh–Tinsukia and Dibrugarh areas (Assam)

Source: Derived from Nishit, "Killer routes of North-East: How Drugs are Brought and Sold in India", *Border Affairs*, October-December 2005.

Impending health crisis: The silent emergency, viz. the health crisis threatens to disrupt normal life in the states of Northeast India. In the states of Manipur, Mizoram and Nagaland, HIV is chiefly concentrated among drug addicts.[3] Since diseases do not respect national frontiers, the spread of malaria, tuberculosis, leprosy in a country with inadequate health facilities is a matter of some concern. This is an area where the international community and the regional community need to lend a helping hand.

The United Nations Programme on HIV/AIDS (UNAIDS) estimates that between 170,000–610,000 people in Myanmar were infected with HIV/AIDS in July 2004 (while the government put the figure at 340,000 only).[4] Since diseases do not respect national frontiers, it is in India's interest that when it initiates AIDS awareness programmes, it is paralleled by a similar programme, preferably by the same agency, on the other side of the border. The two countries initiated AIDS awareness programmes in NW Myanmar (including Tamu town).[5] By the end of October 2004, 18,853 HIV cases and 1,701 AIDS cases including 462 resultant deaths were detected in Manipur.[6] The threat in Myanmar is real but international organizations are reluctant to provide funding. The Geneva based international organization Global Fund (whose funds were being managed by UNDP) terminated its $98 million five-year programme in Myanmar in 2005.

Table 7.5: AIDS Cases in North East India (as reported on July 31, 2005)

Sl. No.	*State*	*Number of AIDS Cases*
1.	Arunachal Pradesh	0
2.	Assam	225
3.	Manipur	2866
4.	Meghalaya	8
5.	Mizoram	106
6.	Nagaland	736
7.	Sikkim	8
8.	Tripura	5
	Total	**3,954**
	India	**1,11,608**

Source: Abstracted from the website of National AIDS Control Organization (NACO), Ministry of Health and Family Welfare, Government of India [http:// www.nacoonline.org/ facts_reportjuly.htm].

The above data is indicative of the seriousness of the problem confronting planners in northeast India. The AIDS figures for Northeast India are serious enough to merit attention of policy planners: in July 2005 Manipur had the highest number of AIDS cases (2866). Other states: Nagaland (736), Assam (225), Meghalaya (8), Mizoram (106), Sikkim (8), Tripura (5), Arunachal Pradesh (0). This requires greater cross-border coordination and implementation of health and AIDS awareness programmes and the greater involvement of international funding agencies in these programmes.

In order to promote the economic development of the Northeast, and to tackle the problem of insurgency at the point of inception, the Group of Ministers Report on National Security sought to encourage border trade by recommending the opening of additional trading points in Tirap and Changlang District of Arunachal Pradesh, Nagaland, Manipur and Mizoram.

The proposal for a road running parallel to the Indo-Myanmar border along its entire length, is also before the Planning Commission for implementation. Existing and potential border disputes between the two countries can be resolved by holding periodic meetings between the Surveyor Generals of the two countries. Mutual problems could be resolved by holding periodic "survey and inspection of boundary pillars, by both the sides" to prevent encroachment.[7] In order to deal with the insurgency situation in the Northeast India the Cabinet Committee on Security had approved the additional force requirements of Assam Rifles.

Immigration Issues

In the early years of independence due to the close understanding between the leadership of the two countries it became possible to resolve issues like Indian immigration to Burma quite amicably. However, under Ne Win due to introduction of nationalisation about 150,000 Indians were dispossessed and had to leave Burma. Later, the third stage began in 1988 when New Delhi came out strongly on the side of the democratic forces in the 1988 uprising and even offered to give shelter to any genuine Burmese refugees who sought it.

Cooperation in Counter Insurgency

The military of India and Myanmar have had some success in some counter-insurgency operations. The problem of insurgency is aggravated by the prevalence of the same ethnic communities across the border enabling easy refuge. Unless the small arms and drugs nexus is dealt with, the northeast insurgent groups will continue to receive arms and ammunition supply of armaments through Myanmarese territory via Thailand (transiting partly by the sea route).

India has had the experience of cooperating with Burma ever since the latter got its independence. U. Nu's autobiography recounts with gratitude India's help in providing arms and ammunition at a time when revolts and rebellions were plaguing Burma.

The need for dialogue becomes evident from the hurdles or near-failures which misunderstandings can create. For instance, an earlier operation in which the two armies cooperated was *Operation Golden Bird* in July 1995 that could only be termed a partial success because of differences which arose. In this 44 day offensive 48 cadres belonging to ULFA, NSCN I-M, and NDFB (National Democratic Front of Bodoland) were killed and about 40 captured in an ambush while they were smuggling arms between Myanmar and Mizoram.[8] Several others were arrested when they were in the process of procuring arms through Bangladesh. In another instance, in November 2001, the two sides held discussions in Kalemyo, Myanmar after Myanmar Army arrested some 40 Manipur insurgents following a raid on three underground camps at Tamu, Namphalong and Khunjao, near the Manipur border. These insurgents belonged to the United National Liberation, Peoples' Liberation Army and Peoples' Revolutionary Party of Kangleipak and were arrested between November 2–10.[9] However, Myanmar refused to extradite them on the ground that they were Myanmarese. When the Indian side accused Myanmar of hosting two Pakistani nuclear scientists on their territory, Myanmar, to India's annoyance, released the insurgents in March 2002.

Sr. Gen Than Shwe assured India (during his October 24–29, 2004 visit) that Burma would not allow insurgents to operate from the territory of

Myanmar. Following that visit, the armies of the two sides cooperated in anti-insurgency operations on their border in November 2004. In February 2005, Myanmar Chief of Naval Staff Vice Admiral Soe Thein visited India and met Indian Navy Chief. Two Indian warships, guided missile destroyer *INS Ranjit* and missile corvette *INS Kuthar* visited Yangon (participating in some basic exercises with Myanmar Navy) from December 22–26, 2005. Myanmar Navy's corvette UMA Anawratha participated in 'Milan 2006', a nine-nation exercise of regional navies off the Andaman coast, January 9–14, 2006.[10]

The two sides held the five day long 11th round of home secretary level talks in Myanmar during October 13–17, 2005, when agreement was reached on cooperation in tackling insurgents, arms and drug smuggling, and proposed infrastructure projects, etc.[11] The 12th round of home secretary level talks was held in New Delhi during September 13–16, 2006. The talks evolved a mechanism to cooperate in security, drug trafficking and border management. The talks dealt with:[12]

- Insurgent groups (of Manipur and Nagaland) operating from Myanmar and the need to clear them out (United Nationalist Liberation Front (UNLF) and the People's Liberation Army (PLA) were specifically mentioned by the Indian side).
- Arms and drug smuggling: It was held in the backdrop of smuggling of Chinese grenades and counterfeit Indian currency through the Myanmar border.
- Border management: Minor differences exist. (i) They pertain to India's objections to the *shifting of border pillars* in Ukhrool and Chandel district of Manipur by the Myanmar Army (which was denied) (ii) *Fencing:* There were plans to fence a 10 km area at Moreh in Manipur but which has not begun. (iii) Rationalisation of the free movement regime between the two countries
- A reappraisal of the various infrastructure projects (road and power sector) in which the two sides are cooperating.[13]

In November 2005 Gen. Joginder Jaswant Singh held talks with his Myanmar counterparts on the issue of security along the Indo-Myanmar border during his five day goodwill visit (October 29-November 2, 2005).

The Indian Coast Guard arrested on Barren Island 55 Arakanese whose boat ran aground while attempting to reach Thailand by boat through the Andaman Sea on February 16, 2006. Another 68 Arakanese had been arrested just prior to Milan 2006 naval exercise in January 2006.[14] The setting up of a 'unified command' on the Andaman and Nicobar Islands in October 2001 would help curb incidents of gun running, poaching while patrolling of the Malacca Strait would place some check on insurgent activity.[15] According to Vice Admiral Arun Singh the C-in-C of the Andaman and Nicobar Command, expansion plans of the military base on Andamans would include three new air bases in addition to the one already existing, enhancing coast guard troop levels and strengthening the infrastructure.[16]

The success of India's counter insurgency operation codenamed 'Operation All Clear' nearly three years back in Bhutan, raised hopes for similar operations on the Indo-Myanmar border. India and Myanmar militaries also maintained close contacts.

So it was hardly surprising when on April 20, 2006, top army officials of the two sides met at the 3 Corps headquarters at Rangapahar to discuss joint operations to flush out Indian militants taking refuge in Myanmar.[17] The Chiefs' visit had been preceded by a friendship dialogue between top army officials of the two sides in Kalewa (October 5–7).

In order for the bordering regions to truly benefit from trade, the infrastructure on both sides needs to be strengthened. It was with this as its objective that the 160-km long Tamu-Kalewa-Kalemyo road built with Indian help was inaugurated on February 13, 2001. It forms an important segment of the proposed Asian Highway linking Singapore with Istanbul. The Border Roads Organisation (BRO) has been entrusted with the task of maintenance of this road for six years. Thailand became part of the India-Myanmar-Thailand Trilateral Highway Project in April 2002 with the planned route covering Moreh (Manipur in India)-Bagan (Myanmar)-Mae Sot (Thailand).[18] BRO has undertaken construction of the Rhi-Tiddim and the Rhi-Falam roads to improve connectivity between the two countries, especially after Champai started functioning as the second border checkpoint.

India has also undertaken the Kaladan river project for which Rail India Technical and Economic Services (RITES) completed a survey in June 2002. A gas pipeline is planned along the Kaladan river from Nengpui in southern Mizoram to Sitwe port. A multi-nodal transport from Mizoram to Sitwe could provide "an alternative outlet to the sea for Northeast India in addition to transit through Chittagong"[19] or through the Siliguri neck and Assam.[20] The Indian railways recently proposed a rail link to Myanmar through the northeast. This involves the construction of the Jirbam-Imphal-Moreh sector by 2010, the Moreh-Segyi sector, and the Segyi-Chaungyu-Myohaung sector. Indian railways also has plans for laying new lines and undertaking conversion to broad gauge in the northeast (depending on resource availability).[21] It also plans to extend the training being imparted to BIMSTEC country personnel to Mekong Ganga Cooperation countries also.[22] Another important project India has undertaken in Myanmar is the Tamanthi hydroelectric project on river Chindwin, which will benefit India's northeastern states. It formed part of the discussions held by the then External Affairs Minister of India K. Natwar Singh during his visit to Myanmar (March 24–27, 2005) when he had stressed on "long term partnership" with Myanmar for bilateral, and regional development.

Market forces and the need to supplement Chinese aid compelled Myanmar to begin wooing foreign capital. Its Foreign Investment Law, 1989 sought to streamline procedures, provide guarantees and incentives and allow repatriation of profit.[23] By February 1, 2006, total foreign investments stood at $7.8 billion with the largest investments in oil and gas and real estate development sectors. The official Myanmar figures list the top investors as the UK, Singapore and Thailand.

The advantage in physically connecting the underdeveloped northeast to the business centres of Southeast Asia is beginning to be appreciated. It could simultaneously address the twin problems of law and order, and chronic underdevelopment. It would also compress the response time in dealing with insurgents.

Myanmar constitutes an important component of India's Look East policy. There is a great potential for improving trade with Myanmar. From a low bilateral trade figure of $87.4 million in 1990–91, India and Myanmar have agreed to raise the bilateral trade from $1 billion to $2 billion over the next three years.[24] India and Myanmar had signed a Border Trade Agreement in April 1994. It led to opening of the first border post at Moreh (Manipur)-Tamu (Sagaing division, Myanmar) in April 1995 and a second one at Champhai (Zowkhathar)-Rhi in January 2004. There is a requirement for additional trading points in Tirap and Changlang district of Arunachal Pradesh, Nagaland, Manipur and Mizoram to deal with the problem of retarded economic development and insurgency.

The potential for mutually beneficial political and economic ties at the bilateral level and through the BIMSTEC were reiterated when Myanmar Foreign Minister U Win Aung paid a three-day visit to India in January 2003. It is significant that India is Myanmar's biggest export market and it absorbs one-fourth of its exports. Myanmar imports primary and semi-finished iron and steel, pharmaceuticals. It exports pulses, beans and wood and wood products to India.[25] But, as relations between the two countries deepen, cooperation in other areas like human resource development, education and biotechnology will need to be emphasized.

India's growing energy requirements and physical proximity to alternative sources of energy in Myanmar indicate the need for exploiting this source for its future requirements but Bangladesh's intransigence in allowing permission for a pipeline through its territory hampered its efforts.[26] It appears to have forced India to finally abandon the option of getting Myanmar gas through Bangladesh and veered towards the more expensive proposal to bring the gas through the north-eastern states.[27] And for this GAIL has invited tenders for a feasibility report for an offshore pipeline to northeast India from Myanmar bypassing Bangladesh.[28] Myanmar's keenness in this regard is seen from the fact that its Energy Minister, Brigadier General Lun Thi visited India twice in

2005 (July and October).[29] The pipeline would be routed through Aizawl (Mizoram)-Guwahati (Assam)-Jalpaiguri (West Bengal)-Gaya (Bihar) and thereafter joining a proposed pipeline from Haldia to Jagdishpur Myanmar will import diesel from India (Bharat Petroleum to supply 120,000 tonnes per annum from Numaligarh Refinery). But its ban on foreign companies prospecting for oil in inland blocks has adversely affected Indian oil companies, which had submitted a bid in June 2005.[30] India and China's competitive thirst for energy became once again evident when Chinese oil company, Petro China signed an MoU with Myanmar Oil and Gas Enterprise (MOGE) to buy 6.89 trillion cubic feet of natural gas from A1 block in offshore Arakan where India's ONGC and GAIL together have 30 per cent shares.

Development of tourism which forms an integral part of India's Look East policy would also serve to stabilise India's northeast. India's northeast accounts for a miniscule proportion of the tourist traffic into the country though it has an excellent natural heritage.[31] Myanmar's national flag carrier – Myanmar Airways International (MAI) suspended its direct Yangon-Delhi flights on September 15, 2005 (which commenced in March 2004) due to declining traffic.[32] Earlier, in December 1995 India had restored the air link with Myanmar after a gap of two decades when Indian Airlines introduced bi-weekly flights between Calcutta and Yangon. India's northeast has to improve facilities in order to attract more tourists.

Increasing interactions between the peoples on both sides of the border has its concomitant problems as well which falls within the ambit of non-traditional security.

Among the important projects India has undertaken in Myanmar is the Tamanthi hydroelectric project on river Chindwin, which will benefit its north-eastern states. It formed part of the discussions held by the then External Affairs Minister of India K. Natwar Singh during his visit to Myanmar (March 24–27, 2005) when he had stressed on "long term partnership" with Myanmar for bilateral, and regional development.[33]

Ensuring Trust for a More Secure Border

There are various steps which India and Myanmar could take to develop greater trust. Besides the many suggestions contained in the Group of Ministers Report pertaining to trade, composite check posts and drugs, the one step which could have lasting impact on Indo-Myanmar relationship would be joint operations to track down insurgents from each others' territory. Tandem operations by the forces of the two countries, instances of which became evident in the recent past is one way to develop durable ties with close neighbours.[34] Taken together all these measures could form the basis of a mature relationship between the two neighbours.

Notes and References

1. For the theoretical nuances of the debate on border issues see, John Williams, "Territorial Borders, International Ethics and Geography: Do Good Fences Still Make Good Neighbours?", *Geopolitics* (London), Vol. 8, No. 2, (Summer 2003), pp. 25–46.
2. Malthea Falco, *Burma: A Time for Change: Report of an Independent Task Force*, Council on Foreign Relations, 2004.
3. HIV prevalence among drug injectors was 24 per cent in Manipur and 14 per cent in Nagaland according to NACO study. See *AIDS Epidemic Update*, December 2005, at www.unaids.org/epi2005/doc/EPIupdate2005_pdf_en/Epi05_06_en.pdf (accessed on December 27, 2005).
4. Irrawaddy website (in English), Bangkok, August 10, 2005, cited in *BBC Monitoring Asia Pacific, Political*, August 11, 2005. According to NACO, 5.1 million Indians were estimated to be living with HIV in 2003.
5. These programmes under the aegis of WHO were coordinated on the Indian side by Manipur AIDS Control Organisation and National AIDS Control Organisation and on the Myanmar side by Chairman, District Peace and Development Council, Tamu.
6. *BurmaNet News* (in English), March 24, 2005, cited in *BBC Monitoring Asia Pacific, Political*, March 27, 2005.
7. Chapter II "Challenges to the Management of National Security", in *Reforming the National Security System: Recommendations of the Group of Ministers*. Government of India, New Delhi February 2001.
8. Wasbir Hussain, "Insurgency in India's Northeast: Cross-border Links and Strategic Alliances", F*aultlines*, Vol. 17, February 2006.
9. *BBC Monitoring Asia Pacific, Political*, November 24, 2001.
10. "India to host multi-nation naval exercises," Rediff.com, December 26, 2005, at http://in.rediff.com/news/2005/dec/26nav.htm (accessed on December 27, 2005); and *The Asian Age* website (in English), Delhi, January 20, 2006, cited in *BBC Monitoring Asia Pacific, Political*, January 21, 2006.
11. *PTI news agency*, New Delhi, in English 1259 gmt 17 October 2005, cited in BBC Monitoring Asia Pacific, Political, October 18, 2005.
12. *PTI news agency*, New Delhi, 10 Sep 06 cited in BBC Monitoring Asia Pacific, Political, September 11, 2006.
13. *PTI news agency*, New Delhi, in English 1151 gmt 12 Sep 06 cited in BBC Monitoring Asia Pacific, Political, September 13, 2006.
14. *The Telegraph* (in English), Kolkata, April 20, 2006, cited in *BBC Monitoring Asia Pacific, Political*, April 22, 2006.
15. Ashok Sharma, "Indian official: Myanmar says it won't support anti-India insurgent groups', *Associated Press*, New Delhi, January 21, 2003. Also see Prakash Nanda, Strategic Significance of the Andamans, *Indian Defence Review*.
16. "Naval Systems: India to expand military bases on Andamans", *Defence & Technology*, April 2006.
17. *The Telegraph* (in English), Kolkata, April 20, 2006, cited in *BBC Monitoring Asia Pacific, Political*, April 22, 2006.
18. K. Subrahmanya, "A Breakthrough Visit", *Deccan Herald*, April 11, 2002.

19. B.G. Verghese, *Reorienting India: The New Geo-Politics of Asia*, Konark, New Delhi, 2001, p. 186.
20. Renaud Egretau, *Wooing the Generals: India's New Burma Policy*, Authors Press, New Delhi, 2003.
21. PTI news agency, New Delhi, March 5, 2006 cited in *BBC Monitoring Asia Pacific, Political*, March 6, 2006.
22. *The Asian Age website*, Delhi, April 23, 2006, cited in *BBC Monitoring Asia Pacific, Political*, April 25 2006.
23. See for details, Aung Than Tun, *Myanmar Laws Digest*, INNWA Publishing House, Yangon, 2001, pp. 81–82.
24. According to Myanmar's Ambassador to India U Kyi Thein, bilateral trade was $328 million in 1997–1998, $428 million in 2001–2002 and touched $480 million in 2003 (financial year). According to him, the target of bilateral trade is $1 billion by 2006.
25. "Win Aung invites Indian business to Burma", Mizzima News, at www.mizzima.com, accessed on January 20, 2003.
26. *The Myanmar Times website* (in English), Yangon, January 16, 2006, cited in *BBC Monitoring Asia Pacific, Political*, January 26, 2006.
27. Myanmar threatened to sell the gas to other countries (such as China or Thailand) if India did not respond quickly. The northeast route will raise the cost by Rs. 1,275 crore. See *Petrowatch: Market Intelligence from the Oil, Gas and Power Sector*, 9 (15), November 3, 2005.
28. The projected route for the pipeline is: Aizawl (Mizoram)-Guwahati (Assam)-Jalpaiguri (West Bengal)-Gaya (Bihar) and thereafter join a proposed pipeline from Haldia to Jagdishpur. See *Petrowatch: Market Intelligence from the Oil, Gas and Power Sector*, 9(17), December 1, 2005.
29. In July, he was on a three-nation tour of China, India and Thailand to interact on energy cooperation. Radio Myanmar, Yangon, July 2, 2005, cited in *BBC Monitoring Asia Pacific, Political*, July 4, 2005.
30. This emerged from the meeting that Myanmar Energy Minister Lun Thi had with Indian Petroleum Minister Mani Shankar Aiyer during his visit to New Delhi in early July 2005. It implied that the bid by Oil India Ltd, Indian Oil Corporation and GAIL for two onshore blocks in Myanmar stood rejected. *PTI news agency*, New Delhi, July 6, 2005, cited in *BBC Monitoring Asia Pacific, Economic*, July 7, 2005.
31. Sobhapati Samom, "Manipur misses the boat," and Krishna Das, "Passage to Bangkok," *North-East Sun*, 7(8), April 15–30, 2002. The tourist arrival figure at the national level was 2.6 million. Only 0.9 per cent of the tourists came from Southeast Asia while 58 per cent came from Europe and 18 per cent from the United States).
32. This happened around the time that Myanmar decided to establish direct air links between Yangon and Kathmandu for pilgrims. "Myanmar Airways suspends flights to New Delhi", *Hindustan Times*, September 7, 2005, at. www.hindustantimes.com/news/7598_1485079,000500020010.htm. Also, "Burma's National Airline to Fly to New Delhi", *Associated Press*, March 12, 2004; and *Xinhua news agency* (in English), Beijing, August 8, 2005, *BBC Monitoring Asia Pacific, Political*, August 9, 2005.

33. Discussions also covered defence, energy and insurgent activity. Economic cooperation forming the backbone of the relationship, issues such as the Kaladan Multi-modal Transport project, the India-Myanmar-Thailand trilateral highway, and cooperation in telecommunications, were also discussed. *PTI news agency*, New Delhi, March 25, 2005, cited in *BBC Monitoring Asia Pacific, Political*, March 25, 2005.
34. *PTI news agency*, New Delhi, October 2, 2006 cited in *BBC Monitoring Asia Pacific, Political*, October 3, 2006.

8

India's Extended Neighbourhood

Baljit Singh

Since 1990s, India has witnessed a major shift in its foreign policy from idealism, third world solidarity, non-aligned and international morality to pragmatism, proximity with west, strategic partnership with the United States, friendship with Israel and neo-liberal ideology as its defining code. This shift is attributed to the changing internal and external environment in which, India has identified the three concentric circles of its foreign policy ranging from immediate to intermediate and then to overarching. The immediate circle is constituted by its neighbourhood, whereas, the intermediate consists of extended neighbourhood and the overarching one includes the global players like the United States, European Union, Russia, Canada and other major players in the contemporary world power structure.

In this paper, intermediate circle or extended neighbourhood is the subject of enquiry. It does not only include the regions beyond India's immediate neighbourhood but also the external players therein and also the bridging states like Afghanistan and Myanmar. Both Afghanistan and Myanmar are the extended part of South Asia and bridge between India and its extended neighbourhood as the former has become the member of SAARC in 2007, whereas the latter joined the ASEAN way back in 1997.

Afghanistan is a bridging state between India and Central Asia, whereas, Myanmar enjoyed that status till it joined ASEAN. Broadly speaking, India's extended neighbourhood comprises the littoral states of Indian Ocean. To be more precise, the West Asia, South East Asia and Central Asia constitute the core of India's extended neighbourhood. However, in the post-independence period, India has grossly and perhaps consciously overlooked the studies and understanding of its non-South Asian neighbouring areas, which traditionally formed 'buffer zones' against external aggression. India has already paid a price for this in the case of Afghanistan.[1] Since 1990s, these regions have emerged as the priority areas of India's foreign policy and it has adopted a pro-active policy towards them.

I

The Persian Gulf was also the area of interest for the foreign policy makers of India during the cold war period. India used to enjoy lot of goodwill, respect and credibility in this region. It was not only a major source of hydro-carbon resources for India but it was also important for India because of its concern for Palestine and solidarity with the Arab World. Its policy towards the Gulf was having pro-Arab tilt and Israel as neglected part. India supported all the resolutions, which the United Nations passed so far for the establishment of Palestine as an independent state. Besides this, India was having more proximity with the Soviet Union in the Persian Gulf. Both India and Soviet Union used to have pro-Arab tilt in their policies towards the Gulf, which were shaped by the close equation between Israel and the United States in the Persian Gulf, apart from latter's equation with several Arab countries as well.

In the post-Soviet world, India's West Asia policy witnessed a major shift for which different explanations are given including rise of religious rightist forces in its politics and their hostility towards the Muslims which was manifested in the demolition of Babri Masjid in December 1992 and the communal riots of Gujarat. This mindset was also reflected in India's policy towards West Asia, which is predominantly inhabited by the Muslims. India, a classical ally of Arabs, decided to have close relations with their arch-rival Israel especially in the areas of security, defence and strategic affairs. Furthermore, India seemed in harmony with US policies in the region and many of these policies were seen as anti-Arab. India under BJP was even prepared to send forces to Iraq to support the Americans but Indian opposition blocked it.[2]

Now the question arises, can this change in India's West Asia policy be explained by referring to the emerging political discourse in its internal politics in the 1990s? It could be the partial explanation because India continued to pursue its changed policy towards West Asia even under the UPA dispensation. India has not only consolidated its relations with Israel but it has also voted against Iran in the IAEA on the issue of latter's nuclear programme. This has led to a debate in India's Parliament and left parties criticized the then government on this issue. Of course India has strongly opposed military action against Iran. Pranab Mukherjee argued that India did not want "another flashpoint in its neighbourhood". He stated that Iran has every right to pursue its nuclear programme for peaceful purposes subject to the fulfillment of its international obligations as a signatory of NPT. He clarified that the row over Iran's nuclear programme should be resolved through dialogue and the ongoing talks between Tehran and UN Atomic watchdog IAEA should be allowed to reach the logical conclusion.[3] The change in the global power structure could be accounted for this radical shift in India's policy towards the Persian Gulf, although the mandarins of South bloc argued that now India has diversified its policy towards West Asia. In its revised form, Israel has emerged as a new area of interest. Despite Indian assurances that its relations with Israel are not at the cost of the Arab cause, even then India's proximity with Israel is a cause of concern for the Arab countries. Although India further clarified that it is committed to the cause of an independent Palestine, yet its new West Asia policy is still a subject of debate not only in the Arab World but also within India. The cooperation between India and Israel in areas such as the economy and agriculture started off with the simple exchange of commodities, which is now growing rapidly, covering trade, technology transfer as well as investments into industry[4] besides the military cooperation.

As mentioned in the beginning, India's policy towards extended neighbourhood does not only deal with the countries or regions falling in it but also deals with external players therein. Therefore, the major challenge in front of Indian policy makers is to avoid becoming junior partner of the United States in the West Asian region which may provide some immediate gain but it will damage India's interest in this region and elsewhere in the long run. If India gets trapped in the American strategy towards West Asia, it will loose its credibility in the region. While supporting United States on some of the issues pertaining to the Gulf, India has already made its credentials doubtful in the region.

Another factor, which compels India to be careful about America in the West Asian region, is the rise of popular sentiment against US there. There is a huge gap between the Indian image and the image of the United States in the region. India's good image in West Asia had provided huge dividends during the cold war. Apart from the anti-American sentiment, the major paradox of this region is that states there do not like to see the emergence of a regional power, meaning thereby that the states in the Persian Gulf do not appreciate the emergence of Iran as a regional power. Hence India's strategic partnership with Iran will be the cause of concern for the rest of the states from the Gulf. Furthermore the United States, which is a dominant player in this region, does not like India's equation with Iran. Its opposition to India-Pakistan-Iran gas pipeline is a case in point.

In March 2005, the US Secretary of State, Condoleezza Rice during her visit to India and Pakistan stated that the US had conveyed its concern to India on the gas pipeline. As an incentive to wean India away from the project, she said, "we believe that a broad energy dialogue should be launched with India". The US made several diplomatic moves on the issue in quick succession thereafter. The US Under Secretary of State Nicholas Burns wrote an article in the *Washington Post* encouraging New Delhi to establish energy ties with Central Asian states and to reduce the lure of long term contracts with Iran.[5]

II

The South East Asian region has been occupying an important place on the foreign policy agenda of India since the early 1990s although the process of normalization of relations with the countries of this region was set in motion in the mid 1980s, when Rajiv Gandhi, then Prime Minister of India, visited Myanmar and Indonesia. Economic diplomacy has been instrumental in reviving India's linkages with the South East Asian countries. The economic reforms introduced by India and the end of cold war were the two major factors which created conducive environment for the emerging equation between India and South East Asia. The changed internal and external environment has led to the articulation of India's "Look East Policy", which has travelled a long way so far. However, in order to analyse India's policy towards South East Asia, it is essential to understand it in a historical perspective.

The cold war politics made South East Asia a distant region for India's foreign policy makers despite the geographic proximity. The US as well as Soviet influence could be the major factor for the low priority of this region on India's foreign policy agenda. The Vietnam war and the estrangement between the US and India had its corrosive influence on India's ties with the South East Asian states. The original five ASEAN states were aligned with the US; others were tilted towards the socialist model propagated by the Soviet Union and China.[6] Because of India's equation with Soviet Union, it was very unpopular amongst the original five of ASEAN. Therefore, India's interaction with this region remained limited, as its policy towards South East Asia was reactive during the cold war period. Nehru regarded SEATO as "harmful to Asia as well as the cause of peace", so much so that India declined to get associated with ASEAN in the 1960s when full membership was offered even before the organization was formed.[7] Apart from the end of cold war, the changing thrust from idealism to pragmatism has made South East Asia a priority area in the realm of India's foreign policy. In response to that India articulated a new policy posture towards this region named as the Look East Policy in which India has tried to overcome the hangover of the cold war. Furthermore, the neo-liberal nature of Indian state since the 1990s has been playing a crucial role in establishing linkages with the South East Asian states. Reason being that the neo-liberal state gives more space to economic diplomacy rather than the traditional diplomacy.

India's Look East Policy has passed through different stages since its articulation. It took shape in 1990s and has given adequate dividends to India. In 1992, India became the sectoral dialogue partner of ASEAN, which was later elevated to the full dialogue partner. In 1996 India became a member of the ASEAN Regional Forum, which deliberates on the security and political issues pertaining to the Asia-Pacific. Initially, this policy was designed to improve India's relations with the ASEAN countries but now it is enlarged to cover the other nations (Japan and Korea) of the region as well so as to facilitate the process of economic and political integration with the region. With the participation of India in the East Asian Summit and from the level of interaction in the 4th India-ASEAN Summit both held at Kuala Lumpur from December

12–14, 2005, it is seen that the Look East Policy is being pursued aggressively and has started yielding results in economic and political fields. India has given a big push to this policy by becoming a summit level partner of ASEAN (2002) and getting involved in some regional initiatives such as the BIMSTEC and Ganga Mekong Cooperation and becoming a member of the East Asia Summit in December 2005.[8]

Within the ASEAN, there are two sets of countries; one set is constituted by its founder members and the other consists of its late entrants like Cambodia, Myanmar, Laos and Vietnam (CMLV). India has special equation with these newer ASEAN states because they are strategically very important to India due to their proximity not only to India but also to other Asian giant, China. Besides this, India has close relationship with Thailand which has closer bilateral interests in the CMLV states than in the other members of ASEAN. India's focus on Thailand and the CMLV states highlights the fact that geographical proximity has a large influence in India's "Look East" policy because the South East Asian states, in particular those along the Mekong River, are also strategically important to China. When Myanmar became a member of the ASEAN in 1997, India came to share a 1500 km, contiguous border with ASEAN. This is how India's engagement with ASEAN states has assumed a different strategic perspective.[9]

Now India do not hesitate dealing with the military regime of Myanmar, its support to democratic forces notwithstanding. Mutuality of interests forced India as well as Myanmar to change their attitude towards each other. Myanmar has become important for India because of various factors: first, its strategic location between India and other states of South East Asia; second, to deal with the insurgent groups in its north east part the cooperation of Myanmar is in utmost necessity; third, to neutralize the influence of China and Pakistan in Myanmar from the strategic point of view. India has become crucial for Myanmar because of political, economic and strategic reasons. As Myanmar is moving towards its economic reconstruction, India could be a great help in this regard. The 100 mile Kalay-Kalaywa-Kyigon-Tamu road in Sagaing Division of Myanmar, built with the assistance of India opened in February 2001.[10] This Indo-Myanmar Friendship Road connects northern Myanmar with India's national highway no. 39 that terminates at Moreh in Manipur state providing better link from Indo-Myanmar border to central Myanmar. India also built a friendship bridge on the Mizoram-Myanmar border to facilitate a new border trade route.[11]

III

Another region that merited attention of Indian policy makers is Central Asia. This region gained significance after the Soviet demise because before that the former was an important constituent of the latter. Because of its geo-strategic and geo-economic profile, this region attracted the attention of many external players. It constitutes the land bridge between Asia and Europe and provides the shortest land route to Europe. Geo-economics of this region lies in its hydrocarbon resources, which are second after the Persian Gulf. This region became crucial for India as well not because of its hydrocarbon resources and strategic location but also because of its security concerns and political uncertainty and external players' power play therein and implications for the South Asian region. Politically, whatever happens there has implication for India because of latter's geographic proximity to Central Asia.

However, India is not having direct physical link with Central Asia, the two routes to approach this area be either through Afghanistan or China. Afghanistan is very crucial for access to India's extended neighbourhood and political instability in it has far reaching implications for Indian security and its neighbourhood policy as well. Keeping in mind its geo-strategic importance, India has been engaging Afghanistan since 1990s. India does not want anti-Indian security set-up to come up in Afghanistan; the former has been playing a meaningful role in the economic reconstruction of the latter. Currently, India spends around $100 million on various projects and $70 million on the reconstruction of a 213 km road from Zaranj to Delaram in Afghanistan. This new silk route road is the result of a project between India, Iran and Afghanistan to develop trade with Central Asian countries such as Uzbekistan, Kazakhstan and Turkmenistan. The route will utilize the Chah Bahar port in Iran to send goods to Afghanistan and to Central Asian countries.[12] Afghanistan is an opportunity as well as challenge for the mandarins at South Bloc. How to exploit this opportunity and to deal with this challenge is an uphill task. Its strategic location between India and Central Asia provides a big opportunity for the former to have access to the latter via Afghanistan. Therefore, whatever India has been spending on the economic reconstruction of Afghanistan is an investment to serve the larger cause, i.e. to have a shortest trade route to Central Asia.

Afghanistan is also a big challenge for India not only because it is listed in the category of failed states but also because the NATO has taken over the responsibility of security of Kabul without having any formal consultation with India before the 19-member military alliance sent the International Stabilization and Assistance Force to Afghanistan. It is the first NATO operation in India's extended neighbourhood.[13] Therefore, India would be faced with the difficult task of either neutralizing or collaborating with NATO both in terms of restoring peace in Afghanistan, as well as, in terms of India's own security calculus.[14]

As compared to South East Asia for which India articulated the Look East Policy, it could not adopt such a policy posture towards Central Asia. But it made efforts to institutionalize relations with the newly emerged countries of this region. The growing international competition amongst the external players for influence in the region has become a security concern for India. India's increasing energy requirements and its desire to diversify its sources of energy supply have made Central Asia an area of attraction. Although, India's strategic, political and economic interests are substantial in this region, its policy towards this region is neither well formulated nor pro-active and its relations with the Central Asian states have remained a low key affair. Thus India's policy towards Central Asia could not go beyond diplomatic mould and was passive in nature. Even the visit of the then Prime Minister of India, Narasimha Rao to this region did not achieve any remarkable breakthrough. Since 1997, India has been taking several key initiatives to gain access to Caspian and Central Asian oil reserves but without any success. The route via Afghanistan is unlikely to become a reality for a long time.[15] Another alternative route to this region is through China, which is having boundary dispute with India.

Of late, India started forging military ties with the countries of this region especially Tajikistan, when the former used latter as a base for its aircraft carrying humanitarian and reconstruction aid to Afghanistan. The most strategically located country from India's security point of view is Tajikistan that shares border with Afghanistan and China. It is also located in close proximity to POK.[16] As far as the military game in the region is concerned, India is a late starter and it has its own limitations because it cannot provide sophisticated weapons, which the other players like USA and Russia can supply to these Central Asian States. At the most, it can provide training facility and can conduct joint military exercises.

Generally, it is argued that China factors in India's policy towards Central Asia. The former has been able to make its presence felt in the region through bilateral as well as multilateral approach. The SCO is the good case of growing multilateral collaboration in the Central Asian region with China as its leader. However, it does not make sense to compare India with China as far as their respective policies towards this region are concerned. China has two major advantages, which are disadvantages for India; one is the direct physical access and other is that Chinese are well versed in the art of diplomacy. India has been pursuing its policy through the bilateral mode and it could not make much progress in multilateralism as an instrument of its policy towards this region. With the support of Kazakhstan and other countries of this region, India is trying to get the membership of SCO, a forum for multilateral interaction. Bilateralism has enabled India to prepare ground for multilateral cooperation in the region.[17]

Instead of India, the United States, Europe, Russia and China figure in the priority of Central Asian states. However, India is neither a competitor to any external player nor a collaborator with them in the region. India wants to have its own place in the region without damaging any one. It primarily looks towards this region from a security perspective, although the region has huge potential of economic dividends along with security. Whereas, the United States has moved into the region in a big way, acquiring major interests in oilfields in the Caspian Sea Region, Kazakhstan presumably would be a major world source for hydrocarbon supplies in the next few centuries.[18]

IV

To sum-up, it can be posited that South East, Central and West Asia regions have figured in India's foreign policy since 1990s. The South East Asian region has become a great attraction for India not only from economic but from security perspective as well. This region is a great business opportunity for India and economic diplomacy has played a great role in engaging countries from this region. Besides this, the South East Asian states are looking towards India from security perspective because of its ability to balance China in the region. The latter is having territorial problem with these states but the former does not have any such problem with them.

Although, West Asia has remained a major source of hydrocarbon resources, this region has witnessed a change in India's policy. India's growing relationship with Israel and its collaboration with the United States in this region is a cause of concern for the Arab world. Although India has clarified that its relations with Israel are not at the cost of Arab countries, Arabs are not satisfied with this logic. Pragmatism with neo-liberal ideology has remained the defining code of India's policy towards West Asia. India's policy towards West Asia has improved its relations with Israel but has made its credentials doubtful in the Arab world because they have started perceiving India as a junior partner of the United States in the Persian Gulf. However, India's relations with Israel are manifestation of realism as well as pragmatism of its policy towards this region.

Central Asia has huge potential for India's energy security and market but India is still pre-occupied with its traditional security concerns from the region. Its policy towards Central Asia has remained confined to diplomatic intercourse. It has not been able to achieve any breakthrough despite the convergence of interests. India's policy response towards this region has remained by and large lukewarm. Lack of direct physical access to this region could be one of the factors. Since late 1990s, India has been trying to gain access to Central Asian reserves but Indian diplomacy has not been able to make its presence felt in this region.

Notes and References

1. P. Stobdan, "Central Asia and India's Security", *Strategic Analysis*, Vol. 28, No. 1, January–March 2004, p. 75.

2. El Sayed Mekkawi, "The Changing Dimensions of India's Image in the Arab World", Anwar Alam, ed., *India and West Asia in the Era of Globalization*, New Delhi: New Century Publications, 2008, p. 195.
3. "India Disfavours Military Action Against Iran", http://www.expressindia.com/latest-news/India-disfavours military-action- against-Iran/216832.
4. Farah Naaz, *West Asia and India: Changing Perspectives*, Delhi: Shipra Publications, 2005, p. 118.
5. Gulshan Dietl, "Transnational Gas Pipelines: Global Context, Indian Experience", Anwar Alam, ed., *India and West Asia in the Era of Globalization*, New Delhi: New Century Publications, 2008, p. 40.
6. C. Uday Bhaskar, "Indian Foreign Policy Orientation in the Twenty-First Century: Continuity and Change", http://www.sueztosuva.org.au/South_asia/2006/Bhaskar.pdf
7. http://www.indianmba.com/Occasional-Papers/OP104/op104.html.
8. *Ibid.*
9. Faizal Yahya, "India and Southeast Asia: Revisited", *Contemporary Southeast Asia*, Vol. 25, 2003, pp. 1–2; http://www.questia.com/googleScholar.qst;jsessionid=HzRGIfQJNbw5hktHvsmmh B6cDhby
10. D. Bhattacharjee, "Challenges in Indo-Myanmar Relations", *South Asia Politics*, June 2004, p. 47.
11. L.K. Choudhary, "Indo-Myanmar Relations: Retrospect and Prospect", *India Quarterly*, Vol. 61, No. 4, October-December 2005, p. 164.
12. Sheela Bhatt, "The Afghan Initiative", http://www.rediff.com/news/2003/aug/01spec.htm.
13. *Ibid.*
14. Stobdan, n.1, p. 69.
15. Stobdan, "Evolving a Look North East Policy: Conceptualizing Sub-Regional Cooperation", *Security and Society,* Vol. 2, No. 1, Summer 2005, p. 102.
16. Stobdan, n.1, p. 70.
17. Baljit Singh, "India's Policy Towards Central Asia", Kuldip Singh, ed., *South-Central Asia: Emerging Issues*, Amritsar: Guru Nanak Dev University Publication, 2005, p. 200.
18. Stobdan, n.1, p. 73.

9

India and the European Union

Rajendra K. Jain

India's initial objectives in establishing diplomatic relations with the European Economic Community (EEC) were to secure better access to the community market and safeguard its access to the UK market in the wake of the British application to join the EEC. Since the conclusion of the non-preferential commercial agreement in 1973, sectoral cooperation with the EEC/European Union (EU) was subsequently expanded both in its content and scope by subsequent agreements in June 1981 and a wide-ranging "third generation" agreement in 1994.

The EU is India's largest trading partner; it accounts for about a fifth of India's total foreign trade, amounting to around € 46 billion in 2006. The European Union has also been the largest source of FDI inflows since economic reforms were initiated in 1991. During August 1991 to 2003, actual FDI from the European Union to India was € 6.2 billion. Numerous Indian companies have also raised Euro-funds to decrease loan liabilities and high interest burdens and to improve efficiency of capital. Sectorally, the EU has a substantial financial stake in industrial machinery, transport, electrical goods and electronics, power, energy, telecommunications, transport, chemicals and consultancy. In recent years, thanks to the emergence of a number of multinational players at the global level, India is now also emerging as a major investor itself, especially in areas like IT. Since 1976, the European commission has committed € 2 billion to India in development assistance.

Greater Political Dialogue

The joint statement on political dialogue (issued along with the 1994 "third generation" agreement on partnership and development) expressed the resolve of India and the European Union to reinforce and intensify their mutual relations in political, economic, technological and cultural fields. Annual ministerial (foreign ministers) and senior officials meeting have carried forward the dialogue. In 1997, it was decided to further enlarge political dialogue by the introduction of five new "mechanisms", viz. (i) Senior officials meetings (which comprises a dialogue on migration and working groups on consular affairs, and on terrorism); (ii) Meetings between the European commission and Indian planners; (iii) Bilateral meetings at margins of multilateral fora; (iv) Working groups of specialists on subjects like export controls, terrorism experts, and consular affairs; and (v) launch of a think-tank network.

The lecturing tone of the EU has considerably declined in recent years partly because India has been willing to engage the EU on developments, problems, and crises in South Asia (e.g. cooperating and collaborating with Brussels, the UK and the United States on dealing with the Maoist insurgency in Nepal). The lecturing tone on human rights violations in India has been toned down considerably because New Delhi has been hitting back at the Europeans by citing the poor track record in this regard of many EU member states.

Recognition of India's growing stature and influence regionally and globally, growing economic interest in a rapidly and consistently growing economy of a billion-plus people with an annual GDP growth rate of over 6 per cent for over a decade, the world's fourth largest economy, acquisition of nuclear weapons, steadily improving relations with the United States, and the acceptance of India as a potential global player in international politics and world trade organization negotiations – all contributed to India's admission into the elite club of nations with which the EU has an annual summit.

The joint declaration of the first India-EU summit (Lisbon, 28 June 2000) resolved that the EU and India shall build "a new strategic partnership" in the 21st century, founded on shared values and aspirations, and characterized by enhanced and multi-faceted cooperation. The Union's first-ever security strategy (12 December 2003) argued that it made sense for the European Union to cooperate ever more closely with each of six countries (including Japan, China Canada and India) as "key international players" in addressing the challenges and objectives identified in the security strategy. This was reiterated in the European Commission's communication on "An EU-India strategic partnership" (June 2004) which urged that India and the EU should forge "a strategic alliance" for the promotion of an effective multilateral approach, proposed "strategic policy dialogues" and stressed the need for "strategic" sectoral dialogues. In its first-ever strategy paper – perhaps because China had given a similar response on relations with an outside entity, India presented a number of proposals for enhancing more meaningful and systematic interaction with the European Union.

At the second summit (November 2001), there were some difficulties in formulating the text of the declaration against international terrorism. During the third summit (Copenhagen, October 2002), the two sides failed to agree on a joint formulation regarding the crisis in South Asia. The Europeans stressed the importance of an immediate resumption of dialogue between India and Pakistan and focused on measures to de-escalate tensions like withdrawal of forces deployed on the borders. The Indians insisted on a mention of the need of Pakistan to end support for cross border terrorism. New Delhi was enraged at the efforts of the EU leadership to pressurize India on talking to Pakistan and exercising restraint through aggressive public diplomacy, by the strident tone of Danish Prime Minister Anders Rasmussen. The larger EU member states pleaded ignorance while the Danes denied this. EU officials subsequently acknowledged the less than adequate handling of the situation.

The strategic partnership was endorsed at the fifth India-EU summit (The Hague, November 2004). The sixth summit (7 September 2005) adopted a new political declaration and a joint action plan divided into four sections (political, trade and investment, economic policy, and cultural and academic) on issues of mutual concern. The action plan sought to promote effective multilateralism, cooperation in UN peacekeeping and in post-conflict political and economic rehabilitation and reconstruction. Apart from a number of sectoral initiatives, a High level trade group was launched to study and explore ways and means to deepen and widen the bilateral trade and investment relationship. It was decided to launch a security dialogue at senior officials' level, which would hold regular consultations on global and regional security issues, disarmament, and non-proliferation "to increase mutual understanding and identify possible areas of cooperation".

The seventh summit (Helsinki, 13 October 2006) led to the tabling of the first progress report of the implementation of the joint action plan. It led to the launching of a CEO round table and endorsement of the recommendation of the high level trade group to begin negotiations for a trade and investment agreement.

India's perceptions of the EU have changed considerably in recent years. It no longer regards the European Union as a mere trading bloc, but increasingly as an emerging actor with a growing political profile in world politics. The EU continues to be weak in terms of projection of hard power, but is currently involved in a number of police missions. India shares European aspirations and preference for a multipolar, rule-based world order, but effective multilateralism continues to be elusive. India has been skeptical towards some major EU initiatives like the international criminal court. Differences in terms of foreign policy goals between the European Union and India will persist since both have different geographical and geopolitical priorities and preferences.

Security Cooperation

There seems to have been a mismatch of expectations since the EU's reluctance to accommodate and incorporate India's strategic concerns and demands were primarily the result of lack of competences by the Union in the field of counter-terrorism since it is essentially the member states which retain competence in this field. This led to frustration amongst Indian policy-makers who expected that there would be quicker cooperation in blocking terrorist financing and curbing money-laundering, and close cooperation with Europol after the establishment of the joint working group on terrorism. However, EU leaders tended to regard proposals by India regarding terrorism to be "ambitious". The new York (11 September 2001), Madrid (11 March 2004) and London (7 July 2005) attacks have undoubtedly reinforced the perception that radical Islamist terrorist events have changed in terms of scale, types of attacks and countries targeted and that many of those involved in Kashmir terrorism also have links with network of terrorism operating in Europe and other parts of the west.

An India-EU security dialogue would tend to be largely declaratory because India and Europe face different security contexts and do not have shared threats. India, thus, confronts traditional security issues that impinge on its territorial integrity, border control, insurgencies and separatist tendencies, the EU more of a security community, mainly confronts non-traditional security threats such as organized crime, terrorism, etc. Because of disparate priorities most EU member states neither share the same urgency nor interest in the immediate and pressing need to cooperate with India. To them, India is neither a genuine security "partner" from halfway around the globe nor a solution to each other's security needs. Thus, given the mismatch of context, concerns and goals, it is difficult to envisage more substantial cooperation in the near future. Initial steps are more likely to be in "soft" areas of cooperation such as money laundering, technical cooperation, and exchange of information. However, the limited prospects of more tangible security cooperation does not in any way whatsoever dilute the value of staying engaged in a dialogue with the EU on regional and global security issues. A dialogue is better than no dialogue at all.

India, EU and the United States

For India, the United States is more important than the European Union because of its global strategic vision for the future, because it is sympathetic to Indian aspirations as a rising power, and because it has the capacity to bring about changes beneficial to India. It is also comparatively easier to deal with the United States on a one-to-one basis which is characterized by effective leadership whereas decision-making in a EU-27 driven forward by committees and compromises. With the EU-India action plan reads like a virtual laundry list of issues which require dialogue, discussions, and greater engagement to attain concrete deliverables.

As India simultaneously engages all the major powers of the world, some are naturally bound to be more important than others. India's growing proximity to the United States in no way implies that it does not regard its relationship with the Union as not important. Indian preferences are in no way unique because as for multitude of other nations Washington is also more important than Brussels. However, a strategic partnership with either the United States or the EU does not imply that Indian perceptions and positions on all major international issues will necessarily coincide.

Europe and the Indo-US Nuclear Deal

The indo-US civilian nuclear cooperation agreement is a good example to illustrate how the United States, as the gatekeeper to various international regimes, is willing to accommodate Indian aspirations as a rising power and assist its quest for ending more than three decades of technological denials. Such a quantum leap would have been inconceivable for the Union, which historically tended to view India as part of the problem of nuclear proliferation and not as an integral part of the solution.

After the conclusion of the so-called "123 agreement" with the United States in July 2007, India has now to negotiate a safeguards agreement with the International Atomic Energy Agency (IAEA) and subsequently get it endorsed by the nuclear suppliers' group (NSG). In both these organizations, EU member states have significant representation. The current 35-member IAEA board includes 12 European nations and the 45-nation NSG has 31 European members. Thus, they will play a significant role when the nuclear deal is taken up for consideration. Some smaller European members of the NSG, especially the Scandinavian countries, face a dilemma in trying to reconcile their traditional position against nuclear weapons with the reality of India's rising strategic profile and the need for a climate friendly energy. Major supporters include France and the United Kingdom, with the former supporting India much before the United States. The Chinese may try to create further complications in the NSG by leveraging such European opposition to the indo-US civilian nuclear cooperation agreement. The combined efforts of the United States and other major members of the NSG, the fence-sitters and the recalcitrants are likely to eventually come around and accept reality. Once approved by the NSG, the deal will enable India to tap the entire spectrum of dual-use technologies, many of which could be sourced from Europe.

The EU, China and India

In the early 2000, external affairs commissioner Chris Patten urged India to shed the so-called narrow "prism of Pakistan" once and for all and develop a wider "world-view like that of China" in order to create a more meaningful partnership of ethnically diverse democracies. Most people in Brussels felt that Indian policy-makers, unlike those from China, appeared to need convincing that the EU is "a player that matters". They felt that, unlike China, India is neither proactive nor entrepreneurial enough to avail of existing opportunities. China is a proactive demander in widening and deepening its dialogue and interaction and relationship with the union in terms of attention and the frequency with which Chinese visitors visit Brussels. EU has neither a strategic vision like the United States towards Asia nor is concerned about managing a rising China.

There is a qualitative difference in the attention and focus given by the European Union to China and India. Many stakeholders in India tend to feel that the EU is obsessed with China, that there is a degree of political discrimination in the European Union's treatment of a democratic India, and in favour of China, with which the Union has few common political values. India's democratic polity does not earn it any brownie points in Europe. The India-EU strategic partnership has not yet reached the "comprehensive" strategic partnership that the EU has with China. India's relationship with China is unlikely to be at the same level as China even though India does not have the problems encountered in the relationship with China (e.g. human rights, a huge trade deficit, the arms embargo, lack of status as a market economy, etc.). Beijing is more central to European interests than India. This is reflected in the dense traffic of EU officials' visits to China—over 200 trips in 2004 alone. China would therefore continue to remain far more important than India because of its political clout, its economic potential, the substantially higher economic stakes and trade, which in many ways defines the degree of political interest that the EU and its member states take in other countries.

Promoting Civil Society Linkages

The Indian elite's perceptions of the European Union – be it culture, politics or society—continue to be essentially conditioned by the Anglo-Saxon media. This precludes a more nuanced understanding of both the processes and dynamics of European integration as well as the intricacies and roles of EU institutions. This has resulted in a rather fragmented and partial view of Europe since it tended to reinforce and sustain traditional stereotypical images and clichés. For the great majority of Indians, however, most of Europe is a strange land, an exotic place for tourism, to which only a privileged layer of society had access.

In recent years, most educated Indians have tended to feel that Europe confronts social and political difficulties in dealing with its diversity of cultures, that multiculturalism does not seem to be working in Europe, and that European societies have not been able to meaningfully integrate non-western ethnic minorities, especially Muslims.

There is a glaring lack of articles on the critical political, socio-economic and cultural challenges faced by contemporary Europe in the English language press. Most of the articles on Europe are informative and descriptive, rather than critical; they tend more to record the event than to analyse it. With over six million Indians travelling overseas, many newspapers and magazines, both in English and the vernacular, now carry regular features on various facets of European culture, places to visit, food, etc.

For most Indians, there is nothing like a European culture, but many cultures and identities. The European Union suffers from weak visibility and low profile in India. The bias is evident in the importance given to Washington in the Indian media and in both intellectual and cultural ties with the United States. Despite a growing information and awareness about the European Union in India in recent years, there still persists a wide gap between peoples partly as a result of mutual indifference.

Recent years have witnessed increasing attempts to overcome the lack of strategic neglect of India for decades by the introduction of innovative programmes. These have included the EU-India Economic Cross Cultural Programme. The introduction of the India window to the Erasmus Mundus programme has generated considerable interest amongst Indian students. There is a growing civil society dialogue, which for the most part is government-driven, but which needs to be broadened and sustained. Nevertheless, there is urgent need to supplement bilateral efforts by more meaningful multilateral initiatives in order to develop more effective synergies.

As the largest democracies in the world, India and Europe have a multitude of cultural similarities – both are multilingual, multicultural, pluralist, secular and complex societies. They are natural partners sharing common values and beliefs, including a commitment to democracy, pluralism, human right and the rule of law. Since culture is most often the window to a country or region, both India and Europe need to foster greater cultural dialogue and exchanges with one another in order to better comprehend our differences and how they can be used in achieving common goals.

Many of the historical and cultural bonds and terms of reference which traditionally linked India with Britain and, in turn, Europe have considerably withered away with time, including globalization and the growing influence of American television and Hollywood. A wired-in middle class is no longer greatly interested in European history, art or society. There is an imperative need to develop a more robust framework of educational exchanges and encourage Indian elites to study in Europe. A key goal should be to induce a greater number of students to study in Europe, which has so far been constrained because of the language barrier and because Europe does not provide a structure of post-doctoral fellowships and employment prospects that is available in the United States. This requires modification of visa restrictions and employment possibilities, at least part-time, during study periods, especially as India's new generation looks mostly towards the United States and hardly towards Europe.

Problems

A key difficulty in transforming the India-EU relations is the problem of leadership which is inherent in a diverse and heterogeneous EU of 27 member states, characterized by conflicts between short-term interests and national rivalries on the one hand and an attempt to forge a common position on the other. India-EU relations are essentially driven by those member states which have substantial trade and economic ties with India since it is they who provide the vision, the ideas and the expertise. Relations with India are driven by "very small circles" in Brussels. The number of officials in the commission dealing with India is only a handful; far less in their number and profile to those dealing with China. The problem is compounded by the fact that there are inadequate numbers of experts who are capable to understand the complex problems that India confronts today. Moreover, since the EU is constant work in progress, Indian policymakers often find it bewildering to deal with it. The EU's approach is inherently gradualist and incremental leading to a considerable time lag in decision-making within the EU because of its compulsion to work by committees and consensus.

Despite the shared values and common ground on many issues, there are basic differences in both perceptions and interests between India and the European Union in many fields, including trade, development and globalization. The EU has taken a stand contradictory to that of India on many issues in the WTO negotiations.

Conclusion

The strategic partnership with India has led to an incremental increase in the number of sectoral dialogues and working groups, which will in due course of time generate an inherent momentum and dynamism which will eventually lead to concrete deliverables. There are bright prospects for greater scientific and technological cooperation. There is considerable potential for India and Europe to move increasingly towards partnership in cutting-edge technologies in a manner which combines India's strengths with European capabilities. Energy is another area of considerable potential between India and the European Union. India hopes that this will lead to the provision and transfer of technologies which can lead to a more efficient and cleaner use of coal and natural gas.

Europe's demographic profile and a graying Europe means that it must consider the problems and opportunities of insourcing immigrants or outsourcing services. India's greatest asset today and in the near future is its demographic profile. With 54 per cent of the population below 25 years of age and 80 per cent of them educated, there is considerable potential for services due to the availability of skilled workforce and the numbers required maintaining current productivity and efficiency levels in Europe.

India and the EU have recently begun negotiations on concluding a comprehensive trade and investment agreement, including not merely goods, but also services, investment, intellectual property rights, public procurement, non-tariff barriers, dispute settlement, etc. Negotiations are likely to be concluded by 2009. And the Confederation of Indian Industry (CII) estimates that a bilateral trade and investment agreement could treble two-way trade to Euro 120 billion, of which trade in services would comprise Euro 75 billion.

Most Europeans are wary of the rise of emerging economic powerhouses in Asia, which tend to be focused on China regarding manufacturing and India in respect of outsourcing. There is considerable exaggeration and lack of informed discussion about the existing and potential danger from India since Europe's economic problems are not merely linked to difficulties in managing globalization, but are intrinsically linked to other issues like competitiveness, economic reform, flexible labour markets, non-sustainability of the current social welfare state, demographics, and so on. The tendency to equate India with China in the sense that they constitute a threat to European employment structures is inappropriate because EU's trade with China is more than six times larger than with India. Growing China and India do pose challenges, but they also provide opportunities since it contributes to greater growth worldwide, it means more exports, especially to a swelling consumerist middle class, which will make more demands of European goods, technology, and services.

10

India and Central Asia

Ashok Kumar

The end of cold war and disintegration of the erstwhile Soviet Union led to the process of setting up of a 'new world order' culminating a radical change in the dynamics of international geopolitics. These consequent changes have not only transformed the whole nature of global politics, but also have dramatically altered the basic parameters in which relationships among states are likely to operate. As a result, India also started facing a new reality in its strategic vicinity following Russia's withdrawal from Central Asia. In this dynamic situation where political-cum-security vacuum existed various regional and global powers have stepped in to gain control in the region.[1] Located in the heartland of Asia, the new states in the form of Central Asian Republics (CARs) of Kazakistan, Kyrghyzistan, Tajikistan, Turkmenistan and Uzbekistan emerged as new entities. This region is situated at the crossroads of ancient silk route[2] linking Russia, China, India and Iran with the West. Besides this region forms a bridge between Europe and Asia. Its location alone is a good indicator of its political and strategic significance and hence draws the attention of the entire political and business community of the world for a stronghold.[3] That is why; it has become crucial for India, much more than before, to moderate the changing security relationship in its extended neighbourhood in this changed regional scenario.

For India, Central Asia is not merely a geographical proximate region but also the one with which it has age-old and profound historical and contemporary relations. Consequently, India cannot remain indifferent to the blatant attempts of external powers to change the geopolitical balance in this region, which is fraught with grave consequences for the strategic balance in South Asia. This change may generate both challenges and opportunities for India in the reorientation of its foreign policy in this region. Despite India having no direct borders with these states, geographical proximity of this region makes the latter to be considered as part of India's extended neighbourhood. Hence, it is imperative for India to look towards this area with more seriousness due to its geostrategic and geopolitical implications for its security. Interests and foreign policies of India for projecting its influence and power into Central Asia are influenced by numerous factors. As it has been rightly observed by R.S. Yadav that,

> The competitive influence-building process by external powers, regional thrust and Pakistan's interest in the area, economic scenario and threats of political instability have led to the emergence of serious challenges for India's security and stability.[4]

Now question arises why and how India is more attracted towards this region? Some geopolitical and economic imperatives might have worked as important determinants for Indian compulsions towards these states. Economically, importance of CARs to India has widely been seen in terms of its enormous hydrocarbon reserves of between 90 to 200 billion barrels of oil and 46 per cent of the world gas reserves.[5] Kazakistan alone possesses a quarter of world's known uranium resources. Uzbekistan treasures the largest goldmine on earth. However, these deposits can be made useable with the help of enormous economic investments and by massive application of sophisticated and advanced technologies. Because of their landlocked status and under developed economy, it is very difficult for them to thoroughly realize their potentials without the support and co-operation of other states. The CARs are trying to diversify their economies and are engaged in new partnerships to enhance economic cooperation. Thus, CARs have the potential to emerge as an important area of economic activity for India. It is likely to be a great center for investment market for joint ventures in the core sector of their economies.[6] Simultaneously, India's energy demand is rising rapidly day-by-day. It is making efforts to look for reliable long-term sources of energy to boost its economy. The pursuit of energy sufficiency and markets are impelling factors for India to look seriously to Central Asia.

Strategically speaking, geographical location, mineral and oil wealth and rise of Islamic fundamentalism make CARs a very important area. Russia, China, Afghanistan and Iran border Central Asia, and it lies only a few miles from the Pakistani and Indian borders. This becomes crucial as it is surrounded by the likely regional powers of the next century, four of which are declared nuclear weapons states. Furthermore, the discovery of oil and gas and possession of nuclear technology by some Central Asian Republics have made this region an area for power politics.[7] The growing international competition for influence in Central Asia to secure energy resources has caused a serious security concern not only for these countries but also for the neighbouring states. The need for peace, stability and greater cooperation have never been as important for Central Asia and its neighbouring countries as it is now. New Delhi can not remain an indifferent onlooker winking at the blatant activities of outside powers. It is because any change in the geopolitical balance in Central Asia is likely to have grave consequences for the strategic balance in South Asia. Besides, India's own rising international profile on account of its size, strategic location, trade interests and a security environment, a desire to play a role in Asia particularly in its extended neighbourhood leads it to look at this region with greater significance than before. Besides, other major issues like terrorism, drug trafficking, security, regional grouping, oil and energy needs, defense interactions, etc. may also determine India's strategic interests in this region.

Politically, demographic composition of CARs is of plural character, where people of different languages, nationalities and ethnicity live to form a composite culture. In view of the poly-ethnic composition of the republics and the artificially drawn state borders dividing people and nationalities in the recent past have invited numerous inter-ethnic tensions and conflicts in this area. Besides, Islam constitutes the major belief of an overwhelming majority of people in these states. The dissolution of Soviet Union has given birth to a sudden resurgence of Islam in whole of Central Asia. The disappearance of Soviet ideology has left a vacuum in the beliefs and value system leaving search for an alternative ideology an inevitable phenomenon in this region. Under conditions of social tensions, there persists a danger of easy conversion of 'folk Islam' into 'political Islam', and through the exploitation of the latter by vested interests, into 'fundamentalist Islam'.[8] Islamic fundamentalists are striving to capture power by coercive means in these countries resulting in civil strife and turbulence, which is likely to have a spillover effect on the Indian state of Kashmir. Any advance by Islamic fundamentalists in this area can invigorate similar activities in Kashmir.

Pakistan has always occupied a central place in India's foreign policy. The support to religious fundamentalism, political extremism, international terrorism and armed subversion have become important components of regional strategy for countries like Pakistan. The fluid situation in Central Asia offers opportunities for Pakistan to enhance its anti-India programme and enlist this region's support for its regional policies. Pakistan is keen to develop its relations with CARs relying on Islamic fraternity. It has supported Islamic revivalism in this area whole-heartedly. The use of Islamic revivalism is more dangerous than the religious unity among the Muslims. These trends have far reaching implications, not only for CARs but also for the neighbouring countries, and a matter of deep concern for both CARs and India's policy makers.

Hence, due to its strategic location, demographic composition and geo-economic importance, this region is considered as a very significant area by the outside powers including India. The discovery of oil and gas and possession of nuclear technology by some Central Asian Republics have transformed it into a fertile region for power politics. Consequently, a struggle for competitive-influence-building by the powers has been underway to establish economic, strategic and political influence in this region. There is absolutely no doubt that Central Asia, whose influence in the past dominated the Eurasian world, is once again going to be a key factor in deciding the future developments in Asia and world. This scenario may have serious ramifications for India in its policy formulations. India is likely to take some initiatives in this direction. Nearly two decades have passed since the Central Asian Republics became independent. Since then objectives of foreign policies of both India and CARs have been to establish dynamic and multi-faceted bilateral relations. Bilateral relations between both regions are marked by understanding and convergence of views on a wide range of issues. The present level of mutual understanding and efforts towards strengthening of existing links in economic, strategic and political spheres between both regions has unfolded significant potential of cooperation between them.

Economic Relations

As far as economic relations are concerned, the foundations for lasting and mutually beneficial relationship between India and CARs have been laid. The dynamics and strength of this relationship are bound to grow, given the historical and significant interest India has evinced in this region. The CARs hold a positive opinion about India's economic development. They all look to India for industrial and technical assistance. Underdeveloped economy and weak socio-economic infrastructure of these countries offer rich opportunities to technically-skilled local labour force and natural resources to Indian entrepreneurs desirous of setting up joint ventures in Central Asia. India has identified a number of sectors in which it has considerable strength for cooperation. These are: automobile ancillary components; textiles; hotels; banking and insurance; drugs and pharmaceuticals; non-conventional source of energy; and electronics. Joint ventures of India and these Republics were envisaged in these areas. Mutual cooperation and 'joint ventures were also envisaged in the areas of railway, science and technology, construction, tourism, aviation, health, ecology, environment, trade and commerce.[9]

India has also offered facilities for training of Central Asian journalists, diplomats and students. A number of Indian companies are already doing good business in CARs in different areas. To boost bilateral economic relations, India offered a moderate financial aid and credit facilities to Kazakistan, Kyrgyzstan, Tajikistan, Turkmenistan, and Uzbekistan despite its own resource crunch. Both India and these states have given 'most favoured nation' status to each other.[10] As far as direct investments are concerned, the level of investments between India and CARs are quite modest in the beginning. Although, India may not have very much investment surplus, but many private companies have ventured into this area, making it one of the major investment destinations for themselves. Indian companies like state owned Indian Oil Company ONGC Videsh Ltd., Ispat Karmat, Larsen and Toubro, Phoenix, Aska International, Tirupati Overseas, Climate Export-Import, Birla Technical, Anjali International among others have varied economic operations in this region. The major Indian presence is in the sectors of oil and gas, hotel industry, light engineering, pharmaceutical and tea markets. Almost all the major pharmaceutical and other Indian entrepreneurs companies have their operations in these states and are increasing their market share every year. They are steadily expanding their activities through opening of their offices, agencies and appointing permanent agents in these states. While CARs have not become the major player in FDI stakes in India, as all these countries have been experiencing difficulties in their economic growth since their inception. They are still working on their disrupted economy and infrastructure.[11]

Beside technical cooperation, India offered its collaboration in the exploration of hydrocarbons and other mineral resources. Both sides have decided that cooperation in the hydrocarbon sector would involve not only exploration but also investments for upgradation and moderation of existing infrastructure facilities such as refineries and pipeline as well as training programmes. India had also signed the treaty on 'principles of inter state co-operation' and Bilateral Investment Promotion and Protection Agreement (BIPA) with each of these Republics for trade promotion in recent years. India and most of these countries have established Joint Commissions to promote economic and technological linkages. Commerce and Industry Ministry of India has launched a Focus CIS Programme at the time of announcement of its EXIM Policy in March 2003. With a view to enhance India's trade with countries of this region, the programme has now been extended further till the financial year 2007–2008. Under this programme, the Government of India extends assistance to exporters, EPCs, business chambers, etc. to visit these countries, organize trade fairs, invite CIS trade delegations to visit India and undertake various other market promotional activities.[12] Besides these agreements on economic cooperation, all of these Republics are a part of the Indian technical and economic cooperation (ITEC) programme, through which a number of students from these countries are availing training programmes in different Indian institutes. Mutual trade fairs and exhibitions are held on a regular basis. The Confederation of Indian Industries (CII) has been regularly organizing 'Enterprise India' exhibitions in the capitals of all the countries of this region to serve as a platform for the Indian small and medium enterprises (SMEs) in Central Asia. It allows Indian companies to explore the economic potential existing in the region.

Trade relations between India and these states of Central Asia are governed by the Bilateral Investment Promotion and Protection Agreements (BIPA) signed with each of the Republics in recent years. It contains normal features of trade agreements, such as mutual Most Favoured Nation treatment, promotion of economic, industrial, scientific and technical cooperation, including in the field of training of personnel, active participation of small and medium sized enterprises in bilateral economic cooperation, and counter-trade, etc. Despite the high economic potential, the scale of trade between India and these countries has been rather modest. The level of trade has been much below their potential. The entire Indian export to these countries is less then 2 per cent of its total exports. The imports also follow a similar picture and account for only 1.5 per cent of the Indian imports on an average basis.[13] The issue of strengthening trade relations between India and these countries have been a cause of concern for policymakers. However, despite the slowdown in India-CARs trade as a whole in the beginning, bilateral trade with some of these countries has grown significantly in recent years. Its trade has displayed dynamism in recent years. Joint Commissions are established on trade, economic, scientific and technological cooperation by India and these countries. Trade flows between India and these states is manifest from the Table 10.1.

Bilateral trade with some of these countries has grown significantly if the figures since 1999 are taken into account. It has more than doubled with each country in these years. The balance of trade had been in favour of these Republics in the beginning. However, after 1998–1999, it has turned in favour of India. Its trade with states of Central Asia stands around 10,2935.39 lakhs rupees as in 2004–2005 it accounts a growth of around 24.47 per cent in comparison to trade of 93,110.34 lakhs rupees in the year 2003–2004. During 2004–2005, there has been an increase in both Indian exports and imports. Indian exports increased to 75,991.29 from last year's exports of 69,769.92 lakhs rupees and import to 26,984.10 lakhs rupees from 23,340.42 lakh rupees during this year.

Above table also reveals that currently trade balance is in favour of India with most of these countries except Uzbekistan. In all Central Asian counties, Uzbekistan is the only country whose trade balance is in its favour, although, it is just around 0.3 per cent of India's total trade. Kazakistan has emerged as main trading partner of India in both imports and exports in these years. While the volume of trade with Kyrgyzstan and Tajikistan has remained far below the real potential. The major commodities of export from India are tea, drugs pharmaceuticals, paper, machinery and instruments, Leather goods and manufacture of metal, etc. are major commodities imported from these countries. Besides, crude minerals, gold and silver, primary steel and non-ferrous metal, etc. are other such commodities coming to India from these states. On the whole, though India-CARs bilateral trade may be small in volume, yet it has been growing steadily over the years and holds potential for further growth and diversification.

India and these countries are also aware of the importance of vast natural resources available in these states, because energy security is going to be fundamental and inevitable requirement for the contemporary world. India is the sixth largest consumer of energy in the world and to sustain its economic growth, it needs a vast amount of energy. As India's energy requirements are going to double in the next few years, it will have to find new options to fulfill this demand. Central Asian Republics possess large reserves of oil and natural gas and are looking for alternative markets where they can get suitable price

Table 10.1: India's Trade with Central Asia Republics

(Valued in Lakhs Rupees)

Year	*Kazakistan*		*Kyrgyzstan*		*Tajikistan*		*Turkmenistan*		*Uzbekistan*	
	Import	*Export*	*Import*	*Export*	*Import*	*Export*	*Import*	*Export*	*Import*	*Export*
1993–94	664	847	0.00	118	241	345	3353	479	2618	469
1994–95	1262	2604	0.00	0.00	662	32	3753	166	2618	2178
1995–96	2657	2987	3	14	1115	1632	920	309	3554	2304
1996–97	4355	1494	406	233	286	258	95	344	924	3323
1997–98	15,686	3269	32	3609	66	415	13	632	922	6471
1998–99	3731	14313	1280	3298	1511	271	45	696	403	5007
1999–2K	5830	11782	787	5979	1012	1032	166	2445	5621	4307
2000–01	6473	22879	2024	8037	248	1623	513	1239	4835	4292
2001–02	3526	21,796	265	5231	638	584	928	2075	928	2075
2002–03	6159	22,687	226	7097	39	4185	2616	4982	9942	2456
2003–04	4256	34,376	250	17,554	1816	2053	4291	8829	12,728	6958
2004–05	6896	35,676	277	22,063	1787	2810	4801	6572	13,223	8832
2005–06	11,643	40,229	653	12,438	2607	2763	5469	8336	11,571	10,820

Source: Monthly Foreign Trade Statistics of India, DGCIS Kolkata, 1999 to 2003. Also see, http://commerce.nic.in/eidb/iecnt.asp

for their raw materials. Therefore, India and these states can be of great help to each other. Convergence on these interests would bring together the main producers and consumers of oil in Asia. India has been striving hard to get access to Central Asian oil and gas reserves.

In this respect, Governments of both India and CARs are making serious efforts to create the right kind of atmosphere to enter this strategic field. Besides the bilateral efforts, both are also taking steps in opening their options by linking themselves to other regional countries. They are discussing this issue with a number of countries to provide access to their oil and gas reserves. Iran and Afghanistan have emerged as the potential ally in this respect. North-South transport agreement among India, Iran and Russia in September 2000, and earlier through a tripartite transport agreement among India, Iran and Turkmenistan in 1995 are such steps in this direction. The signing of a trilateral agreement between India, Iran and Afghanistan in January 2003 is another important step in this direction.[14] Another transit route option, has been added with the signing of an agreement with China for the use of its road to Kyrgyzstan through the Xinjiang province.[15] This proposed 'energy highway', with the distance of 890 mile and estimated worth of $2 billion, would run from Russia via Kazakistan, Uzbekistan and Kyrgyzstan, and on to Kashmir through India-China Line of Control.

Besides this, various projects of oil and gas production and laying down of pipelines are under consideration.[16] The governments of both India and CARs are taking keen interest in the construction of oil and gas pipelines linking these states with India. The proposed Iran-Pakistan-India gas pipeline or Turkmenistan-Afghanistan-Pakistan gas pipeline projects have assumed new significance for India as an alternative source of gas.[17] Once the problem of connectivity gets resolved, the linkages between India and these states will take a new turn for the benefit of both. Thus, both India and CARs are making effort to create right kind of atmosphere to improve the connectivity.

Strategic Relations

The new scenario of 'sphere of influence' has made the states of Central Asia strategically significant in present times. The instability in this region may have immense implications for the regional balance in South Asia. The growing international competition for influence in Central Asia causes a serious security concern for India as well as Central Asia and its adjoining areas. The combination of religious fundamentalism, nationalist separatism and international terrorism pose the greatest threat to the security and stability of this region. Both India and states of Central Asia are the victims of religious extremism and international terrorism and there is considerable similarity in its nature, source, pattern and methodology. Both share two sides of the hotbed of international terrorism, i.e. the states of Pakistan and Afghanistan. So, they face a common threat from cross-border terrorism from Islamic extremists abetted by neighbouring countries. In this regard convergence between India and the states of Central Asia may emerge on this issue.[18] CARs wish to become partners of the Islamic regional alliance to the extent it suits their respective national interests, alongwith their survival and autonomy in international relations. Consequently, they reiterate that the global fight against terrorism must also address those who instigate, assist or acquiesce as much as those who perpetuate terrorism. They affirm their faith in secularism and pledge to fight fundamentalism.[19] Leaders of both India and these states have expressed their common resolve that Afghanistan may not be allowed to be used as safe haven for terrorism. They are of the view that further efforts are needed for the long-term establishment of a broad-based multi-ethnic and independent government in Afghanistan. There lies a great amount of understanding between both regions in relation to the arising security problems in the region.

Besides, lucrative drug trade of opium in this region also poses a major threat to stability in CARs and its adjoining area. The terrorist groups, particularly in Afghanistan, regard the drug production and sales as the most appropriate means to earn money to purchase armaments. It has become the biggest transit point for drug delivery between Central Asian Republics and other neighbouring countries. Tajikistan and Kyrgyzstan have also developed important opium routes and become significant opium producers themselves. Fergana Valley in Uzbekistan is becoming the distribution centre of drugs from where the latter are re-distributed and redirected along several routes to Russia and to the Western world via Kyrgyzstan, Uzbekistan and Kazakistan.[20] This narcotics trade has linked CARs with global market. It is considered to be an easy source to finance the growth of terrorism and religious fundamentalism in the Indian state of Jammu and Kashmir and the Central Asian Republic of Tajikistan as well. New Delhi is worried about the flow of arms and narcotics from this war torn area into Kashmir. On this issue as well as on the issue of jointly combating the cross-border terrorism there is a compatibility of interests between India and CARs. That is why, India has signed agreements on joint working groups against terrorism with most of these countries. It is sharing its experience regarding counter-terrorist activities, intelligence expertise and giving training to their military personnel. Common approach on this issue can provide a firm foundation for mutual cooperation. In this direction, India is taking advantage of this situation and trying to form permanent relationship and working groups with these states to contain drug trafficking and combat terrorism.

In fact, these problems are not only being addressed at the bilateral level but also in various regional forums like CIS collective security, Shanghai Five, Conference on Interaction and Confidence-building Measures in Asia (CICA) and Bishkek International Conference on Enhancing Security and

Stability in Central Asia. In this regard, the CICA summit is a landmark in bringing the concerned states together in collectively countering the threat of terrorism with the shared goodwill between India and CARs with like-minded countries.

Interests of both India and CARs, thus, converge in terms of their ideas on defense and security and stability in this area. Both have adopted a policy of maintaining a balance in the region, in view of the rising influence of other powers. It may safely be asserted, on the basis of the foregoing analysis, that India, like this region, wants to become an area of cooperative and developmental activities rather than an object for scramble for influence and plundering of its rich natural resources and an arena of a new great game.[21]

Political Relations

The region of Central Asia constitutes a composite culture, cohering as a distinct entity by ethnic, linguistic and religious affinities. The predominantly Muslim population of all the states has drastically changed the political scenario of this region. The ethnic orientation of these Republics is further marked by sub-divisions within the main groups themselves. It is not only going to have impact on their own systems, but also have significant consequences for adjoining states. Similarly India is a plural society where Muslim population also forms an important component of its population. As a result, India is baffled by the developments in this area. In the past, chequered history of Central Asian region had spillover impact on its neighbouring states, as well as on India. It will have serious implications for India's policies in future as well.

In this context the shared demographic beliefs and values amongst them may provide a binding framework to these diverse manifestations. India and CARs share a common perspective on various issues such as threat of religious fundamentalism, ultra ethno-nationalism, and trans-boarder terrorism alike as both are plural societies surrounded by fundamentalist regimes. The best course for such societies is an open, liberal, secular and democratic political system. India, to a large extent, has succeeded in establishing and experimenting with such a system. The Central Asian leadership, at present, seems to be committed to establish such a political system and India can play a positive role in helping them by offering training facilities to acquaint them with a functioning democracy in a developing society. Thus, they are working for such a countering mechanism that encourages ethnic, religious and linguistic discord to be resolved among different sections of people. Both are of the view that only democratization in these states can resolve their problems. This area can be stabilized if each of Republics consolidates itself, preferably as a plural, democratic polity, free from discrimination on religion, ethnic or other ground. Hence, they support the emergence of any kind of democratic, liberal and participatory tendencies to contain the harmful tendencies. Therefore, interests of India and these countries converge in terms of their common democratic beliefs for the survival of multi-cultural ethos. Consequently, they are vocal supporters of secular ethos, which is fundamental for the growth of democratic culture in these states. Thus, their policies are likely to be directed towards promoting democratic culture, secular values and pluralistic system in CARs. India's political and security interests require that the Central Asian states consolidate their newly attained independence without interference from out-side powers in the name of religion or ethnicity.

Both India and these countries share similar views on most of the questions dealing with the dynamics of emerging 'new world order'. Such questions include the world stability, liquidation of the areas of armed conflicts, regional and global integration of countries and also welfare and prosperity of the peoples. Beyond this, they have similar opinion to withstand the rising global dominance of the USA in international relations. They are of the view that emerging new order has to be based on democratic principles and cooperation among all the members of international community. India and these countries would work together, towards a multipolar world based on territorial integrity and non-interference in internal affairs by outsiders and sovereign equality of all states.[22]

Political interaction between India and countries of Central Asia has been regular and mutually supportive in UN and other international organizations on various international and regional issues. They also support the increasing role being played by the UN in international affairs and positively assess its efforts in resolving the global and regional issues. They consider as central the role of the UN in the preservation of international peace and security in accordance with its Charter. India and these states expressed their determined opposition to unilateral use or threat of use of force, in violation of the UN Charter and intervention by powers. On the issue of democratization of UN, India and most of these Republics agree to the expansion of the Security Council to make it more representative and efficient. All these countries, noting the role being played by India in the world affairs, support India as an appropriate candidate as a permanent member of a restructured UN Security Council.[23]

Thus, India's relations with each country of Central Asia have developed in a unique and specific way. The success achieved during the past years in the growth of bilateral cooperation is ample proof of it. Co-operation between both regions have several promising directions, which are of great interest to both India and CARs. There is unending scope to derive multifarious benefits via a two-way union with this region. The dynamics of these individual relationships was, however, influenced by some common problems and constraints faced by the region as a whole. Lack of direct transportation system, language barrier, inadequate transit facility, and modest progress made both in liberalization and privatization, inadequacy of information about business opportunities, lack of direct and regular interaction among the business entities and inadequate banking facilities in these countries are some of the major problems which hinder the existing relations. However, several initiatives have been taken jointly with the countries of Central Asia to facilitate promotion of bilateral trade over the last few years. This change has provided both challenges and opportunities for India in the reorientations of its foreign policy goals. So, it is imperative for India to look towards this area with more seriousness. India would like the region to become an area of cooperative developmental activity of all interested international powers rather than an object for influence and plundering of its rich natural resources. India should favourably respond to initiatives of these states to evolve any regional formations.

To sum up, for India Central Asia constitutes a very important geo-strategic region with which India has age-old ties. Following the break up of former Soviet Union the Central Asian Republics are busy in developing and diversifying their relations with the world in general and neighbouring countries in particular. Large-scale strategies are being framed; deals are being signed for exporting strategic materials and energy from Central Asia in all directions. On the basis of prevailing goodwill among these states India should capitalize on it and take concrete and bold steps to strengthen its economic, political, scientific and cultural relations with Central Asian Republics. India's basic thrust towards this region should be one of positive engagement. The relaxation of tension in the post-cold war era is likely to strengthen their bilateral ties in a more constructive manner. However, the changing global and regional politics, along with the changed domestic scenario in CARs and India's pace of economic reforms are likely to determine the future course of their relationship.

References

1. P. Stobdan, "Central Asia: Emerging Strategic Equation", *Aakrosh Quartly*, Vol. 2, No. 4, July 1999, p. 57.
2. Great silk-road is an agreed name for a trans-continental land road of ancient and Middle Ages, which existed for about 15 centuries. The ancient route of economic and cultural ties linked three parts of world – Asia, Europe and Africa passing from the Far East through Central and Middle Asia, India, Afghanistan, Iran, Western Asia to Mediterraman countries. This road got its name as 'Silk Road" from the main trade article Silk and Silk goods, which originated from China. For more detail see, Nasir Raza Khan, "India's Connection with the Silk Route", *India Quarterly*, Vol. LXI, No. 1, January–March 2005, p. 83.
3. Svantee E. Cornell, "Geopolitics and Strategic Alignments in the Cacucasus and Central Asia", *Perceptions*, Vol. IV, No. 2, June–August 1999, p. 105.
4. R.S. Yadav, "India and the Central Asian Republics: Challenges and Opportunities," in B.G. Gafurov: *Dialogue of Cultures and Civilizations*, Moscow: Embassies of India and Tajikistan in Russian Federation, 2000.
5. K. Warikoo, *Ethnicity and Politics in Central Asia*, New Delhi, South Asian, 1992, p. 80.

6. Poonam Mann, "Central Asia: The Region in Focus, Role for India" in Mahavir Singh, ed., *Asia Annual*, New Delhi, Shipra, 2003, p. 86.
7. Warikoo, n.5, p. 80.
8. Devendra Kaushik, "India and Central Asia: Renewing a Traditional Relationship", *South Asian Survey*, Vol. 5, No. 2, 1998, p. 240.
9. Madan Mohan Puri, "Central Asian Geopolitics: The Indian View", *Central Asian Survey*, Vol. 16, No. 2, 1997.
10. R.S. Yadav, "India and the Central Asian Republics", *World Focus*, Vol. 20, Nos. 10-11-12, Oct.-Nov.-Dec. 1999; Also see Shams ud Din, "India and Central Asian Republics: Prospects for Cooperation", in Riyaz Punjabi, et al., eds., *India and Islamic World*, Radient, New Delhi, 1998.
11. Meena Singh Roy, "India-Kazakistan: Emerging Ties," *Strategic Analysis*, Vol. xxvi, No. 1, Jan.-March 2002; Also see, Puri, n.9, p. 251.
12. "Focus CIS: A Programme for enhancing bilateral trade between India & CIS." in http://commerce.nic.in/focus_cis.htm
13. Welcome Remarks by Nagesh Kumar, "India-Central Asia Economic Relations", RIS-CII Seminar, New Delhi, October 17, 2003.
14. Poonam Mann, n.6, p. 91. Also see, "India Iran and Afghanistan agree to develop new Silk Route," http://www.gasandoil.com/goc/news.htm/308999.htm; http://www.hindu.com/2005/04/ 06stories/2005046064211OO.htm; and, http://www.hinduonnet.com/thehindu/2003/11/15/stories /2003111502361100.htm
15. Roy, n.11.
16. R.S. Yadav and Suresh Dhanda, "Oil Politics of Caspian Sea and Central Asia: Policy Options for India," *Contemporary Central Asia*, Vol. x, No. 2, August 2006.
17. *Ibid.*; Also see, Shah Alam, "Pipeline Politics in the Caspian Sea Basin", *Strategic Analysis*, Vol. 26, No. 1, Jan-March, 2002.
18. Poonam Mann, "Fighting Terrorism: India and Central Asia", *Strategic Analysis*, Vol. xxiv, No. 11, Feb. 2001, p. 2036.
19. R.S. Yadav, "Democratization of Central Asian Republics and India", *Kurukshetra University Research Journal*, Vol. xxviii–xxx, 1994–95, p. 228. Also see, Meena Singh Roy, "India's Interest in Central Asia", *Strategic Analysis*, Vol. xxiv, No. 12, March 2001, pp. 2276, 77, 78; and, CICA, Declaration on Eliminating Terrorism and Promoting Dialogue among Civilizations, 5 June, 2002, Alamaty.
20. *Ibid.*
21. *Ibid.*, Also see, Statement by the Prime Minister Atal Bihari Vajpayee at the CICA Summit in Almaty, www.indianembassy.org/special/cabinet/Primeminister/2002/pm_june_04_2002.htm.
22. M. Imanaliev, "India and Kyrgyzstan in constructive cooperation", *Himalayan and Central Asian Studies*, Vol. 2, Nos. 3–4, July–December 1998. Also see, Askar Akaev, "Kyrgyzstan on The Eve of The Twenty First Century: Principal Trends of Reforms", *Himalayan and Central Asian Studies*, Vol. 2, Nos. 3–4, July-December 1998.
23. India-Kazakistan Joint Declaration, 12 February 2002, New Delhi (Ministry of External Affairs of the Government of India, 2002). Also see, http://www.hindu.com/2005/04/06/stories/2005040606421100.htm; and, "India offers $5 m to Tajikistan", *The Hindu*, May 11, 2001.

11

India and SAARC

Suman Sharma

India's approach to regional cooperation in Asia can be well analyzed with its reference to the broader framework of SAARC. The roots of regionalism in Indian policy can be traced back to the years of its struggle for independence. The emergence and evolution of SAARC have been examined keeping in focus India's early responses and subsequent approaches and priorities – economic, cultural, political and strategic. Here an attempt has been made to analyse how post-cold war developments have affected India's approach to regional cooperation process in Asia in general and SAARC in particular. India's initiatives and interest in both sub-regional and wider Asian groupings like ASEAN and Indian Ocean Rim Association have been taken into account to examine how it would affect SAARC.

Historical Perspectives

India's independence in 1947 and the process of decolonisation of Asia and Africa thereafter induced a desire among the newly independent states to forge a unity for reconstruction of the nations ravaged by Western colonialism. The Indian leadership, even before the dawn of independence, wove the visions of world peace and an equitable international order on the edifice of Afro-Asian unity. The Indian National Congress spearheading the struggle for Indian independence dreamed of an Asiatic Federation.

The All India Congress Committee (AICC) in its Bombay session held in July 1921 took note of a resolution passed by the citizens of Bombay in April 1921 urging AICC 'to promote feelings of amity and concord with neighbouring states with a view to establish goodwill and sympathy to formulate a clear and definite foreign policy for 'India'.[1] Realising that Britain was using India's position and resources to promote its imperialistic designs in India's neighbourhood, the AICC in a historic declaration in Delhi on 4–5 November 1921, affirmed that the Congress let it be known to the neighbouring and other non-India states:

(i) that the present Government of India in no way represent Indian opinion and that their policy has been traditionally guided by considerations more of holding India in subjection than of protecting her borders;

(ii) that India as self-governing country can have nothing to fear from the neighbouring states or any state as her people have no designs upon any of them, and hence, no intention of establishing any trade relation hostile to or not desired by the people of such states; and

(iii) that the people of India regard most treaties entered into with the Imperial Government by neighbouring states as mainly designed by the latter to perpetuate the exploitation of India by the Imperial power, and would, therefore, urge the states having no ill-will against the people of India and having no desire to injure her interest, to refrain from entering into any treaty with the Imperial power.[2]

Anti-imperialism became the cornerstone of the foreign policy of Congress and provided an opportunity for the states of Asia to come together. Gandhi observed that the common lot no less than territorial homogeneity and cultural affinity was bringing the Asiatic races wonderfully together and they seemed determined to take their fullest share in the world politics.[3] The INC saw the emergence of a great Asiatic Federation as inevitable and participation of India in the union of the oppressed nationalities of Asia as the precursor to the freedom of every nationality to bring about world peace. The Congress world-view maintained that no nation on earth can really be free when other nations are held in bondage.[4]

Pursuing the idea of an Eastern-Federation Congress discussed political ideas that scaled the ramparts of the Himalayas and most of the surrounding seas to recognize that the freedom of Asiatic nations would contemplate the organization of an Eastern-Federation.[5]

India's role in the fight against imperialist repression was pivotal since she was considered to be the leading state fighting against imperialism. The leadership of Indian national movement before and immediately after Indian independence set before themselves an agenda for regional cooperation and unity in Asia. The INC nursed a sense of grievance that despite India's importance and leadership against colonialism, India could not secure its rightful place as a member of the Security Council of the United Nations on account of its colonized status. The CWC in July 1945 adopted a resolution expressing strong resentment against the position allotted to the smaller nations in the United Nations Organisation. The Committee observed that the Great-Powers not only dominated and completely controlled the new organization but were placed above and beyond the law they had themselves helped in framing. In accordance with its perception of India's role in national and international fields, the CWC felt that India must attain the status of an independent and sovereign state, having a place in the highest council of nations, and in a position to contribute to the maintenance of peace, security and freedom.[6]

It was in keeping with this grandiose image of India that the INC considered India to be the central actor in Asia. Thus Jawaharlal Nehru, who more than anyone else represented Congress views on foreign policy matters, observed that "whether one talked of the Middle East or Southeast Asia or China, all impinged on India and all depended on India economically, politically and strategically. They could not help looking at India and India could not help looking at them. In the modern world it was inevitable for India to be the centre of things in Asia."[7] Nehru also maintained that the small states of the future world had no future in store and they were certain to be reduced to the status of the satellite states. He advocated the creation of a South Asian Federation of India, Iraq, Iran, Afghanistan and Burma.[8]

Inspired by Jawaharlal Nehru, a landmark Asian Relations Conference (ARC) was organised on the eve of Indian independence in March 1947 to discuss issues like National Movement for Freedom, Racial Problems and Inter-Asian Migrations, Transition from Colonial to National Economy, etc.[9] This conference was attended by twenty eight countries including Soviet-Asian Republics. The basic objective of India under Nehru's leadership was to proclaim Asia's resurgence, the need for Asian unity and greater cooperation, and to work for larger ideal of 'one world'. India's strong desire for Asian unity was underlined by her move in convening a New Delhi Conference on Indonesia in 1949 against Dutch police action in Indonesia and continued efforts to organise the newly independent states of Asia and Africa which process culminated in the historic Bandung Conference held in Indonesia in 1955. In the backdrop of cold-war rhetoric between the East and the West unleashed in the aftermath of the Second World War, Nehru's India put forth the five principles of peaceful co-existence (later known as Panchsheel) as an alternative world-view to the 'immorality' of the cold-war.

These initial efforts to unite Asia failed primarily due to the power politics of cold-war ideology, Sino-Indian rivalry, victory of communist movement in China and the threat perception of some Asian countries from rising tide of communism. There was also lack of clarity about the specific region which was sought to be evolved into a collective identity."[10] The high ideals of 'Panchsheel' and a strong anti-colonial sentiment failed to counter the strong pulls and pressures of the cold-war and Asia failed to evolve a regional platform.

A pioneer in studying India's regional policy, Sisir Gupta, reflecting on the problems and prospects of regional integration in Asia, found that in developing countries like India, foreign policy was not the function of mass opinion but rather of modernized elite groups often represented by one man or a group of men who represented the urges and aspirations of the elite. The foreign policy of India was thus largely seen as creation of Jawaharlal Nehru. The lack of communication among the elites of different Asian countries and the tendency of the Indian elite to identify with European values and problems were seen as a serious difficulty in the process of regional integration in Asia.[11]

The cold-war conflict which impeded the process of regionalism in Asia, facilitated the same in Western Europe. Blessed by the patron saint of Western bloc, the United States of America, Western Europe embarked on post-war reconstruction by evolving a common identity in search of peaceful and prosperous Europe devoid of war and blind nationalism. The European Economic Community was launched in 1957. Three and a half decades later, through a painstaking long process, fifteen countries of Western and Central Europe in 1993 launched a European Union (EU) with an array of impressive regional institutions like a European Council of Heads of State/Government, a European Parliament, a European Court of Justice, a European Commission – the bureaucracy, and a common currency with a Central European Bank. The EU has ambitious projects to evolve a common foreign and security policy and a common policy in the field of justice and home affairs. The Western Europe thus achieved a significant level of political and economic integration.

Emergence of SAARC

A universal realisation among the third world countries for self-help and collective help in pursuing the goals of economic progress and development, impelled the countries of South Asia to forge a regional grouping despite their earlier misgivings and apprehensions. India with her experience of initial efforts to organise the Asian community and recent history of conflicts in the region cautiously welcomed the initiative of Bangladesh in 1980 for an association of South Asian nations, namely, India, Pakistan, Sri Lanka, Bangladesh, Nepal, Bhutan and Maldives.[12] Five year later, after a painstaking, gradual step-by-step progress, the seven South Asian nations launched South Asian Association for Regional Cooperation (SAARC) in 1985.

The initial years of SAARC were marked by significant political developments in the world culminating in the demise of the cold war and dismemberment of the Soviet Union. The end of the cold war brought about a fundamental change, a paradigm shift in international relations. The predominant strain was of the primacy of economics in a market driven international politics. There have also been significant attempts by the world's rich to consolidate 'regionally' in order to prepare for the global future. Almost every country in the rich club of the Organisation of Economic Cooperation and Development (OECD) is a member of some sort of regional cooperative arrangement. As already noted, Western Europe achieved an advanced state of economic integration and much more after the creation of European Union (EU) in 1993. The emergence of a free trade area of North American continent (NAFTA) has further fuelled the phenomenon of regional cooperative arrangements. In fact, nearly all countries of Latin America, Caribbean and continental Africa are also involved in some form of regional cooperation. The dynamic economies of South East Asia had already come together into a successful Association of South-East Asian Nations (ASEAN). The Gulf countries are bonded together in a cooperative arrangement called Gulf-Cooperation Council (GCC). There is a Southern Cone Market (MERCOSUR) in Latin America, a South African Customs Union (SACU) and an upcoming powerful bloc of Asia-Pacific region – Asia Pacific Economic Cooperation (APEC). In fact, with APEC and the newly emerging Indian Ocean Rim-Association for Regional Cooperation (IOR-ARC) an entirely new dimension of 'open-regionalism' has been added to the concept of regionalism. Open-regionalism seeks to promote the objectives of free-global trade without attempting to form a trade bloc as such. It is thus found that the urge to merge into some form of cooperative arrangement seems to have become almost universal.[13]

India's Policy Response to Regional Cooperation in South Asia

The proposal for regional cooperation in South Asia was made by Bangladesh in 1980 in the wake of significant political developments in the region.[14] Soviet invasion of Afghanistan in 1979 had intensified East-West divide and brought the cold war conflict on the door-steps of South Asia. The West led by United States wanted a regional security arrangement in South and South-West Asia. This was a critical and crucial time for Indian policy in the region. In pursuance of its policy of non-alignment India never wanted to get embroiled in East-West cold-war and also was in favour of keeping at bay the influence of extra-regional powers in South Asia. India's friendship and commonality of interests with the Soviet Union inhibited her free expression of condemnation of Soviet action in Afghanistan. India's suspicion of possible Western sponsorship of the proposal for regional cooperation and also of neighbours 'ganging up' against her made her respond cautiously to the proposal. Analysing India's dilemma and policy predicament S.D. Muni has rightly observed that:

> India could not reject the proposal either because the idea of regional cooperation in itself was a positive one and could play a useful role in India's own regional policy. An outright rejection of the proposal by India could also give legitimacy to the neighbouring states going ahead with it on their own. This in effect would have made the forum an instrument of neighbours "ganging-up" against India. It would also have aggravated India's isolation in the region, which was already becoming pronounced on issues such as the Indian Ocean, Kampuchea and Afghanistan. India, therefore, had to be careful in its response to the proposal. It activated its diplomacy to see that the proposal was moderated and redefined so as to become compatible with essential aspects of its perceived interests in the region.[15]

India, thus, favoured a slow, gradual step by step approach and put forth two important preconditions for regional cooperation in South Asia. These pre-conditions were that no bilateral contentious issues be discussed in the proposed regional grouping and that all decisions be taken on the basis of unanimity. India wanted to shut out politics and contentious bilateral issues from regional cooperation. In a very forthright and pragmatic manner the Indian Foreign Secretary put forth two important pre-conditions for regional cooperation in South Asia when he said:

> At this stage it would also be useful to stress that we reach unequivocal agreement on what I would call the "ground rules" which should govern regional cooperation exercise and which in fact appear in the Bangladesh paper itself. Here I would submit that the principle of avoiding discussions in regional framework of all bilateral and contentious issues and of unanimity as the principle on the basis of which decisions in regard to regional cooperation are taken should be followed scrupulously.[16]

India's approach was to soften the political and strategic divergence in South Asia through greater economic and cultural cooperation. In line with India's cautious approach, which was shared by Pakistan as well for its own reasons,[17] the bureaucracy of the seven nations tried to identify and evolve the possible areas of cooperation in the fields such as agriculture, rural development, telecommunication, meteorology, health and population activities. This process went on for three years till 1983 when the baton was passed on to the political establishment to push further the agenda for regional cooperation. The Foreign Ministers of seven South Asian countries adopted a declaration on South Asian Regional Cooperation (SARC)[18] in August 1983 with the objective to promote the welfare of the peoples of South Asia and improvement in the quality of their life. Significantly, the two pre-conditions proposed by India were incorporated in the declaration. The SARC declaration also provided for an institutional arrangement of Technical Committees for each area of cooperation, an Action Committee for implementation of projects and a Standing Committee of the Foreign Secretaries for the co-ordination and monitoring of an Integrated Programme of Action (IPA) in the identified areas of cooperation. Two years later in December 1985, after an intensive political interaction and adequate spade work, the seven South Asian nations launched South Asian Association for Regional Cooperation (SAARC) at a Summit Meeting of the Heads of State/Government in Dhaka, Bangladesh. Thus despite the absence of some acknowledged essential ingredients like common ideological/political perception and common foreign policy orientations, the move for regional cooperation in South Asia reached its launching stage due to compulsions of international political and economic situations where South Asia was threatened to be left out of the global march to peace and progress. The Indian Foreign Secretary mentioned 'trade' as a field of great importance for regional cooperation. He said:

> In fact, in many other regions of the world, cooperation in trade was established at a relatively early stage starting with certain specific sections. As developing countries we all have understandable difficulties in liberalising trade flows which might necessitate drastic changes in our trade regimes. But it should be possible to consider limited cooperation based on a regional system of trade preferences, cooperation among state trading agencies and trade related institutions and cooperation in the marketing and processing of commodities of interest to countries of the region.[19]

The issue of 'trade' for India was an important element of regional cooperation. However, this was excluded from the initial process of cooperation due to fear of India's neighbours that a liberal trade regime would work to the advantage of 'big' India. India's approach was to suggest a carefully balanced inter-dependence and a division of labour based on local factors that could provide strength to the region's economic base and infrastructure. India, nevertheless, did not force the issue since her policy was to hasten slowly the process of regional cooperation in South Asia.

The size, power potential and centrality of India in South Asia makes her the most significant feature of SAARC. While India shares the typical features of underdevelopment with her South Asian neighbours, she also shows characteristics sharply distinguishing her from them. India has laid down a vast industrial infrastructure, has a strong military machine, a large scientific and technological manpower and a relatively stable democracy with a vast, politically stabilizing middle class having significant purchasing power. Such an India, seeking a global role after exercising her nuclear option, gives rise to serious misgivings about her objectives and role in South Asia among her smaller neighbours, particularly Pakistan, Bangladesh, Nepal and Sri Lanka.[20] SAARC with this 'baggage' of Indo-centrality and a region prone to the intra-state and inter-state conflicts, made a modest beginning by adopting a Charter in 1985 Dhaka Summit enunciating the objectives and the principles and an institutional framework for SAARC.[21] The principal objectives of SAARC being socio-economic welfare and cultural development of the South Asian peoples, emphasis was laid on the achievement of the goal of collective collaboration in the economic, social, cultural, technical and scientific fields.

The institutional framework for SAARC provides for pyramidal structure with Summit of the Heads of State/government at the apex, supported by the Council of Ministers (Foreign Ministers of the Member States) and the arrangement of the Standing Committee and Technical Committees as earlier mentioned in the SARC declaration. The Charter also provided for setting up a Secretariat with Secretary General, seven Directors and General Services Staff. This came into being rather quickly when it was set up in Kathmandu in 1987 to coordinate and monitor implementation of SAARC activities and to service the meetings of the association. The most significant feature of the

Charter is considered to be the provision that the Heads of State/Government would meet once a year, or more often, if necessary. This provides an excellent opportunity to give a political direction to the regional cooperation process as well as to informally discuss the contentious, bilateral issues on the sidelines of the Summit meetings.

During the period 1985–1990 SAARC process moved slowly through five Summit meetings with expansion of activities including those incorporated in the Integrated Programme of Action (IPA), and institutionalization of SAARC. Apart from the IPA, this period witnessed promotion of people-to-people contact, setting up of SAARC regional institutions like Agricultural Information Centre, Meteorological Research Centre and Institute of Rural Technical and Regional Software Centre, a Centre for Human Resource Development etc. A SAARC Food Security Reserve of 2,21,480 metric tonnes meant for emergency situations like droughts and floods was established and a Regional Convention on Suppression of Terrorism was ratified.[22]

During this period India continued to pursue her objectives in SAARC and emphasized on cultural and tradc cooperation and the exclusion of divisive and contentious politics in SAARC. However, in the Fourth Summit at Islamabad in 1988, India expressed her frustration at the slow pace of cooperation and lack of cooperation in economic areas in SAARC. This was reflected in the Prime Minister's statement when he said:

> We also need to strengthen linkages between ourselves to give us strength, individually and as a region. This calls for increased economic exchanges within our region, covering the gamut of economic activities from agriculture to industry, infrastructure, technology and human resource development. Economic cooperation must lie at the heart of a regional cooperation. There has to be a degree of harmonization to ensure that complementarities in our economies are matched to give strength to our respective economies and strength to our voice and influence in world forums.... Yet we shy away from trade and economic cooperation.[23]

Pakistan and Bangladesh continued to oppose inclusion of 'trade' among areas of cooperation. Trade with India, for them, was a sensitive issue which was not confined to mere economic arguments. Their opposition to freer trade regime in the region symbolised the political resistance to possible Indian domination. These initial formative years also provided the first test for Indian policy of insulating SAARC from contentious bilateral issues when in 1989 Sri Lanka refused to host the SAARC Summit due to a dispute with India on the withdrawal of Indian Peace Keeping Force (IPKF) from the island nation. This force was stationed in Sri Lanka in accordance with an agreement to facilitate resolution of Tamil-Sinhala ethnic conflict in Sri Lanka.[24] The SAARC process survived this crisis and the Summit meeting was held in Male in Maldives in 1990 after the withdrawal of IPKF from Sri Lanka.[25]

The second half of 1980s coinciding with the formative years of SAARC witnessed erosion and disappearance of cold war, consensus between US-USSR on major international issues, indications of Soviet withdrawal from Afghanistan and an increasing thaw in Sino-Soviet relations. However, South Asia could not reap the benefits of this global detente. The conflict situation between India and most of her neighbours, politico-strategic divergence in their foreign policies, exclusion of bilateral contentious issues from SAARC agenda and the failure to develop any policy consensus marked slow growth of SAARC during these initial years.

Post-Cold War Indian Policy

The end of the cold-war coinciding roughly with the beginning of the last decade of the twentieth century brought about a fundamental paradigm shift in international relations. Some analysts argue that with the end of the cold-war the 'geo-politics' of the cold-war got transformed into the 'geo-economics', i.e. into competitive areas of de-regulation and free trade.[26] The world's largest economic and military power, the United States of America, emerged as a clear hegemon in the global politics. This further reinforced the political, economic and ideology of the countries of the North. With the collapse of the competitive power bloc of Soviet Union, the capitalist ideology became fiercely assertive and we saw the ascendance of the neo-liberal 'Washington Consensus' prescribing the ideology of the free-market for economic progress and development. The champions of this new world order coined a new phenomenon of 'globalization' to explain and propagate the western world-view of resolving the problems of mankind through unhindered and free market forces.

The ascendance of the process of globalization saw the decline in the power of the 'State' and erosion of the role of the United Nations. The efforts of the UN agencies to promote the ideology of the New International Economic Order (NIEO) envisaging a just and equitable international economic order were superseded by the new market fundamentalism operationalised by the Bretton Woods institutions (IMF and World Bank) and the World Trade Organisation (WTO).

The process of regional cooperation in South Asia and India's policy regime in this regard could not remain immune to these historic developments of great political and economic significance. In 1991 India, as a matter of deliberate design or probably compelled by the consequences of the profligacy of 1980s, announced a change in her economic policy dispensation to dovetail her policies with the phenomenon of global marketisation. The new logic of globalization also impelled the governments of other SAARC Member Countries to embark on a process of economic policy change to open up their markets and economies to the outside world. With the exception of Sri Lanka where this process started much earlier, the decade of 1990s represents a turning point for all countries of South Asia where major political parties of these countries committed themselves to the path of economic liberalisation and globalization.[27]

South Asia also witnessed significant political changes during this period. With the revival of representative democracy in Pakistan (1988) and victory of democratic movements in Nepal (1990 and 2006) and Bangladesh (1991), the forces of representative democracy seemed to bring hope and positive sentiments for regional cooperation process. During 1991–2006, SAARC process despite serious road-blocks created by intra-state and inter-state conflicts, went through eight Summit meetings. It moved into core areas of economic cooperation, established a SAARC Preferential Trade Arrangement (SAPTA), a SAARC Fund for Regional Projects (SFRP), a South Asian Development Fund (SADF) and SAFTA. Some very significant decisions were taken at the latest Dhaka summit. These are South Asian Free Trade Area (SAFTA), the SAARC convention on terrorism, cooperation on the issue of admission of new member (Afghanistan) to SAARC and granting of observer status to China and Japan. It may be mentioned here that Pakistan establishment has refused to ratify SAFTA treaty with India. South Asian regionalism, therefore, has been a victim of conflictual regional relationships between India and her neighbours.[28] There seems to be a set pattern of such relationships with neighbours suspecting India's objectives[29] in the region and India feeling that her sensitivities and genuine security concerns are not respected by her neighbours, particularly by Pakistan. The asymmetry between India and her neighbours is perceived to be the biggest negative factor which inhibits normalisation of relations between them and consequently retards the SAARC process.

The post cold-war imperatives of economic liberalization and globalization, as well as absence of great power rivalry in South Asia, probably provided a greater opportunity to India to give desired shape to SAARC. India during a brief phase of 1996–97 experimented with a new doctrine to break the log-jam of her bilateral disputes with neighbours. This doctrine known as Gujral Doctrine (after the name of Inder Kumar Gujral who was the Foreign Minister and later the Prime Minister of India during 1996–97) envisaged, among other things, a more accommodating and generous Indian policy without demanding reciprocity from neighbours in resolving long-standing bilateral disputes. While the practice of Gujral Doctrine helped in improving India's relations with Bangladesh, Nepal and Sri Lanka, her relations with Pakistan remained mired in traditional animosity. The bonhomie and warmth generated by the Lahore visit of Indian Prime Minister in 1999 proved short-lived due to subsequent fierce Kargil border conflict between India and Pakistan and return of military dictatorship in Pakistan. The shift in Indian policy approach may not bring any meaningful breakthrough in Indo-Pak relations but certainly brings hope for revival of SAARC process in near future.

In the context of the slow growth of SAARC process in economic areas and a positive political climate generated by India's adoption of Gujral Doctrine, an idea for sub-regional cooperation involving India, Bangladesh, Bhutan and Nepal was mooted. Thus, a large number of projects were identified for implementation under the aegis of SAARC Regional Project Fund. However, due to serious misgivings and reservations about the concept of a sub-regional groupings within SAARC among other member countries, the idea of a South Asian Growth Quadrangle (SAGQ) involving India's North-East, Bangladesh, Bhutan and Nepal has not taken off. India has also been looking to other trans-regional groupings like ASEAN, APEC and IOR-ARC to pursue its goal of a larger Asian and probably global role in the world affairs. India is a full dialogue partner of ASEAN but could not secure the membership of the rich club of APEC. She has become a member of Bangladesh, India, Myanmar, Sri Lanka, Thailand Economic Cooperation (BIMSTEC) which is considered to be a link between SAARC and ASEAN. India is also a member of IOR-ARC which was formed in 1997.[30] In pursuit of its 'Look East' policy India launched a new cooperative forum – The Mekong Ganga Cooperation (MGC) forum – with five of its eastern neighbours, namely, Myanmar, Thailand, Laos, Cambodia and Vietnam in the year 2000. Some observers see this as an Indian effort for battling Chinese influence in Indo-China. Some critics consider relevance of SAARC in respect of reducing bilateral tensions, enhancing regional security and promoting economic well-being of people as almost negligible. Its structure as an inter-government body is seen as limiting its role and merely embodying the relationship of forces between member countries and their inter-state tensions. India as the largest state of South Asia has been making efforts to soften the political and strategic divergence among SAARC member countries through greater economic and socio-cultural cooperation. SAARC has generated considerable dynamism at the social, NGO/Civil Society levels. India has taken a lead in this respect. But the Achilles' heel of Indian policy thrust in SAARC has been the attitude and policy of Pakistan whose ruling establishment seems determined to thwart any Indian attempt for promotion of regional cooperation.

Conclusion

The end of cold war seemed to have provided greater leeway to India to promote her perception of South Asian regionalism through SAARC. However, the bilateral disputes between India and other SAARC countries, particularly between India and Pakistan, are deep rooted and defy the general global trend towards lessening of tensions in the post-cold war period. The core issue between India and Pakistan does not seem to be Kashmir (as claimed by

Pakistan) but a more fundamental difference on the nature of the 'States' of India and Pakistan – the contradiction between the State of Pakistan created artificially on the basis of religion and the secular ideology of Indian State. However, despite Kargil border conflict or because of it, a realisation would grow that military confrontation cannot resolve the territorial dispute between the two neighbours now possessing sophisticated missiles and nuclear weapons. It is quite probable that paradoxically nuclear terror (as in case of Europe) brings in peace and an end to war in South Asia. This could be an ideal ground for the sane civil society to step in and create a bond of friendship and amity in South Asia.

The bilateral disputes between India and other members of SAARC, particularly between India and Pakistan, will continue to impede and torment SAARC process. India's neighbours expect her to play down the big-brotherly attitude and keep a low-key but positive profile in SAARC. India, on the other hand, distrusts her neighbours, particularly Pakistan which is seen as attempting to undermine the secular basis of the Indian State and harbouring and sustaining cross border terrorism and proxy war against India. Probably India feels that she has much more at stake than the smaller nations of SAARC and a mere South Asian regional status may not fulfill her global aspirations. This explains her 'Look-East Policy' and pursuit of sub-regional and trans-regional cooperation. This might prove to be detrimental to the growth of SAARC process. However, the future of SAARC will depend not only on Indo-Pak relations and the contours of future global economy but also on the intervention of the civil society and non-government initiatives in South Asia to promote peace, harmony and economic progress.

Notes and References

1. A.M. Zaidi, *INC: The Glorious Tradition*, Vol. II, (1922–1927) Texts of Resolutions passed by the INC, The AICC and CWC, New Delhi, 1987, p. 34.
2. *Ibid.*, p. 38, Also see, Bimla Prasad, *Origins of Indian Foreign Policy*, Calcutta, 10.
3. M.K. Gandhi, "The Spirit of the East", *Young India*, Ahmedabad, April 14, 1920, Navjeevan Trust, 1981, Vol. II.
4. For details refer to the Presidential Address of C.R Das in the INC of 1922, in A.M. Zaidi and S.G. Zaidi (ed.), *The Encyclopaedia of the Indian National Congress: India at the Cross Roads*, Volume 8, 1921–1924, New Dew 1981, pp. 117–118.
5. Mohamed Ali Presiding over INC, 1923, n.4, p. 287.
6. Please *see* CWC resolution passed in its meeting July 3–15 at Simla. A.M. Zaidi, *INC: The Glorious Tradition*, Volume IV, pp. 207-208.
7. Jawaharlal Nehru, "Inter-Asian Relations" *India Quarterly*, October 1946.
8. Please see J.S. Bright (ed.) *Before and After Independence*, New Delhi, 1950, p. 379. These views were expressed by Nehru in August 1945.
9. "Asian Relations" – Report of the Proceedings and Documentation of the First

Asian Relations. Conference, New Delhi, March-April, 1947, *Asian Relations Organisations*, New Delhi, 1948, p. 3; Also see Jawaharlal Nehru, *India's Foreign Policy: Selected Speeches (1946-April 1961)*, New Delhi, 1961, Venatramni, "Forty years of Asian Relations Conference 1947", in Eric Gonsalves (ed.) *Asian Relations*, New Delhi, pp. 71–75.

10. S.D. Muni & Anuradha Muni, *Regional Cooperation in South Asia*, New Delhi, 1984, p. 12.
11. Sisir Gupta, *India and Regional Integration in Asia*, Bombay, 1964, pp. 85–113.
12. *Declaration of SAARC Summits (1985–1995)*, SAARC secretariat, Kathmandu, March, 1997, pp. 1–6.
13. For details see Percy S. Mistry, "Regional Integration and Development: Panacea or Pitfalla?" *RIS*, New Delhi, 1995.
14. President Zia-ur-Rahman discussed the issue of a South Asian regional approach in respect of Afghanistan situation with Indian Prime Minister Indira Gandhi in New Delhi in January 1980. (This was followed by the visit of a senior Indian official for further talks in Dhaka.) President Rahman also discussed the question with King Birendra of Nepal in Dhaka in March 1980 and sent his envoys to other South Asian countries to explore the possibilities of a regional arrangement. His call for a six nation summit (Maldives did not figure in this call) in May 1980 was the product of these exploratory talks. For details *see* S.D. Muni, "SAARC: Building Regionalism from Below", *Asian Survey*, Vol. XXX No. 4, April 1985, pp. 391–405.
15. Muni, *Ibid*., p. 396.
16. Statement by R.D. Sathe, Foreign Secretary of India at the First Meeting, Colombo, 21–23 April, 1981 (official text) as published in Muni and Muni, n.10, p. 109.
17. For a detailed Pakistani view point see Ross Masood Hussain, *SAARC – Evolution and Prospects: A view from Pakistan*, FES, Islamabad, 1991.
18. The acronym 'SARC' is used for referring to the regional grouping in the formative years prior to the official designation of an Association in December 1985.
19. Statement by M.K. Rasgotra, Foreign Secretary of India at the Third Meeting of Foreign Secretaries, Islamabad, August 7–9, 1982.
20. For details on India's 'hegemonic' role in South Asia see, Leo Rose and S. Kumar, "South Asia" in W.J. Feld and G. Boyd (ed.) *Comparative Regional Systems*, New York, 1980, pp. 264–268; B. Buzan, *South Asian Insecurity and the Great Powers*, London, 1986, pp. 9–14; Mohammad Ayoob, "India in South Asia: The Quest for Regional Predominance", *World Policy Journal*, 1990, pp. 107–134.
21. "Dhaka Declaration", *Declaration of SAARC Summits (1985-1993)*, SAARC Secretariat, Kathmandu, March 1997, pp. 1–6.
22. For details, see, "The SAARC Record: Retrospect and Prospect", Report by Ambassador K.K. Bhargava, Secretary General of SAARC on Activities of the Association and Secretariate, Kathmandu, November 1990, pp. 11-16.
23. Prime Minister's Address at Fourth SAARC Summit at Islamabad on December 29,1988, *Foreign Affairs Record*, 12 December 1988, p. 426.
24. A.P. Venkateswaran "SAARC in Crisis", *The Indian Express*, 23 July, 1989; Also *The News Times*, 29 July, 1989; For Sri Lanka's point of view see, Editorial, *The Daily News*, 3 July, 1989.
25. In May 1990 Sri Lanka insisted on hosting the SAARC Summit and even

threatened to boycott it if held elsewhere. On the other hand Maldives was not prepared under any circumstances to forgo its claim to host the 1990 Summit because it coincided with silver jubilee of its independence. Under these circumstances Sri Lanka mooted the proposal of two meetings – one in Colombo in the first half of the year to dispose of SAARC agenda and the other in December in Male to consider the impact of the momentous global developments on the region However, the consensus emerged for one Summit to be held in the third week of November 1990 in Male; For further details see, K.K. Katyal," Crisis over SAARC Summit Deepens", *The Hindu,* 5 May, 1990; Also Partha S. Ghosh, "An Experiment worth Pursuing", *The Financial Express,* 18 November, 1990.

26. For details see Gills Boquerat and Indra Nath Mukherji, "SAARC: Economic and Political Atlas," *Pondy Paper in Social Sciences*, (20), Pondicherry, 1996.
27. For details see, Sugata Bose (ed.), *South Asia and World Capitalism,* Delhi, 1990; Moazzem Hossain, et al. (ed.), *South Asian Economic Development: Transformation, Opportunities and Challenges*, Routledge. London, 1999; Ric Shand, *Economic Liberalisation in South Asia: Performance and Prospects*, Research and Information System for the Non-Aligned and Other Developing Countries, New Delhi, 1998.
28. For detailed analysis also see, K.K. Bhargava, "The Maturing of SAARC", *The Economic Times*, 17 May 1997; "SAARC Comes of Age" (editorial), *The Deccan Chronicle,* 17 May 1997.
29. Mohammed Ayoob, "India Matters", *Washington Quarterly,* Winter 2000, pp. 27–39; Also see K.K. Bhargava, "India and its South Asian Neighbour: Obligations and Privileges", Paper presented at the national seminar on India's Pivotal Role in South Asia: Optimising Benefits and Minimizing Apprehensions, CASAC, New Delhi, April 21, 2000.
30. For a detailed analysis of 'Look East Policy' see V. Suryanarayana, "Prospects for a Bay of Bengal Community", C. Raja Mohan, "The Asian Balance of Power", and A.N. Ram, "Historical Perspectives", in Seminar, March 2000, New Delhi; Sanjaya Baru, "India's Neighbourhood: Economic and Cultural, Not Physical", *The Times of India*, February 5, 2000; Muchkund Dubey and Nancy Jetley (eds.), *South Asia and its Eastern Neighbours: Building a Relationship in the 21st Century,* FES, New Delhi, 1999.

12

India's Response to Terrorism in the Post - 9/11

Kulwant Kaur

Terrorism has been redefined since 11 September 2001 as "Global Terrorism" and from then onwards it has become the dominant area of concern in the world politics. It has been regarded as the greatest challenge before humankind in the new millennium. But states, like India, have been at the receiving end of even 'non-global' terrorism since long before it acquired 'global' dimension. India has been a victim of terrorism in the Northeast, Punjab, Jammu and Kashmir and now it is spreading to other parts of India too. Consequently, New Delhi has been waging a fight against this menace of terrorism in its own ways. The questions that occur in ones mind are: Is there any specific strategy that has been evolved by India in response to the problem of terrorism after it has acquired transnational character? Whether the paradigm shift that has transformed the nature and dimensions of terrorism has any positive impact in facilitating India's fight against terrorism? Is there any rearrangement in India's strategy of fighting against the phenomenon of cross-border terrorism that has undergone a change from national to trans-national in character? In other words, whether the anti-terrorist strategies that have been devised and used by the United States at the 'global' level to meet the threat of 'global terrorism' have also been relevant and effective to redress India's concerns in this regard? Broadly, these questions have been examined in this article. However, before an analysis of these issues, the concept of terrorism and some of critical concerns for India in this context, have been examined.

Conceptual Muddle

Terrorism means different things to different people. Subjective and political considerations in looking at the phenomenon of terrorism have made the concept more controversial and contentious. In fact, it has been perceived and addressed from different perspectives. A terrorist for some people, can be a freedom fighter for the others. Lack of consensus over its meaning and definition makes the task of addressing it more tough and complicated. The League of Nations, the United Nations and South Asian Association for Regional Cooperation have made efforts to define it, but all these institutions have failed to agree and arrive at a common understanding of what constitutes terrorism.

Walter Lacquer has pointed out that there are 109 definitions of terrorism provided between 1936 and 1981. He has defined terrorism as "the use of threat of violence, a method of combat or a strategy, not an ideology, to achieve certain goals, that its aim is to induce a state of fear in the victim, that it is ruthless and does not conform to humanitarian norms and that publicity is an essential factor in terrorist strategy."[1]

According to A.O. Schmidt, an expert in the crime branch of the UN:

> Terrorism is an anxiety - inspiring method of repeated violent action employed by clandestine individuals, groups and state actors for idiosyncratic, criminal or political reasons, where by – in contrast to assassinations – the direct targets of violence are not the main targets. The immediate human victims of violence are generally chosen randomly or selectively from the target population and serve as message generators.[2]

The illegitimate use of force to intimidate, hurt or kill the innocent persons or damage the property for certain ends or perceived grievances can be called terrorism. However, in several situations, it is difficult to differentiate between the just and unjust grievances, good and bad ends. Meaning is given and intentions are defined in accordance with the affiliations and bonding of an individual, group or community and a state. Use of force is justified or condemned on the basis of subjective considerations and perceptions. Lack of objectivity and international consensus do often allow the sympathy to even the most proactive use of violence. However, no noble goal can ever justify the use of violence against non-combatants. Terrorism is a kind of asymmetric warfare.

Terrorism cannot and should not be associated with any religion, nationality, civilization or ethnic group. These attributions should not be used to justify terrorism or counter-terrorism measures. Criminal acts and use of violence intended or calculated to provoke a state of terror are unjustifiable, whatever the considerations or factors that may be invoked to justify them.

From these and many other definitions of terrorism, however, a few characteristics become noteworthy and salient. These are:

- It is calculated and planned use of violence;
- to create fear and terror not only in the minds of targeted ones but also in general public and common masses;
- methods employed are cruel, ruthless and barbarian;
- motives can be either political, economic, social or ideological or a combination of all these;
- targets are usually non-combatants, such as political figures, bureaucrats, or innocent bystanders; and

- It is secretive; the perpetrators belong to clandestine groups or are secretly sponsored by states.

Major Critical Concerns

The size of the country, the nature of its society and polity make India the biggest victim of terrorist activities in the world. It is estimated that around 70,000 people have lost their lives to terrorism in India and majority of them in Jammu and Kashmir. Nearly 11,000 security personnel laid down their lives fighting with the terrorists.[3] More than half a million people were forced to leave their homes and got displaced in their own country. The terrorists had threatened the democratic structures and put the rule of law at peril. The attack on the Legislative Assembly of Jammu and Kashmir on 1 October and on the Indian Parliament on 13 December 2001, were indication of their abhorrence towards democratic institutions. The then Home Minister, L.K. Advani described the attack on the Indian Parliament as an attempt to "wipe out the entire political leadership of India".[4] Prime Minister Vajpayee told the US government that India's patience was wearing thin. These attacks had brought the terrorists literally at war with the rule of law, democracy and established norms of civil society. These attacks have serious implications for the Indian polity and its people.

11 September 2001 marked the beginning of a new phase in the United States policy towards Southern Asia. General Pervez Musharraf and Islamabad acquired strategic importance in the counter terrorist strategy of the United States. The US State Department's "2001 Report on Foreign Terrorist Organizations" lists 28 groups, including *Al-Qaida* as terrorist. Pakistan under General Musharraf was expected to play a major role in capturing Bin Laden and other prominent figures in *Al-Qaida*, who had received shelter in Afghanistan from the Taliban government. Besides geography, Pakistan's hold and influence over the Taliban made Musharraf indispensable to the Bush Administration in its fight against terrorism. For Pakistan, it was not much a question of choice, when President George Bush declared, "either you are with us or you are with the terrorist". Certainly, it was a tough decision for Musharraf to join the United States in defeating and destroying the same very forces –Taliban – who were once created, trained and equipped by his own country.[5]

Musharraf addressed his people on television on 20 September 2001 and said:

> Pakistan is facing a very critical situation and I believe that after 1971 this is the most critical period. The decision we take today can have far reaching and wide-ranging consequences.... The negative consequences can endanger Pakistan's integrity and solidarity. Our critical concerns, our important concerns can come under threat. When I say critical concerns I mean our strategic assets and the cause of Kashmir....[6]

General Musharraf's decision to join the US led coalition against terrorism had conferred on Pakistan a 'frontline state' status and also the status of Major Non-NATO Ally. For India, the US support to the military regime of General Pervez Musharraf had two serious fallouts. One, Bush Administration's acquiescence to Pakistan's engagement with the Taliban [7] and other *Jihadi* groups led to accentuation of terrorist attacks in India. The promises made by General Musharraf[8] neither brought any change in perspectives not dismantlement of the terrorist infrastructure in Pakistan. The pronouncements and commitments were only tactical moves to minimize Islamabad losses. Pakistan had in fact adopted a dual policy of privately supporting the *Jihadis* and publicly fighting with them,[9] so as to receive billions of dollars from the United States as a result of its cooperation. This policy had resulted in resurgence of the Taliban in Afghanistan and more frequent and widely spread terrorist attacks in India. The attacks in Hyderabad, Delhi, Ahmadabad, Varanasi, Jammu, Mumbai and other parts of India pointed out the spread of terrorist network and determination of Islamabad to destabilize India despite its commitment to global counter-terrorism. In fact, terrorism has proved to be a low cost, low risk, cost effective and potentially high yielding means of winning tactical objectives. Two, Bush Administration's over reliance on General Musharraf had pushed Pakistan into the hands of Islamic fundamentalists and extremist forces and undermined the moderate, democratic elements in Pakistan.[10] The overall developments in Pakistan like legitimization and consolidation of military rule, upsurge in radical Islamists, strengthening of mullah-military alliance[11] and continuation of terrorist infrastructure in Pakistan have serious implications for India. Lack of Pakistani elite's willingness[12] or its inability to freeze the assets of individuals or groups engaged in terrorist activities have undermined the civilian authority within Pakistan on the one hand and on the other hand, their increasing lethal power has affected the security of the whole subcontinent. Their twin objectives of making *Jihad*[13] in Kashmir a success and setting of an Islamic state have led to growth of fundamentalist and sectarian forces in the whole region. Their activities pose a threat to the on-going peace process in the Indian subcontinent endangering communal harmony, national integrity and unity of the states in the region.[14]

Combating Terrorism

To meet the menace of terrorism, concerted and coordinated national efforts, regional and international cooperation are required. A national strategy based on a broader consensus among various political parties, societal groups and state and central governments could only help to fight the danger and threats posed by terrorism. Unfortunately, even in the wake of terrorist attack on the Legislative Assembly of J&K and on the Indian Parliament in October and December 2001 respectively, India could not evolve a national strategy and failed to take effective and credible steps against the terrorists and the state sponsoring these acts of terrorism. Even 'Operation Parakram' that was an exercise in coercive diplomacy to compel Pakistan to stop cross-border terrorism and renounce it as an instrument of state policy against India failed to obtain its objectives[15] and elicit support of all political groups within the nation. In fact, within the country, there is disagreement regarding how to counter the challenges of terrorism. According to some politicians and strategists, India cannot isolate itself from the United States and others who are fighting the 'global' war against terrorism,[16] even if New Delhi does not approve their tactics and strategies. They view that any victory of extremist elements, Bin Laden or Taliban, would mean Talibanisation of the Islamic nations of West and South Asia. Such a development is not going to be in India's national interest as the essence of Taliban ideology is against the principles of democracy, pluralism and secularism.[17] India has stakes in stable, peaceful and democratic Afghanistan and Pakistan. Resurgence of Taliban poses a serious threat to India's interest not only in Afghanistan but also in Central and West Asia. Robert Gates, the US Defense Secretary, also admitted recently that in the last two or three years there had been a constant increase in the overall level of violence and that *Al-Qaida* is resurfacing in Afghanistan after defeat in parts of Iraq.[18] The greatest challenge for India is not to loose strategically located Afghanistan to unfriendly extremist and fundamentalist forces by helping to build peace, restoring political stability and democratic government and ensuring economic reconstruction.

On the other hand, there is another viewpoint contended by some sections of people, leaders and strategists that India will have to fight its own battle of terrorism. The US war against terrorism is focused on its own strategic, economic and global interests; that it adopts a selective self-centered approach,[19] that it was the US and CIA that propped up the Taliban[20] to bleed the Soviets in Afghanistan and that it was a blunder to start the war in Iraq before ensuring the complete emasculation of *Al-Qaida* and Taliban from Afghanistan, Pakistan and other areas of the subcontinent. It was in this context that Congress-led coalition government in India refused to send forces to join NATO troops. Moreover, Islamabad that became ally and strategic partner of the US in the latter's war against terrorism has been exporting terrorism to India as well as Afghanistan. Therefore, large chunks of people in India feel, that the US is complaisant regarding Pakistan's involvement and is applying double standards in its 'global' war against terrorism. India's concerns will never be taken seriously as long as support of Pakistan is essential for the US in its fight against *Al-Qaida* and Taliban.

Out of the above two options, i.e. either cooperation with the United States or isolation from it, none alone could serve India's national interest. India will have to construct a coherent national counter-terrorism policy based on its own experience and needs.[21] The first option is marked with a number of limitations, i.e. the international coalition against terrorism has been forced by the world's hegemon unilaterally rather than getting it forged through the international organization or involvement of international community; goals, tactics and strategies have been drawn by the sole superpower itself keeping in view its own national interest rather than the overall objective of defeating and countering terrorism throughout the world. Moreover, the pre-emptive action against Iraq in the absence of any evidence either of the presence of *Al-Qaida* members[22] or any weapons of mass destruction cannot be supported by India. Similarly, India cannot afford the second option of getting isolated from the United States. One, because both the countries are facing the challenge of terrorism; two, both uphold the same principles of democracy, secularism and pluralism and three, India knows that the US can exert pressure on Pakistan to stop cross-border terrorism in India[23] and lastly because of the mutual benefits of sharing intelligence, experience and helping each-other in countering terrorism. Therefore, India should evolve its own profound, comprehensive national strategy based on broader consensus to face the challenges posed by the terrorists in different parts of the country. Terrorism flourishes in environment of discontentment, exclusion, poverty, political oppression, human rights abuses and in situation of regional conflicts; hence, state capacity to improve governance and to address the issues should be improved. Conditions conducive to terrorism that are exploited by the terrorists to mobilize recruits and justify violence, should be properly taken care of at the initial stage.

Moreover, national efforts are to be supplemented with the regional and international ones. At the regional level, in response to the United Nations Security Council Resolution 1373 of 2001, South Asian Association for Regional Cooperation (SAARC) had adopted Regional Convention on suppression of Terrorism. During the 12th SAARC Summit at Islamabad on 4–6 January 2004, the Council of Ministers signed the Additional Protocol to the SAARC Regional Convention on Suppression of Terrorism.[24] This came into force on 12 January 2006 after ratification from the member nations. India and Pakistan have also constituted a joint 'Anti-Terror Mechanism' (ATM) in pursuance of the decision taken between the President of Pakistan and the Prime Minister of India in Havana on 16 September 2006.[25] The first meeting of the Indo-Pak Joint Anti-Terror Mechanism was held in Islamabad on 7 March 2007 and the second one at New Delhi on 22 October 2007. India is not very satisfied with the outcome of these meetings[26] as it felt that its concerns were not addressed and that the terrorist infrastructure in Pakistan and POK continued to be used by terrorist outfits like JeM, LeT and *Al-Badr*, etc. and that Islamabad refused to discuss and include the terrorist activities in J&K within the framework of ATM. However, it will be pointless to give up such a mechanism as it could prove to be an important source of sharing intelligence periodically and keeping a check on the network of terrorist outfits. Even the UN Charter, the several resolutions passed by the General Assembly and other organs and more specifically the UN Global Counter Terrorism Strategy adopted on 8 September 2006[27] urge all the states to fulfil their obligations under International Law and International Humanitarian Law in the combat against terrorism. The broader framework of the United Nations, that urge the member states to refrain from organizing, instigating, assisting, financing or participating in terrorist acts in the territories of other states and refraining from encouraging activities within their territories directed against other states, should be used to exert and sustain pressure on Islamabad to refrain from allowing the use of land in Pakistan and POK for organizing terrorist violence against its neighbours.

In a nutshell, the menace of terrorism has to be attacked at all levels, i.e. national, regional and international. A well-formulated national policy along with coordinated efforts at the regional and international levels will be essential to counter terrorism. Complacency, lack of adequate efforts, resources and coordination, easy availability of small arms could lead to boost terrorism. On the other hand, following steps may be helpful in countering terrorism:

(i) to develop intelligence capabilities and promote better coordination among the various agencies involved in this task;
(ii) to spread education and awareness among citizen;
(iii) to encourage religious tolerance and mutual understanding by having greater inter-faith dialogue;
(iv) to build an active civil society;
(v) to increase the capacity building of the state to address the issues of the people and to deliver socio-economic justice;
(vi) to find solution to the regional conflicts and lastly;
(vii) to encourage the role of regional, international organizations and specialized agencies for countering terrorism.

In conclusion, it can be pointed out that overall India lacks an effective national strategy and national preparation to face the challenges posed by terrorism. The 9/11 attacks on the World Trade Centre and Pentagon that had made terrorism transnational and more destructive, attracted the attention of the world community. Nevertheless, this in no way facilitated India's fight against terrorism. There is not only constant increase in violence but also it is becoming widespread in different parts of the country. Despite this, India fails to respond effectively against the terrorist as well as the state(s) sponsoring terrorism. It has neither enacted any stringent laws against terrorists nor formulated its policy at the national level to tackle terrorism. The US counter-terrorism strategy also in no way helps or intends to fight terrorism against

India as a part of its 'global' counter terrorism. However, in the post 9/11 there is an international public opinion against violence and terrorism and for the first time America denounced terrorism in Kashmir and refused to treat it as part of the national struggle of the Kashmiris. This stance of the United States should be used by India as a window of opportunity to justify its position in Kashmir and to enhance pressure on Islamabad to stop cross border terrorism.

Notes and References

1. Walter Lacquer, "Reflection on Terrorism", *Foreign Affairs*, Fall 1986, p. 88.
2. Cited in A.C. Bose, "Roots of Terrorism and What the Terrorists Aim At", in Kulwant Kaur, ed., *Global Terrorism: Issues, Dimensions and Options* (New Delhi: Kanishka, 2005), p. 4.
3. Ajit Doval, "Terror Tactics Change, But do We?", *Hindustan Times* (New Delhi), 11 September 2007.
4. Statement made in the Indian Parliament on 18 December 2001. See, http:www.rediff.com/news, 19 December 2001.
5. For details see Kulwant Kaur, "US War on Terrorism in Afghanistan: A Human Rights Perspective," in Mahendra Gaur, ed., *Terrorism and Human Rights,* (New Delhi: Anamika, 2003), pp. 27–36.
6. For the full text of the speech, see, www.pak.gov.pk/public/president address, 19 September 2001.
7. Washington wanted the military regime in Pakistan to cooperate in the US efforts to dismantle the Taliban – *Al-Qaida* terrorist infrastructure in Afghanistan and Pakistan. For details see "US-Pakistan Counter–Terrorism Cooperation: Dynamics and Challenges", *Strategic Analysis*, vol. 30, no. 3, July–September 2006, pp. 525–561.
8. In a historic speech, Musharraf declared: "no organization will be allowed to indulge in terrorism in the name of Kashmir. We condemn the terrorist acts of September 11, October 1 and December 13. Anyone found involved in any terrorist act would be dealt with sternly. Strict action will be taken against any Pakistani individual, group or organization found involved in terrorism within or outside the country," For the full text of his speech, see www.pak.gov.pk/public/president address.htm, no. 40, 12 January and 27 May 2002. Also see, "Unfulfilled Promises: Pakistan's Failure to Tackle Extremism," *International Crisis Group, Asia Report*, no. 73, 16 January 2004, www.crisisgroup.org.
9. With the connivance of ISI, Pakistan army had allowed the flow of arms, oil and other essential items to Talibans in Afghanistan even after Pakistan had joined the US-led coalition. *The Telegraph* (Calcutta), 10 December 2001.
10. For details see Shanthie Mariet D'Souza, "Mush – Bush Ambushed," *State Times* (Jammu), 2 October 2007.
11. For details see Kalim Bahadur, "Regional Implications of the Rise of Islamic Fundamentalism in Pakistan", *Strategic Analysis*, vol. 30, no. 1, January-March 2006, pp. 7–29.
12. In fact, it was Washington that took the lead in freezing the assets of the *Lashkar-e-Toiba* (LeT) and designating it along with the *Jaish-e-Mohammed* (JeM) as 'foreign terrorist organizations.' Subsequently, President Bush called upon Musharraf to take action against the LeT and the JeM and other terrorist

organizations and their leaders and the sources of their finances. *The Hindu* (Delhi), 23 December 2001 and *Hindustan Times* (New Delhi) 27 December 2001.

13. It was Syed Abdul-Ala Maududi, who disoriented the definition of *Jihad* from man's struggle against evil from within to a struggle to seize power for the establishment of Islamic order.
14. For details see K. Warikoo, "Islamist Extremism: Challenge to Security in South Asia", *Strategic Analysis*, vol. 30, no. 1, January-March 2006, pp. 30–45.
15. S. Kalyanaraman, "Operation Parakram: An Indian exercise in Coercive Diplomacy," *Strategic Analysis,* vol. 26, no. 4, October-December 2002, pp. 478–488.
16. India's offer to provide support and assistance in the US-led campaign against terrorism in the wake of 9/11 was considered essential in its national interest.
17. For details, see Kalim Bahadur, n.11, pp. 18–25.
18. *State Times* (Jammu), 5 December 2007.
19. J.K. Baral and J.N. Mahanty, "The US War Against Terrorism: Implications for South Asia," *Strategic Analysis*, vol. 26, no. 4, October-December 2002, pp. 508–517.
20. Osama Bin Laden, *Al-Qaida*, *Lashkar-e-Toiba*, Taliban and many other terrorist organizations in Pakistan and Afghanistan are the creations of America. All the weapons left in Afghanistan have been used by these outfits. For details, see Shyam Chand, "Globalization of Terrorism", *Mainstream*, vol. XLIV, no. 48, 18 November 2006, pp. 25–29.
21. K.P.S. Gill, "National policy Wanted to Counter Terror," *Hindustan Times* (New Delhi), 10 September 2007.
22. Moreover, while America has been engaged in Iraq, the international terrorism network has been active and got strengthened in other parts of the world. For details see, Bruce Hoffman, "Al-Qaida and the War on Terrorism: An Update," *Current History*, vol. 103, no. 677, December 2004, pp. 423–427.
23. Though the United States restrained India from taking action against Pakistan in the wake of terrorist attack on Parliament yet for the first time it accepted that the terrorists in J&K are not the 'freedom-fighters' and exerted pressure on General Musharraf to get a promise that he would not allow the territory of Pakistan including that of POK to be used for exporting terrorism against any other country.
24. "SAARC Regional Convention on Suppression of terrorism and its Additional Protocol," http:/www.saarc-sec.org/main.php?t=2.4
25. "Pakistan–India Anti-Terrorism Mechanism Meeting: Joint Statement," http://counterterrorismblog.org, 7 March 2007.
26. *State Times* (Jammu), 25 September 2007.
27. For details see "Uniting against Terrorism: Recommendations for a Global Counter–Terrorism Strategy", a report submitted by the Secretary General to the General Assembly A/60/825. For the plan of Action and Measures to be adopted to promote comprehensive, coordinated and consistent responses at the national, regional and international levels to counter terrorism, http://www.un. org/terrorism/strategy-counterterrorism.html.

13

India's Security Concerns

Rajpal Budania

Understanding National Security

The term national security has been used widely.[1] National security is both a rhetorical phrase and a policy objective. It generally means the ability of a nation to protect its core values from external as well as domestic threats. The field of study, therefore, extends to the analysis of the manner in which nations plan, make, and evaluate the decisions and policies designed to increase this ability.

Traditionally, national security has been defined as protection from external attack; primarily viewed in terms of military defences against military threats. This view is based on the concept of maximizing national power in conflict situations and has led to the assumption that a nation can be secure only if it increases its own power at the expense of another nation or nations. National security, therefore, was considered as the ability of a nation to protect only its internal core values from external threats. Walter Lipmann noted: "A nation has security when it does not have to sacrifice its legitimate interests to avoid war and is able, if challenged, to maintain them by war."[2] This kind of an understanding of national security suited stable nation-states of the industrialized West but inadequately explained the problem of security faced by a heterogeneous and developing nation-state like India. This is a narrow definition of security. It led one into believing that the way to increase security is merely to increase military power, and peace and development need not to be the supreme end of the foreign and security policies.

It is well accepted that military power is a very important component of security. But it is only one facet. History is replete with examples of arms race and military build-up which resulted in less, rather than more, of security. By now it is well established that arms race is associated with escalation of conflict to a high probability of war. Quantitative analysis of international disputes indicates that the disputes preceded by an arms race are more likely to lead to war than those without.[3] Hence, arms race contains seeds of insecurity, resulting into security dilemma and zero-sum game.

Today a broader definition of national security is needed as security is not just the absence of war or preparedness for war. The concept of national security has been broad-based by the inclusion of non-military and internal threats to security. It has non-military dimensions at economic, diplomatic, environmental, and social-political level. A broader definition of national security is articulated by Arnold Wolfers thus: "Security, in an objective sense, measures the absence of threats to acquired values, in a subjective sense, the absence of fear that such values will be attacked."[4]

The broadened scope of security is justified due to the challenging nature and the magnitude of non-military threats as the chances of large-scale military confrontations have receded somewhat. Arguably the prominence of non-military threats in the concept of national security has increased as the danger of all-out military conflicts has, as a result of the end of the Cold War rivalry, relatively decreased. Many more people die from preventable diseases and natural calamities than from war. Security against one's own anti-national and anti-social elements is as important as dealing with external threats to the state's core values. Barry Buzan says about the broadened concept of security that we should have "more concern about the sources of threat, rather than just ways to fend off the threats themselves, and more awareness of the role of one's own state in generating threats. On this level the national security problem defines itself as much in economic, political and social terms as in military ones. Domestic as well as foreign factors loom large in the matter, and the military aspect of security is seen to be merely part of a bigger picture."[5]

Today there is a strong view that the security of individuals, groups and states has an interdependent nature.[6] Nature of attacks on the security of the individual, groups and states is also interdependent and requires collective mechanisms for safety. Moreover, insecurity is associated with instability and disorder. Insecurity of individuals and of groups is detrimental to the stability of the state, and the instability of a state creates a latent danger for the security of other states or international security.

State lies at the core of all aspects – military or non-military – of security. To protect individuals from instability and disorder it has multitude of functions to perform. State is also primarily responsible for conditions of war or peace in the world politics which is anarchic in nature (i.e. there is no superior organisation to control the behaviour of the states).

India's first Prime Minister, Jawaharlal Nehru, was far ahead of his times in perceiving broad-based definition of security. He highlighted the importance of non-military aspects of security both at the national and international levels at a time when the leadership of the great powers was defining national security in terms of military power based on Morgenthau's realism. Nehru followed a development-oriented political economy and hence sought to do away with internal socio-economic causes of insecurity. His belief in development, 'one world', confederal solution to the problems of South Asia and peaceful coexistence had seminal impact on India's conceptualisation of security. First, India sought to defend its national security through building internal strengths. Second, it highlighted the transnational threats or aspects of security and overcoming them through non-military and collective efforts of nations. Third, it based its national security on the principle of 'security with each other' rather than 'security against each other'. Finally, India has consistently believed in the efficacy of political approach to managing or resolving inter-state or intra-state threats to its national security. India as a post-colonial state has essentially based its conceptions of security on transnational cooperation and development. Its rise as a military power is a natural reaction for self-defence in the wake of worsening international and regional security environments.

The International Conference on the Relationship between Disarmament and Development, convened by the United Nations General Assembly in New York from August 24 to September 11, 1987, adopted a definition of security that encompasses non-military aspects. In its final document, which was adopted by consensus by the representatives from the 150 participatory states, the Conference stated:

> Security is an overriding priority for all nations. It is also fundamental for both disarmament and development. Security consists of not only military, but also political, economic, social, humanitarian and human rights and ecological aspects. Enhanced security can, on the one hand, create conditions conducive to disarmament and, on the other, provide the environment and confidence for the successful pursuit of development. The development process, by overcoming non-military threats to security and contributing to a more stable and sustainable international system, can enhance security and thereby promote arms reduction and disarmament. Disarmament would enhance security both directly and indirectly. A process of disarmament that provides for undiminished security and progressively lower levels of armaments could allow additional resources to be devoted to addressing non-military challenges to security, and thus result in enhanced overall security.[7]

The document further states:

> Recently, non-military threats to security have moved to the forefront of global concern. Underdevelopment and declining prospects for development, as well as mismanagement and waste of resources, constitute challenges to security. The degradation of the environment presents a threat to sustainable development. The world can hardly be regarded as secure so long as there is polarization of wealth and poverty at the national and international levels. Gross and systematic violations of human rights retard genuine socio-economic development and create tensions which contribute to instability. Mass poverty, illiteracy, disease, squalor and malnutrition afflicting a large proportion of the world's population often become the cause of social strain, tension and strife.[8]

Security has to be understood not only as the ability to overcome the threats to core national value of physical survival of a nation-state but also as a psychological problem. "The problem of security is mainly psychological, and as a matter of fact, it is met only to a very small degree by coming to agreements of a military nature regarding it. It is in fact the dramatic form of a deep-seated suspicion that no country is really safe from the machinations of others."[9] Security is not just 'the condition of being protected or not exposed to danger, but is also freedom from fear, anxiety, or apprehension; a feeling of safety.'[10] Therefore, what we are concerned with is not just a state of strategic affairs, but also a state of mind. "States need to feel as well as actually to be secure; indeed the search for a sense of security, the need to assuage fears is an important determinant of policy in its own right."[11]

Dietrich Fischer suggests that security has two aspects: (1) the absence of objective dangers, and (2) the absence of subjective fears, whether or not they are justified.[12] He further says that ignorance or denial of dangers does not provide security. Nor does a false claim of a threat of aggression, sometimes deliberately invented or exaggerated, justify military expenditures; it exposes a country to real danger. Nevertheless, what determines governments' policies is their perception of threats and dangers, even if they may be under-estimated or over-estimated. Hence, both perceived and actual threats are important in national security perceptions and approaches.

The term 'national security' is often used rather casually for embracing whatever concerns happen to be fashionable. Due to this reason, building a sound theory of national security has been a problematic proposition. The term security is often used for rhetorical purposes rather than for analytical value. Moreover, national security is primarily a term of political convenience. It is more respectable to talk about national security than military power.[13] Big powers have increased their military power under the pretext of national security for pursuing hegemonic objectives. The realist school of thought was quite active during the Cold War and furthered the principle that security is a derivative of the struggle for power. In the post-Cold War period, India and Pakistan have declared themselves as nuclear weapon states, citing national security as the main objective for doing so.

Therefore, the concept of national security has remained unquantifiable; the meaning of which is more readily sensed than defined. The unquantifiable characteristic of the concept of security has also acted as a negative factor in the development of a sound theory of security. Moreover, the lack of a sound theory of security has adversely affected the formulation and the adequacy of security policies to deal with the threats to national core values.

The concept of national security must take into account the present day realities. Main sources of instability today are not conflicts of inter-state but those of intra-state nature. Former UN Secretary General, Boutros Boutros-

Ghali warned about the threats to national security from multi-ethnic societies. He described certain characteristics of likely intra-state conflicts as 'the collapse of state institutions, especially the police and judiciary, with resulting paralysis and chaos.'[14] In this context, it is pertinent to take note of the recommendations of the Report of the Commission on Global Governance, according to which "...Security must be broadened from its traditional focus on the security of the states to include the security of people and the planet."[15] It further says: "All people, no less than all states, have a right to a secure existence, and all states have an obligation to protect those rights."[16] In fact, this view about people's security is based on idealistic norms for security policies in the new international order. The concept of security necessarily envisages an interdependent world order needing a common security regime to be achieved through the collective efforts of mankind.

Nature of Security Concerns

In the past the general tendency was to primarily focus on the threat of military aggression from across borders and on military means to defend oneself against such threats. But no more so. Today we find increasing volume of literature being focused on the non-military dangers to security and non-military means to meet such dangers. Many more people die from preventable diseases, domestic conflicts and avoidable natural calamities than in war. However, a military threat must not be underestimated. This is particularly true of India which has faced aggressions from China and Pakistan. Military threats to India have not ceased; therefore, it has no alternative but to prepare against any eventuality.

Threats to security are classified variously depending on whether their source is internal or external, intentional or unintentional, military or non-military, natural or man-made. The most common classification of threats to security is based on their geographic *source*, namely, internal or external. The classification based on military or non-military aspects of security is based on the *object* of the danger. If the object is war or threat of war then it is termed as military threat and if the object is danger to economic well-being, environment, human rights, communal harmony and civilizational survival, then it is termed as non-military threat to security. Non-military aspect of security includes the threats to the development of the state and society.

India faces serious external and internal threats to its national security. Based on the duration of the threat they are judged as immediate, temporary, long-term and permanent. The core values or vital national interests of India are of permanent nature and they must be defended at any cost.

Moreover, the factors that may have an adverse impact on national security are divided into *objective* and *subjective* by their nature. Further, they are divided into *real* and *perceived*. The policy of ensuring and extending national security aims at identifying and eliminating any threat or threats at the 'probable' stage of its origin. National security policy must be aimed at reducing or preventing objective threats by the timely elimination of subjective threats. Undue emphasis on one factor may result in misperception of the nature of threat, with disastrous consequences for policy. Therefore, for greater security it is important to take into account all the dimensions of a threat such as military, political, economic, social and ecological, and their impact on the core values.

External Threats

The nature and magnitude of India's internal vulnerabilities are bothersome. These vulnerabilities have induced external intervention. India has faced the external threats and intervention to its security since its independence from the neighbouring country Pakistan and great powers in both covert and overt forms. India's concept of security includes managing and minimising these threats.

A state is vulnerable to instability, internal conflict, dismemberment and also external intervention when there is serious disagreement over the organizing ideology or the purposes of the state. Political violence and struggle for power among the competing groups can lead to external interference. In a situation of internal strife, the domestic contestants – insurgents and the incumbent regime – may seek external aid in support of their respective causes on the basis of ethnic, religious or ideological affiliation, or strategic need. Insurgents in India's North-east, Punjab and Kashmir have sought and achieved external support along these lines. In the sub-continent global powers have sought to further their vital security interests and create a sphere of influence. For this, they have helped perpetuate regimes of their preference, as US has done in the case of Pakistan's non-democratic regimes. Intervention in the internal affairs has been a frequently used instrument of policy particularly during the Cold War period. Even after the end of the Cold War, India faces subtle means of intervention in its internal affairs.

India faces both military and non-military external threats to its security. Disputes and conflicts with the neighbouring states have shaped India's external security perceptions and policy choices. Developments within its neighbours also bother India. Recently the Annual Report of India's Ministry of Defence has noted: "India has taken suitable steps to meet the challenges and opportunities arising out of its rapidly changing security environment. While our peace effort with Pakistan has maintained strategic stability in our west, developments in Nepal and Bangladesh… have caused concern, mainly in border regions with these countries."[17] India is getting very concerned at the spectre of terrorism getting foothold in Bangladesh. The rise of Islamic fundamentalism and terrorism and political violence with its attendant repercussions on the security of India is bothering the country's security management apparatus.[18] India is also getting concerned at the rise of militant Islam in Maldives. Growing numbers of young men from Maldives are going to Pakistan and Afghanistan-Pakistan border for training with *jihadi* groups.[19]

India's national security has given high priority to the country's defence against the military threats from Pakistan, and also China after the 1962 war. Despite the broad-basing of the concept of security by the inclusion of the non-military threats, India continues to place the military threats at the top of the scale of threats to its security. The anarchic nature of international order, confrontationist policy of Pakistan towards India, nuclear capabilities of Pakistan and China, military collaboration between China and Pakistan, and the US arms supply to Pakistan are the main factors determining India's perception of military threats to its external security. The causes and conditions of war are still present in the region. Moreover, the policies of great powers still pose a serious challenge to India's core national values.

Therefore, assessing the capabilities, motives, and the policies of the adversary states and seeking appropriate strategic response to the challenges arising out of these external factors forms an important objective of India's national security.

External threats that may adversely affect the security of India are:[20]

1. Armed aggression (including nuclear one) or threat of such aggression from any state, but particularly from Pakistan and China due to their proximity and hostility to India.
2. Abetting transnational terrorism (including narco-terrorism) and subversive activities and espionage against India.
3. Imposition by any state of its own interest and policies on India or attempts to resolve disputes by force.
4. Policies aimed at the destruction of India's social, economic, political and ideological structures.
5. Emergence of any global, regional and sub-regional crises and conflicts which may affect India.
6. Disputes and conflicts between India and the neighbouring states, and also the effects of internal conflicts and crises in the neighbouring state or states.
7. Massive inflows of migrants from neighbouring state as it happened during the Bangladesh crisis.
8. Threats from natural and ecological calamities spilling over to India and spread of animal or human diseases.
9. Restricting or impeding the development of foreign trade and economic cooperation and also direct dependence on any one country in economic or technological branches of strategic importance.
10. Dissemination of false information by external sources for sowing dissensions and creating internal instability in India.

11. Threats to India's population and its gene pool due to probable transgression of radioactive substances, chemical pollution, acid rains and epidemics through atmosphere.

Internal Security Concerns

Most of the developing countries face challenges to their security arising out of the domestic conflicts. In the case of the developed countries we find relative harmony among the interests of the individual, groups and the state. In the developed countries, vital components of the state, namely, the idea of the state and its institutional expression, the physical base comprising both territory and population, and sovereignty, are accepted as legitimate both domestically and internationally.[21] The state authority enjoys popular support and broad-based legitimacy. Consequently, challenges to state authority and the degree of internal vulnerability are quite low in these states. Contrary to this, the internal vulnerabilities in the developing world are quite high, so are the challenges to the state authority and the socio-economic and political objectives of the state.

Internal security in India and most of the developing world is problematic mainly due to three reasons: First, they do not conform to the idea of homogeneous socio-political units. Second, they are extremely vulnerable due to their economic weakness and uneven regional development. Third, these states have limited capabilities to deal with internal threats to security. As a result, there has been considerable disharmony among the interests of the individuals, groups and the state. Some of the internal threats like separatism have threatened the very basis of India as a single unit. Importantly, India's internal vulnerabilities and conflicts have invariably invited external intervention. Sub-nationalism and separatist tendencies in India have been characterised by the intrusive role of external powers particularly Pakistan. As such, India's nation-building process has acquired transnational dimension and concerns.

It is sometimes argued that internal challenges, such as regionalism, separatism, communalism and casteism, are really various forms of struggle for political power, and therefore, they should not be described as threats to national security. However, given the nature of separatism in Kashmir, Punjab and elsewhere wherein external powers have been involved, the argument that they are just ambitious struggles for political power becomes utterly untenable. Obviously, they are challenges to India's national security rather than mere movements for political power as they threaten the organizing ideology of the state and the very survival of Indian state.

As enshrined in the Indian constitution, the idea of the Indian state comprises of secular democratic republic and to secure to all its citizens: Justice – social, economic and political, Liberty – of thought, expression, belief, faith and worship; Equality of status and of opportunity, and promote among all fraternity, assuring the dignity of the individual and the unity and integrity of the Nation. These values enjoy broad societal consensus. However, all these values are still in the process of development. Indian multi-ethnic society, economy and polity still suffer from serious limitations and drawbacks to realise these values. Consequently, we find multifaceted and multidirectional threats to India's internal security.

Apart from the external threats, India faces the enormous task of safeguarding its national security from internal threats which have their roots at the domestic level. Since partition India has faced the challenge of overcoming the causes which divide the plural society. The task of national integration is not easy and it remains unachieved so far. India's diversity of culture, language and religion give the country a distinct identity, but at the same time they have posed serious challenges to India's coherence, hence threat to security. Robert W. Bradnock rather pessimistically explains:

> India's very diversity severely inhibits the emergence of a coherent national identity. It lacks the rallying cry of fundamentalist religious belief that exists in some Islamic countries. Nor does it have the cultural unity bestowed by a predominant language and universally shared history, as in China. Without such strengths, India, it is argued, with its predominantly Hindu population but with a secular constitution designed to give equal rights to divergent minorities, cannot summon up the nationalist vigour to become a force in the wider world. Rather it will remain locked in introspection, struggling with its own political identity and viability.[22]

Narrow nationalism and sub-nationalism have contributed to instability. Population explosion, acute poverty and ignorance, deteriorating ethos and values in society, questions about credible defence capability, secessionist problems in Jammu and Kashmir and North-eastern states, uncertainty caused by the demands for greater regional autonomy, widespread corruption, criminalization of politics,[23] exploitation of religion and caste for partisan purposes, and environmental degradation have seriously undermined India's progress and security. To make matters worse, there is a collapse of the administration in many parts of the country such as Bihar and Uttar Pradesh. One analyst says: "The Government appears to have lost its moral authority and our society is enveloped in an atmosphere of debasement of all values, rampant corruption at all levels and sickening and unabashed culture of sycophancy. The picture is very grim indeed. Unfriendly people have already started referring to India as a flabby giant tottering to its fall."[24] Added to this scenario is the failure of politics in the management and resolution of domestic conflicts in a pacific and satisfactory manner.

Conflicts and discord are inherent in a country like India where diverse elements are present. But living together they must develop a spirit of reasonable tolerance and understanding. Somehow lack of tolerance and understanding or lack of emotional integration continues to bother India's survival. Hence the pessimistic argument that India is only a geographical entity lacking the sense of unity or cohesion. Explaining the threat to India's unity from regional chauvinism, Kuldip Nayar says: "The states are unaccommodative and behave like strangers. The way the Karnataka – Tamil Nadu water dispute burst on the scene, the way it defied any solution for days and the way even the Prime Minister's award was questioned or accepted under protest – all this shows how flimsy is the very concept of India. Some lakh cusecs of water had nearly washed away the indivisible links in the southern part of the country."[25] His views came in the wake of intense intransigence, and even rivalry, over the sharing of Kaveri river waters between Tamil Nadu and Karnataka states of the Indian Union. Showing concerns about the lack of unity in India, he further states: "There was a sense of Indianness which motivated those who guided our destiny then. No leader is now prepared to rise above his or her personal and political considerations. The word 'country' does not evoke the kind of emotion it used to in the past. Today the centre and the states are ruled by pygmies. Ideals of social, political and economic equality would have strengthened the bonds of people in different parts, but then all this has been stalled by politics."[26]

Acute internal threats to India's security prompted the CIA (Central Intelligence Agency) of America to conclude that India was among the sixteen countries which might fall apart under certain circumstances.[27] The CIA report was based on some key findings: "Democracy generally lowers the risk of state failure while autocracy increases it, poor democracies are more unstable than either rich democracies or poor non-democracies, and poor democracies that do not improve living standards are exceptionally vulnerable."[28] Contrary to this, Indian argument is that 'the notion that poverty and democracy cannot go together has been decisively disproved by the Indian experiment in the past five decades.'[29] The CIA report may have been motivated, but to brush it aside as a figment of Westerners' imagination will hardly be conducive to objectively assessing and overcoming the weaknesses in Indian democracy.

This lack of cohesiveness and a sense of unity in India raises the important question whether India has followed the path of state-building or nation-building and whether such a strategy has paid India in terms of ensuring its long-term objective of survival or security.

One important aspect of the nature of threats to India's national security is that there is a definite link between external and internal threats. India's internal vulnerabilities such as communalism, regionalism and linguism have been the target of external intervention, particularly by Pakistan. General K.V. Krishna Rao argues:

> While internal threats to the Nation could be many and from different sources, a most serious threat is posed by subversion. While in most cases this is

> carried out by external forces, they generally operate through internal agencies. This is one case where it is difficult to draw a definite link between external and internal threats. Many a time, much more can be achieved by an adversary by internal subversion than by going to a war; and it is, therefore, much more cost effective. Subversion is carried out in many ways. Religious groups, social organisations, farmers' bodies, trade unions, student organisations, and so on can be penetrated. Indeed, the intelligence organisation of the country itself can be infiltrated into.[30]

This causes a definitional problem as on the one hand we have a link between the external and internal threats while on the other it is difficult in some cases to distinguish between external and internal threats. In India's case, the separatist tendencies have domestic roots, but they are sustained and flared up by the external sources. Thus, these are internal vulnerabilities and threats exploited by external factors. In this regard India's threat perception about the separatist and secessionist movements supported from outside is becoming more realistically estimated and efforts are afoot for formulating effective and comprehensive internal security policies.

In a totalitarian state, ideologies and values other than that of the State are viewed as threats to national security. But India is a liberal democratic state where individuals and groups are free to espouse their preferred values and ideologies within the accepted framework of the Indian Constitution. Hence we find the presence of rightist, centrist, leftist, communal, secular, local and national ideologies in India's domestic politics. Political and religious rights of the Indian people are not normally considered as threats to national security. But India has witnessed problems when the political and religious rights have been directed at the idea or the very basis of the state in cases such as insurgency in Kashmir, North-east, Punjab and earlier Tamil Nadu. However, not all political movements undermine security. Movements for separate states within the framework of Indian Constitution may increase security rather than undermine it as the local people will have larger share in power and development, increasing administrative efficiency and economic well-being. It is believed that creation of new states such as Jharkhand, Uttarakhand, and Chhatisgarh will have a salutary effect on the security of the people and Indian state overall.

In India the military dimension of threats to security is the most visible and highest on the agenda of its security. The military threats to security have attracted greater attention of Indian policy-makers and observers for various reasons, such as:

1. History of wars and covert and overt intervention since ancient times, accentuated by Pakistan and China after independence.
2. Conflictual relations with Pakistan and China.
3. Involvement of Pakistan in Western military alliances, and its strategic collaboration with China.

4. US arms sale policy and arms supplies to Pakistan.
5. Existence of a situation of nuclear asymmetry in the South Asian region and India's lack of a credible nuclear deterrence for a considerable time until May 1998 when it forced its way into the nuclear club.

As the concept of security has been broad-based there are differences over some threats or problems whether they need to be addressed as threats to national security when they do not directly threaten any of the components of the state. Moreover, social and ecological threats are more difficult to identify and articulate than the military threats. Although non-military threats, such as the question of sustainable development or a disease like AIDS, may not directly and immediately threaten the idea or stability of the state, even an indirect threat is a concern, which in the long-term may transform into a potent threat for a nation's security.

There is no end point in the quest for national security. A developing state like India does not have a significant degree of control over the global system. It has to be on guard towards the dynamics of both the international and domestic environments and adjust continually to the realities of the situation. It is an important strategic objective of a state to influence the environment, particularly in the immediate region, in order to enhance the national security interests.

India has faced three wars from Pakistan and one from China. More recently, it has fought a limited war in Kargil against Pakistan. That apart, it perceives nuclear threats from both Pakistan and China. Pakistan's own nuclear capabilities and its nuclear and strategic collaboration with China have posed serious external military threat to India. Mainly for these reasons, India continues to place military threats on top of the scale of threats to its national security. Notwithstanding that, India's perception of security has been broadened and it has increasingly given importance to threats of non-military nature from within the country, which create various vulnerabilities for her and prepare ground for external intervention.

Given the magnitude of internal and external threats, India's national security is based on national power, which comprises of military, economic, political and social components. Moreover, India has sought to solve the internal dissent and conflicts mostly within a democratic political framework. Democracy has been an important instrument to solve India's problems, be they political, economic or social. Therefore, for India, national security does not only mean the ability of the state to maintain its independence and sovereignty but also includes the ability to take action that will make possible the peaceful resolution of political, economic, religious, social or lingual problems and thus facilitate peaceful coexistence among its citizens. The pursuit of India's national security requires a secure and effective system of governance, a strong military force, an effective foreign policy, rapid economic progress and social justice. India will be more secure if it steps up the process of nation-building and develops harmonious ties at the sub-state, regional and international levels. Emphasis must be laid on building inner strength to reduce and eventually eliminate internal threats and vulnerabilities, and simultaneously minimise the opportunities for external intervention and interference. In other words, India needs a sound and an integrated approach to security.

Notes and References

1. For understanding the concept of national security, see: Jasjit Singh and Thomas Bernauer (eds.), *Security of Third World Countries* (United Nations Institute for Disarmament Research (UNIDIR): Dartmouth, 1993); Muthiah Alagappa, *The National Security of Developing States* (Dover, Massachusetts; A.H. Publishing House, 1987); Mohammed Ayoob (ed.), *Regional Security in the Third World* (London, Sydney: Croom Helm, 1986); Barry Buzan, Gowher Rizvi *et al., South Asian Insecurity and the Great Powers* (London: Macmillan, 1986); Barry Buzan, *People, State and Fear: An Agenda for International Security Studies in the Post-Cold War Era* (Boulder, Colorado: Lynne Reinner, 1991); Sridhar K. Khatri (ed.), *Regional Security in South Asia* (Kathamandu: Centre for Nepal and Asian Studies, Tribhuvan University, 1987); and Edward E. Azar and Chung-in Moon (eds.), *The National Security in the Third World: The Management of Internal and External Threats* (Cambridge: University Press, 1988).
2. Walter Lippmann, *US Foreign Policy*(London: Hamish Hamilton), 1943, p. 32.
3. *Ibid.*, p. 16.
4. Arnold Wolfers, *Discord and Collaboration: Essays on International Politics* (Baltimore: Johns Hopkins University Press, 1962), p. 150.
5. Barry Buzan, *People, State and Fear: The National Security Problem in International Relations* (Brighton, Sussex: Wheatsheaf Books Ltd., 1983), p. 253.
6. This view about the interdependent nature of relations has promoted the concept of common security at the regional and international level. For details see, Radmila Nakarda and Jan Oberg (eds.), *Surviving Together: The Olof Palme Lectures on Common Security, 1988* (Lund University Peace Research Institute (LUPRI): Dartmouth, 1989); Joseph Rotablat (ed.), *Coexistence, Cooperation, and Common Security: Annals of Pugwash 1986* (Pugwash: Macmillan, 1988); and Bjorn Moller, *Common Security and Nonoffensive Defense* (Boulder, London: Lynne Rienner Publishers, 1992).
7. Quoted in Dietrich Fischer, *Nonmilitary Aspects of Security: A Systems Approach* (UNIDIR: Dartmouth, 1995), pp. 9-10.
8. *Ibid.*, p. 10.
9. Peter Mangold, *National Security and International Relations*, London (New York: Routeledge, 1990), p. 1.
10. Wolfers, n.4, p. 151.
11. Mangold, n. 9, p. 6.
12. Fischer, n.7, p. 10.
13. Mangold, n. 9, p. 3.
14. Boutros Boutros-Ghali, *An Agenda for Peace 1995* (New York: United Nations, 1995), p. 9.

15. *The Report of the Commission on Global Governance: Our Global Neighbourhood* (New York: Oxford University Press, 1995), p. 78.
16. *Ibid.*, p. 84.
17. Ministry of Defence, India, *Annual Report, 2005-2006*, p. 2.
18. *Ibid.*, pp. 8-9.
19. Praveen Swami, "Maldives: militant Islamists on the rise," *The Hindu*, 24 November, 2007.
20. Rajpal Budania, *India's National Security Dilemma* (New Delhi: Indus, 2001), p. 28–29.
21. Barry Buzan identifies components of the state in these terms. According to him 'the idea of the state' denotes the purpose of the state and is embodied in the organizing ideology which provides the political and socio-economic principles for the organization and functioning of the state. See his, *People, State and Fear*, n.5, pp. 36-65.
22. Robert W. Bradnock, *India's Foreign Policy Since 1971*, Catham House Papers (London: The Royal Institute of International Affairs, Pinter Publishers, 1990), p. 12.
23. The Vohra Committee Report has made startling revelations about the criminalization of politics in India and the presence of a parallel government of the criminals–politicians–bureaucrats–police nexus. For details see *India Today*, February 15, 1996, pp. 28-57.
24. Lt. Gen. S.K. Sinha, "Threats and Strategy" in Maj. Gen. Rajendra Nath, *et al.*, (eds.), *Indian Security: Threats and Strategy* (Chandigarh: Panchand Research Institute, 1990), pp. 43-44.
25. Kuldip Nayar, "Regional Chauvinism: Threat to India's Unity," *Indian Express*, 8 January, 1996.
26. *Ibid.*
27. "Indian will fall apart, feels CIA," *The Hindustan Times*, 9 February, 1996.
28. *Ibid.*
29. Clinched Forecast', *The Hindustan Times*, 10 February, 1996.
30. Gen. K.V. Krishna Rao, *Prepare or Perish: A Study of National Security* (New Delhi: Lancer Publishers, 1991), p. 286.

14

India's Nuclear Policy

Suresh Dhanda

The May 1998 tests marked the dramatic shift in India's nuclear policy. Through these tests India asserted its nuclear weapons capabilities overtly and declared it as a nuclear weapon state. This has been an apparent departure from its decades old declared policy. Since then India is seriously engaged in revising its plans and enhancing its weapons capabilities to build a credible minimum deterrence against Pakistan and China. Simultaneously, it is talking about disarmament and non-proliferation. Hence, it becomes pertinent to know the various aspects of its nuclear behaviour. The present paper is a modest attempt in this direction. For the sake of clarity, the paper has been divided into six parts. The first part deals with the historical perspective of India's nuclear programme. In the second part, changing dynamics of India's nuclear policy have been analysed. Third part describes the nuclear weapons capabilities, fissile material and future weapons potential. In the forth part, issues like nuclear force structure, custody, command and control, nuclear doctrine, etc. have been discussed. The next part debates the efforts and intentions of India towards non-proliferation regime, particularly NPT, CTBT and FMCT. And finally, conclusion is recorded with future trends in India's nuclear policy.

I

India's nuclear programme can be traced back to mid 1940s when a small group of influential scientists grasped the significance of nuclear energy and persuaded the political leaders to invest resources in the nuclear sector. After independence in 1947, the quest for nuclear capability had begun with Prime Minister Nehru and Atomic Energy Commission (AEC) Chairman Homi Bhabha who took keen interest in nuclear science. From the beginning, India's nuclear programme was ambitious and envisaged having capability for covering the entire fuel cycle. Thus, India has developed facilities for mining uranium, fabricating fuel, manufacturing heavy water, reprocessing spent fuel to extract plutonium and enriching uranium. The programme never lost sight of military uses of atomic energy. As early as 26 June 1946, Jawaharlal Nehru said, "As long as the world is constituted as it is, every country will have to devise and use the latest scientific devices for its protection. I have no doubt that India will develop her scientific researches and I hope Indian scientists will use the atomic force for constructive purposes. But if India is threatened, she will inevitably try to defend herself by all means at her disposal."[1]

India's keen interest in nuclear programme can be viewed in its decision during 1950s when it procured a Candu-type CIRCUS reactor from Canada for its atomic energy programme, which went critical in 1960 and provided India with access to unsafeguarded plutonium.[2] The other important plant was constructed at Trambay and commissioned in mid 1964.[3] These two facilities allowed India to acquire the fissile material to construct a nuclear explosive device. The Chinese detonation of an atomic device in 1964 led India to seek nuclear umbrella for its security as latter was humiliated by former in 1962 war.[4] After the failure of security guarantee from US and erstwhile USSR, India adopted the policy of keeping its nuclear option open. In November 1964, the then Prime Minister Lal Bahadur Shastri authorized theoretical work on the Subterranean Nuclear Explosion For Peaceful Purposes (SNEPP). The SNEPP project culminated in the peaceful nuclear explosion during the Prime Ministership of Mrs. Indira Ghandhi. Hence, India took ten years to make an ambiguous response to China's maiden nuclear test of 1964.[5] The *Pokharan-I* test in 1974 was officially declared as peaceful nuclear explosion (PNE) but there have always been doubts and nobody believed it to be PNE.[6]

India's nuclear weapons programme was put on hold during the brief tenure of Janata Party government (1977–79). However, the weapons programme was resumed after Indira Gandhi returned to power in 1980, she authorized preparations for additional nuclear tests in 1982 but the tests were cancelled for reasons never explained publicly. However, in the late 1980s advances in Pakistan's efforts to acquire nuclear weapons, as well as the oblique nuclear threat issued by Islamabad in the wake of 1986–87 Brasstacks crisis, appears to have persuaded then Prime Minister Rajiv Gandhi to authorize weaponization of India's nuclear capability.[7]

The Indian government revived the missile programme in 1980 by launching the Integrated Guided Missile Development Programme (IGMDP) under the aegis of Defence Research and Development Organization (DRDO) in 1983 to develop a family of strategic and tactical guided missiles.[8] By may 1994, India acquired the capability to deliver nuclear weapons using combat aircraft and by 1996, Indian scientists also succeeded in developing a nuclear warhead that could be mated on to the army's ballistic missile *Prithvi*-I.[9] In the winter of 1995, in an apparent reaction to the indefinite extension of the nuclear non-proliferation treaty (NPT) and advances in negotiations on the Comprehensive Test Ban Treaty (CTBT), the Narasimha Rao government considered a crash programme of nuclear tests. However, India's test preparations were detected by US intelligence agencies and subsequently, Rao's government postponed the tests under US pressure.[10]

During the brief period of BJP government coming to power in 1996, plans for testing were renewed. However, Vajpayee government was unable to win a parliamentary majority and decided not to go through with the tests as they would create a political crisis for the incoming successor government. However, when returned to power in 1998, the BJP finally authorized two rounds of nuclear tests in May 1998, after which it formally declared India's nuclear status. Subsequent to the tests, the Vajpayee government declared that India would build a credible minimum deterrence. Since then, Indian government also formally articulated a nuclear doctrine of "no-first-use" and spelled out the broad outlines of India's nuclear command, control and communication framework.

II

The May 1998 tests in Pokharan signaled a dramatic shift in India's nuclear posture. It brought India's nuclear capability from the realm of a quiet and covert military programme to a publicly known status. The reasons behind this shift revolve mainly around the issues of national security. However, the sense of prestige or status that nuclear weapons bring in international relations can not be ruled out. As far as national security is concerned, for a country pursuing an independent foreign and security policy, potential challenges posed by existential and specific nuclear weapons threat can be adequately addressed only either through global abolition of nuclear weapons or by reliance on nuclear deterrence to ward off such challenges. The former does not seem feasible so only the later was the available option left with India. Hence, it followed the same.

Jasjit Singh, former director of IDSA, has listed various factors that pushed India towards overt nuclear weapons deterrence: First, the China factor played an important role in this direction. India had to formulate its nuclear policy in the context of those nuclear weapon states with China as a central factor which undoubtedly pose the biggest strategic challenge. India needed to take prudent precautions so that the situation of 1962 did not repeat itself. The historical, strategic and ideological motivations that resulted in China's aggression in 1962 may not have fully dissolved. Territorial dispute with China still persists. While China signed an agreement with India in 1993 for both countries not to use their military capabilities against each other, it is not entirely clear what will be the status of this commitment in times of tension and crisis, especially in territories which China claims and depicts as Chinese territories. This is made more complicated by China's declared policy in a different context where it is completely unwilling to renounce the use of force for reunification and treats reunification as a sacred duty. China's internal tension related to Tibet and Xinjiang also has a negative impact on India's security.

Nuclear conventional force modernization has been progressing at a fast pace, especially with access to Russian military technology since 1992. Moreover, Chinese transfer of nuclear and missile systems including technology to Pakistan even after its accession to the NPT in 1992 has been a source of serious concern for India's security. More than 96 per cent of China's nuclear forces and ballistic missiles have relevance only for its immediate neighbours.

Second, increasing nuclear proliferation worldwide also motivated India to shift its nuclear policy towards military purposes. Iraq was suspected, rather, almost successful in acquisition of nuclear weapons in violation of treaty obligations with technology transferred from NPT members mostly from West Europe and North America. In case of North Korea, it pursued a clandestine nuclear programme in violation of its treaty obligations and was seen to be rewarded with nuclear power reactors. Iran is suspected by the West of pursuing a nuclear weapons programme in spite of its NPT commitments. Saudi Arabia was also reportedly pursuing nuclear ambitions at one time. China and France violated solemn assurances to exercise the "utmost restraint" in nuclear testing to validate plans for new warheads. China, infact was cynical in carrying out a nuclear test within hours of giving this assurance at the NPT extension conference, while France regressed from its earlier moratorium.

Nuclear delivery systems, specially ballistic missiles, have been transferred by China and North Korea to Pakistan, Saudi Arbaia and Iran.[11] China has continued to proliferate nuclear weapons technology even after it acceded to the NPT in 1992.[12] Pakistan reached successful nuclear weaponisation by 1987 when it tested a nuclear device at Lop Nor in China.[13] Over two years, evidence has emerged of significant transfers of nuclear weapons technology to Pakistan from West as well as from China. On April 6, 1998, Pakistan fired a nuclear capable IRBM across its populated areas with the US responding only with mild regret compared with strong pressures brought to bear on India by the G–7 to give up its indigenous missile programme.[14]

Third, the end of the cold war unfortunately demonstrated a negative trend and the withdrawal of the international community in general and nuclear weapon states in particular from the commitment of global nuclear disarmament. Permanent extension of NPT without firm commitments to disarmament, unwillingness to hold the fourth UN special session on disarmament, blocking the opening of negotiations for disarmament at the conference on disarmament (CD) and a host of other indications clearly demonstrated the unwillingness of the nuclear weapon states to move firmly towards global abolition of nuclear weapons. For India, if a nuclear weapon free world was not likely or feasible, the only other option to ensure its security was through acquisition of nuclear weapons. Moreover, the dominant strategic doctrines of the major powers mostly started to re-emphasize the role and likely use of nuclear weapons even in non-nuclear situations. Russia resiled from its earlier commitment of no-first use and defensive doctrine and has come to rely more heavily on nuclear weapons than ever before. NATO has continued to shy away from a no first use commitment in spite of dissolution of Warsaw pact and dramatic degradation in potential conventional capabilities of its possible adversaries. China has moved towards the doctrine of limited deterrence. NATO's new strategic concept and corresponding nuclear doctrine reaffirms the doctrine for an expanded role of nuclear weapons.

Fourth, the post-cold war strategic environment inevitably disturbed the earlier balance but in the absence of any over-arching ideological or strategic challenge, it was expected to become more benign and co-operative. Devaluing of the UN system and unwillingness to institute reforms in tune with the altered geo-political realities and evolving a more co-operative international order has forced countries outside the alliance system to think more seriously about autonomous national capabilities. Efforts to impose unipolarity have increased apprehensions about the international order managed more by denial regimes and punitive action than democratic values. The effect of the new strategic environment was increasingly narrowing national sovereignty. India's efforts at cooperation did not bring about adequate understanding of its security concerns. It was increasingly forced to rely on its national options.

Fifth, the most critical impact of aggressive non-proliferation and counter-proliferation without disarmament during the 1990s came to pose an extremely serious threat to India's policy of keeping its nuclear option open. India faced a dual challenge after 1990 to which it had to either submit and go down the slippery slope to being disarmed without any solution to its security concerns or cross the threshold that it had preferred not to do for three decades. The first challenge India was facing since 1964 was of how to build strategic capabilities at the very minimum level as an interim measure while working for global nuclear disarmament. This policy took the shape of keeping the nuclear option, not weaponising and working for disarmament. It was perhaps not adequately appreciated that this was a policy of restraint. The second challenge was added since the beginning of the 1990s of protecting the policy of restraint from the western liberal democracies, led by the USA, targeting this policy in pursuit of their own agencies. India was specifically targeted under these non-proliferation policies thus creating a threat to the continuity of the policy of keeping the option open at the non-weaponised level.

Sixth, the negotiated draft of the CTBT as it emerged in June, 1996 not only violated the original mandate of the 1993 UN General Assembly, but also failed to address India's concerns. That's why India was unwilling to sign the CTBT but made it clear that it would not come in the way of the treaty coming into force. However, in violation of all norms, the international community brought forth a draft at the end of the July that sought to impose the CTBT on India through the stipulation of article XIV, making India's (among others) signature essential to the treaty coming into force. Concurrently, an implicit threat of punitive action was held out in the shape of measures to be taken if the treaty did not enter into force three years later. Thus, CTBT clock timed to September 1999 was ticking whereby India could face punitive measures if it did not sign the CTBT even if it did not weaponise. This created a time bound imperative for declaration of weapons capability. The BJP's assumption of power facilitated the decision which was further propelled by the test of intermediate range ballistic missile *Ghauri* by Pakistan to which USA responded with only mild regret.[15]

III

The size and composition of India's nuclear arsenal is difficult to determine as there are no official figures for weapon stockpiles at any stage of development. The only figures that can be offered are either explicit estimates made from considerations of India's probable ability to produce critical raw materials and consideration of likely production plans or are unofficial statements of uncertain provenance and authenticity. India claimed that the first three tests conducted on 11 may 1998 achieved yields of 43 kiloton (a thermonuclear device), 12 kiloton (a fission device) and 0.2 kiloton (a low yield device). The figures were later revised to 45 kiloton for the thermonuclear device and 15 kiloton for the fission device. However, these figures have been suspected by some independent analysts by claiming that the cumulative yield of the tests was more likely between 20–30 kiloton which indicates that the thermonuclear test was likely to have been a failure.[16] India carried out two more tests of sub-kiloton devices on 13 May to generate additional data for improved computer simulation of designs and for attaining the capability to carry out sub-critical experiments. However, observers doubt whether such a small number of tests are sufficient for India to have collected all the necessary data to conduct sub-critical experiments successfully.

The fissile material for India's nuclear stockpile is most likely obtained from its two research reactors; the 40 MW CIRUS and 100 MW Dhruva, which went critical in 1960 and 1985 respectively. The CIRUS is capable of producing 9–10 kg. of weapon grade plutonium annually while Dhruva 20-25 kg. The irradiated fuel from the reactors is probably reprocessed at either the plutonium reprocessing plant at Trambay or the reprocessing plant at Kalpakkam.

Though India has not made any official statement about the size of its nuclear arsenal, the Natural Resource Development Council (NRDC) estimated that by 2002, India was having a stockpile of approximately 30–35 nuclear warheads.[17] The same figure of nuclear arsenals has also been estimated as on 2002 by another prestigious magazine *Bulletin of Atomic Scientists*.[18] Carnegie Endowment for International Peace, a well reputed organization, estimated in

2002 that India had produced enough weapon-grade plutonium for 50–90 nuclear weapons and a smaller but unknown quantity of weapon-grade uranium.[19] A report by US Department of defense 2001, contends that India probably has a small stockpile of nuclear weapon components and could assemble and deploy a few nuclear weapons within a few days to a week.[20] Another study by Ashley J. Tellis in 2001 asserts that India does not have or seek to deploy a ready nuclear arsenal.[21] An article appearing in *Jane's Intelligence Review* in May 2002, reports that India's objective is to have a nuclear arsenal that is "Strategically active but operationally dormant" which would allow India to maintain its retaliatory capability within a matter of hours to week, while simultaneously exhibiting restraint.[22] However, the study also maintains that in future, India may face increasing institutional pressure to shift its nuclear arsenal to a fully deployed status. According to one more study India is estimated to have 50–100 nuclear devices; its 100 MW Dhruva reactor has been operational since 1985, and has probably produced enough plutonium for 100 nuclear devices and continues to produce sufficient plutonium for 5–7 nuclear devices annually.[23] Rodney W Jones, a noted scholar, assumes that by the year 2000 India was having up to 100 nuclear weapons that can be prepared for use on short notice.[24] By projecting these numbers out to coming years by the same methodology would suggest even higher figures than the conservative stockpiles. Another reputed journal *Nuclear Nonproliferation Review* is of the view that India had 100–500 warhead equivalents.[25]

Beside these above estimations, some other organizations too have speculated about the nuclear arsenal of India.[26] One of the major studies about nuclear weapons in South Asia was done by David Albright at the Institute for Science and International Security (ISIS) Washington DC in 2000.[27] This is a pioneering work which has been widely referred by a number of other authors. Albright calculated the size of India's stock of weapon grade plutonium to fix the number of warheads. He has derived India's inventory by estimating the total production of weapon grade plutonium in the CIRUS, Dhruva and power reactor and by subtracting draw downs from nuclear testing, processing losses and civil uses of weapons grade plutonium.[28] The median value, which is the value midway between the smallest and largest value, is about 310 kg of weapon-grade plutonium at the end of 1999 based on range of value between 5th and 95th percentiles, which are 240 kg to 395 kg.[29] In other words, it was 90 per cent certain that the true value of India's inventory at the end of 1999 was between 240 and 395 kg where the median value was about 310 kg (See Table 14.1).

Albright employed the measurement of 4.5 kg weapon grade plutonium per nuclear weapon to calculate total number of nuclear weapons that India could have made using the available fissile material. Accordingly, the median estimate was about 65 weapons and the 5th and 95th percentiles were 45 and 95 weapons respectively. Albright estimated that CIRUS and Dhruva together

Table 14.1: Estimate of Nuclear Capabilities of India

Weapons grade Plutonium		*Weapons grade Uranium*		*Nuclear Weapons Equivalent*	
Median (kg)	5th–95th Percentiles (kg.)	Median (kg)	5th–95th Percentiles (kg.)	Median (kg)	5th–95th Percentiles (kg.)
310	240–395	Insignificant	Insignificant	65	45–95

Source: David Albright, *India's and Pakistan Fissile Material and Nuclear Weapons Inventories, End of 1999*, Institute for Science and International Security, Washington DC, 11 October 2000.

produced 410 kg of weapon-grade plutonium, the power reactors produced about 25 kg and the draw down was about 125 kg.[30] In his calculation, Albright ignored any highly enriched uranium produced by India as insignificant. By using similar methods Albright has also estimated potential nuclear weapons capability of India. Using the measure of 8 kg of civil plutonium per weapon, he estimated that India could have produced 8300 kg of civil plutonium up to 1999 which is equivalent of 1040 weapons. However, he acknowledged that civil plutonium is spent fuel and thus not suitable for use in nuclear weapons.[31] The estimation of potential nuclear arsenal in the future depends upon the production of weapon-grade plutonium by India (See Table 14.2).

Table 14.2: India's Fissile Material Stocks and Nuclear Arsenal Potential

Year	*Weapon-grade Plutonium (kg)*	*Number of Weapons*
1995	330	66
1996	350	70
1997	370	74
1998	390	78
1999	410	82
2000	430	86
2001	450	90
2002	470	94
2003	490	98
2004	510	102
2005	530	106
2006	550	110
2007	570	114
2008	590	118
2009	610	122
2010	630	126

Source: David Albright, *Fact Sheet: India and Pakistan-current and Potential Nuclear Arsenal*, ISIS, Washington DC 13 May, 1998.

Up to the end of 2010 India will be able to produce 630 kg of weapon-grade plutonium sufficient to build 126 nuclear weapons. However, it is important to note that India has not been employing the whole of its available capacity to produce weapon-grade plutonium as its programme has a significant civil nuclear energy component also.[32]

IV

India has configured its nuclear devices as aerial bombs or missile warheads. At present, India's nuclear deterrent is based on a small number of land-based bombers and land-based short and medium-range ballistic missiles. However, in the long term India envisions a minimum deterrent based on a triad of land, air and sea based nuclear forces.

India reportedly has a number of different types of aircraft but it apparently chose Soviet built MIG-27M Flogger aircraft with a range of 800 km and the Anglo-French Jaguar aircraft with a range of 1600 km to deliver nuclear aerial bombs.[33] The Sukhoi 30 MKI aircraft with a capacity to carry out a 800 kg payload and with a normal range of 3200 km and air-to-air refueling range of about 700 km, gives India a nuclear deep strike capability and some experts believe that India acquired the Sukhoi to counter China's deep strike capability.[34] Mirage-2000 H can also be equipped with nuclear bombs but is more likely to be used for air defence missions.[35]

But aircrafts have several disadvantages as delivery vehicles. An aircraft may be destroyed on the ground in a conventional or a nuclear attack, or an airbase runway may be destroyed, preventing take off. Protection from a conventional attack may be possible by hardening shelters for airplanes, putting them under cover to hide them, or dispersing them to a number of bases to complicate the targeting problem for a potential attacker. Even so, aircraft has several weaknesses as a secure second-strike delivery vehicle. They may be vulnerable to both nuclear and conventional attacks, and because of their reliance on runways, may not be able to respond if the runway is destroyed. Moreover, connectivity with flying aircraft, through two-way radio communication, is not as assured as is landline communication with a fixed and hardened facility. However, assuming surviving command posts and the absence of communications degradation from prior atmospheric nuclear blasts, connectivity with aircraft can be maintained with moderate effectiveness.

So, besides aircraft, India has also developed nuclear capable ballistic missiles as delivery systems.[36] India has an extensive largely indigenous ballistic missile programme, including infrastructure for both solid and liquid fuelled missiles. India's existing missiles are of *Prithvi* and *Agni* series. India has *Prithvi*-I with a range of 150 km capable of having a payload of 1000 kg, *Prithvi*-II with a range of 250 km capable of having a payload of 500 kg and *Prithvi*-III, a naval version named *Dhanush*, (reportedly under development) with a range of 350 km.[37] India probably has deployed only one type of short range ballistic missile (SRBM) *Prithvi*-I (SS-150). Some experts insist that both *Prithvi*-I and II are nuclear capable. Other analysts believe only the *Prithvi*-II can carry nuclear warheads and express doubts that the *Prithvi*-I would be nuclear tipped, given its short range, mobility and liquid fuel supply. But the CIA has assessed only *Prithvi*-I as having a nuclear role.[38]

India's second family of ballistic missiles is the *Agni*-I, II and III. The *Agni* missiles are designed to extend the reach of Indian nuclear capabilities, particularly to China. However, one more variant of *Agni*, now officially (and confusingly) referred to as *Agni*-I is specifically designed for missions against Pakistan and was tested with a capacity of 1000 kg payload on January 8, 2003 to a range of 700 km.[39] India reportedly intends to retrofit its Brahmos adaptation of Russian supplied Yakhant anti-ship cruise missile so that it can be fired either from naval ships or from SU-30 MKI attack aircraft. This cruise missile apparently could be used as a stand off system with either conventional or nuclear weapons.[40] For technical details of India's missiles, see the table given below (Table 14.3).

Keeping in view certain limitations of *Prithvi* series of missiles like logistic burdens, fuel toxicity, short-range, liquid fuelled engine and handling the weapon system in the field India seems to rely on *Agni*-I, II and III ballistic missiles as its land based missile force in the future. In comparison to *Prithvi*, each of these variants of the *Agni* missile combines the advantages of longer range, higher payload and solid-fuelled payloads. India is also developing an Inter Continental Ballistic Missile (ICBM). As part of a programme to develop a secure, sea-based second strike capability, India is developing a submarine launched missile: the *Sagarika*. The *Sagarika*, which is expected to arm India's Advanced Technology Vessel (ATV), is suffering from programme delays and is not expected to become operational before 2010.

India is also pursuing Ballistic Missile Defence (BMD) system to get a shield against the threat of ballistic missiles. For this purpose it has taken two routes: one to acquire missile defence systems from abroad; and second to develop the system indigenously. Through first route, it is trying to get variants of Russian S-300 BMD system, the Israeli Arrow BMD and the American Patriot Advanced Capability-3 (PAC-3). While its indigenous efforts are centered on the domestically designed, *Akash*, surface to air missile (SAM).

Currently, India does not maintain a constituted nuclear force on a heightened state of alert. The nuclear capable missiles, non-nuclear warhead assemblies and fissile cores are maintained in a de-alerted state by the individual armed services, the DRDO and the Department of Atomic Energy (DAE) respectively, with plans to reconstitute them rapidly during an emergency or national crisis.[41] After much debate, deliberations and delay, the Indian government has entrusted operational control of India's nuclear missiles force

Table 14.3: Profile of India's Missiles

Name	*Type*	*Range/Payload*	*Propellant*	*Status*	*Origin*
Prithvi-I	SSM	150 km/1000 kg	Liquid	Operational	Indigenous
Prithvi-II	SSM	250 km/ 800–1000 kg.	Liquid	Operational	Indigenous
Prithvi-III/Dhanush	SSM	350 km/ 500–1000 kg	Solid	Development/ Tested	Indigenous
Agni-I	SSM	700–850 km/ 800–1000 kg	Solid	Development/ Tested	Indigenous
Agni-II	SSM	2000–3300 km/ 800–1000 kg	Solid	Serial Production	Indigenous
Agni-III	SSM	3000–5500 km/ 600–1800 kg	Solid	Development/ Tested	Indigenous
Agni-IV/Surya	SSM	5000–6000 km/ 600–1800 kg	Solid	Under-development	Indigenous
Akash	SAM	27 km/60 kg	Ramjet sprocket booster	Under-development/ Tested	Indigenous
Nag	Anti-Tank	4–6 km	Solid	Under-development/ Tested	Indigenous
Astra	AAM	100 km/15 kg	Solid	Under-development/ Tested	Indigenous
Trishul	SAM	9 km/5.5 kg	Solid	Under-development/ Tested	Indigenous
Brahmos	Cruise	300 km/250 kg	Solid	Development/ Tested	India/Russia
Sagarika	SLCM	350 km/500 kg or 1000 km/500 kg	Liquid	Under-development	India/Russia

Source: Federation of American Scientists, Washington DC; *Nuclear Threat Initiative*, Washington DC; Arms Control Association, Washington DC; and Government of India, Ministry of Defence, *Annual Report 2006–07*, New Delhi.

to the Indian Army. Although the Indian Air Force deploys an undisclosed number of nuclear capable bombers and is actively planning to upgrade the air leg of the dyad, it has lost the inter-organizational battle with the army for custody of India's nuclear missile force.[42] The Indian government is also considering a proposal to place all nuclear-capable land based missiles under the consolidated control of a strategic rocket command within the army.

India's nuclear force is administered by a tri-service Strategic Force Command (SFC).[43] Chief of Defence Staff (CDS), who heads the tri-service command, reports to the chairman of the chiefs of staff committee. SFC will report to the CDS who will act as the single point military advisor to the Indian government and act as the interface between the civilian executive and the armed services.[44] At the level of the civilian executive, India's Nuclear Command Authority (NCA) is responsible for the management of its nuclear forces and for making all decisions pertaining to the use of nuclear weapons. The NCA is a two-layered structure. It comprises a Political Council (PC) and an Executive Council (EC). The PC is chaired by the Prime Minister and is the "sole body, which can authorize the use of nuclear weapons." The decisions of the PC are conveyed to the EC, headed by the Prime Minister's National Security Advisor, who then interfaces with the SFC to execute the political directives of the PC.

At doctrinal level, India has declared a nuclear "no-first-use" policy on 17 August 1999, and is in the process of developing a nuclear doctrine based on "credible minimum deterrence."[45] The contents of the "draft report" were partially revised and then embraced for the first time as government policy more than three years later in January 2003.[46] The National Security Advisory Board (NSAB), the main architect of draft, represented a cross section of India's military, political, intellectual and scientific community. Indian doctrine is based upon a retaliatory, no-first use policy with the goal of deterring nuclear attacks, although other reasons to use nuclear weapons may not have been ruled out completely. India may not have thought about other contingencies such as Pakistan using nuclear weapons on its own territory in response to an Indian invasion.[47] The main cornerstones of the doctrine include survivability, robust command and control, effective intelligence and early warning capabilities, planning and training, and finally the will to employ these weapons should deterrence fail.[48]

India's views on nuclear weapons are much different those of Pakistan's, and may be designed for political utility, as well as for deterrence value. Targeting philosophy is not specifically spelled out in the draft nuclear doctrine, but there is a theme of punitive response and massive retaliation that would seem to imply a counter-value strategy. Pakistan's major cities and industrial areas could be readily targeted and attacked with either aircraft or ballistic missiles.[49] Alternatively, India could target Pakistan's nuclear facilities in a counter force attack given the short ranges and knowledge of Pakistan's military capabilities.[50] The survivability of India's nuclear forces may be ensured through secrecy and dispersal, including separating weapons from delivery systems. India's nuclear doctrine may be in a state of transition, since it has mentioned a nuclear triad and command and control functions that may not currently exist.[51]

V

The Indian leadership, over the years, has been deeply conscious of the dangers posed by nuclear weapons.[52] The first Prime Minister of India, Jawaharlal Nehru stressed, while speaking in Lok Sabha on 10 May 1954, "I would like the House to remember that use of technology for peaceful purposes is more important for a country like India whose power resources are limited than for a country like France, an industrially advanced country."[53] Although, India was one of the countries which first proposed a ban on nuclear testing, it has been unwilling to sign global treaties that were discriminatory because they allowed a few countries to hold nuclear weapons indefinitely. In 1965, India, along with a group of non-aligned countries, had put forward a proposal for an international non-proliferation agreement under which the nuclear weapon states would agree to give up their arsenals, provided other countries refrained from developing or acquiring such weapons. In 1961, India supported UN General Assembly resolution 1653 of 24 November 1961 which called on the Secretary General to ascertain the views of member states on the possibility of convening a special conference for concluding a convention on the prohibition of use of nuclear weapons. In 1978, India proposed negotiations for an international convention that would prohibit the use or threat of use of nuclear weapons.

India has seen total elimination of nuclear weapons as the only durable, non-discriminatory and comprehensive non-proliferation order. That's why India had refused to sign NPT when it became clear that instead of addressing the central objective of universal and comprehensive non-proliferation, the treaty only legitimized the continuing possession and multiplication of nuclear stockpiles by those few states possessing them. However, India, while opposing the NPT, has reiterated its resolve to undertake nuclear disarmament as part of a time bound and comprehensive worldwide effort in that direction. India, however, remained constant in its opposition to the NPT. It also opposed the indefinite extension of this treaty in May 1995.

India also supported the idea behind Comprehensive Test Ban Treaty (CTBT) when it was first proposed in the 1950s but Indian government changed its stand when negotiations on CTBT moved towards a resolution. During discussions in the Conference on Disarmament, India wanted to ensure that the CTBT did not legitimize existing nuclear arsenals as the NPT does.

In India's view, the CTBT must be an integral step in the process of nuclear disarmament. Developing new warheads or refining existing ones after a CTBT is in place, using innovative technologies would be as contrary to the spirit of CTBT as the NPT is to the spirit of non-proliferation. The CTBT must contain a binding commitment on the international community, especially the nuclear weapon states, to take further measures within an agreed time-frame towards the creation of a nuclear weapons-free world. The Indian government also objected the provision of entry into force, as well as clauses which allow nuclear weapon states to conduct further experiments to ensure the safety and reliability of their nuclear weapons. In fact, India wanted a genuine CTBT without any loopholes. India holds that mere expression of intent have not been enough to make the nuclear weapon states come to the negotiating table, and the treaty should, therefore, clearly include a time-bound framework for total nuclear disarmament. However, with respect to the CTBT, India declared a voluntary moratorium soon after the 1998 tests. It declared that India would not be the first state to resume nuclear tests.

India was one of the few countries which supported the idea behind Fissile Material Cut Off Treaty (FMCT). Initially, it had linked the FMCT with disarmament but after the tests of 1998 it dropped the linkage between the two. India also rejected to abide by an informal moratorium on fissile material production. Since India does not possess sufficient stock of fissile material for its proposed minimum credible deterrence against Pakistan and China, it will not start these negotiations. The crucial concern for India in this regard is the scope of verification procedure in the proposed treaty. Through official statements, India has taken a position that the proposed treaty should incorporate a verification mechanism in order to provide the assurance that all countries are complying with their obligations.

VI

India's nuclear programme has gradually shifted its postures during various political regimes. The reasons for this slow movement include the rate of funding, the technology denial regimes imposed especially after *Pokhran*-I, the desire to be totally self-reliant and a reluctance to pursue military nuclearization except when forced by circumstances. But nuclear tests of 1998 at *Pokharan* have signalled a dramatic shift in India's nuclear behaviour. These tests brought India's nuclear capability from the realm of a quiet and covert military programme to a publicly known status as a nuclear weapon state. After that India seems to increasingly think and make policy like a nuclear weapon state. Variety of reasons with focus on national security have played the role behind this shift in nuclear policy.

Indian government has divided the nuclear weapons and delivery systems among the armed forces, civil defence and atomic energy department. Nuclear doctrine has also been declared. Command and control arrangements have also been spelled out. In fact, strategic elites in India have started to think the reality that nuclear weapons are not mere political instrument but may be used as weapons in real sense during warfare. Now, India's focus is on developing a nuclear trial to get a sure second-strike capability. However, at this point, it is unclear whether India is seeking to acquire a global nuclear strike capability in the long term or its nuclear deterrence will be technically restricted to deter nuclear threats from Pakistan and China. India may go for some more nuclear tests in the future to clear the controversy regarding thermonuclear capability and to get additional data for sub-critical experiments, as well as to design and validate a new class of nuclear warheads. Though, India has assured the NSG members at Vienna, on 6 September 2008, not to conduct nuclear tests in future, but neither the NSG waiver nor the 123 agreement between India and USA debar India from retaining the nuclear weapons. India has a right to conduct more tests, and to develop more weapons, if it faces a serious threat to its security. Although, India has not signed NPT and CTBT, but it never opposed the global nuclear disarmament. Even in future, it is always in favour of a time-bound universal treaty for the abolition of nuclear weapons.

Notes and References

1. Lorne J. Kavic, *India's Quest for Security: Defence Policies 1947–1965*, University of California Press, Barkeley, 1967, pp. 27–28.
2. CIRUS (Canadian-Indian, US), a 40 mwt research reactor that was offered to be built by Canada in 1955 as part of the "Colombo Plan"(Colombo plan was an initiative by the rich commonwealth nations to help the poor commonwealth nations of South and South-East Asia. The US contribution in this direction was the heavy water to moderate the reactor). US agreed to supply 21 tonnes heavy water for this reactor in February 1956 under the Eisenhower plan "Atoms for Peace". The acquisition of CIRUS was a watershed event in nuclear proliferation and was specifically intended by India to provide herself with a weapons option, and this reactor produced the plutonium which was used in the PNE of 1974.
3. Prime Minister Nehru in July 1958, authorized the project "phoenix" to build a plant with a capacity of 20 tonnes of fuel a year sized to match the production capacity of CIRUS. The plant was based on the US developed purex process, and an American firm "vitro international" prepared the plan for it.
4. The Chinese have two major claims on Indian territory. One claim, in the western sector, is on Aksai Chin in the northeastern section of Ladakh District in Jammu and Kashmir. The other claim is in the eastern sector over a region included in the British-designated North-East Frontier Agency, the disputed part of which India renamed Arunachal Pradesh and made it into a state. In the fight over these areas, the well-trained and well-armed troops of the Chinese People's Liberation Army overpowered the ill-equipped Indian troops, who had not been properly acclimatized to fighting at high altitudes.
5. The first Chinese nuclear test was conducted at Lop Nor on 16 October 1964. It was a tower shot involving a fission device with a yield of 25 kilotons. Uranium 235 was used as the nuclear fuel, which indicates Beijing's choice of the path of creating high-yield nuclear weapons right away.
6. Jyotirmoy Banerjee, "Pokharan-II: Fallout and Implications," *World Affairs*, Vol. 3, No. 3, July–September 1999, p. 120.
7. In 1986–87, India mobilized a quarter of a million troops just 20 miles from the Indo-Pak border opposite the Pakistani province *Sindh* in a military exercise code named "Brasstacks." The scale of military mobilization by India was unprecedented during peace-time. Indian troops carried live ammunition, worsening the fear in

Pakistan that India was likely to attack Pakistan along its Southern borders. At the time Pakistani experts thought that India might be preparing to relieve pressure in its Punjab province by attacking Pakistan. Indian scholars believed that the exercise was intended to stop Pakistan from allegedly interfering in the Sikh insurgency in Punjab by threatening to retaliate against Pakistan's domestic 'trouble spot' in *Sindh*. More recent disclosures, however, suggest that brasstacks was staged by India as a deliberate policy of provoking Pakistan for war, so that India would have a pretext to attack and undermine Pakistan's self confidence and perhaps its territorial integrity. This threat was blocked by Pakistan's counter deployment of its armed forces and issuance of veiled nuclear threat. For a detailed account of brasstacks crises see "Brasstacks and Beyond: Perception and Management of Crises in South Asia," *Acids Research Report*, Programmes in Arms Control, Disarmament and International Security, University of Illinois at Urbana-Champaign, Urbana, 1995.

8. The Indian government revived the missile program in 1980 by launching the Integrated Guided Missile Development Programme (IGMDP) under the aegis of DRDO in 1983 to develop a family of strategic and tactical guided missiles. The IGMDP involved the development of two strategic ballistic missile systems: two variants of a short-range ballistic missile (*Prithvi*), and a medium-range technology demonstrator (*Agni*). Under the programme, the DRDO also sought to develop medium and short-range SAMs (*Akash* and *Trishul*), and a third-generation ATGM (*Nag*).
9. *Nuclear Overview, India*, NTI, Washington D.C; http://www.nti.org/e_research/profiles/India/Nuclear/index.html
10. *Ibid.*
11. In the early 1990s, the NDC, a subsidiary of the PAEC, acquired complete though unassembled M-11s and possibly an undisclosed number of M-9 SRBMs from China. Chinese assistance extended to training Pakistani missile crews in the assembling, maintenance, and simulated launches. During the mid-1990s, China apparently transferred an entire production line for M-11s and possibly M-9s to the NDC. Chinese assistance most likely encompassed equipment and technology transfers in the areas of solid-fuel propellants, manufacture of air frames, re-entry thermal protection materials, post-boost vehicles, guidance and control missile computers, integration of warheads, and the manufacture of TELs for the missiles. Though China subsequently agreed to abide by MTCR guidelines under US pressure, yet it has interpreted those guidelines narrowly. Beijing has apparently agreed not to supply category-I or complete ground-to-ground missiles, which would not cover air-launched cruise missiles. It also does not abide by the MTCR's key technological annex. Indeed, CIA has alleged that Chinese missile-related assistance to Pakistan increased in the wake of the latter's May 1998 nuclear tests, and that such assistance is critical for the success of Pakistan's medium-range, solid-fueled ballistic missile programme. R. Jeffrey Smith, 'China Linked To Pakistani Missile Plant; Secret Project Could Renew Sanctions issue," *Washington Post*, 25 August 1996, Section-A, p. A01; Tim Weiner, "US Says It Suspects China is Helping Pakistan With Missiles," *New York Times*, 26 August 1996, p. 6; "Pakistan's Missiles," *Pittsburg Post-Gazett,* Pittsburgh, Pennsylvania, 27 August 1997, p. A-4; in Lexis-Nexis Academic Universe, 26 August 1996,

http://www.lexis-nexis.com/; Steven Erlanger, "US Wary of Punishing China For Missile Help To Pakistan," *New York Times*, 27 August 1997, p. 6; and Douglas Waller, "The Secret Missile Deal," *Time*, 30 June 1997; http://www.cnn.com/ALL POLITICS/1997/06/23/ time/missiles.html

12. For details on NPT, see, Mahmed I. Shaker, *The Nuclear Non-Proliferation Treaty: Origin and Implementation 1959–1979*, 3 Vols., Oceana, New York, 1980.
13. It is also reported that a Pakistani nuclear device was tested at the Chinese testing site at Lop Nor in Sinkiang in 1987 eleven years earlier to its open test in 1998. By 1992, Pakistan started claiming through Abdul Quadir Khan and other senior officers like Pakistani foreign secretary Shahryar Khan that Pakistan is a nuclear weapons capable state. If it was true then the events of May 1998 at *Chagai* hills had only formalized the existing situation. J.N. Dixit, *India's Foreign Policy: 1947–2003,* Picus Books, New Delhi, 2003, p. 439.
14. India had to put its IRBM program on hold after 1994, reportedly under US Pressure. Agni-II (2500 Km) was tested finally in April 1999.
15. The missile was believed to have been transferred from China/North Korea and tested on April 06, 1998 across inhibited territory. The orders to undertake the nuclear test were apparently issued in New Delhi two days later.
16. Senior Indian scientists such as P.K. Iyengar have also publicly suggested that it is likely that the fusion device burned only partially. However, the former head of India's Atomic Energy Commission (AEC) R. Chidambaram has claimed that a "post-shot" analysis of the Pokhran II tests confirmed that the May 1998 tests yielded about 60 kilotons. Chidambaram subsequently asserted that the tests provided India with "the capability to design and fabricate nuclear weapons [in the range] of low-yields up to 200 kilotons."
17. In case of India's nuclear arsenal see, "India's Nuclear forces-2002," *NRDC Nuclear Note Book, 2003*. In case of Pakistan see, Pakistan's Nuclear forces 2001, *NRDC Nuclear Note Book 2002*, For the data of nuclear yield from May 1998 tests see, Terry C. Wallace, *The May 1998 India and Pakistan's Nuclear Tests,* Southern Arizona Seismic Observatory (SASO), University of Arizona, July 1998.
18. "India's Nuclear Forces, 2002", *Bulletin of Atomic Scientists,* Vol. 58, March 2002, p. 1. Also see, "Missile Proliferation and the Strategic Balance in South Asia," *CRS Report for Congress,* RL 32115, 17 October, 2003.
19. Joseph Cirincione et al., *Deadly Arsenals,* Carnegie Endowment for International Peace, June 2002, pp. 191–206.
20. "Proliferation: Threat and Response" *Report of US Defense Department,* January 2001.
21. Ashley J. Tellis, *India's Emerging Nuclear Posture,* RAND, Santa Monica, 2001. This study discusses India's pursuit of a "force in being" nuclear posture, which falls somewhere between a ready arsenal and a recessed deterrent – a collection of unassembled nuclear warheads, all kept under strict civilian control and separate from delivery systems.
22. T.S. Gopi Rethinaraj, "Nuclear Diplomacy Returns to South Asian Security Agenda," *Jane's Intelligence Reviews,* May, 2002.
23. Dinshaw Mistry, "Nuclear Asia's Challenges," *Current History,* April 2005, p. 178.
24. Rodney W. Jones, *Minimum Nuclear Deterrence Postures in South Asia: An*

overview, Final Report by Policy Architects International for DTRA/ASCO, October 2001; http//www.dtra. mil/abut/organiza tion/souty_asia.

25. Arian L. Pregenzer, "Securing Nuclear Capabilities in India and Pakistan: Reducing the Terrorist and Proliferation Risks," *Nonproliferation Review,* Vol. 10, No. 1, Spring 2003, p. 125. Also see, Duncan Lennox, "Comparing India and Pakistan's strategic Nuclear Weapon Capabilities", *Jane's Strategic Weapon Systems,* May 30, 2002; http//www.janes.com/security/international_security/news/jsnes 020530_1_n.shtml
26. Raju G.C. Thomas, "India's Nuclear and Missile Programme: Strategy, Intention and Capabilities", in Raju G.C. Thomas and Amit Gupta, eds., *India's Nuclear Security,* Vistaar, New Delhi, 2000, p. 110; G. Balachandran, "International Nuclear Control Regimes and India's Participation in Civilian Nuclear Trade: Key Issues," *Strategic Analysis* Vol. 24, No. 4, October-December 2005, p. 570; Davin T. Hagerty, "South Asia's Nuclear Balance," *Current History,* April 1996. Also See, Franoise Heisbourg, "The Prospects for Nuclear Stability Between India and Pakistan", *Survival,* Winter 1998-1999; and Amit Gupta "South Asia Nuclear Choices: What Type of Force Structures may Emerge?", *Armed Forces Journal International,* September 1998.
27. David Albright, *India's and Pakistan's Fissile Material and Nuclear Weapons Inventories, end of 1999,* Institute for Science and International Security, Washington DC, 11 October 2000.
28. US officials have recommended strongly that India's Cirus and Dhruva plutonium production reactors have a lifetime capacity, factor of about 40 per cent while Indian officials have stated that the average capacity factor is significantly greater, as large as 60 per cent. In this estimate, the most likely choice is selected as 40 per cent with values up to 60 per cent having a diminished probability of occurring. On the other end, a lifetime capacity factor of less than 30 per cent is viewed as highly unlikely. In the case of Pakistan, total enrichment capacity at the Kathua and the newer Gadwal facilities, a wide range of possible values is given equal probability of occurring. David Albright, India's and Pakistan's Fissile Material and Nuclear Weapons Inventories, End of 1999, *Defence and Technology,* Vol. 1, No. 6, October 2002, p. 10 and 11.
29. The range in the values can be understood by considering the set of all values, which in this case vary between 180 kg and 480 kg. Because values in the tails of the range carry a very low probability of being true, often only the values that fall between the 10th and 90th percentile are considered, which in this case are 250 kg and 375 kg respectively. To be more certain that the actual value lies in the range, the 5th and 95th percentiles can be selected, which are 240 kg and 395 kg, respectively. One way to interpret the results is that in the latter case, there is 90 per cent certainty that the true value lies between 240 and 395 kg of weapons-grade plutonium, where the median value is about 310 kg. *Ibid.*
30. David Albright, *India's and Pakistan's Fissile Material and Nuclear Weapons Inventories, end of 1999,* Institute for Science and International Security, Washington DC, 11 October 2000. Also see, Raju G.C. Thomas and Amit Gupta, eds., *India's Nuclear Security,* Vistaar, New Delhi, 2000.
31. David Albright, *India's and Pakistan's Fissile Material and Nuclear Weapons*

Inventories, end of 1999, Institute for Science and International Security, Washington DC, 11 October 2000.

32. See, George Perkovich, *India's Nuclear Bomb*, OUP, New Delhi, 2000.
33. Robert S. Norris, et. al., "India's Nuclear Forces 2002," *Bulletin of The Atomic Scientists,* Vol. 58, No. 2, March/April 2002, p. 2.
34. Srinjoy Chowdhury, "Sukhois Capable of Hitting Chinese Targets," *Statesman*, 28 September 2002.
35. Raj Chengappa's account suggests that India first attempted to mate externally carried nuclear weapons pods with the Jaguar and later shifted to the Mirage-2000 for this mission. Raj Chengappa, *Weapons of Peace: The Secret Story of India's Quest to be a Nuclear Power*, Harper Collins, New Delhi, 2002, pp. 327 and 382–384.
36. Since the early 1990s India and Pakistan have been steadily moving their nuclear deterrence from aircraft based to ballistic missile based with potentially devastating results for the South Asian stability. The introduction of nuclear capable ballistic missiles on a significant scale adds to the negative variables that collectively raise the risk of an inadvertent nuclear war breaking out in a region that is unstable principally due to the Kashmir territorial dispute. Ben Sheppard, "Ballistic Missiles: Complicating the Nuclear Quagmire," in D.R. Sardesai and Raju G.C. Thomas, eds., *Nuclear India in the Twenty First Century,* Palgave-Macmillan, New York, 2002, p. 189.
37. The *Prithvi* class of missiles is a road mobile, single stage, liquid fuelled, short range missile that employs propulsion technology from the Soviet SA-2 surface to air (SAM) missile. The *prithvi* is otherwise Indian in design. The *prithvi* program began in 1983 and was test fired in 1988. Three basic types *prithvis* currently exit. The *Prithvi*-I has a range sufficient to strike any significant target if deployed anywhere along the Indian border. The Indian army has reportedly ordered 100 of these missiles, which entered into serial production in 1997 and reportedly can be equipped with 5 types of warheads. A longer range variant of *Prithvi*-I, the *Prithvi*-II (SS-250), an air force version, has also been developed. Under development is a *Prithvi*-III (SS-350), which will be used for naval purposes. This third variant, also known as Dhanush, may be solid fuelled. It is believed to be derived from the Russian SA-2. Published reports in September 2000 indicated an Indian government decision to proceed with production of 300 Prithvi missiles. "India to Make 300 Prithvi Missiles," *The Hindu,* 8 September, 2000.
38. Robert S. Norris, et. al., "India's Nuclear Forces 2002," *Bulletin of The Atomic Scientists,* Vol. 58, No. 02, March/April 2002. p. 3.
39. The *Agni* missiles have been developed, reportedly with distant China as well as nearby Pakistan in mind, and have been tested in three versions, with a fourth, intended to be of longer range, is under development. The first variant, *Agni*-I, was demonstrated in various tests to ranges between 900 and 1200 km, and the second variant, *Agni*-II, to ranges between 1200 and 2000 km, each with notional payloads of 1000 kg. A third variant referred again as *Agni*-I is Pakistan specific with a range of 700 km. This Pakistan specific missile reportedly weighs twelve tons and evidently uses only solid fuel propulsion. It is presumably lighter in weight than the variants with the liquid fuel engines, and easier to mount on road-mobile transport-erector-launchers (TELs) or on the railroad launch cars, India

reportedly has been developing. A fourth variant, *Agni*-III intended for ranges closer to 3000 km (using three solid fuel stages) with a 1000 kg payload has been tested, and is underdevelopment. See *The Military Balance 2003-04,* IISS, London, 2003, p. 131.

40. Brahmos missile is a product of an Indo-Russian joint venture. Brahmos is a cruise missile which cruises horizontally and travels only in the atmosphere. It is a two stage vehicle that has a solid propellant booster and liquid propellant ramjet system. The Brahmos is the first and the only supersonic cruise missile that uses liquid ramjet technology. It cruises in the atmosphere at the speed faster than sound. It has been rated at 290 km in range when surface launched using the supersonic boost state, it may be capable of longer ranges if used only in sub-sonic mode or when launched from aircraft. It has been configured to launch from ground including silos and ships, submarines and aircrafts. Besides, it can blast off from a mobile platform on land, that is, from a vehicle. One may assume it as a nuclear capable, if equipped with a small enough nuclear warhead. For details, see Rahul Datta, "India to Go in for Cruise Missiles," *The Pioneer,* 15 June 2001; "Brahmos Launch a Big Breakthrough," *The Hindu*, October 30, 2003; "Before You Can Say Brahmos," *Hindustan Times*, 30 October 2003; "Brahmos Flight Tested," *The Hindu*, 30 October 2003; "Anti-ship Version of Brahmos Proves it Mettle," *The Hindu,* 3 December 2003, and R. Prasanam, "India Enters The Cruise Missile Race; Hyplane Avatar Reaches Planning State," available at http://www.google.com
41. Ashely J. Tellis, *India's Emerging Nuclear Posture: Between Recessed Deterrent and Ready Arsenal,* Rand, Santa Monica, 2001, p. 251.
42. "Indian Govt. to Hand over Agni Missiles to Army," *Press Trust of India,* 2 September 2003, Nationwide International News; in Lexis-Nexis Academic Universe, 23 September 2003, http://web.lexis-nexis.com/.
43. "India Establishes Strategic Forces Command," *Press Trust of India*, 4 January 2003, Nationwide International News; in Lexis-Nexis Academic Universe, 5 January 2003, http://web.lexis-nexis.com/; Edna Fernandes, "India Sets Up Nuclear Arsenal Command Structure," *Financial Times,* 6 January 2003.
44. Rajat Pandit, "India All Set to Set up Nuclear Forces Command," *Times of India*, Mumbai, 31 December 2002, http://timesofindia.indiatimes.com/.
45. *India's Nuclear Doctrine,* Government of India, Text released to the press in New Delhi on 19 August 1999.
46. Also see, http://www.mea.India.nic.in
47. For example see, P.R. Chari, "India's nuclear Doctrine: Confused Ambitions," *Nonproliferation Review*, Vol. 7, No. 3, Fall-Winter 2000, pp. 123–135. Official doctrinal statements do not even mention critical issues such as missile defence and the relationship between nuclear and sub-nuclear levels of conflict.
48. For detail see, Waheguru Pal Singh, "India's Nuclear use Doctrine" in Peter R. Lavoy et al., eds., *Planning the Unthinkable: How New Powers will use Nuclear, Biological and Chemical Weapons,* Cornell University Press, Ithaca, 2000; and Lt. Gen. Pran Pahwa, *Command and Control of Indian Nuclear Forces,* United Services Institution of India, New Delhi, 2002.
49. *India's Draft Nuclear Doctrine,* National Security Advisory Board on Nuclear Doctrine, 17 August, 1999.

50. Rodney W. Jones, *Minimum Nuclear Deterrence Postures in South Asia: An overview,* Final Report by Policy Architects International for DTTRA/ASCO, October 2001, pp. 29–30.
51. Andrew C. Winner and Toshi Yoshihara, *Nuclear Stability in South Asia,* The Institute for Foreign Policy Analysis, Spring 2002, p. 33.
52. J.N. Dixit, *India's Foreign Policy 1947–2003*, Picus Books, New Delhi, 2003, p. 280.
53. *Ibid.* p. 281.

15

India's Kashmir Policy

Ajay Singh Manhas

The state of Jammu and Kashmir has been one of the most strategic places due to its unique geo-political status in the Indian sub-continent in Asia. The state is encircled by China (sinkiang and Tibet), Afghanistan and Pakistan. It forms the extreme northern part of the Indian Union and thereby is strategically important for the defence of northern India. Due to its contiguity with many important countries of Asia, Jammu and Kashmir state occupies a great importance even in the global politics.

During the last six decades, Jammu and Kashmir has become a bone of contention between India and Pakistan over which both have fought four wars and till date, no sign of permanent resolution of the issue is visible. The perceptual gap between the two countries due to their ideological divergence and external environment of cold war politics in fifties complicated the issue. The rigid stand taken by both India and Pakistan over Kashmir has made the resolution difficult. India considers it a symbol of its secular character as Jammu and Kashmir is the only Muslim majority state in India. Pakistan, on the other hand, considers that with the merger of the state of Jammu and Kashmir, a Muslim dominated state, it will be able to defend the "Two Nation Theory", according to which the British Indian Empire was divided into two – India and Pakistan. Besides ideological, it is due to the geo-strategic, economic, political and psychological considerations that, both the countries conceived Kashmir as inevitable part of their existence. No one is ready to make any compromise and the result is a protracted conflict.

It is because of the on-going conflict and its influence on national, regional and even international politics, that it is important to understand the issue of Jammu and Kashmir and its historical background. To understand the complexities of the issue and dynamics and nature of the conflict, it is important to throw some light on the genesis of its conflict.

At the time of the division of the sub-continent, the Jammu and Kashmir became an issue between India and Pakistan. The princely state of Jammu and Kashmir, that was a Muslim majority state,[1] was under the rule of Maharaja Hari Singh, a Hindu ruler. Both India and Pakistani leaders tried to convince Hari Singh to accede Jammu and Kashmir to their respective states. Even

Lord Mountbatten (Governor General of India) during his visit to the state in July 1947 advised Maharaja to make up his mind about accession to any of the dominions before 15 August 1947.[2] But Maharaja Hari Singh followed the policy of biding time and could not decide to accede to either of dominions.

In the meantime, Pakistan in order to annex the state by force, invaded the state by sending tribesmen along with its regular forces on 12 October 1947.[3] This swift changing milieu, which had cast a dark shadow over his kingdom and after weighing the complexity of the situation, Maharaja Hari Singh signed the instrument of accession with India on 26 October 1947.[4] However, the government of Pakistan contested the validity of accession, despite the fact that the accession was legal and valid.[5] Moreover, the instrument of accession signed by Maharaja Hari Singh and accepted by Lord Mountbatten on behalf of government of India, was also duly endorsed by the Head of the emergency administration led by Sheikh Abdullah on behalf of the people of state, and Maher Chand Mahajan, the Premier of the state representing Maharaja Hari Singh, the hereditary ruler of the state.[6] The legality of the instrument of accession, therefore, cannot be questioned as it had been endorsed by legitimate authority in the state.

Meanwhile, in order to avoid a direct conflict with Pakistan on matter of invasion of her territory, the then Indian Prime Minister Pandit Jawaharlal Nehru, on the advice of Lord Mountbatten, decided to lodge a complaint to the United Nations.[7] After long deliberations in the United Nations on the Kashmir issue, both India and Pakistan accepted the option of plebiscite to resolve the issue.[8] India's acceptance of the offer of plebiscite under the United Nations resolution of 13 August 1948 [9] was conditional in the sense that according to this resolution, the option of plebiscite was to be carried out only when Part I and Part II [10] of the resolution are implemented.

However, it should be noted that Nehru took the Kashmir issue to the United Nations Security Council for its settlement, but, it resulted only in the internationalization of the issue. Moreover, by accepting the option of plebiscite in Jammu and Kashmir, the government of India itself put a question mark over the validity of accession of the state to the Indian Union. This offer of plebiscite was to be given inspite of the fact that from the legal point of view, only the ruler of the state was competent to execute the instrument of accession and he had attached no such condition on joining the Indian Union. Moreover, Nehru's policy on Jammu and Kashmir at the time of independence was shaped by British Viceroy Lord Mountbatten, as, he used the special relationship of his wife Edwina with Nehru to mould his policy towards Kashmir.[11]

However, the option of plebiscite in Jammu and Kashmir was not carried out because Pakistan on its part, failed to fulfil the required conditions for plebiscite[12] and later on, even refused to accept United Nations resolution of 13 August 1948 to withdraw its forces from Pakistan Occupied Kashmir.[13]

Moreover, later on, a change occurred in the milieu in the sub-continent due to Pakistan's joining of Western alliances (September 1954, SEATO and February 1955, Baghdad pact, later known as CENTO). With these alliances, Pakistan received substantial military and economic aid, which changed the whole context of Kashmir issue and this brought the USA-USSR cold war to the doorsteps of the Indian subcontinent.[14]

With the change of the environment in the subcontinent, India decided to withdraw from the commitment it had made to the United Nations regarding plebiscite. As according to a reputed expert on Kashmir, Surendra Chopra, the Indian representative (Menon) invoked the doctrine of *rebus sic stantibus* when he argued that "holding of a plebiscite was out of question since circumstances had changed" due to Pakistan's military alliance and its acquisition of weapons from United States.[15] Hence, the logical conclusion was the withdrawing of the plebiscite offer.

After being failed in its efforts to acquire Kashmir through United Nations with the support of the western powers, Pakistan decided to acquire it with force. So, firstly in 1965 and then in 1971, it tried to merge Kashmir with it through war. On both the occasions, India adopted tough postures and repulsed the Pakistan aggression. The war of 1971 resulted in the disintegration of Pakistan and signing of Shimla agreement in 1972.[16] Under the agreement, both agreed to settle their differences by peaceful means through bilateral negotiations.[17] Thus, India tried to solve the long-standing issue of Jammu and Kashmir with Pakistan, as for the first time, Pakistan accepted Kashmir as a bilateral issue to be solved by discussions between the two countries.

Here, it is to be noted that after the war of 1971, India succeeded in making the Kashmir issue, a bilateral one, yet it failed to take the leverage of its winning position. India had about 93,000 Pakistan Army personnel as prisoners of war and large area of Pakistan was under Indian control.[18] The meekly surrender of advantage was a colossal blunder in its policy as far as Jammu and Kashmir was concerned, as it was the best opportunity available to India to settle the Kashmir issue forever.

After Shimla Agreement, there was not much progress with regard to Jammu and Kashmir and there was a situation of stalemate. As far as Pakistan is concerned, after its failure to acquire Kashmir by force, in late eighties it changed its tactics to capture Kashmir and adopted the policy of "bleeding India through thousand cuts."[19] The discontentment emerging at that time in Jammu and Kashmir against the government of India was fully exploited by Pakistan to avenge the humiliation inflicted upon it by India in East Pakistan in 1971 war. Therefore, Pakistan started aiding secessionist elements in the state of Jammu and Kashmir and provided every support to the insurgents.[20] Violence and the terrorist activities increased day by day. By using its principal agency Inter Services Intelligence (ISI), Pakistan also sent its citizens and

Afghan cadres that it had developed or trained during Afghanistan war, to Jammu and Kashmir. As, after the signing of Geneva Accords, and with the withdrawal of the erstwhile Soviet army from Afghanistan in 1989, Pakistan was left with large number of militants and terrorists unemployed and huge stock of all kinds of weapons.[21] These weapons were diverted for equipping both Kashmiri militants and other *mujahideens* who were earlier busy in Afghanistan. There was thus increase in aid to militants in Kashmir from across the border and Pakistan continued its approach of supporting cross-border terrorism. But, the government of India adopted a soft policy on terrorism. This is indicated by the way the government of India tackled the issue of kidnapping of Rubaiyya Sayeed, the daughter of then Home Minister, Mufti Mohammad Sayeed, in 1989.[22] The surrender of the Indian government by releasing top five militants in exchange of release of Rubaiyya Sayeed signified the weak policy of the government towards terrorism in Jammu and Kashmir. The soft attitude towards terrorism legitimized kidnapping which became common thereafter. We can also take the example of Kandhar Hijack episode of 1999, where the government of India released top militant Masood Azhar along with Ahmed Omar Sheikh and Mushtaq Ahmed Zargar in exchange of passengers and crew members of IC-814 Airlines.[23] Masood Azhar, after the release, formed *Jaish-e-Mohammed* which is responsible for many terrorist attacks in Jammu and Kashmir and other parts of the country.

Apart from these, there is no consensus regarding the Kashmir issue in India. There are certain persons who favour the option of taking back the part of Jammu and Kashmir from Pakistan by using force, others favour status-quo, which means that we should retain what we have at present. But, the Parliament resolution of 1994 clearly states that the whole of Jammu and Kashmir including the parts occupied by Pakistan is an integral part of India.[24] But the policy adopted by Government of India during the Kargil war, i.e., we will maintain the sanctity of Line of Control,[25] sidelined the resolution of the Parliament.

Again, on the issue of third-party mediation in Jammu and Kashmir, India does not have any clear policy. Through Shimla agreement, the issue of Jammu and Kashmir was made a bilateral issue, but in reality, at different times, New Delhi had asked the international community, particularly the United States, to put pressure on Pakistan to stop-cross border terrorism. Also during the Kargil intrusion, there was a clear indication that government of India was asking the United States to compel Pakistan to withdraw from the areas occupied by it and maintain the sanctity of the Line of Control. Moreover, after the 13 December 2001 attacks on Indian Parliament, the deployment of forces along the international border and Line of control in full military preparedness, was with a purpose of pressurising the United States and other Western powers to coerce Pakistan to stop cross border terrorism against India.[26]

Moreover, Pakistan since 1948, has been projecting the Kashmir problem and the rights of the people in Jammu and Kashmir in various international fora, but India on its part, failed to project the problem of Pakistan occupied Kashmir or highlight Islamabad's annexation of Northern Areas of Pakistan occupied Kashmir and its merger with the mainland. As such, the government of India failed to project its national interest as far as Kashmir issue is concerned. There is no proactive and consistent policy of the government of India to deal with the Jammu and Kashmir issue. The policy of government has been very feeble and always defensive and reactive.

However, in the present globalised world, no country can live in a perpetual war like situation. Since the restoration of the bilateral dialogue in early 2004, the relationship between India and Pakistan has improved. The Confidence Building Measures (CBMs) have become the catchword for the peace process evolving between the two countries. Since than, a plethora of new CBMs have been either in place or have been suggested by one or other side. Under the CBMs, like the opening of borders, transfer of Line of Control (LoC), bus service, increase in people-to-people contacts by easing some visa restrictions, increase in trade and movement across LoC, creating meeting points for divided families, increased pilgrimages and cultural interactions, etc.[27] have been carried out.

These CBMs have created a "feel good" atmosphere between the two countries. This changed situation and the easing of tensions after the peace process between India and Pakistan, have allowed the leaders of both the countries to move a little bit from their long-standing positions over Jammu and Kashmir. This change has been clearly stated by Pakistan's President Pervez Musharraf when he offered to drop Pakistan's traditional demand for a United Nations plebiscite in Kashmir, and meet India "half-way" in a bid to resolve the Kashmir, dispute. Musharraf stated, "...we are for the United Nations Security Council resolutions whatever it stands for. However, now we have left that aside".[28] After the US President George Bush's visit to Islamabad in March 2006, President Musharraf at the time interaction with media insisted that his government was willing to "think outside the box" solutions for resolving the Kashmir issue.[29] Moreover, Musharraf has expressed his views that he is ready to give up Pakistan's claim over Kashmir.[30] This changed position of Pakistan was clarified by Islamabad's Foreign office spokesperson Tasnim Aslam when she said that her country had never claimed Kashmir to be an integral part of Pakistan.[31] All these annotations clearly state a change in Pakistan's policy on Jammu and Kashmir, which since long has been stating that Kashmir is a disputed territory and the resolution of the United Nations regarding plebiscite must be implemented for the resolution of the dispute.

However, on India's part, in a joint press statement of 6 January 2004, on the sidelines of the Twelfth South Asian Association for Regional Cooperation (SAARC) summit in Islamabad, New Delhi undoubtedly agreed that Kashmir was a disputed territory by unambiguously agreeing that Kashmir was to be settled "to the satisfaction of both sides".[32] Again, responding to the General Musharraf's aspirations on Kashmir, Manmohan Singh told British journalist Jonathan Power, "Short of secession, short of redrawing boundaries, the Indian establishment can live with anything".[33] Moreover, Prime Minister Manmohan Singh has stated many times that "borders cannot be changed, but they can be made irrelevant". He further elaborated, "...there cannot be question of divisions or fresh partitions, but the Line of Control can become a line of peace with a freer flow of ideas, goods, services and people."[34] These comments clearly state a shift in India's policy on Jammu and Kashmir, as since independence, India has been stating that whole of Jammu and Kashmir (including Pakistan Occupied Kashmir) is part of Indian Union.

This flexibility in the long stated rigid stands of both New Delhi and Islamabad, positive approach towards the issue, peace process and the Confidence Building Measures, etc. have created a positive bent of mind, of the people of both the countries in support of peace. This change in the milieu, in the long run, will force the political leaders to settle the conflicting issues once for all, which will facilitate the process of regional cooperation and economic integration of South Asian states.

To conclude, it is time, for both India and Pakistan, to take advantage of the conducive atmosphere, take the peace process ahead, come up with more confidence building measures, introduce more trade links, and introduce measures that will mutually benefit the two nations. Moreover, in an era of globalization, the national boundaries are bound to melt due to the increasing value of economics in the world. With the stabilization of the region, an economically developed Jammu and Kashmir can become a connecting link for economic union in the subcontinent. Jammu and Kashmir can act as a catalyst for a South Asian Union on the lines of European Union.

Notes and References

1. According to the 1941 census, out of a total 4,021,616 population of the state, 3,100,000 were Muslims and 809,000 Hindus. Cited in Gowher Rizvi, *South Asia in a Changing International Order* (New Delhi: Sage, 1993), p. 45.
2. Ram Krishen Kaul Bhatt, *Political And Constitutional Development Of Jammu and Kashmir* (Delhi: Seema, 1984), pp. 155–156.
3. Notedly, it is admitted by a retired Major General Akbar Khan of Pakistan Army, who played a key role in engineering and managing the tribal infiltration in Kashmir, in his book, "*Raiders in Kashmir*" (Islamabad: National Book Foundation, 1975) – as cited in J.N. Dixit, *India – Pakistan In War And Peace* (New Delhi: Books Today, 2002), p. 113, and also see, Jagmohan, *My Frozen Turbulance In Kashmir* (New Delhi: Allied, 1996), pp. 85–86.
4. For the text of The Instrument of Accession, see, Justice A.S. Anand, *The Constitution of Jammu and Kashmir, Its Developments and Comments*, Third

edition (New Delhi: Universal Law Publications, 1998), Appendix-III, pp. 382–383.

5. As according to the Indian Independence Act, 1947, the rulers were free to join either India or Pakistan as with the lapse of the British paramountcy, the Princely states were free to join either of the dominions. For details see the text of "The Indian Independence Act, 1948", as cited in V.P. Menon, *The Transfer of Power in India* (Calcutta: Orient Longman, 1997), Appendix-XI, pp. 516–532.
6. Somnath Dhar, *Jammu and Kashmir* (New Delhi: National Book Trust, India, 1999), p. 77; also see Bhatt, n. 2, p. 167.
7. Dixit, n. 3, p. 116, and Anand, n. 4, p. 81; also see C. Dasgupta, "Kashmir's 1947: Whodunnit Mountbatten, not Nehru, as villain", *The Times of India* (New Delhi), 10 November, 2001.
8. K.K. Misra, *Kashmir and India's Foreign Policy* (Allahabad: Chugh, 1979), p. 105.
9. For Text of the United Nations Resolution of August 13, 1948, see S.M. Jaffar, *Kashmir Sold and Resold* (New Delhi: Book Land India, 1993), Appendix-I, pp. 257–260.
10. Part I and Part II of the resolution required that all forces regular and irregular under the control of both India and Pakistan shall cease-fire; Pakistan would withdraw its troops, it would endeavour to secure withdrawal of tribesmen and Pakistan nationals and India will withdraw bulk of the forces once United Nations Commission for India and Pakistan (UNCIP) confirms that the tribesmen and Pakistan nationals have withdrawn and Pakistan troops are being withdrawn. *Ibid.*
11. This becomes clear from British Viceroy Lord Mountbatten's daughter Pamela Mountbatten's book – "India Remembered: A personal Account of the Mountbatten's during the Transfer of Power", Cited in "Nehru-Edwina were in deep love, says Edwina's daughter", *Daily Excelsior* (Jammu), 16 July, 2007; also see, "The 370 Noise", *State Times* (Jammu), 5 September, 2007; and "Pamela Mountbatten on the Jawaharlal-Edwina relationship", *The Hindu* (Internet Edition), http://www.thehindu.com/2007/07/18/stories/2007071862131300.htm, 18 July 2007.
12. "Pakistan Wrecked Plebiscite Prospects: Yaswant", *Hindustan Times* (New Delhi), 16 March 2003.
13. *Ibid.*
14. Surendra Chopra, *U.N. Mediation in Kashmir: A Study of Power Politics* (Kurukshetra: Vishal, 1971), pp. 124–125.
15. *Ibid.*, p. 136.
16. For text of the Shimla agreement, see Ved Marwah, *Uncivil Wars: Pathology of Terrorism in India* (New Delhi: Harper Collins Publishers, 1995), Appendix-A, pp. 437–440.
17. *Ibid.*
18. Rizvi, n.1, p. 72.
19. Ashwani Kumar, "Cross Border Terrorism – Historical Perspective", in V.D. Chopra, ed., *Global Challenge of Terrorism* (New Delhi: Gyan Publishing House, 2002), p. 63.
20. For details see, Sumit Ganguly, "India's Territorial Dispute with Pakistan and China: Understanding Security Relations", in P. Sahadevan, ed., *Conflict and*

Peace Making in South Asia (New Delhi: Lancer, 2001), pp. 201–202, and G.M. Shah, "Geo-political and Socio-economic causes of Militancy in Jammu and Kashmir," in V.D. Chopra, ed., *Ibid.,* p. 193.

21. For proliferation of small arms in South Asia, see, Kulwant Kaur, "Proliferation of Small Arms and Light Weapons in South Asia", in Kulwant Kaur and Baljit S. Mann, ed., *South Asia: Dynamics of Politics, Economy & Security* (New Delhi: Knowledge World, 2006), pp. 279–290. These weapons were made available to Pakistan by the United States, Saudi Arabia and other foreign countries to supply to mujahideen to fight the Soviet Union in Afghanistan. Surinder Singh, *Fighting the New Evil of Terrorism* (Jammu: Trikuta, 2000), pp. 302–303; also see Chander K. Khanduri, "The Kashmir Problem and An Approach Towards Solution: Realities and Perspectives", in V.D. Chopra, ed., *Genesis of Indo-Pakistan Conflict on Kashmir* (New Delhi: Patriot, 1990), p. 193.
22. Victoria Schofield, *Kashmir in the Crossfire* (New Delhi: Viva Books, 1997), p. 240.
23. Prabhu Chawla, "Relief and Surrender", *India Today,* Vol. XXV, No. 2, 4–10 January 2000, p. 33.
24. For Text of the Parliament Resolution, see website http://www.aryawat.com/kashmir/parliament.htm.
25. Sunil Narula and Nitin A. Gokhale, "A Step Across the thin line?", *Outlook,* Volume V, No. 25, 5 July 1999, p. 18; also see Colonel Ravi Nanda (AVSM), *Kashmir and Indo-Pak Relations* (New Delhi: Lancer Books, 2001), pp. 144–145.
26. Muchkund Dubey, "Needed: A Kashmir Policy-II", *The Hindu* (Delhi), 22 August 2002.
27. Amit Barwah, "India-Pakistan Peace Process 'Irreversible'," *The Hindu* (Delhi), 19 April 2005, (Internet Edition), http://www.hindu.com/2005/04/19/stories/2005041906030100.htm.
28. "Pakistan makes Kashmir Concessions", *B.B.C. News*, at http://news.bbc.co.uk/2/hi/South_asia/333031.stm, 18 December 2003.
29. "President Musharraf's media interaction after US President visit", Islamabad, at http://www.presidentofPakistan.gov.pk/FlesPressRoom/PressConferences/39200632758AMMedia6thMarch.Pdf, 5 March 2006.
30. "Clues to Kashmir peace puzzle", *The Hindu* (Delhi), 13 December 2006; also see Nirupam Subramanian, "Kashmir How Pakistanis View the Shift", *The Hindu* (Delhi), 15 December 2006.
31. *Ibid.*
32. "India-Pakistan Joint Press Statement", at http://www.indianembassy.org/press_release/2004/Jan/07.htm, 6 January 2004.
33. G. Parthasarathy, "Pak Nuclear Blackmail Remains: Natwar Singh's Doctrine is Unrealistic", *The Tribune* (Internet Edition), http://www.tribuneindia.com/2004/20040617/edit.htm, 17 June 2004.
34. "Singh Pledges to Work with Pakistan for Kashmir Peace", International The News, http://www.thenews.com.pk/top_story_detail.asp?Id=9048, 24 October 2007.

16

India's Energy Security Policy

R.S. Yadav

The end of cold war has not only led to bizarre transformations in the international system, but also brought change in the concept of security. During the cold war era security had been perceived mainly as territorial and military oriented, whereas in the present it is variously called comprehensive security, human security, non-military security, non traditional security, etc. not restricted to military affairs but incorporating political, social, economic and environmental issues.[1] As a result, threat to security has not only been limited to territorial sovereignty but also includes poverty, oppression, social injustice and ecological degradation. Therefore, objective of security goes beyond achieving an absence of war to encompass the attainment of democracy, sustainable economic development, social justice and protection of environment. Hence, energy security became one of the major components of security by the state. This became all the more important in case of India with the adoption of structural reform process since 1991. In the current process of globalization India has projected 8 to 9 per cent growth target of its GDP in the next decade. This is likely to involve large scale progress both in its infrastructural and industrial development. For this consumption of huge energy is not only required to meet out this demand, but it will be an area of prime concern for the policy makers in the country. Consequently, due to the above twin development, energy security has acquired important place in India's foreign policy orientations in the post-cold war era. Besides, its importance also lies with the fact that "unlike other non-military aspects of security, energy security has had the most direct connection with the narrow, military concept of security."[2] Thus, due to the growing demand for energy for the economic development of the country as well as the competitive-influence-building policies of the powers to capture the economic resource rich areas have made it a matter of serious concern for the policy makers in India. That is why, here a modest attempt has been made to analyze and evaluate India's energy security policy vis-à-vis its comparative position with other key players. Simultaneously, an effort is made to examine how India's foreign policy is going to project its energy interests in this unequalitarian order not only by fulfilling its own needs but also by prolonging the development by preserving the environmental concerns of the humanity.

I

Economic development is the core objective of any country's foreign policy after territorial security. In this context, energy security acquires prominence. In broad sense it is the assurance of continuous flow of resources to meet the energy needs of the country. It is to be sustained by developing the available sources in the country, as well as, getting the deficit obtained from outside. It involves all types of activities like exploration, production, import, acquisition of acreages, strategic resources, etc for the perennial flow of energy. Thus, energy security has been well defined by European Commission as "the ability to ensure that future essential energy needs can be met, both by means of adequate domestic resources worked under economically acceptable conditions or maintained as strategic reserves, and by calling upon accessible and stable external sources supplemented where appropriate by strategic stocks."[3]

Before a detail analysis of India's energy security policy is made at the outset it must be categorically clear that: (i) India's energy security issue should be understood in the over all context of global availability of various resources and the competitive-influence-building activities of the major powers; (ii) availability of these natural resources should be looked into the context of demand for sustainable development; and (iii) the exploration and development of resources should be linked to global concerns for environment.

The common sources of India's energy are coal, oil, natural gas, nuclear, thermal, solar, wind, geothermal, tidal and hydroelectric. But major sources which have foreign policy linkages are oil, natural gas and nuclear fuel. Hence, present discussion is limited to explore these three issues and their likely fallout for India's foreign policy in general and energy security in particular.

Oil

(a) *Domestic Production:* India had 5.6 billion barrels of proven oil reserves as of January 2007, the second largest amount in Asia-Pacific region (behind China). Much of its crude oil reserves are located off the Western Coast (Bombay High) and in the Northeast (Assam) of the country, although substantial undeveloped reserves are located in the offshore Bay of Bengal and Rajasthan. But with the impressive growth rate during the last few years, India is also becoming a significant consumer of energy resources. Presently, it is fifth largest consumer of oil in the world. Its annual oil production is about 32 to 33 million tonne, while its consumption is approximately 135 to 140 million tonne. Hence, the gap between its production and consumption is very huge and having tremendously increasing annually which is evident from following Figure:

Figure 16.1[4]: India's Oil Production and Consumption, 1990-2006

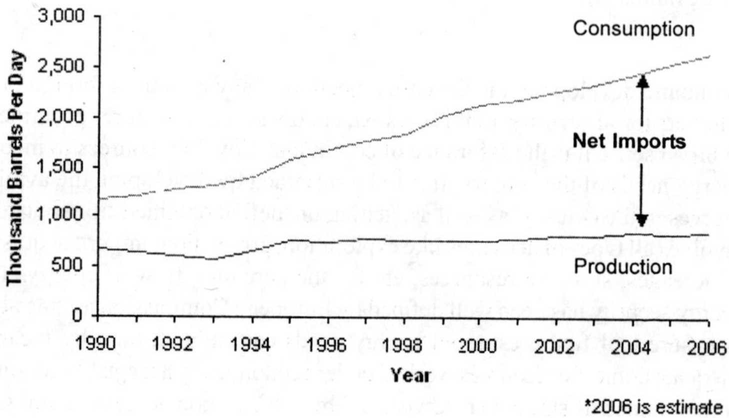

Source: EIA *International Energy Anuual 2004; Short-Term Energy Outolook* (Jan. 2007)

The above gap is being filled up from the import of oil from outside. Hence, India imports 70 per cent of its crude needs mainly from the Gulf States and it is being projected that by 2020 India's dependence on oil imports is likely to be around 91 per cent. This huge imports has serious bearing for its economy as it is likely to have tremendous increase in the import bill, which is manifest from the Table 16.1.

Table 16.1[5]**:** The Rising Import Bill

Year	*Quantity (mmt)*	*Value (Rs. crore)*
1996–97	33.9	18,337
1997–98	34.4	15,872
1998–99	39.8	19,907
1999–2k	57.8	40,028
2000–01	74.1	65,932
2001–02	84.9	80,116
2002–03	90.0	85,042
2003–04	95.0	93,159
2004–05(estimated)	100.5	1,30,000

To meet out the deficit, India has involved private companies in domestic explorations and overseas exploration and production. However at domestic level, except for Reliance, most of the production remained in the hands of Indian Oil Cooperation. Hence, scenario did not change much.

(b) *Oil Exploration and Import:* At external level, Approach Paper to Ninth Five-Year Plan (1997–2002) recommended the acquisition of acreage in other countries.[6] As a result, by January 2007, ONGC Videsh Ltd. (OVL) has acquired 25 oil and natural gas projects in 17 countries spanning Africa, Asia and Latin America. Consequently, India is making an annual investment of US $ 1 billion in Sudan, Russia, Libya, Vietnam, Iran, Syria, Lebanon, Kazakhstan, Indonesia, Iraq, Myanmar, Bangladesh and Sri Lanka. India's major equity stakes are:

- India invested US $750 million to acquire 25 per cent equity in Sudan's Greater Nile Petroleum Operating Company (GNPOC) in 2003. The GNPOC acreage in Sudan holds proved crude oil reserve of more than one million barrels, and current production levels from the 8 main GNPOC fields exceeds 3 lakh bbl/d. This company also operates a 935-mile crude oil pipeline that pumps oil to Port Sudan for export. India has its largest investment in this region and already four shipments have been received by now.
- India's OVL has obtained a 20 per cent stake in Sakhalin-I in Russia at a cost of US $1.7 billion and the field became operational in 2005 and reached a production of 2,50,000 bbl/d till 2007. India is involved in the project through a consortium arrangement with Exxon-Mobil, Sodeco and the Russian Companies R N Astra and SMNG. Exxon Mobil is the operator. India's share in the first six or seven years is about 5 million tonnes a year, which included Russia's share as part of the repayment for a loan to the Russian government. After the loan is paid, India's share tapers off to 2.5 million tonnes a year. Gas production in this region also started this year.
- In Kazakhstan, OVL has submitted a bid for minority stakes in Kurmangazy oil field which is being shared by Russia and Kazakhstan. This venture is likely to give India a toehold of recoverable reserves. It is also considering acquiring a 15 per cent stake in Alibekmola, a discovered field, currently controlled by Canadian firm Nelson Resources. To support energy security interests in Central Asia, India has already stationed troops in Tajikistan, provided it with US $40 million aid package and undertook to refurbish an air base near Tajik capital Dushanbe.
- Other state in Africa from where India is importing around 15 million tones of oil annually is Nigeria. Since August 2000 the contract with Nigeria is being renewed annually.[8] With Angola it tried hard to enter into agreements but failed. It also has agreements with Ivory Coast and Ghana about oil explorations.

Despite its explorations elsewhere, West Asia continues to be India's greatest source of energy need as it continues to import at least 65 per cent of its oil from this region. Saudi Arabia, Iran and Iraq continue to be its biggest source despite turbulence in this area.

(c) *Strategic Petroleum Reserve* – India is also planning a strategic petroleum reserve and for this construction of storage tanks with 36.7 million barrels of crude oil has been approved. Mangalore, on the western coast, has been considered as site for such purpose. About the actual quantity of reserve and when to fill up such tanks are yet to be decided by the government. It is being handled by a state owned organization Indian Strategic Petroleum Reserve Cooperation Limited.

Natural Gas

(a) *Domestic Scenario* — As on January 2007, the proven natural gas reserves of India have reached 38 trillion cubic feat (tcf). The bulk of India's production comes from Bombay High, Assam, Andhra Pradesh and Gujarat. If 2004 statistics are taken India produced 996 billion cubic feat (bcf) and consumed 1089 billion cubic feat (bcf). India is making explorations in offshore Bay of Bengal, Krishna-Godavari basin and Mahanadi Basin. Though government owned companies are doing the main task, yet partnership of private sector is also being invoked by involving Reliance Company in the Krishna-Godavari basin. BG International and Reliance are also jointly working to expand production at the Tapti, Panna and Mukti fields in Bombay High. Through various exploration activities, it is expected that by 2009 India is going to double its production of natural gas. Despite the large gas explorations, however, most observers feel that India's demand is likely to outstrip its production soon. During the last five years its consumption of natural gas is increasing very fast.

(b) *Gas Imports*— India imports natural gas from abroad to meet its current needs and future demands. In this context, it is seriously working on imports through pipelines. Though pipelines are generally the most economic mode of transportation, yet it involves the problem of route security, huge investments and has serious political implications.[9] At present discussions on the construction of three pipelines are going on and final decisions have not been arrived at. One such project is to build a Iran-Pakistan-India pipeline to the length of 1700 miles to run from South Pars fields in Iran to the Indian state of Gujarat. The discussions are going on since 1994 but variety of political and economic issues, involving both global and regional politics are preventing the finalization of such process.[10] Since February 2006, India is also making efforts to join Turkmenistan-Afghanistan-Pakistan 1050 mile pipeline originating from Turkmenistan's Dauletabad-Donmext natural gas fields. But the security threats emanating from instability and terrorism from Afghanistan and Pakistan are major irritants in this project. Besides, availability of adequate quantity of gas from Turkmenistan is also preventing the finalization of such deal. In March 2006, India signed a deal with

Myanmar, but specific about pipelines, whether through Bangladesh or through its eastern border to Tripura, is yet to be finalized. Import of small amount of natural gas from Bangladesh is also feasible, but internal politics in that country is preventing its decision in favour of New Delhi.

(c) *Import of LNG*— Currently India is also involved in the purchase of Liquefied Natural Gas (LNG) from abroad and building of terminals to receive such imports. Since 2004 it is importing LNG from Oman and Qatar to its Dahej terminal in Gujarat. This facility is being owned and operated by Petromet LNG, a consortium of state-owned Indian Companies and international investors. Its second terminal, which became operational in 2005, is again in Gujarat near Surat, It is being operated by Hazira LNG, a joint venture of Shell and Total. India is also building another such terminal at Kochi, which is likely to be completed by the year 2009.

Nuclear Energy

India launched its nuclear programme, under the leadership of Homi Bhabha, for nation's security and self-reliance in its energy needs. As a result, its nuclear power programme commenced in 1963 with the building of Tarapur Atomic Power Stations (TAPS I & II) employing Boiling Water Reactors (BWRs) with American assistance. Later, Rajasthan Atomic Power Stations (RAPS I & II), based on Pressurized Heavy Water Reactors (PHWRs), were established with the help of Canada. At present, India has 15 operating nuclear power reactors and 8 more under various stages of construction or commissioning.[11] Through these reactors India has planned to attain 10,000 mws nuclear power by 2010; 20,000 mws by the year 2020; and, 50,000 mws by the year 2050. But presently it is just producing 8,400 mws from its 12 reactors with a capacity of 700 mws each. In the given scenario, at very conservative estimates, India requires at least 1000 mws from each reactor in addition to its existing capacities. Despite all these India's meeting of energy target has been very low to the tune of approximately 3 per cent, where as US nuclear share of electricity generation is about 19 per cent, Japan utilizes about 30 per cent, and France utilizes nearly 78 per cent and the over all electricity generation by nuclear powers in the world is 17 per cent.[12]

But main problem for India, to enhance its nuclear energy use, is the shortage of nuclear fuel in the form of uranium. It is because the known uranium resources in Jaduguda mines are depleting fast and Department of Atomic Energy (DAE) is unable to start fresh mining in Domiasiat in the Northeast and Nalagond in Andhra Pradesh due to local opposition to uranium mining. Besides, Indian natural uranium ores are of very low grade nature. Finally, the uranium produced in India is roughly six to seven times more costly as compared to the prices available in the international market.[13]

Consequently, India has been in desperate need for nuclear fuel to meet out its future energy needs. Most important priority at this stage is to give attention to three important issues: (a) procuring natural uranium fuel for its PHWRs to consolidate the indigenous three-stage nuclear power programme envisaged by Bhabha; (b) continuity of enriched uranium fuel supply for Tarapur reactors at least for the next 10 years; and (c) to seek US assistance in facilitating nuclear supplier groups (NSG's) clearance for opening of the way to imports of nuclear fuel.[14] In the light of these requirements, India started making efforts to collaborate with the USA in the area of nuclear programmes. In the post-*Pokhran*-II era, USA was also interested in engaging India in the nuclear non-proliferation activities, not insisting on signing the NPT or CTBT.[15]

As a result, during Manmohan Singh's Visit to the USA on 18 July 2005, both India and America agreed to cooperate in the area of "peaceful nuclear energy related initiatives".[16] Later on 2 March 2006, during the visit of President George Bush to India, both countries agreed to proceed further by agreeing to separate India's civil and military nuclear programmes. India agreed that by 2014, it will separate its nuclear reactors into two categories of civilian and military use reactors and 65 per cent of them, put in civilian category, will be placed under the inspection of IAEA.[17] Later on due to some compulsions of domestic politics on 18 December 2006 'Henry J. Hyde, US-India Peaceful Atomic Energy Cooperation Act of 2006' was passed by the USA, which placed certain restrictions on India. As a result, it invoked serious criticism by different strata of society in India.[18] But continuous diplomatic efforts on both sides did not allow the process to derail, rather on 1 August 2007 both signed a draft agreement for cooperation in the peaceful uses of nuclear energy between the two countries.[19] But in India, Left parties, the coalition partners of the UPA government, made serious criticism and did not allow the ruling party to enter into such agreement. And when they failed to prevent the government to sign such agreement, they left the coalition partnership in protest. Besides, they also made public the notes exchanged between the UPA and Left committee on this issue.[20]

But if an objective analysis is made in this regards then one can find that India's military alignment with the USA has not evolved due to the current 123 agreement, rather it evolved through numerous military-to-military cooperation activities pursued by India and the USA initiated in the form of Kickleighter proposal 1991; ten-years defence agreement 1995; incident of 9/11; formation of High Technology Cooperation Group (HTCG) 2002; development of Next Step in Strategic Partnership (NSSP) 2004; and finally defence framework cooperation agreement of June 2005.[21] In continuation of its earlier efforts, Government of India sent a draft proposal for its approval to the IAEA on 7 September 2008, which got passed through consensus voting in the international body.[22] Later the similar agreement got waiver from the 45-member body of NSG. As a result, India signed bilateral agreements on civil nuclear energy cooperation with France (30 September 2008), USA (10 October 2008) and Russia (5 December 2008). Though some expert are still of the view that signing of 123 Agreement with the USA is not going to allow India a level playing field as both domestic laws of the US and involvement of NSG Countries at implementation stage are bound to make India Vulnerable to the vagaries of the global market and undue pressure from the USA.[23] Whatever be going to be the politics in future, it is certain that present deal has provided opening for India's import of nuclear fuel from 45-member NSG countries. Besides, at this stage it was very essential for India to meet out its both present and future energy requirements. Moreover, it is viewed that fresh uranium supply from these states is going to boost power generation of existing six nuclear plants. Presently, they are functioning at almost one-third of their installed capacities due to lack of fuel, but with the receipt of likely supply of uranium by April 2009 they are likely to work with their full capabilities.[24]

Coal

Coal is the predominant energy source for power production in India, generating approximately 70 per cent of its total domestic electricity needs. Visualizing the energy demands of the future, coal, along with oil and natural gas, is going to remain an important source of power generation. Current production of coal in India is 290 million tones per year, but its demand is going to be more than double by the year 2010. Major coal fields are found in Jharkhand, West Bengal and Madhya Pradesh. The Indian government controls almost all coal production, which has been plagued by low productivity, distribution problems, and an increasing loss of domestic market share to higher quality and less expensive imports. Nearly all of India's 390 mines are under Coal India Limited (CIL), which accounts for about 90 per cent of the country's coal production.[25] Though in terms of use of coal in power production India is going to remain self-sufficient in the next 100 years, yet because of higher ash content and the peculiar chemical and combustion properties of Indian coal will necessitate substantial modification of the technologies available with foreign companies to suit India's fuel resources.[26] To this limited extent foreign policy outlook of India will be affected in the context of development of energy through coal.

II

Policy Options for India

Now questions arise: What are the strategies needed for the Indian policy makers? What are the initiatives required at this juncture to meet out the energy security requirements of the country? How India is making re-orientation in its foreign policy in the changed context? These are facts that presently Indian foreign policy is making efforts to adjust itself into the changed regional and global milieu. It is also making efforts to realize its changed priorities in the contemporary world order. To attain its core objectives in appropriate manner India's policy makers need to adopt multi-pronged strategies making new permutations and combinations visualizing changes both in the regional and global power structure. In the realm of energy security following options seem imminent for its policy makers.

(i) Changed scenario reveals that presently most of the energy sources are located in Asia and Africa. The new regions in Africa, Central Asia and states in Southeast Asia are emerging as new centres of natural gas and oil, besides the already existing West Asian oil. In this context, new India-China partnership could serve as the foundation for an Asian energy union, as both are not only emerging as fast growing economies, but are also competing for oil exploration and production in these states. By signing an agreement on 12 January 2006 between ONGC Videsh Limited and CNPC for joint bidding of oil exploration projects, at the time of visit of the then Indian Minister of Petroleum and Natural Gas to Beijing, both have made a good beginning. Such kinds of agreements may open the new vistas for energy cooperation in the form of recovery technologies for ageing oil fields and basin evaluation and drilling rigs by China and IT-enabled exploration and production services of India. Both can also help each other in transport mechanism including pipeline and use of backhaul cargoes in very large crude carriers. Ultimately this cooperation may facilitate the growth of Asian market. Though role of Western powers and their border problems may work as irritants, yet the larger economic interests may overcome such hurdles.

(ii) Developments in last few years show that Russia under Putin is emerging as world's biggest single producer of hydrocarbons. It is also positioning itself for the role of main motor and coordinator of new global strategy for energy security. In this context, it is eager to link itself with the Asian countries by offering to help guarantee the energy security and its readiness to provide long term and stable supplies of energy resources. It is also eager to join with them in joint projects of exploration of oil and natural gas fields in Russia and a third country. It is keen on evolving joint venture for the construction of pipelines for transportation of oil and gas. India being a close friend of Russia can explore these possibilities in a very positive manner. As explained earlier, it has already invested US $1.7 billion for the exploration of Sakhalin-I and is reaping the fruits of such cooperation since 2005. Emerging India-China and India-Russia Cooperation, along with their commonalities of interests in Central Asian Republics, can work as cementing force to strengthen their ties.

(iii) Availability of oil surrounding Caspian Sea has brought Central Asia to the forefront of global oil diplomacy.[27] Competitive-influence-building efforts of powers have begun in Central Asian Republics (CARs) due to the availability of natural resources in the form of oil and gas. Multinational companies of Italy, Britain, USA, along with Russia's Gazprom started fighting for their influence. Even the states surrounding Caspian Sea are fighting for their sovereign rights and pipeline issues. The USA is also making efforts in devising pipelines in a way to deprive Russian hold. But developments in last few years have consolidated the Russian hold more than anybody else. Even in the regional forum like SCO, Russian predominance is clearly manifest. China through building pipelines and rail road linkages has established its hold in some of the republics. Here China is also collaborating with Russia in its anti-Western outlook in the SCO. India is also making efforts by collaborating with some of the republics and also joining the SCO as an 'observer' country. But it has to do a lot more to take benefit of this region's oil and gas resources. It has to give clear support to pipeline construction from this region to South Asia, despite USA's opposition to such activities.

(iv) India's ONGC Videsh Limited is making huge investment in 17 countries abroad for exploration and production of oil and gas. But geography plays very important role in creating impediments for utilization of such resources. Even if that is overcome costs rise to prohibitive level. Therefore, there is need that India's energy security be ineluctably linked to its neighbourhood. This reality should not be ignored by the policy makers. Fortunately India is ringed by gas rich neighbourhood—Myanmar, Bangladesh, Turkmenistan and Iran. Concentration on these neighbours, on the one hand, will make the easy availability of oil and gas at cheap rates, and on the other hand, the goodwill with them will ensure supply through pipeline from far off lands in non-interruptive and continuous manner. The promise of collateral gains from the 'peace pipeline' is indeed too alluring to be ignored by any one of them. Hence, in a world that is decisively gravitating towards regional coalitions and groupings based on economic cooperation, India's linking of its energy security benefits with its neighbours can not be ruled out.

(v) In the given scenario nuclear energy can work as a very important component in India's energy security, it is because India's nuclear programme since its inception had major focus on its civilian use. However there is scarcity of availability of fuel for indigenous energy production. In this context, stalling the signing of Indo-US nuclear civil energy deal seems to based on ignorance[28] and misperception among people and officials.[29] Even the objections by the left parties, as discussed earlier, which consider this deal as against India's strategic national interest also do not seem tenable. Experts are of the view that these apprehensions are baseless.[30] Visualizing it as very important for the pursuit of nuclear technologies for the benefit of the nation even prominent nuclear scientists have made an open appeal to parliamentarians to clear this deal.[31] Besides, without opening with NSG to run a nuclear programme on a large scale is not possible. Even opening IAEA inspections in no way affects our secrecy, as six reactors are already working under such inspection. Moreover, this deal is permitting the supply of nuclear fuel to India without signing the NPT and in no way restricts India's options to the US alone. Rather the majority of reactors in India are PHWRs type for which US has no expertise. Thus, leaving India outside the international regime is not going to resolve its energy needs.[32]

III

But to exercise the above policy options is not without problems. Numerous geo-political and geo-economic issues are going to affect future course of energy security of India. Following factors are likely to work as major irritants in this process:

(i) For its energy needs India is mainly dependent on import of oil from West Asia. This region, due to its geo-strategic location and geological resources, is highly politicized and threat prone. Inter-state and intra-state rivalries and warfare, including interventions by the powers, has been routine affair in this area. Even embargoes on the production and supply of oil have been very frequent. Consequently, continuous political instabilities and turmoil are not ruled out. However one can't deny this fact that political stability works as an important ingredient in oil production and price stability. Prices are also affected by the scarcity of availability of these resources in future. Both these factors have raised the price to an exorbitant level of more then US $100 from nearly US $20 a decade ago. Therefore, the growing instability in the region and soaring prices of oil may create problem of availability and financial difficulties for India.

(ii) The region of West Asia is criss-crossed with the oil pipelines and dotted by oil and gas fields, handling facilities and export terminals. Presently, India is also planning to import oil and natural gas from West Asia and Central Asia through pipelines. But most of the pipelines have to pass through the turmoil prone countries of Afghanistan and Pakistan. The presence of terrorism in these states has made the task more difficult. Sometimes even politics and need of huge financial investments are also creating problems. Even natural gas from Myanmar, being off shore, it can be accessed only after laying a pipeline undersea or overland through Bangladesh. But whether Bangladesh would be willing to allow the pipeline to be routed through its territory and the security of such a pipeline would be paramount concerns which would decide the pace of monetization of this available gas.

(iii) Use of piped gas or liquefied natural gas (LNG) will be dependent upon the associated infrastructure (LNG regassification facilities or pipelines) and the price of the gas. Though India is importing huge LNG from Oman and Qatar, it is much costlier as compared to the cost of natural gas. This also requires construction of LNG terminals which pose serious security risks and are attractive targets for terrorists. In terms of price, India follows dual producer pricing formula. While international oil companies (IOC) producing gas in India are paid a price that is linked to an index of fuel oils, whereas domestic gas producer (ONGC) is paid a cost plus price. Besides, ONGC absorbs the difference between the price paid to IOCs and the price charged to domestic consumers. But as share of IOC gas in the total domestic gas production goes up and LNG imports increase, it would be difficult to maintain dual pricing system. [33] This increase in price may create problem in Indian market as well, as it may make cost of electricity generation through gas a prohibitive option.

Above problems can be resolved by taking steps in the direction of policy improvement and domestic reorientations. At policy level, formulation of *Hydro-Carbon Vision 2025* is good beginning but a lot needs to be done to formulate an integrated and comprehensive energy security policy. A full desk dealing with oil diplomacy on regular basis must be set up in the MEA to coordinate such activities of different concerned ministries. Such policy should focus on the activities like developing relations with energy resource countries, ensuring uninterrupted supplies of oil and gas, making strategies to deal with oil organization regimes, etc. It should also make effort to evolve collective thinking for sustainable development of energy resources. It should also try to create a balance between nuclear technologies and fuel dominant group led by the USA and the emerging hydrocarbon suppliers' states of Russia and China. As India is in need of both nuclear power, as well as, oil and natural gas for its energy requirements, a delicate balance between them is not only essential, but inevitable.

Simultaneously, policy initiatives are also required at domestic level. Its present dependence on imported oil must be reduced by the use of renewable energy sources available in the country. Utilization of clean coal technologies should be encouraged. Shift may be made towards next generation fuels from bio-mass technologies. To make improvement in the production of domestic oil and gas, efforts are also needed to enhance energy efficiency mechanisms at various levels. Through various fiscal, legal and regulatory methods an attractive environment for FDI and joint ventures should be created. Improvement in the overall basic infrastructure, suited to the new global business culture, is also needed. Thus, efforts at both the levels are pre-requisite for the growth of a healthy, long term, and smooth energy security policy.

IV

From the above it can be concluded that the end of cold war has led to redefining the concept of security and beginning of the process of globalization. Now considering security as a holistic concept, energy security has become its important component. Impressive growth of Indian economy, as a result of globalization, has further boosted its energy needs. These changes have led to reorientation in India's domestic and foreign policy outlook. The issue of energy security has become very important, in the context of its increased need for oil, natural gas and nuclear fuel, which has resulted in a shift in India's foreign policy. Among the three segments oil will continue to affect its foreign policy decisions in the times to come. Hence its foreign relations with the countries of West Asia and Central Asian Republics will continue to remain important. This thrust will also consolidate ties with Russia and China to great extent. Even its regional cooperation through forums like SCO and consolidation with Asian energy groups are likely to strengthen. The need for energy will also work as compulsions to take policy initiative towards the improvement of relations with neighbouring states in the West (Afghanistan and Pakistan) and East (Myanmar and Bangladesh). Simultaneously, India's thrust to fulfill its nuclear fuel requirements is likely to consolidate its ties with the NSG countries in general and USA, France, Russia in particular. Though efforts may be made at domestic level to enhance alternative fuel and renewable source of energy, yet for some more time its focus is likely to remain on the above three core areas. Accordingly, India's foreign policy options remain directed towards the optimum utilization of its available resources in the context of changing energy security needs vis-à-vis new emerging global milieu.

Notes and References

1. For details see, Kanti Bajpai, "The Idea of Human Security", *International Studies*, 40(3), 2003; Dipankar Banerjee, "Towards Comprehensive and Cooperative Security in South Asia", *South Asian Survey*, 6 (2), 1999; and Takashi Inoguchi, "Political Security: Towards a Broader Conceptualization", *International Studies*, 40 (2), 2003.
2. Gulshan Dietl, "New Threats to Oil and Gas in West Asia: Issues in India's Energy Security", *Strategic Analysis*, 28 (3), July-September 2004, p. 374.
3. Cited in Gawdat Bahgat, "Central Asia and Energy Security", *Asian Affairs*, 37 (1), March 2006, p. 1.
4. Source: Energy Information Administration, *International Energy Annual, 2004* (Washington, 2005).
5. Source: Govt. of India, Ministry of Petroleum & Natural Gas, *Annual Report, 2005* (New Delhi, 2005).
6. Govt. of India, Planning Commission, *Approach Paper to the Ninth Five Year Plan, 1997–2002* (New Delhi, 1997).
7. This equity was purchased from Candian Talesman Energy Inc. which had to

withdraw from Sudan on pressure from Human Rights Group in their country. Other stoke holders in that company are China National Petroleum Company (CNPC 40%), Petrones (30%) and Sudan National Oil Company (Sudapet 5%).

8. India's detailed imports from Nigeria from 1999 to 2005 has been as under:

India' Oil Import from Nigeria

Year	*Quantity (mmt)*	*Value (US $ mn.)*
1999–2000	15.450	2595.7
2000–2001	12.570	2140.4
2001–2002	11.320	2001.9
2002–2003	11.578	2389.0
2003–2004	11.074	2393.0
2004–2005	15.081	N.A.

Source: Ruchita Beri, "Africa's Energy Potential: Prospects for India", *Strategic Analysis,* 29(3), July-September 2005, p. 381.

9. For details see, S.D. Muni and Girjesh Pant, *India Search for Energy Security* (New Delhi, Rupa, 2003); Kuldip Singh, "Iran-Pak-India Gas Pipeline and Energy Security", *Punjab Journal of Politics*, 30(1), 2006; and Rahul Roy Chowdhary, "An Energy Security Policy for India: The Case of Oil and Gas", *Strategic Analysis*, 21 (II) February 1998.
10. For details see, Singh, *Ibid*, pp. 1–20, Also see, Bhagyashree Pande, "US Threatens Sanctions Over Indo-Iran Gas Pipelines", *The Pioneer*, 22 May 2005; and, Seema Sudhir, "Iran-India Pipeline: One Step Forward, To Steps Back", *Mainstream*, XLIII (30), 3 September 2005.
11. Details of the Indian power reactors are as under:
    (i) Pressurised Heavy Water Reactors (PHWRs) 18 (Canada & Indigenous)
    (ii) Boiling Water Reactors (BWRs) 02 (USA)
    (iii) Pressurised Water Reactors (PWRs) 02 (USSR)
    (iv) Prototype Fast Breeder Reactors (PFBRs) 01 (Indigenous)
    A. Gopalakrishnan, "Indo-US Nuclear Cooperation: A Non-Starter?", *Economic and Political Weekly*, 2 July 2005, p. 2935.
12. "N-Power Generates 17 per cent of World's Electricity", *Times of India*, 25 July 2005.
13. Gopalakrishnan, n.11, p. 2936.
14. *Ibid*, p. 2937.
15. This is very much evident from 14 rounds of talks held between Jaswant Singh, the then External Affairs Minister of India, and Strobe Talbott, the then US Deputy Secretary of State of the USA, during 1999 to 2001. For detail see, Strobe Talbott, *Engaging India: Diplomacy, Democracy and the Bomb*, (New York: Brookings Institution Press, 2004)
16. For details see, "Prime Minister Manmohan Singh's Visit to the US", *Strategic Digest*, 35(8), August 2005; and, http://meaindia.nic.in/treatesagreconent/2005/18ta 1807200507.tm
17. For details see, Venkateshwaran, "Indo-US Relations: Recent Developments", IPCS Special Report no. 19, May 2006, www.ipcs.org/countspecialreport. Also see Ajey Lele, "Nuclear Indulgence to India: Will US Congress Relent?",

www.ipcs.org.article no. 1975, 22 March 2006; and, Manish Dabhade, "Indo-US Nuclear Deal: New Realism", www.ipcs.org.article no. 1958, 7 March 2006.

18. For details on Left Parties Statement on the Indo-US Bilateral Nuclear Deal, see, www.mainstreamweekly.net/article 277.html.
19. "Agreement for Cooperation Between the Government of India and the Government of the United States of America Concerning Peaceful Uses of Nuclear Energy", http://wwwhindu.com/nic/123agreement.pdf.
20. Communist Parties feel that this arrangement is likely to make India an ally of the US hegemonic design of power expansion in the post-cold war era. For details see, Communist Party of India (Markist), *et al.*, *Left Stand on the Nuclear Deal: Notes Exchanged in the UPA-Left-Committee on India-US Civil Nuclear Cooperation,* New Delhi, July 2008. Also see, Suresh Srivastava, *Agreement 123: Bharat Ke Gale Ki Fans*, New Delhi, Confluence International, 2007.
21. For details see, Kanti Bajpai, "India-US Relations: Where Are India and the US Heading?" *Economic and Political Weekly*, 6 August 2005, pp. 3577–3581; Achin Vainaik, "Significance of Framework Agreement on Defence", *Economic and Political Weekly*, 6 August 2005, pp. 3581–3585; Verghese Koithara, "India-US Defence Cooperation: Expectation and Prospects", *Economic and Political Weekly*, 6 August 2005, pp. 3585–3589; and, Sukumar Muralidharan, "Partnership and its Discontents", *Economic and Political Weekly*, 6 August 2005. pp. 3589–3591.
22. For details see, "Agreement Between the Government of India and the International Atomic Energy Agency for the Application of Safeguards to Civilian Nuclear Facilities", http://mea.gov.in/pressrelease/2008/07/07pro2.htm.
23. R. Ramachandran, "Nuclear Issues: Waiting Trap", *Frontline*, 7 November 2008, pp. 113–117; and T.S. Subramanian, "Nuclear Issues: Contentious Clauses", *Frontline*, 7 November 2008, pp. 118–120.
24. Proposed capacity and existing status of power generation from six-nuclear reactors it as under:

*Power Generation Capacity of Nuclear Reactors**

(*in MWe*)

Sl. No.	*Name of Reactor*	*Proposed Capacity*	*Existing Output*
1.	Tarapur	1400	511
2.	Kakrapara	440	117
3.	Narora	440	73
4.	Rajasthan	740	252
5.	Kaiga	660	237
6.	Kalpakkam	440	205
	Total	**4120**	**1395**

* *The Hindu*, 30 October 2008

25 "Economic Recovery Propels India's Energy Demand", *Energy Today*, 1(1), March-April 2005, p. 54.

26. A. Gopalakrishnan, "India and the US: For Synergy in Energy", *Frontline*, 31 March 2000, p. 82.

27. For details see, R.S. Yadav and Suresh Dhanda, "Oil Politics of Caspian Sea and Central Asia: Policy Options for India", *Contemporary Central Asia*, X (2), August 2006.
28. O.P. Sabharwal, " Nuclear Ignorance: MPs Must update their knowledge", *The Tribune*, 8 November 2007.
29. Inder Malhotra, "Stalled Nuclear Deal: Gap Between Official and Private reaction", *The Tribune*, 2 November 2007.
30. V.P. Malik, "Strategic Aspect of N-Deal: India Must be Guided by National Interest", *The Tribune*, 7 November 2007; and, Arundhati Ghose, "The 123 Agreement: No Threat to India's Strategic Interests", *The Tribune*, 12 November 2007.
31. These scientists were: H.N. Sethna, M.R. Srinivasan, P.K. Iyengar, A. Goptalakrishanan, S.L. Kati, A.N. Prasad, Y.S.R. Parsad, Placid Rodriquez. "Appeal To Parliamentarians on Nuclear Deal", *The Hindu*, 15 August 2006.
32. M.R. Srinivasan, "Can the Impasse on the Nuclear Deal be Broken?", *The Hindu*, 26 December 2007.
33. Sudha Mahalingam, "Energy and Security in a Changing World", *Strategic Analysis*, 28 (2), April-June 2004, pp. 267–268.
34. For details see, Shebonti Ray Dhadwal, "India's Energy Security Policy: A Case for Nuclear Power", *Strategic Analysis*, 23(8), November 1999, pp. 1289–1303.

17

India's Foreign Economic Policy[1]

Anand P. Mavalankar

The economic policy of a sovereign state in its external sector assumes special significance when the concerned nation chooses to recast its policy measures both in response to the country's political and economic environment, as well as a growing consensus within the country about the content and direction of its overall domestic and foreign economic policy. India's foreign economic policy in the 1990s resembles this 'scenario. In July 1991, the Congress Government's Central Budget for the 1991–92 financial year had specific provisions to liberalise India's economy, in terms of decontrolling certain industries as well as ensuring greater liberalisation of India's foreign trade. It marked a genuine departure in India's quest for liberalisation, thereby integrating India's economy with the world economy. This essay aims to identify and discuss some of these policy changes, with the ultimate objective of elucidating the underlying rationale and nature of India's foreign economic policy in the 21st century.

Background

At the time of India's independence, the prevailing international, political, strategic and economic environment had a bearing on India's role in the post-World War II global order. During the Cold War between the United States and the former Soviet Union in the 1950s, the main concern of India's economic diplomacy was to formulate and implement a "non-aligned" foreign economic policy. It meant that India would secure economic assistance (by way of foreign aid) from all major developed countries for bringing about planned development in its political economy in the formative years of its independence.

In the late 1960s, India's economic diplomacy had to undergo a certain transformation in regard to its external sector. Severe food shortages and other compulsions of domestic political economy forced India to devalue the Indian rupee, as per the advice of the World Bank. In other words, the role of the international financial organizations was critical to the change in India's exchange-rate policy, which was effected on grounds of shoring up India's balance-of-payments position in the long run. It was also considered vital in terms of ensuring that concessional assistance from the World Bank would flow uninterrupted into the Indian economy, thus filling the gap between domestic savings and the needs of investment for the ongoing economic development in India. While it indicated India's commitment to "development" in adverse economic conditions, it underscored "India's compromise with its self-reliant' economic posture in regard to pursuing a ruthlessly independent foreign economic policy.

In the 1970s, certain key developments in the world economy had distinct consequences for India's foreign economic policy. The collapse of the Bretton Woods system in the early 1970s and introduction of flexible exchange-rates affected India's trade position in the world economy, on account of the trade-reducing effects of floating exchange-rates. Secondly, in the wake of the two oil-shocks in 1973 and 1979, India had to pay higher import prices for oil to the "Organization of the Petroleum Exporting Countries (OPEC). As a consequence, India's foreign exchange reserves were considerably" depleted. It produced severe balance of payments difficulties for India at that time. Slower growth in the United States and West European countries in the 1970s led to lesser Indian exports to those countries. On account of the recession in the advanced industrial states in the 1970s, there was a sharp rise in international interest rates. Consequently, the developing countries had to pay higher interest on commercial loans borrowed from the advanced industrial states.

The net effect of the above developments in the international economic environment of India in the 1970s was two-fold. In the first place, severe balance of payments difficulties occurred due to higher import prices and lower export prices. Secondly, India had to borrow loans on higher interest rates, which was an added burden to India's political economy;

In addition to the exogenous shocks to the Indian economy indicated above, there were several endogenous shocks to the economy as well. First of all, India's fiscal and monetary policies were excessively lax, resulting in huge unproductive budgetary expenditures and uncontrolled money supply in the economy. Secondly, there were a variety of price distortions in the domestic economy, which affected the process of resource allocation and public distribution of goods in the economy. Thirdly, public enterprises in the economy were making huge losses. Fourthly, due to excessive protection of the economy, certain gains from international trade were foregone. And last, but not the least, the level of foreign borrowing had gone up as well. These trends severely undermined the growth potential of the Indian economy. Indeed, it led to the questioning of the manner in which India's planned development had been undertaken.

By the end of the 1970s, sharp increases in oil prices and the decline in commodity prices (thus affecting India's export earnings) considerably affected India's balance-of-payments position. India's position was indeed unfavourable, especially due to the second oil shock of 1979–80. Deterioration in terms of trade for India's agricultural commodities, recession in the developed industrial countries and sharp rise in international interest rates – these developments brought about a foreign exchange crunch in India's balance-of-payments (BOP).

India was obliged to negotiate a record loan of $5.6 billion from the International Monetary Fund in November, 1981. The borrowing of the IMF loan in the early 1980s was aimed at stabilising the BOP position of the Indian economy. Due to sharp criticisms in India over the IMF conditionality clauses and some improvement in the foreign exchange position, India did not avail of the last tranche of about $1.1 billion. Apparently, there was no policy consensus in regard to borrowing another IMF loan in the late 1980s under the Rajiv Gandhi government. Notwithstanding India's short-term balance-of-payments difficulties, the V.P. Singh government did not seem inclined to go to the IMF, as it considered the option of borrowing the IMF loan to be detrimental to the overall well-being of the Indian economy.

As far as India's foreign trade in the 1980s was concerned, India's exports to the outside world reached only 6710.7 crores in 1980–81, while imports from the outside world reached 12,549.2 crores. In 1988–89, India's exports to the outside world reached 20,288.9 crores, while its imports reached 27,692.2 crores. India's share of world exports had declined from 2.4 per cent in the early 1950s to 0.4 per cent by the end of the 1980s. The rise in India's imports was due to the liberalisation of the imports policy, as well as the implementation of the New Economic Policy, which paved the way for the external sector to play a significant role in the modernisation of industry.

India's Foreign Economic Policy: A Conceptual Framework

In the above section, the nature of the internal economic environment till the 1980s is briefly alluded to, by way of providing the setting in which India's foreign economic policy (FEP) was to evolve in the 1990s. Before we dwell upon specific components of such policy, it is worthwhile to conceptualise FEP for a fuller understanding of the nature of the FEP of India vis-à-vis the international economic environment, as well as India's internal political-economic landscape.

A sovereign state is usually interested in formulating its FEP with other states as well as international economic institutions within the global economic and financial system. The less-developed countries (LDCs), are particularly in need of financial resources from the advanced industrial states and international economic institutions to fill the gap between domestic savings and the huge sums required for meeting the needs of economic development at home. Secondly, the LDCs have to earn as much foreign exchange as possible by increasing exports to the rest of the international community. This is also vital for paying towards imports of capital goods and other essential items necessary for large-scale industrialization and economic growth in India. Clearly, this constitutes the basic motivation for moulding the FEP of LDCs, such as India.

The foreign economic policy, then, can be defined in the following way. It consists of those economic dimensions of a country's foreign policy, which are determined by domestic political and economic considerations, as well as external political and economic compulsions. So, while aiming at meeting the multiple requirements of the national economy, it responds to the changing international economic environment in accordance with a given state's overall economic and other objectives.

Since the foreign economic policy of a given state evolves amidst the prevailing international economic system, the conceptualization of the FEP must proceed from the systemic level of analysis. As there is unequal distribution of economic needs and capabilities (of states) in the international system, there are bound to be different degrees of dependence upon trade as a component of overall economic activity (proportion of total economic activity accounted for by exports and imports). Secondly, all sovereign states in the system are interdependent in terms of acquiring resources and commodities from other states. In other words, sources of supply and external markets remain outside the boundaries of a sovereign state. By acquiring such resources and generating necessary capabilities, nations tend to acquire economic and political strength in their respective political economies. Notwithstanding the proclamations of "self-reliance" on the part of the sovereign states, states do tend to rely on other states to acquire scarce economic resources and fulfill certain kinds of economic needs.

The prevalence of this "systemic" condition impinges upon the FEP of a given sovereign state. Whether the state can disregard the condition would depend on its various capabilities and the diverse needs of its political economy. The distinction between the advanced industrial states and the LDCs is pertinent here, in the sense that reliance of the LDCs on other states and international economic institutions in the system is quite critical. For one, the LDCs need natural resources (such as minerals) and other economic resources to carry out certain economic tasks in their respective economies. Secondly, they need capital, machinery and technological know-how to develop and modernise their economies. And last, but not the least, they need to diversify their exports to various states, so as to avoid economic dependency on a particular major power.

So, the foreign economic policies of the LDCs evolve in the light of above considerations. The specific foreign policy actions of such states reflect their foreign policy orientations. The term "orientation" denotes "a state's general attitudes and commitments toward the external environment, its fundamental strategy for accomplishing its domestic and external objectives and aspirations."[2] In this connection, Holsti makes the following observation about the choice of a particular strategy by the sovereign state:

> At least four conditions or variables can help account for the selection of any particular strategy. First is the structure of the international system. The patterns of dominance, subordination, and leadership of an international system establish some limits on the freedom of action of the component units. Second, a state's general policy strategy can be linked to the nature of domestic attitudes and social and economic needs. Third, the degree to which policy-makers perceive a persisting external threat to their own values and interests will have great bearing on their orientation toward the external environment. Finally, a state's geographic location, topographical characteristics, and endowment in natural resources can often be linked to its choice of orientations.[3]

So much for the basic elements that need to be woven into the conceptual framework of a given state's foreign economic policy. Keeping them in view, a conceptual framework of India's foreign economic policy can be spelled out in the following way:

(i) The "systemic" condition impinging on India's FEP must be addressed as a key independent variable to explain the overall thrust of FEP at a given point of time. As we have discussed in the first section of this paper, the international economic environment in the 1980s influenced the manner of thinking of the FEP in the 1990s. In fact, the FEP in the 1990s had been geared to realise the objectives of structural adjustment in India's political economy. These objectives include the reduction of a balance of payments deficits, resumption of higher rates of economic growth and achievement of structural changes that would prevent future payments and stabilization problems.

(ii) The dependent variable of FEP must be explained by the nature of the political economy of a given sovereign state. Here, the priorities, needs and interests of the LDCs are clearly distinguishable from those of advanced industrial states. As far as India's foreign economic policy in the 1990s is concerned, India's dependence on oil-imports, need for capital, machinery etc., and the vital necessity of diversification of exports suggest the linkage between the nature of its political economy and its foreign economic policy direction.

(iii) The FEP strategy is conditioned by the structure of the international system, nature of domestic attitudes and social and economic needs, the policy makers' perception of a persisting external threat to their own values and interests and the state's geographic location, topographical characteristics and endowment in natural resources. The decline in concessional assistance, and domestic socio-economic pressures for containing inflation and promoting economic growth, are factors that have shaped the outline of India's foreign economic policy strategy in the 1990s.

The above elements of the conceptual framework of India's foreign economic policy are discussed in the subsequent sections, with special reference to India's FEP in the 1990s in specific policy areas such as trade and foreign investment.

In addition, such a conceptual framework should address the whole question of "foreign policy objectives" in a systematic manner. This relates specifically to the dependent variable of FEP, which ultimately affects the character and direction of the political economy of a state's foreign relations. Broadly speaking, there are three categories of objectives. In the first place, there are "core" values and interests that commit the very existence of states, and which must be preserved or extended at all times. Achievement of these values or interests may or may not impose demands on others. Secondly, there are middle-range goals, which normally impose demands on several other states. Commitments to their achievement are serious and some time-limits are usually attached to them. And lastly, there are universal long-range goals, which seldom have definite time limits.

As regards India's FEP, there have been certain "core" values and interests that constitute its mainstay. Such "core" values are economic justice to all states, peaceful resolution of bilateral and multilateral economic disputes, and economic growth/development of all states. As regard certain abiding interests, India's continuing interest has been to achieve economic development at home in a "non-aligned" manner. The basic motivation is that of maintaining India's economic independence in dealing with the advanced industrial states, as well as international financial institutions. Further, India's major interest is to contribute towards a "just" and "equitable" world order. In the 1990s, the above-stated "core" values and interests have shaped India's foreign economic policy.

Secondly, as regards middle-range goals, India's foreign economic policy aims to generate enough foreign exchange earnings to pay for India's imports from the rest of the world. Secondly, it seeks to deal with balance of payments difficulties faced by the economy from time to time. Thirdly, it aims to diversify its exports to various markets in the outside world, so that it does not have to rely on a few states for selling its goods and services. Fourthly, it seeks to devise suitable exchange-rates and other macro-economic policies to realise a "structural adjustment" of the domestic economy with the changing international economic environment. As regards India's universal long-range goals, it seeks to make efforts to facilitate the creation of a "just" and "humane" international political and economic order to serve the interests of all the developing countries.

We may now assess some key dimensions of India's foreign economic policy in the 1990s. Inflation and balance of payments (BOP) constraints were two major economic crisis-areas facing the Indian government by the end of the 1980s. In the 1990–91 budget, the balance-of-payment position management was accorded priority, and proposals were introduced to "keep the current deficit (the source of the BOP crisis) within manageable limits, by encouraging the export of goods and services, avoiding non-essential imports and improving the fiscal balance."[4] According to the economic survey (1989–90), it was indicated that the strain on the balance-of payments was particularly severe since 1988–89. Several adverse medium-term factors had contributed to the situation. Two important factors were the declining self-sufficiency in the production, consumption of crude oil and petroleum products from the peak attained in 1984–85 and the steady erosion of surpluses in the invisible account. Net invisible receipts had financed 92 per cent of the trade deficit in 1978–79 and only 55 per cent of the deficit, on an average, during 1982–85. During 1985–88, invisibles could finance just 36 per cent of the deficit.[5]

The Iraqi annexation of the tiny oil-rich kingdom of Kuwait in August, 1990, and the subsequent Gulf War in early 1991, had very adverse consequences for India's balance-of-payments position.[6] At the time of the installation of the Rao government of June 1991, India's balance-of-payments situation was indeed precarious.

Transformation of India's Foreign Economic Policy since July, 1991

In the wake of India's 10th General Elections (of May–June, 1991), P.V. Narasimha Rao's Congress (I) Government introduced, in June 1991, a package of reforms which aimed to introduce full blooded economic liberalization with an overall purpose to achieve 'stabilisation' and 'structural adjustment.' These policies were introduced to bring about 'a successful transition from an essentially inward-looking posture to an outward-oriented economy, exploiting foreign trade and investment opportunities fully.'[7] Further, it signified a 'new policy framework which will promote greater efficiency, growth and a surer and deeper attack on poverty alleviation.'[8] The underlying rationale was that if the reforms are pursued resolutely, economic dynamism, growth and development will follow, and that these will be sufficient, in themselves and without major state intervention, to reduce significantly if not eliminate poverty.[9]

The roots of the liberalisation programme of June 1991 were, however, in an earlier period – the liberalisation of the trade regime in the late 1970s under the Janata government, the new regime of industrial policies of the early 1980s, initiated by Indira Gandhi after she returned to power in 1980; and the so-called New Economic Policy of the Rajiv Gandhi government in 1985.[10] The liberalisation programme of the early 1990s was a deliberate and open attempt at a root and branch transformation of the economy's institutions and functioning.[11] The policy package covered a combination of short-term stabilisation measures and medium-run, or long-term structural adjustment economic reforms, each designed to achieve the goals stated above. The two sets of measures were not mutually exclusive, and each indicated policies that bore upon the other set of goals. Some of these measures were highly complementary in nature. As Bhagwati and Srinivasan put it, 'the question of direct foreign investment is related to the question of trade and industrial policy, reforms in one suggesting and even requiring reforms in the other.[12] The stabilisation measures included devaluation (the rupee was devalued by 20 per cent in July 1991), restraint on public expenditure (for instance, reducing subsidies on food, fertilisers and petroleum), reduction of the fiscal deficit, and removal of restrictions on the flow of foreign capital. These were meant to overcome the immediate crisis in terms of stabilising India's balance-of-payments position and securing macro-economic stability of the economy. At the same time, far-reaching micro-economic measures were required to strengthen the long-term growth-potential of the Indian economy.

As regards long-run, structural adjustment measures, a wide range of reforms were effected in these sectors. In trade policy, certain licensing controls were eliminated and partial convertibility of the rupee was introduced. In industrial policy, industry was deregulated and freed from a number of controls and licences. In the public sector, its scope was narrowed by reducing reserved areas from 17 to 8, along with disinvestment of public sector equity in profit-making enterprises, withdrawal of support from those making losses, and greater freedom in fixing prices. In the tax system, there were reforms in direct taxes and in excise and customs duties.

Further, specific policies were pursued to promote the inflow of direct private foreign investment, wherein such investment was considered as a non-debt inflow, giving access to international technology and markets. All these measures were meant to reduce rent seeking, integrate the Indian economy into the world economy, and make the Indian industry more efficient and competitive.

Such transformation in India's economic policy was in accordance with the advice offered in the World Bank's October 1990 *Report on the Indian Economy*,[13] and was congruent with the conditions attached to the World Bank Structural Adjustment Loan and the IMF Stand-by-Loan negotiated by India in 1991, during the external debt crisis, and with the likely conditions of the later Extended Fund Facility (EFF), for which the Rao government was expected to apply. In 1993, the Ministry of Finance issued a discussion paper on the economic reforms,[14] which was 'really an attempt to prepare the ground for the far tougher conditionalities to which the country is to be subjected as the price for the EFF and ESAF (Extended Structural Adjustment Facility) borrowing from the IMF and the loan for financial sector reform from the World Bank.[15] In the event, as pressure on the Indian balance of payments, eased, the EFF was not negotiated and the ESAF borrowing not sought, but the influence of the Bank and the Fund, whether actual or prospective, is clear.[16]

India's policy response to the 1991 crisis and the advice of the Bank and the Fund merit detailed examination. For the purposes of this paper, however, we shall confine ourselves to certain major themes of India's foreign economic policy in the 1990s. Before alluding to them, we provide a brief account of the factors and forces responsible for the transformation in economic policy.

Explaining Foreign Economic Policy Transformation in the 1990s

To begin with, the factors contributing to a policy movement towards full-blooded economic liberalisation can be subsumed under Marxist explanations. Drawing on O'Connor's thesis on the fiscal crisis of the state,[17] Baru takes the view that "the budget deficit for 1985–86 reveals the inability of the state to raise resources more than its inability to control expenditure... the state's inability to tax the rich and retrieve for itself at least part of its expenditure is one part of the problem, its inability to raise resources from its own enterprises is the other."[18] According to him, 'the fact of this crisis is then used as a justification for a further atrophy of state participation in the economy,' and therefore the trend towards liberalisation. This politically rooted crisis inhibits the growth of public investment, thus retarding the expansion and technological modernisation, hence efficiency and profitability of the public sector, thereby worsening the fiscal crisis. Faced with a decline in public investment, the private corporate sector seeks new growth opportunities in liberalisation; consisting of growth at the expense of the public sector through either pre-empting the latter's growth by free entry into hitherto reserved areas or by privatisation of the public sector.

On the other hand, Prabhat Patnaik emphasises the aggressive push by the rich towards liberalisation for new growth opportunities. According to him, "Together with intensified external pressure, and perhaps even more decisive as a contributory factor, has been a strong build-up of internal pressure in favour of liberalisation."[19] In the context of the fiscal crisis restricting public-investment derived growth opportunities, "big business finds the growth of its investment opportunities constricted relative to the growth in its command over capital."[20]

As regards 'liberal' explanations, the theme of 'deinstitutionalisation' has acquired salience for explaining the loss of the credibility of the state apparatus to lead the way for economic transformation. It basically refers to the decay, decline or undermining of political institutions, processes and norms. In this regard, the formulation of the Rudolphs suggests that the increase in the demands made on the state's limited resources, coupled with the state's inability to mobilise resources by taxing the urban and rural rich and the burgeoning middle classes, results in a demand overload on the state and eventually leads to the retreat of the state.[21]

So much for the two broad ideological explanations relating to the transformation in India's foreign economic policy. Now, let us briefly turn to the shift in India's choice of economic model and the overall strategy of economic development. Under the Mahalanobis planning model, there was a deep disbelief about foreign trade ever becoming an engine of growth – a disbelief that expressed itself in a policy of systemic import substitution. The policy that went along with the Mahalanobis planning model, was that of Import Substituting Industrialisation (ISI)"[22] Guha characterises the ISI as "a phase in the development process – a phase which constituted an adaptation to both the external environment and internal endowments at the outset of Indian planning."[23] Guha's exposition brings out contradictions in the dynamics of the ISI. Firstly, the efficiency of the Indian state was severely limited by the extreme heterogeneity of Indian society. According to him, "Diversity of this scale fostered a compromise and concession nurtures democracy, but it also generated a soft state in which central authority was hostage to a multitude of sectional interests."[24]

Furthermore, Guha points towards changes in the world economy in the 1960s and 1970s, which undermined the foundation of the ISI model itself. According to him, a central premise of the model was the segmentation of the world market into national and regional units by distribution costs – a segmentation which made it difficult for producers located in poor markets to achieve economies of scale.

The globalisation of the world economy from the seventies onwards changed this. The information revolution demolished the information barrier between markets and suppliers in different countries. Distribution costs due to packaging and pilferage were reduced by containerisation. A unipolar world economy centered at the Atlantic was replaced by a polycentric system with the Pacific and the Middle East as its other foci: this reduced the spatial and cultural gaps that producers in poor countries had to bridge in reaching richer markets. Living standards too rose all over the world. Demand became more differentiated and sophisticated with quality, variety and exclusiveness counting more than ever before. Mere cheapness was no longer a decisive consideration and economies of scale, associated as they are with long production runs and standardised products, dwindled in relative importance. Changes in both tastes and technology reduced the material and mineral intensity of output and therefore the share of transport cost in delivery price. These changes included a growing taste for high value-added products (ranging from diamonds to electronic goods) as well as for light high-value components added to standard products (e.g. electronic equipment and cars).

Finally, the micro-electronic revolution led to flexible specialisation and to the use of micro-electronically controlled general purpose versatile machinery to produce small batches of differentiated products almost as cheaply as in long production runs.[25]

As Guha goes on to say, "the upshot of the unification of the global market was that domestic market size began to count less as a determinant of export advantage and labour costs began to count for more." He is of the view that India was relatively much slower to adapt to these changes. In fact, India's share in world exports plummeted from 2 per cent in 1950 to 1.1 per cent in 1960, to 0.65 per cent in 1970 and to 0.42 per cent in 1980.[26]

Foreign Trade Policy

India's foreign trade policy constitutes one of the key components of India's foreign economic policy in the 1990s. Earning foreign exchange through foreign trade would necessarily influence the balance-of-payments position of the country. Technically, sustainability in the balance-of-payments position in the external account can be ensured via capital inflows. Ultimately, repayments or outflows must be met with hard currency. This can come about only via secure improvements in the trade balance. As regards the external sector of the Indian economy, two indicators are worth mentioning – (i) the level of external debt outstanding and (ii) the debt-service to exports ratio. The first is a clearly defined target of the stabilisation policy, and the second captures, in a summary way, the economy's capacity to repay and/or bear the burden of its debt. The outstanding level of international debt is actually growing at a faster rate. On the other hand, the debt-service ratio has fallen marginally since the beginning of the stabilisation programme, but continues to remain high enough for India to be designated a severely indebted economy by the World Bank.[27]

India's continued dependence on external borrowing in the absence of a well-defined strategy for repayments, constitutes a major problem in India's foreign trade policy. In 1991, in the wake of the installation of the Rao government, the major policy pronouncement referred to the changed orientation to 'foreign trade', rather than 'foreign aid' in India's foreign economic policy. In other words, promotion of India's exports, became a core goal of India's foreign economic policy. The experience of the People's. Republic of China in accelerating its exports, was an eye-opener to India's policy-makers. China's has adopted several specific policies to achieve this objective: geographical targeting, sectoral targetting, direct export rights, foreign exchange retention rights, and export quotas. Policy initiatives at the local level also influence exports. Clearly, the need for right incentive structures is felt by the community of exporters in India. This area has, however, remained largely unattended in the Indian foreign economic policy establishment.

The connection of foreign trade policy to India's balance-of payments position needs to be clearly spelled out. By March 1997, foreign currency reserves (including SDRs) have touched $21.18 billion, surpassing the earlier peak of $20.82 billion, reached towards the end of March 1995. In terms of import cover, the current level of reserves is equal to some seven month's imports, which compares favourably with the earlier peak level of March 1995.[28] All the same, India's balance-of-payments position has not yet acquired the required resilience and enduring strength. This can be indicated by the following pointers.

Firstly, exports in dollar terms have grown by a measly 5.6 per cent in the first months of 1996–97. As regards the quality of exports, they have not been able to make a dent in the international market for capital-intensive and high-technology products. Secondly, there has been a sharp fall in imports in 1996–97. Thirdly, the likely decline in the current account deficit from 1.7 per cent of GDP to 1.3 per cent in 1996–97, is the result of a fall of $1.5 billion in the deficit in the merchandise balance from $9 billion to $7.5 billion. It is projected that net invisible receipts are likely to have gone up from $7.5 billion in 1995–96 to $8.5 billion in 1996–97. The rise in private remittances has led to improvement in balance-of-payments position and build-up of reserves.[29] Further, the cost of portfolio inflows and even NRI deposits, has been significantly higher than that of commercial debt. The focus of foreign direct investment has been on the domestic market. However, due to large import dependence and relatively low export earnings of Indian industries, the pressure on India's trade balance continues to remain ominous.

Indeed, in view of the above trends, India's external sector remains vulnerable in the present economic regime of dear money, free markets and fiscal compression. The basic reality still persists, in the sense that accumulation of foreign exchange reserves through costly capital inflows, is noticed. In a capital scare economy, acquiring costly capital and then investing it in the international money markets at low yield rates, does not present a cheerful picture. The whole difficulty seems to be that capital cannot be absorbed productively in the economy itself; it can be augmented only if aggregate domestic savings rise over time.

As a matter of fact, the balance-of-payments outlook for India in the medium term rests upon two factors:

(i) The imperative to sustain rapid export growth to assure external sector viability. This can be achieved by increasing the base of India's exports in a difficult international trading environment in the coming years.
(ii) The importance of petroleum, oil and lubricants (POL) in the total import bill and the uncertainty surrounding the future of international oil prices.

Conclusion

By way of conclusion, one can say that India's foreign economic policy in the 1990s has undergone a transformation in the wake of the changed international political and economic environment. While accounting for the transformation, we have alluded to certain key dimensions of India's policy, such as foreign trade and balance of-payments. However, we have not referred to other equally vital dimensions, such as foreign direct investment and 'South-South' trade.

As regards the "core" values in India's foreign economic policy, efforts have been made to achieve them in the present post-cold-war world order. In the 1990s, the 'trade' orientation of India's foreign economic policy has been clearly dominant. In this essay, we have confined ourselves to developing a broad understanding of the policy. A critical perspective to deconstruct such a policy, can be advanced only in a different sort of essay.

Notes and References

1. Reprinted with permission from Usha Thakkar and Mangesh Kulkarni, eds., *India and World Affairs: Towards the 21st Century.* Mumbai, Himalya, 2008
2. See K.J. Holsti, *International Politics: A Framework for Analysis,* Eaglewood Cliffs, New Jersey, 1972, p. 102.
3. *Ibid.,* p. 103.
4. See *Economic Times*, 22 March 1990, p. 1.
5. *Ibid.*
6. The price of Brent crude oil-which is an indicator of the price for much of the world's crude-surged to as high as $25 per barrel, in the wake of the Iraqi annexation of Kuwait. In fact, in late July 1990, the Brent crude fetched only $15 per barrel. The crude price rise was triggered by fears of shortages in the oil-market because of disruption in supplies from Iraq and Kuwait which together accounted for about 9 per cent of the total world production, and roughly 20 per cent of the OPEC crude oil production. Prior to the crisis, however, the OPEC member had agreed in July 1990, to maintain the oil prices at $21 per barrel, with daily output of around 22.5 million barrels a day. The OPEC members had then favoured a graduated increase in crude oil prices from the prevailing $16 per barrel to $21, and that too only in genuine response to the market situation, so that the world was spared the oil shocks of the 1970s. Moreover, due to excessive production, importers were saddled with huge stocks, so that a steep upsurge in prices seemed out of the question. But the Iraqi invasion of Kuwait upset all such calculations and oil cost rose to $23 per barrel. See The Economic Times, Ahmedabad, August 18, 1990, p. 14.
7. See J.N. Bhagwati and T.N. Srinivasan, *India's Economic Reforms.* This report was commissioned for the Ministry of Finance by Dr. Manmohan Singh, 1993, p. 66.
8. *Ibid.,* p. 11.
9. See J.N Bhagwati's Radhakrishnan lectures, delivered in Oxford, June, 1992, and published as India in *Transition: freeing the Economy*, Oxford, Clarendon Press, 1993; and T.N. Srinivasan, 'Indian Development Strategy: An Exchange

of views,' *Economic and Political Weekly*, 3–10 August, 1991; T.N. Srinivasan, 'Reform of Industrial and Trade Policies,' *Economic and Political Weekly*, 14 September, 1991; and T.N. Srinivasan, '*Indian Economic Reforms: Background Rationale and Next steps*,' mimeo, Economic Growth Çenter, Yale University, 1993.

10. See Vijay Joshi and I.M.D. Lettle, *India, Macroeconomics and Political Economy, 1964–1991*, Delhi: Oxford University Press, pp. 57, 62–63, 154, 269, 270. For a further understanding of the nature and significance of earlier measures, see Deepak Nayyar, *Economic Liberalization in India: Analytics, Experience and Lessons*, Hyderabad: Orient Longman, 1996; and C.T. Kurien, *Economic performs and the people*, Delhi: Madhyam Books, 1996, pp. 3, 10.
11. See Kurien, 1996, pp. 3–4, 10; As regards Indira Gandhi's measures, it reflected a 'Shift from planning the economy to management of the economy.' See Kurien, 1996, p. 10. Rajiv Gandhi's new economic policy added greater latitude for the purchasing power of the upper income groups.
12. See Bhagwati and Srinivasan, n. 6, p. 44.
13. See World Bank, *India: Trends, Issues and Options, Country Economic* Memorandum 1.
14. See Bhagwati and Srinivasan, n. 6.
15. EPW Research Foundation, 'Sugar Coating for Tougher Conditionalities to come,' *Economic and Political Weekly*, 27, 31 July, 1993,
16. For a detailed look at India's dealings in these various respects, see policy watch, 'IMF Stand-By Loan conditions,' *Economic and Political Weekly*, 26, 52, 28 December, 1991; BM, 'Towards Neo Colonial Dependency, *Economic and Political Weekly*, 26, 31, 32, 7 and 10 August 1991; see BM, 'Double-Talk on EEF,' *Economic and Political Weekly*, 28, 21, 22 May 1991; See JM, "Discussing Economic Reforms. Achievements and future intent, *Economic and Political Weekly*, 28, 31, 31 July 1993, and C.T. Kurien, 1996, pp. 6–7.

    An IMF Stand-By arrangement represents the fund's third line of credits. The first two lines-the reserve or gold tranche and the first credit tranche carry no conditionality. A Stand-By loan does, and requires a government to adopt a stabilization programme agreed by the Fund Management and Executive Board, and includes various performance criteria. Performance is carefully monitored, and if the performance criteria are not met, access to the stand-by facility is denied until the stabilization programme is renegotiated. Such a loan is usually drawn down over a single year and is generally repayable over five years. An Extended Fund Facility (EEF) Provides balance-of-payments support for longer periods and in large amounts. Here tougher conditionality holds. Extended Structural Adjustment Facility (ESAF) loans are given by the World Bank and the IMF jointly. On this, see Laurence Harris, Banking on the Fund – the IMF. Open University Third World Studies, U 204, Case Study 9, Milton Keynes: Open University Press, 1983; Tony Killick, Ed., *The Quest for Economic Stabilisation, the IMF and the Third World*, London: Gower in association with the Overseas Development Institute, 1984, pp. 183–84; Frances Steward, *Adjustment and poverty, options and Choices*, London and New York: Routledge, 1985, p. 19.
17. See James O' Connor, *The Fiscal Crisis of the State*, New York: St. Martin's Press, 1973.

18. See S. Baru, "The State in Retreat," *Economic and Political Weekly*, 20, 13 (1985), p. 705.
19. See Prabhat Patnaik, "New Turn in Economic Policy: Context and Prospect," *Economic and Political Weekly*, 21, 23 (1996), pp. 1–15.
20. *Ibid.*, p. 1017.
21. Llyod Rudolph, and Susanne Rudolph, *In pursuit of Lakshmi, The political Economy of the Indian State*, Chicago: University of Chicago Press, 1987
22. See Ashok S. Guha, "The import Substituting Industrialisation Model: Its Rationale and Limitations," in Mihir Rakshit, Ed., *Planning and Economic Policy in India-Evaluations and Lessons for the future*, New Delhi: Sage Publications, 1996, p. 88.
23. *Ibid.*, p. 89.
24. Guha, n. 21, p. 92.
25. *Ibid.*, p. 98.
26. Guha, p. 99.
27. See the relevant World Debt Tables of the World Bank. The World Bank tends to use the debt service to exports ratio as opposed to the debts service to current receipts ratio used by the Government of India.
28. See *Economic and Political Weekly*, March 22, 1997, p. 555.
29. *Ibid.*

18

India's Response to Environmental Concerns

Anand Mathur

Progress and pollution go together. The economic growth is essential to combat poverty and deprivation but has exerted considerable pressure on the environmental sustainability. With industrialization, energy consumption has increased, prosperity resulted in building more houses and using more vehicles; all this deteriorated the quality of environment. The burning question before the World and more particularly before developing nations is how to achieve target of economic growth without polluting the environment. In this context, what are major global concerns associated with the problem of environment and how India is responding to them in terms of its foreign policy is a matter of serious concern for us. Present essay is a modest attempt in this direction.

I

Global Environmental Concerns

It is universally acknowledged that protection of environment is a global problem and should be solved globally. Since Stockholm declaration of June 1972, the World is grappling with the issue of correcting damage caused to environment. Earth Summit at Rio-de-Janerio in 1992 and Johannesburg in 2002, Kyoto protocol of 1997 or Gleneagle meet of July 2005, all discussed the ways and means of protecting environment. Similarly, national governments enacted laws replicating these international declarations. But due to national priorities, moral convictions and compulsions developed and developing nations have divergent perceptions on environment related issues and find themselves at daggers drawn. For example, the first Earth summit was called to work out a World Schedule for saving the environment, combating the depletion of the ozone layer and reducing 'greenhouse gas' emission (Carbon dioxide, methane and chlorofluoro carbons (CFCs). The participants were to adopt an "Earth Chapter" to protect the environment in the 21st Century, called Agenda-21. The southern nations hold the rich nations responsible for environmental mess and questioned about their efforts for controlling greenhouse gas emission and curbing the export of hazardous waste.[1] They also look with suspicion on Global Environmental Facility (GEF), set up for cleaning the globe. Because the decision-making in GEF rests with developed countries only. G-15 meeting was called in Geneva in March 1994 before signing the final act of Uruguay Round in Marrakesh. Third World countries cautioned against the attempts of OECD countries to use environmental standards as a means of non-trade barriers. Several eco-testing, eco-labeling and eco-standards setting organizations are coming up. In a position paper called "World Trade Organization: Trade and Environment" presented to GATT Director General of the Third World Network (TWN) states that inclusion in the WTO agenda of new areas as environment, labour standards and human rights is being sought by the North, "not for advancing the noble cause of protecting the environment or people's rights but to use them to reduce the competitiveness of the South in (its) home markets and enlarge the market space for transnational corporations in the world".

The developed Countries are imposing their 'values' on less developed nations in the name of biodiversity, the Tuna/Dolphin Case[2] and Shrimp/Turtle Case[3] are examples of "eco-imperialism". The US had laid an embargo on imports of tuna fish from Mexico because they were caught in purse-seine nets which cruelly killed dolphins or it (the US) imposed a ban on the import of shrimps from India, if caught in the vessels without a "turtle excluder device. It is a sort of "moral militancy" of environmentalists who are imposing trade sanctions unilaterally on other nations, who do not share their 'values' or 'preferences'.[4] The depleted state of global fish stocks has become a major economic and environmental concern. For decades, Europe has leased fishing rights from Senegal, Mauritania and other West African nations. In contrast, no limit has been set to the amount of the fish the Europeans can catch – "a slightly acceptable colonialism". Some of the West Africa's fisheries are heading for collapse. The $500 million that Europe will pay Senegal for the rights to fish its waters from 2001 to 2006 will no doubt, come in handy. The Country has few saleable assets and depends on the EU cash to help pay some of its overseas debts. Fish as food and job in fisheries are going down. The size of EU vessels are increasing, though the EU specified in the contracts that some of the money be earmarked for 'development' of local fishing industry. The gesture would be laudable if Europe's trawlers left any fish for the locals.

Similarly, the developed countries are exporting their industrial waste into poor southern countries. Instead of reprocessing it at home, they prefer to dump it into less developed countries, where there is no effective environmental regulatory system. India has become a major dumping ground for such toxic waste. The Basel ban of March 1994 prohibits the trans-border movement of hazardous waste from OECD to non-OECD even for "recycling" after 1997. India – one of the first few countries that raised its voice against this toxic dumping, was battling under the influence of its domestic industry, which 'recycles' OECD waste, to support a Norwegian resolution under the Basel

Convention at Geneva on September 22, 1995 because India has become a "willing recipient" of this toxic waste.

World Climate is changing due to global warming caused by the greenhouse effect. Kyoto Protocol on Climate change required the participating Countries to cut back emission of Carbon dioxide by 2012 to 5.2 per cent of 1990 levels. The US and Australia refused to ratify Kyoto Protocol in February 2005 under the influence of their short sighted businessmen. Economic slow down consequent to signing the protocol is given as the reason for staying away from moves to save the planet.[5]

If poor countries hold the rich nations responsible for environmental mess, the rich nations argue that poverty and underdevelopment are the greatest source of pollution. G-8 countries accounts for 47 per cent of world's carbon emission but the US supported studies have held developing countries responsible for environmental devastation. The example of "Asian Brown Haze" has been given in this regard.[6]

The Max Planck Society reported in their Indian Ocean Experiment (INDOEX) that a dense brown pollution haze upto one to three kilometers above the ocean surface was noticed. The haze layer covered most of the northern Indian Ocean including the Arabian sea, much of the Bay of Bengal and the equatorial Indian Ocean to about 5 degrees south of the equator. The results indicate that the build-up of the haze, a mass of ash, acids, aerosols and other particles, is disrupting the weather system including the rainfall and wind patterns. The blanket of pollution is reducing the amount of solar energy hitting the earth surface by as much as 10 to 15 per cent. The haze may reduce precipitation over North-West India, Pakistan, Afghanistan, Western China and the neighbouring Western Central Asia region by 20 to 40 per cent.

Klaus Toepfer, Executive Director of United Nations Environment Programme said, the haze is formed in the region where the population is around 5 billion and where emission of rapidly growing economies is very high. The haze is the result of forest fires, burning of agricultural waste, dramatic increase in the burning of fossil fuels in vehicles, industries and power stations and emission from millions of inefficient cookers, burning wood, cow dung and 'bio fuels'.[7] Surprisingly, the report of INDOEX was published only a few days before the Earth summit of Johannesburg; the reason may be to suggest that the developing countries of this region are responsible for the pollution and they should play a greater role in cleaning of the environment.[8] The Northern nations were playing the "good governance" card as a way of blaming developing countries for fouling up their own environment, and as a conditionality for development assistance. T.R. Baalu, Indian Environment and Forest Minister informed that the developing countries have agreed to adhere to the official development assistance (ODA) of 0.7 per cent of their respective GDPs and will route this money through the global environment facility.

The Asian Brown Haze was considered a major environmental hazard not only for Asia but for entire world because a pollution parcel like this can travel halfway around the globe in a week. It is a controversial study. The chairman of Intergovernmental panel for climate change Rajendra Pachauri said, "It could very well be that these are being generated in North America or even in Europe and travelling all the way. Recently, similar to "Asian Brown Haze", pollution cloud has been spotted in other parts of world also. It has been renamed as "Atmospheric Brown Cloud".[9] It is interesting to assess who is more responsible for greenhouse gas emission – energy guzzling appliances and heavy industries of North or smoke emitting *Choolas* and methane expelling animal waste fuel of poor countries. People cut forests because they need the wood, they fish because they need to eat and because they need the money. Whatever may be the position, it is the duty of one and all to preserve and protect this invaluable gift of nature. The presence of haze has highlighted the need for more research on how to achieve economic growth without sacrificing the long term health and natural wealth of the region.

The prudence demands that the developed and developing countries should leave confrontationist approach and work together for the protection of the environment. The global temperature is increasing 0.3 celsius per year. The World-watch Institute of Washington DC in its annual report (1995) prepared by noted environmentalists included India in the list of environmental powers – four developed (US, Russia, Japan, Germany) and four developing (China, India, Brazil, Indonesia) that will play a pivotal role in determining the quality of the global environment. The then US Vice President Al Gore, who is deeply interested in environmental issues, said that while developed countries like the US and the EU should take on greater responsibilities, India and China should also share this responsibility.

Three "Es" are very important for the future welfare of humanity; they are Economic prosperity, Environmental quality and social Equity. It means that economic growth must be pursued in a manner that ensures the protection of socio-ecological system. Evolution of such strategy that harmonizes economic, environmental and equity considerations into a synergistic whole is essential for the sustainable development of the world.

The friction between 'environment' and 'development' has been resolved through the principle of sustainable development. The World Commission on Environment and Development (Brundtland Commission, 1987) defines sustainable development as "meets the needs of present without compromising the ability of future generations to meet their own needs". This explains that the present generation must be accorded an equal opportunity for economic growth involving no depletion of natural resources or eco system so as to leave the planet ecologically viable for the posterity. We should not take from the earth more than we give back. Thus, the concept of sustainable development strives for a perpetually stable resource base and a perpetually stable economic growth. In short, the development should not only be growth oriented, it should be environment friendly, then only the objective of sustainability will be achieved.

The new global currency of power is sustained economic growth. The reckless exploitation of natural resources for economic growth is detrimental to environmental sustainability. With economic growth and environmental sustainability, the social dimension of sustainable development is equally important. Mere economic progress is not an end in itself. Beyond the formal growth statistics, what is needed is not only increase in gross national products but also gross national happiness. Carl Frankel, author and US editor for *Tomorrow* magazine, considers social equity as 'vertical' dimension of sustainable development. With 'horizontal dimension of economic growth', he said, we need to do justice to subjective and soulful aspect of development.

Economic growth depends on availability of energy. Traditionally, fossil fuel is used for energy generation. It emits obnoxious gases that cause global warming, ozone hole and acid rain. With industrialization, energy consumption has increased. The scarcity of energy is a worldwide problem. China alone is consuming 12 per cent of the world's energy (*World Energy Outlook* 2005). India too occupies sixth position as an energy consumer in the world. The US insist that India and China, which are growing at the rate of seven to eight per cent annually must not be exempted from quota deadline of Kyoto Protocol. Ken New Combe, the World Bank's senior adviser for sustainable development, while expressing his views in a meeting in Paris in June, 2005 said, "a new global climate management regime must include limiting the emission of greenhouse gases in rapidly industrializing countries such as India, China, Mexico and Brazil. India is the 6th largest emitter of green house gases. The growing economy of India needs more energy. The fossil-fuels are limited, so there is need to replace fossil-fuels with bio-fuels and other renewable resources of energy. Solar, wind, wave, biomass, geothermal and nuclear are other resources of energy generation. The introduction of eco-friendly alternatives of windmills and solar panels are the best long term solutions as their capability of regeneration is enormous. Similarly nuclear energy is most efficient, abundantly available, sustainable and cost effective energy source. President Bush and Manmohan Singh advocated for emission free nuclear energy as an alternative to the fossil-fuels during summit conference at Gleneagle. On July 18, 2005 India and the US entered into a civilian nuclear energy cooperation deal. An agreement for providing nuclear fuel and reactors for Indian nuclear energy plants was assured provided India separate its civilian and military nuclear facilities and place its civilian nuclear facilities under IAEA safeguards. The purpose of deal was mainly to release the pressure on the global hydrocarbon resources. India, which is suffering nuclear isolation, could not produce much nuclear energy. It is merely 3 per cent of its total energy production. If access to eco-friendly nuclear power would not be given to India, it will be forced to burn coal and other fossil fuels to meet its energy needs. The French President Jacques Chirac during his visit to India said, "if we do not help India produce electricity using nuclear power, we would let develop in India a chimney for greenhouse gases."

At global level, the share of nuclear power is about 18 per cent of the total electricity production. The US generates only 20 per cent nuclear energy whereas France produces nearly 78 per cent nuclear energy of the total production. So, there is lot of scope for nuclear energy generation worldwide. The nuclear energy cooperation is thus very important for energy-security, self-sufficiency and environment sustainability.

The growth in human population, the growing demand for nature's resources and the spread of environmentally damaging technologies were contributing to the "growing threat" to planet Earth.[10] In developing countries, people burn fossil-fuel and animal dung for keeping their homes warm and cooking their food, due to which respiratory illness accounts for 10 per cent of global deaths. Some NGO distributed new and improved stoves in a village of Kenya at the cost of 1 dollar a piece. The clean burning stoves reduced the death rate to half.[11] There is need to replace environmentally inappropriate and polluting technologies by "clean technologies." India and other nations of South bargained to get the sophisticated non-polluting, environment friendly technologies that have been developed in recent years in the North; but clean technology does not come cheap. Many of the clean devices have been patented and available for sale in global market at very high price. Manmohan Singh while inaugurating the 94th Indian Science Congress on 2nd January 2007 in Chidambaram, Tamil Nadu said now environment friendly technologies being developed across the world must be shared and made available to all so that Earth is saved. Thus, free flow of technology, pooling of resources and data, exchange of knowledge between developed and developing countries is essential to fight the threat of environmental menace which is as compelling and imperative as nuclear arms control.

The wisdom of our forefathers has much to offer in pursuing an environment friendly and sustainable development path. In a folktale a wise farmer said he placed one third of his income in God's feet, other one third for personal use and last one third he used to throw in a well. Offering a portion of income to God means paying tribute to ancestors who walked before us on Earth and who left this planet ecologically viable for us, other portion of income is for growth and enjoyment of present generation, 'throwing in well' means to pay for conservation of the environment so that the posterity could enjoy the bliss of pollution free environment. The countries of South Asia have capability as well as traditional knowledge for preservation of environment.

One of the provisions of Kyoto protocol, known as the Clean Development Mechanism (CDM) establishes a framework within which the industrialized countries can meet a part of their carbon dioxide emission reduction requirements by purchasing certified emission reductions (CERs) from India and other developing countries. In fact South Asian countries can offer to the rest of world valuable lessons on green practices, that are part of their traditions.

Cicero has rightly said, "Nature has granted the use of life like a loan, without fixing any day for repayment."[12] It reminds us that gift of life is not an absolute right, it is coined with duty also, duty to take care of fellow beings and duty to preserve all resources for the future descendants, in other words ensuring intra- and inter-generational equity. In the words of Mahatma Gandhi, "the earth provides enough to satisfy every man's need, but not for every man's greed".

R.S. Pathak, Judge, International Court of Justice has cautioned and reminded us of our responsibility of saving this planet. He said, we have inherited the planet and we are the beneficiaries of those who walked the earth before us. At the same time we also hold this beautiful world on trust, as trustees for the generations who will come after us. Inter-generational equity exists side by side with intra-generational equity. Both form part of a common scheme, and both together simultaneously define the true proportion of our rights, obligations and responsibilities.

Manmohan Singh said that measures the global community took to protect the environment and deal with climate change should be equitable in their impact on the development prospect of developing countries. He said, "we can and must use the inventiveness and ingenuity of our knowledge to find new pathways to growth. But this must be a shared effort. It must be an effort that enables the poor to improve their quality of life, their well-being, their consumption levels, without being forced to pay the price for the profligacy and excessive consumption of the rich and the super rich.[13]

The earth and its environment are God's munificence and should be treated with sanctity. Only with collaborative efforts and shared responsibilities the environment could be saved. Anthropologist Ruth Benedict said, "human beings have an endless capacity to invent and learn". The countries of world can learn from environmentally progressive Sweden, who has announced to completely end its dependency on oil by 2020.[14] It gets almost all its electricity from nuclear and hydro-electric power. Its paper and pulp industries use bark to produce energy and sawmills burn wood chips and sawdust to generate power. These attempts put Sweden at the top of world Green League Table. Iceland hopes by 2050 to power all its cars and boats with hydrogen made from electricity drawn from renewable resources, and Brazil intends to power 80 per cent of its transport fleet with ethanol derived mainly from sugarcane within five years. The use of CNG in auto rickshaws of Delhi reduced pollution level in the atmosphere considerably.

Similarly, many useful and environment friendly items can be produced by recycling of waste. Bio-degradable material can be easily converted into organic manure. Chemical fertilizer slowly turns the soil saline. Organic fertilizer produced from bio-degradable garbage processing not only reduces pollution, eliminate stench and disease but also restores the health of the soil.[15] Through innovative ideas and continuous research many useful and environment friendly items can be produced from recycling of non-biodegradable waste. Beautiful paper items can be made out of waste paper pulp. Coir and ply board can be produced from coconut. Its husk and slurry can be used for producing bio- gas. Flying ash, a pollutant of thermal power house can be used for making cement and bricks. It can also be used in construction of roads. Now, scientists have invented bio-degradable plastic also. The "eco-feminism" is very important in this regard as they prepare many attractive and useful items from waste materials. These efforts not only curb environmental pollution but also provide cleanliness.

Conservation of environment does not only mean to retain whatever is left but it involves whole range of activities aimed at protection and ensuring the intrinsic quality of resources through the proper and scientific use. Reforestation, protection of wild life, prevention and control of water, air pollution, soil conservation, etc. must be part of comprehensive environment policy. Implementation of polluter pays principle, precautionary principle, public trust doctrine, sustainable development principle and evolving other new principles for environment sustainability, is desirable.

Britain had made climate change a central issue in the G-8 Summit at Gleneagles on July 6–8, 2005. India, China, South Africa, Mexico and Brazil were also present in the meeting. The Asian Brown Haze or Atmospheric Brown Cloud (ABC) was considered a major environmental hazard. The countries of world including India agreed to work on the project to tackle ABC's threat. Research suggests that the impact of the haze will intensify over the next 20 years. It is hoped that with such collaborative initiative, the world would successfully face the challenge of environmental menace. Instead of compartmentalized way of thinking, an integrated approach is needed for equitable development and environmental protection.

II

India's Response and Policy Options

India's response to above global environmental concerns are reflected in three-fold manners: (i) protection of environment; (ii) preservation of natural resources; and (iii) to meet out its own energy needs.

(i) The issue of protection of environment became an important area in international politics since 1970s. India is also aware about its responsibilities and sensibilities towards this issue. Since then India is making serious efforts to facilitate and promote the cause of environment by observing all the concerns raised during four important international conferences: Stockholm (1972), Nairobi (1982), Rio-de-Janeiro (1992) and Johannesburg (2002). It is equally concerned about the major crises faced by the global environment in the form of ozone layer depletion, global warming, greenhouse effects, earth degradation, etc. It is observing all the norms to facilitate preservation of environment both at bilateral relations with other states and at numerous multilateral forums of United Nations and other such bodies.

(ii) Like all developing countries India is also concerned about its economic development as one of the important objectives of its foreign policy. Consequently it is also bothered about the just and equalitarian distribution of resources available in nature. In this context, India is aware that there is a threat of misappropriation of these resources by the developed world due to their technologically advantageous position. Hence it is also in favour of policy of sustainable development as propounded by different international bodies. It is of the view that without such policies the developing countries may lose their share and ultimately may face serious deprivations due to lack of such resources. Simultaneously, India is in favour of improvement in the degradation of the environment through concerted efforts. While contributing towards this end, it is in favour of the principle that 'polluters must pay'.

(iii) Energy security is an important factor in India's foreign policy, as it is in need of huge energy for its economic development. Given the current process of its economic reforms with a target of 8–10 per cent of GDP growth this requirement is going to enhances substantially in the times to come. At present India's most energy needs are fulfilled with the oil, of which it is already a net importer. Of the total oil consumption 70 per cent is imported and only 30 per cent is produced indigenously. If the projection of consumption of oil is made then by the year 2011 India's requirement will be around 150 million tones out of which 65 to 70 million will be met through indigenous production. As a result, India would have to import substantial quantities of oil amounting to roughly 1.5 million barrels per day by the year 2011.[16] Though India is making efforts to boost its alternative sources of energy, yet oil continues to remain one of the most dependable source in India. Consequently, it has to make effort that its flow of oil remain as it is, as well as, it may continue to augment its domestic needs.

Now question arises – how India can meet the above challenges? What are the foreign policy options available to India to realize the goals affecting its national interests? In this context, India seems to be in need of multi-pronged strategies in the following manner:

(a) Firstly, India should make efforts at the global level to form a joint strategy with the important players to do away with the problems affecting the growth of clean environment. It should play an important role to initiate global negotiations on climate change by using various forums of the United Nations. Simultaneously, it should also make concerted efforts with the developing counties to get some important protocols, like Kyoto protocol, to be operationalized. Since it is the joint responsibility of both the developed and developing countries, hence the latter must put pressures on the former to bring about technology transfer to the third world. As a result, foreign policy needs to be formulated in this area on the basis of considerable scientific study and on the coordinated action of the developing countries, which are most vulnerable to exploitative actions by the North.

(b) Secondly, natural resources can be protected for a longer period only if the coordinated efforts are made by both the developed and developing world. India is a developing country and is placed at present at the threshold of developed world in certain technological (like nuclear and information technology) innovations and uses. Hence, it can play the role to bridge the gap between the counties of North and South. Though in the present era of globalization it seems quite difficult, yet given its potential to be the second largest market it is at least in a position to initiate such a process. Simultaneously, it should coordinate the scientific knowledge of both the 'North' and 'South' in such a way that it can be beneficial for all the countries of the third world. In this era of increasing interdependence among different countries of the world; initiation of such ideas can work out some form of transformations as all the states want preservation and sustenance of resources for longer period.

(c) Finally, economic strength is not only necessary for the development, but also essential for the effective use of its foreign policy options. India, therefore, is in dire need of energy security both for its domestic growth and to act as an important player at global level. Hence, on the one hand, it is striving hard to enhance its energy output by making investments abroad in oil exploration companies in Russia, Vietnam, Sudan, Central Asian Republics, and Nigeria, etc. and, on the other hand, signing different agreements in the area of oil and natural gas supplies through pipelines from different parts of the world. Simultaneously, it is busy in enhancing alternative sources of energy, especially its nuclear energy programmes. Consequently, its recent signing of civil nuclear energy deals with France, America and Russia are not only aimed at procuring nuclear fuel from the USA but to opening of its trade with US, France and Russia along with other nuclear supplier group (NSG) countries for continuous boost of its energy needs for times to come.[17]

Thus, it can be concluded that non-conventional priorities like environment have acquired a significant place in the formulation of India's foreign policy in the post-cold war era. On the one hand, India's policy has been conscious of the emerging negative challenges as a result of environmental concerns, whereas, it is equally aware of its responsibilities and future needs having linkages with the environmental issues. Since the magnitude of the problem is so complex there is need to take bold steps both at bilateral and multilateral levels. Therefore, there is urgent need not only to acknowledge the importance of these new efforts to realize them, but also to safeguard the future interests of the country.

Notes and References

1. Bunker Roy, "Earth Summit: Crucial Questions North must Answer", *Indian Express*, May 16, 1992.
2. A.K. Kaul "Environmental issues in International Trade" in Satish C. Shastri, ed., *Human Rights, Development and Environmental Law – An Anthology*, Bharat Law, Jaipur p. 29.
3. *Ibid.*, p. 33.
4. Anand Mathur, *Indo-American Relations – Foreign Policy Orientations and perspectives of P. V. Narsimha Rao and Bill Clinton*, Jodhpur Scientific Publishers, Jodhpur, 2003 p. 190.
5. Zero Hour, "Remember, the face of Surat," *Hardnews*, New Delhi, Vol. 3 No. 11 October 2006, p. 1.
6. Anand Mathur, "Environmental Management: A Challenge before Developing countries" *SAJOSPS*, Vol. 7 No. 1 July–Dec. 2006 p. 75.
7. "Pollution cloud over South Asia threatens Economy," *National Geographic News*, August 12, 2002.
8. Anand Mathur, "Growing Importance of Indian Ocean in Post-Cold war era and its implication for India," *Strategic Analysis*, Vol. 26, No. 4, Oct-Dec. 2002, pp. 558–559.
9. *Hindustan Times*, February 16, 2006.
10. Jaya Menan "West's green drive cannot be at poor World's cost: PM" *Indian Express*, January 3, 2007.
11. Fred Guteral, "Put out the dung fire", *Newsweek*, September 2, 2002 p. 37.
12. Thomas, William L, "Green Nexus Financers and sustainable development," *Georgetown International Environmental Law Review*, Summit 2001.
13. *The Hindu*, Delhi, January 4, 2007.
14. *Hindustan Times*, New Delhi, February 9, 2006 p. 9.
15. Pranab Roy "Management of Municipal Solid waste" *SAJOSPS*, July-Dec. 2004, pp. 108–110.
16. K. Pachauri, "The Environment: Energy Challenge", in Lalit Mansingh, et al., *Indian Foreign Policy: Agenda for the 21st Century*, (Vol. I), Konark, New Delhi, 1997, p. 334.
17. For details see, Anand Mathur, "Indo-US Civilian Nuclear Cooperation Deal: Reflection of Changing Matrix of Relationships in Polycentric World Order," in Anand Mathur and Sohan Lal Meena, eds., *India's Profile in Polycentric World Order*, Jaipur, RBSA, 2008.

19

India's Refugee Policy

Ram Niwas Beniwal

The Back Ground

Human Rights are freedoms which are granted equally to all persons without distinction. In a sense, human rights are universally recognized standards of behaviour. The violation of these standards by states, or other agents, may give rise to situations which lead to the creation of refugees. Refugees, by definition, are victims of human rights violations.[1] Viewing the refugee problem in the context of human rights is clearly relevant. In fact, the origin of the international system of refugee protection, as codified in international refugee law, grew out of concern for the plight of refugees feeling the troubles of post-war Europe. Regrettably, protecting and assisting victims of human rights violations which result in forced displacement is as relevant today as it was some six decades ago. Refugees are not simply victims of human rights violations, but they also represent a distinct group of individuals who are without the protection of a national state. Hence the international system of refugee law was adopted in order to replace the protection which is normally provided, or is at least the responsibility of national governments for their citizens.

Though the phenomenon of population displacement is quite old, yet the forcing of people from their established and known habitat emerged with the birth of a territorial nation-state[2], gradually assuming religious, racial or ideological character and identity. The very process of the emergence of such identity has resulted in discriminatory practices against minorities and those groups of people who do not share the ideological or religious predilections of the dominant groups. This process of refugee generation continued as the conflicts of state formation spilled over into inter-state conflicts and tensions and stabilization of territorial boundaries of ethnic, religious and ideological defined state.

It is one of the greatest failure of modernity that millions of people around the world continue to experience what Euripides called "the loss of a native land," i.e. refugees. Although the condition of refugeehood has always existed in some form or another, a comprehensive international legal regime aimed at the protection of refugees has only existed for about seventy years. Indeed, refugee law is a relatively new branch of international law. Historically, the refugee issue had been defined as a matter of sovereign privilege. It was dealt with unilaterally or bilaterally between the state of origin and the host country. The inadequacy of this approach became evident in the aftermath of the first world war when the breakup of empires and the onset of the Russian revolution unleashed large scale refugee flows. The problem coincided with the birth of League of Nations and the notion of an international community based on international cooperation and solidarity. It was in this climate that the first office of the High Commissioner for Refugees was created. Similarly, when the United Nations came into being after the devastation of the second world war, the international community came together to create a permanent international refugee regime. In 1950, the present day Office of the High Commissioner for Refugees was created by the United Nations General Assembly through its resolution number 428(v) and began its operation on 1 January 1951. Its mandate is to provide international protection to refugees and assist governments in finding permanent solutions to the problem of refugees.[3]

Derived from the Latin word 'refugium' the word 'refugee' literally means "shelter, security, or a haven".[4] According to the 1951 Convention, a refugee is one who owing to well founded fear of being persecuted for reasons of race, religion, nationality, membership of a particular social group or political opinion, is outside the country of his nationality and is unable or, owing to such fear, is unwilling to avail himself of the protection of that country; or who, not having a nationality and being, outside the country of his former habitual residence as a result of such events, unable or, owing to such fear, is unwilling to return to it.[5]

Broadly speaking definition of the term refugee now includes a variety of different groups: internally displaced and war-affected populations, asylum seekers, stateless people and others whose nationality is disputed as well as returnees/refugees and displaced people who have been able to go back to their homes, but who still require some support from the international community.[6] Although numerous private and governmental agencies exist to attend to the needs of refugees on the local, national and international scales, the oldest, most prominent and best funded global agency for the purpose is UNHCR.

UNHCR aims to provide protection and ensure the respect of fundamental rights for all those under its concern. In the case of refugees, the most basic need is protection from refoulement or forcible return to a country in which they have reason to fear persecution or attack. It also provides assistance to those persons of concern who cannot meet their own basic needs, and when there are no other resources available. The types of assistance include emergency help for major influxes; case and maintenance programmes that meet basic needs on a more routine basis; voluntary repatriation; local settlement assistance to promote self-sufficiency and local integration in host countries; and resettlement in third countries for refugees who cannot return to their homes and who face particular protection problems in their country of first asylum.[7]

In South Asia, though most of the countries have acceded to the major international Humanitarian and Human Rights instruments, yet none of them ratified the 1951 UN Convention and 1967 Protocol. However, at least three of them (India, Pakistan and Bangladesh) are the members of the Governing body of the UNHCR. This alongwith the absence of permanent institutional structure to oversee issues of refugees, the grant of refugee status has been at the discretion of the political authorities. Some of these countries have rejected refugee's status on narrow political grounds. In the process, they have reduced the status of fleeing humanities to political arbitrariness. For example, Pakistan gives refugee status only to Afghans. Others are mostly declared as illegal immigrants not eligible for work permits or public education.

In India, refugee problem has been there since its inception as an independent nation-state. The process of nation-building and state-building in the South Asian region has been responsible for producing a vast number of refugees. Besides, war, famine and political oppression have been the other reasons contributing to population displacement.[8]

From a theoretical perspective, problem of refugees has been caused due to following six fold factors: (i) anti-colonial wars and self-determination movements; (ii) international conflicts; (iii) revolutions, coups and regime changes; (iv) ethnic, communal and religious conflicts; (v) creation and restructuring of state boundaries, and (vi) population transfers[9]. Besides the above factors, Muni and Baral have identified three broad categories of refugee-generating factors in South Asia,[10] which obviously apply to India as well.

(a) First, the breakdown of colonial rule and the rationalization of some of the colonial legacies. In this context, exodus of large numbers of refugees created due to partition or creation of new states due to independence. Partition of British India into the states of India and Pakistan and refugees caused due to aftermath of Independence of Burma and Sri Lanka are such examples.
(b) Second factor is related to state and nation-building processes, which precipitated not only political, ethnic and religious conflicts but created economic and environmental conditions that forced people to migrate within or outside their respective countries. The largest refugee flow witnessed by India caused due to above factors was the migration of large population from East Pakistan in 1971. Similar is the case of Sri Lanka, where the state, through a gradual process beginning in 1950, acquired a

Sinhala-Buddhist identity. The simmering ethnic conflict that exploded in July 1983 sent more than 220,000 refugees to India and 75,000 outside the South Asia. Later, Bangladesh drifted towards authoritarian political order and assertive Islamic identity strengthened the flow of Hindus and Buddhist Chakmas to India. A vigorous policy of Bhutanisation has led to massive outflow of the Southern Bhutanese of Nepali origin. Approximately, 25,000 to 30,000 Nepalese of Bhutan have taken refugee in India's West Bengal and Assam provinces. Besides, there have been economic migrants from the neighbouring countries to India.

Finally, developments outside the region have also been responsible for refugee generation. Such extra-regional refugees have come from Tibet, Afghanistan and Myanmar. Basically, India's democratic polity, large size, secular state system, federal constitutional structure, porous borders and better economic opportunities accounted for the flow of refugees in this country.

Indian Policy

India is not a party to either the Refugee Convention of 1951 or the Protocol of 1967. In translating the international obligations into action, different behaviour of states have been observed on International law or International Relations. They are:

(i) States become parties to international treaties/conventions and follow them by making suitable legislation;
(ii) States become parties to international treaties/conventions but do not follow them;
(iii) States do not become parties to treaties/conventions but by and large respect the philosophy behind such international treaties /conventions; and
(iv) States do not become parties to treaties/conventions, and do not respect them.

With regard to the international obligations concerning 'refugees', India falls under the third category as mentioned above. India has not yet become a party to the international obligations in the treatment of refugees and as such has not passed any comprehensive legislation on refugees. At the same time India has provided 'safe haven' to the refugees in need from the beginning. The experience of partition and the consequent movement of population and their belongings from one state to another, had been a matter of concern for both the countries (India & Pakistan) at that particular point of time. Thereafter, India has accommodated refugees from Burma (Myanmar), Bangladesh, Afghanistan, Sri Lanka, Tibet, Iran, Somalia, Sudan and from other countries.

India's refugee policy can be understood by analyzing four-fold components, which directly and indirectly provide a complete framework for its policy. These components are:

I. Provisions in Indian Constitution

Notwithstanding the fact that India is not a party to the 1951 Convention, it has acceded to certain international covenants, treaties and instruments, which by implication are also available to refugees and bind Government of India to respect refugee rights. For instance, in April 1979, India acceded to the 1966 International Covenant on Civil and Political Rights (ICCPR) and the 1966 International Covenant on Economic, Social and Cultural Rights. Article 13 of the ICCPR instrument deals with the expulsion of a person lawfully present in the territory of the state. India reserves its right under this article to apply its municipal law relating to aliens. In December 1992, India acceded to the 1989 Convention on the Rights of the Child. Article 22 of this Convention deals with refugee children and refugee family reunification. The 1963 Convention on the Elimination of All Forms of Racial Discrimination was ratified by India in 1969, and the 1979 Convention on the Elimination of All forms of Discrimination against Women was ratified in 1993.

Applicable non-binding international human rights instruments include the 1948 Universal Declaration on Human Rights whose Article 14(1) states that, "Everyone has the right to seek and to enjoy in other countries asylum from persecution."[11] Also included are: The principle of non-refoulement incorporated in the Asian-African Legal Consultative Committee's 1966 Principles Concerning the Treatment of Refugees (Bangkok Principles)[12], which specifically includes non-rejection at the frontier. More recently, the Declaration and Programme of Action of the 1993 Vienna World Conference on Human Rights included a special section on refugees which reaffirmed the right of every person to seek and enjoy asylum, as well as the right to return to one's own country.[13]

The then Secretary General, Indian Centre for Humanitarian Laws and Research, New Delhi Rose Verghese, has noted that while India lacked a formal legal framework for refugee protection, its administrative policies over the years have generally been in line with international refugee law principles. However, most of these policies are directed toward refugees from South Asian countries, the problems of asylum seekers from countries outside the immediate region are not addressed in a systematic manner. Even with respect to the former group of asylum seekers, in the absence of legislation, there are some discrepancies and treatment of refugees is affected by domestic or foreign policy considerations. While courts in the country have been humanitarian in their treatment of asylums seekers, they have been hampered by their inability to enforce provisions of international human rights instruments and refugee law norms in the absence of accession to relevant treaties or incorporating national legislation.[14]

Article 37 of the Indian Constitution provides that the Directive Principles of State Policy in Part IV are fundamental to the governance of the country and that it shall be the duty of the state to apply these principles in making laws. Article 51(c) in Part IV of the Constitution provides that the state shall endeavour to foster respect for international law and treaty obligations.[15] Thus, while Indian courts are not free to direct the making of legislation, they do adopt principles of interpretation that promote rather than hinder the aspirations enshrined in Part IV of the Constitution.

It is also true that India has not passed refugee-specific legislation to regulate the entry and status of refugees with the result that it has no general legislation on refugees. They are treated under the law applicable to aliens.[16] The principal Indian laws relevant to refugees are: Foreigners Act, 1946 (Section 3, 3A, 7, 14); Registration of Foreigners Act, 1939 (Section 3.6); Passport (Entry into India) Act, 1920; Passport Act, 1967 and Extradition Act, 1962. Though jurisdiction over issues of citizenship, naturalisation and aliens rests with the Union Legislature vide item 17 of the Union List,[17] Influxes of refugees have been handled by administrative decisions rather than through legislative requirement. This administrative decision is exercised within the framework of the 1946 Foreigners Act, and refugee policy in the country has essentially evolved from a series of administrative orders passed under the authority of section 3 of the said Acts.[18]

Now the question arises – what are the rights available to foreigners or aliens, which by implication are available to refugees in India? In its judgement in the case *Luis de Readt Vs Union of India* as affirmed later in *Khudiram Chakma Vs Union of India*, the Supreme Court of India, held that article 21 of the Constitution of India which protects life and personal liberty by stating that they may not be deprived except according to procedure established by law, is applicable to aliens in Indian territory as well.[19]

II. Decisions by Indian Judiciary

Various judicial decisions have, in the absence of a concrete legislative structure, tried to provide solutions to the problems of refugees, primarily with regard to the principles of non-refoulement, right to seek asylum and voluntary repatriation. The courts have, however, arrived at their decisions without entering into a discussion of international refugee law. It may be noted, however, that courts cannot ·take treaty provisions mentioned earlier into account. More recently the Hon'ble Supreme Court, in *National Human Rights Commission Vs Union of India*,[20] appears to have gone further in establishing protection to refugees in the face of Imminent expulsion from the country, The All Arunachal Pradesh Student Union (AAPSU), a nongovernmental body, had issued – quit India notices to all alleged foreigners including the Chakma refugees living in the state, with the threat of use of force if its demands were not acceded to. Justice A.M. Ahmadi held that as the constitutional rights in Articles 14 and 21 are available even to non-citizens, the state is bound to protect the life and liberty of every human being, be he a citizen or otherwise, and it cannot permit anybody or group of persons, e.g. the AAPSU, to threaten the Chakmas to leave the state. The Court recognised that the "quit India" notices amounted to a threat to life and liberty as understood by Article 21, and that Chakmas could not be evicted from their homes except in accordance with law.

The decision is limited to threats of expulsion posed by an activist student union and it does not enter into a discussion of issues pertaining to expulsion notices issued by the central government even if they constitute a violation of Article 21. Nevertheless, protection even against expulsion orders issued by the government has been provided to refugees through a staying of deportation orders. In *Malavika Karlekar Vs Union of India,*[21] twenty-one Burmese facing deportation from the Andaman Islands filed a writ petition with the Supreme Court pleading a violation of their rights under Article 21. The Court directed that the deportation order was to be stayed to allow the asylum seekers to approach UNHCR for refugee status. In some instances, detainees have been granted leave to travel to New Delhi, where the Office of UNHCR is located, in order to seek determination of refugee status, e.g. *Khy-Htoon and others Vs the State of Manipur*, Gauhati High Court, 1990; *Bogyi Vs Union of India*, Gauhati High Court, 1989; and *Zothansangpuli Vs the State of Manipur*, Gauhati High Court, 1989. In *Bogyi Vs Union of India,*[22] even in the absence of a pending application for refugee status, the Gauhati High Court ordered the temporary release of a Burmese man from detention for a two-month period so that he could apply for refugee status with UNHCR.

The petitions in these cases usually allege violation of Article 21 of the Constitution in the event that' the deportation orders are carried out. While the absence of reasons given in passing these interim motions staying the deportation orders results in an unclear legal position with respect to non-refoulement, the implication of the decisions would appear to be that a successful application for refugee status by an asylum seeker preempts refoulement. That is why B.S. Chimni is right when he observed that, "In the context of refugee rights, it can be argued that Article 21 encompasses the principle of non-refoulement which requires that a state shall not expel or return a refugee in any manner whatsoever to the frontiers of territories where his life or freedom would be threatened on account of his race, religion, nationality, membership of a particular social group or political opinion".[23]

However, Indian courts do not have the authority to enforce the provisions of the above mentioned international human rights instruments unless these provisions are incorporated into municipal law by the legislature, and this process of incorporation in the Indian context has been largely ignored with respect to the above treaties. Parliament is under no obligation to enact law to give effect to a treaty, and in the absence of such law judiciary is not competent to enforce obedience of the treaty obligations by the Executive. Thus, while India has the duty to carry out in good faith its obligations arising out of international law, the Indian government cannot offer acts or omissions on the part of their legislative or executive organs as an excuse for failure to fulfill the above obligations. In the event of failure of the government to bring its municipal law in line with its International obligations, international Law does not render such conflicting municipal law null and void.

Benefits granted to different groups of refugees in India appear to be determined by the' situation of the refugees in relation to the local people, e.g. ethnic ties between refugee groups and the local population impacts upon assistance provided and to the relative burden they impose on the states concerned. This is particularly true for subjects like education that fall under the State List in the Indian Constitution. Thus the Chakma refugees in Tripura are worse off economically than are the Sri Lankan refugees in Tamil Nadu.

Administrative discretion is also paramount in the treatment of issues like the regulations of stay in the country of foreign nationals who are recognized as refugees under UNHCR's mandate. Afghan refugees recognized by the UNHCR in New Delhi have their residential permits regularly extended on the basis of renewal of their refugees certificates while Sudanese refugees with the UNHCR are often issued "Leave India" [24] notices by the government upon the expiry of their student visas.

III. NHRC and Refugee Issue

The 1993 Protection of Human Rights Act established a recommendatory body called the National Human Rights Commission that has power to inquire into the "violation of human rights or abetment thereof."[25] The Commission is not restricted to investigating issues of concern to citizens only and, in fact, it has visited both the special camps for Sri Lankan refugees in Tamil Nadu and the camps for Chakmas in Tripura to investigate living conditions there. It has also filed a petition in the Supreme Court on the threatened expulsion of Chakmas in Arunachal Pradesh. An issue here is whether a body like the Human Rights Commission may be used to take up cases of discriminatory treatment between refugees, especially in light of the fact that some of the areas involved are related to primary education, fall clearly within the preview of recognized human right.

An examination of the potential role of the National Human Rights Commission is also pertinent in the face of recent judicial decisions establishing standards with respect to non-refoulement and voluntary repatriation. As these judgments may be limited in their scope of application to particular refugee groups in identified areas of the country, a standardization of the norms established may take place through recommendations of the Commission. A denial of non-refoulement and voluntary repatriation standards applicable to other groups of refugees in the country, especially if these are other groups of refugees recognised by the governments, is clearly violative of human rights norms.

In this context, it needs to be stressed that repatriation should only be voluntary and be carried out in conditions of absolute safety. In the only case decided on the issue in India, the Madras High Court, in *Pedumaran and Dr. S. Ramadoss Vs Union of India*, has set standards with regard to the repatriation of refugees by emphasising the voluntary character of repatriation.[26] A writ petition was filed seeking interim relief in the form of an induction to restrain the authorities from repatriating refugees against their will. It was argued by the petitioners that the Indian government was using force by reducing rations, limiting movement of refugees, and stopping the financial assistance that was previously given. The court in its findings established that Indian government had acted properly and in accordance with international law, laid special emphasis on UNHCR's role as an impartial third party in verifying the voluntary repatriations and on the fact that individual refugees had signed forms in English and Tamil where they had expressed their willingness to return. The state government was, however ordered to translate the decision in Tamil language and circulate it in refugee's camps. The court also ordered that a circular in Tamil be posted in all refugee campus indicating that no refugee would be forcibly repatriated.

The court did not address the issue of whether reduction of rations, limitation of movement and the stoppage of financial assistance constituted coercion so as to render the repatriation involuntary. However, by presuming from the start that repatriations are necessary to be voluntary, and by examining whether the government's actions had sufficiently established "voluntariness", standards governing voluntary repatriations have been set by the court. The moot question is whether these standards are extendable to all other refugees in the country? The Court in this case was asked to pronounce judgment upon a very specific situation where the government already had in place a repatriation policy. In its judgment, the Court merely approved the policy and did not make any observations about the larger refugee context in the country.[27]

IV. Working of UNHCR in India

UNHCR began its operations in 1951 on the initiative of the UN General Assembly.[28] Subsequent to independence Government of India followed a cloistered approach in permitting voluntary organizations to assist refugees. Department of Rehabilitation monitored most of the assistance to refugees. However, this cloistered approach was relaxed in 1969, when India permitted UNHCR to open its first branch office in India at New Delhi. When relations between China and India began to deteriorate and the hope of Tibetan refugees to return home early waned, UNHCR was asked to assist and accelerate the process of permanent settlement of Tibetan refugees. The other time when UNHCR and Government of India happened to closely interact was in the case of the erstwhile East Pakistan refugees. In April 1971, India received about 10 million refugees from Bangladesh on humanitarian grounds. India raised the issue to the international consciousness and attention to mobilize support from UNO and other countries. Pakistan registered its protest in the UNO on 29 April 1971. In spite of the protest, UN Secretary-General designated UNHCR to act as a co-ordinating agency between the needy refugees and helpful voluntary organizations. The then High Commissioner, Prince Sadruddin Aga Khan visited India and Pakistan in June 1971. He also made consultations with governments of both the countries on relief measures and voluntary repatriation. He made a second visit to India in November of the same year.

Since February 1969, UNHCR has been caring for the hordes of refugees coming to India, officially as well as unofficially. It has been involved with numerous categories of refugee: Tibetan, Bangladeshi, Afghan and Sri Lankan. Since 1995, India has also become a member of 53 member EXCOM of the Office of the UNHCR.[29] Today, UNHCR operates in India through its Office of Chief of Mission at Delhi and also has a sub-office at Chennai, which is basically meant for repatriation of refugees from Sri Lanka. The Chennai office works under a Repatriation Officer.

The office of the UNHCR in India is mainly composed of four units: (a) Legal Unit; (b) Social Service Unit; (c) Programme Unit; and (d) Public information unit.[30]

(a) The Legal Unit, as the name suggests, deals chiefly with the determination of refugee status and promotion of the protocol. All asylum seekers are individually interviewed by Legal Officers at UNHCR. Those found to have genuine fear of persecution, arising out of serious human rights violations in their country of origin, are recognized as refugees. They are issued refugee certificates for identification.[31]

The 1951 Convention and its 1967 Protocol are the principal international instruments for the protection of refugees. They have been ratified by 134 countries. India has neither ratified the Convention so far, nor it does have any specific domestic laws on refugees. Refugees are dealt with under the Foreigners Act, 1946, which does not distinguish between refugees and other foreigners. In order to raise awareness about these issues, and to build a favourable public opinion, UNHCR has been undertaking a host of promotional activities. These include interactive activities with the academia, including students, researchers and teachers of international law and international relations as well as with NGOs and others such agencies and institutions. The Unit is led by a Legal Officer aided by two Assistant Legal Officers. As on January 1999, there were about 17,700 refugees registered with UNHCR, Delhi.

(b) The Social Service Unit consists of a Social Service Officer and five workers. It looks after various aspects of the needs of refugees such as healthcare, education, employment and settlement. Assistance is provided to the refugees through projects implemented by NGOs. For instance, the Young Men's Christian Association (YMCA) assists refugees with educational and vocational training, social counselling and income generation activities. Another NGO, Voluntary Health Association of Delhi (VHAD) provides medical assistance, referral and medical services and medical counselling to refugees.

A legal NGO, Public Interest Legal Service and Research Centre (PILSARC) offers legal counsel to refugees facing legal protection problems in India. The entry, stay and departure of refugees are handled by the foreigners' section of the Ministry of Home Affairs and Foreigners Regional Registration Officers throughout the country.[32] In some cases involving detention and deportation of refugees, UNHCR intervenes directly with the Government of India to secure their release and seek appropriate solutions. In some cases UNHCR provides financial assistance to refugees for a limited period of 6–12 months, and to those suffering from disability, chronic illness or other forms of vulnerability.[33]

(c) Programme Unit mainly looks after the overall administration of various projects and programmes undertaken by UNHCR for refugee welfare as well as the financial aspects related thereto. Public Information Unit consisting of a sole Public Relations and Information Officer, undertakes various usual public relations exercises apart from those related to refugee welfare. It also interacts with students, researchers and any other person interested in the informational aspects of the UNHCR. In India it is led by a Chief of Mission assisted by a Deputy Chief of Mission who is also responsible for programming. The total number of staff at UNHCR, Delhi is 25 including 7 project staff from UNDP and excluding 20 contracted staff. The total budget for its India operation is US $1.6 million which it gets from the UN and donor countries and institutions.

Since 1981, UNHCR has been associated with about 50,000 refugees of whom over 30,000 have been repatriated. Some of them are also resettled in India and other countries. For this, UNHCR works in association with various embassies in India who take refugees as per the quota of their country. But as far as possible, it strives for their voluntary repatriation by arranging their passage.

(d) One of the thrust areas of UNHCR's advocacy efforts in India has therefore been to highlight the absence and the need for laws to protect the rights of refugees. In this endeavour it has over the years built an institutional relationship with the judicial community in India. In collaboration with well-known lawyers, it has organised several seminars and workshops on Refugee Law and International law relating to refugees. One of the key partners in this effort has been SAARC Law, together with whom it held a major seminar in 1997. UNHCR has also sought the services of PILSARC as an implementing partner, to provide legal assistance to refugees facing protection problems.

The Indian Centre for Humanitarian Laws and Research (ICHLR), another implementing partner of the UNHCR in India, has been conducting seminars, workshops and conferences on refugee issues throughout the country. ICHLR, in collaborating with the Informal Consultations on Refugees and Migratory Movement in South Asia, has also brought out a draft National Model Law on Refugees for countries in South Asia. To disseminate the draft National Model Law, it, plans to support NGO efforts to translate it into the national languages of various South Asian countries. It is also supporting NGO efforts to bring out a handbook on well-known court cases in India relating to refugees. This will serve as useful references in future cases relating to refugees.

UNHCR, also collaborates with the National Human Rights Commission (NHRC) of India to strengthen the protection of refugees, who are very often victims of human rights violations. It is consciously working towards building a legal framework to protect refugees. Stressing on the importance of a legal framework, it has also endowed a Chair on Refugee Law in the National Law School at the University of Bangalore in 1996. Similarly, it has supported the Centre of Refugee Studies, Department of International Law, Jadavpur University, Calcutta, in conducting several short courses for lawyers and law professors. It also interacts with the Department of Rehabilitation in Chennai. Apart from such efforts, it has encouraged the print media to take up refugee issues. Under an agreement with the Government of India, it monitors the voluntary repatriation of Tamil refugees returning to Sri Lanka.

UNHCR has slowly developed a network to help refugees. It has arrangement with All India Institute of Medical Sciences for providing medical assistance to refugees. Upon recommendations of UNHCR, the International Committee of Red Cross provides travel documents to refugees, who have been offered third country settlement. UNHCR also collaborates with National Human Rights Commission, an establishment under Government of India, which monitors the human rights scenario in the country. The NHRC played a prominent role in protecting the Chakmas.[34]

However, despite the substantial involvement of UNHCR with refugees in India, India has not yet acceded to the 1951 Convention on the Status of Refugees.[35] Notwithstanding this, India has been cooperating with UNHCR in the administration of refugee situation in the country in a significant manner. She has been more of a refugee receiving than a generating country due to its easily accessible borders, socio-cultural identities, economic opportunities and a democratic and soft state.

India's experience of coping with refugee problems goes back to the partition of the subcontinent, when eight million refugees, from the areas which are now Pakistan and Bangladesh, moved into India and were successfully integrated into the population.[36] However, like other South Asian countries, India is not a party to most of the international refugee conventions.[37] According to one scholar, "part of the reason for India not ratifying the 1951 Convention was ideological in nature and related to the politics of the Cold War. Since with the end of cold war old compulsions of global politics are no more, hence it is expected that India may enter into such agreements.[38] According to a report, India, in fact, is considering signing the 1951 Convention on Refugees; this because of growing complexities over the refugee issues in the SAARC (South Asian Association for Regional Cooperation) region and the absence of a national legislation on refugees. Ministry of External Affairs sources said that the Government is examining the issue of refugee protection and India's international obligations, including the option of signing the 1951 UN Convention.[39]

Need for Perspective

The Primary objective in India should be to seek a formal accreditation of the former and extend its role by gaining access to all refugee groups in the country and secure accession of India to the 1951 Convention and 1967 Protocol. In fact, it has been actively soliciting greater Indian participation in refugee affairs and trying to create public interest on refugee issues through a vigorous programme of promotional activities relating to the discrimination of refugee law, encouragement of research and studies on refugee issues and creating awareness of refugee problems with local institutions of higher learning, NGOs and professional bodies. Complimenting the Indian response to refugees, a study of the US Committee for Refugees observed:

> Despite the curbs on international assistance and monitoring, India has accorded a welcome to asylum-seekers that is as generous as for any refugee groups in Asia. The record is not unblemished, to be sure. There have been instances of pushback and coercive measures to promote repatriation, but it has largely been the case that any person, who has landed on the shore and asked for refuge, has been granted refuge.[40]

Despite this India has faced and is still facing acute refugee problem; leaving aside their minor influxes, it is neither a party to the 1951 Refugee Convention or 1967 Protocol and nor has a specific legislation on Refugee Law. The government generally meets its humanitarian obligations towards refugees and asylum seekers, but prefers to do so as a matter of administrative policy rather than as a legal requirement. It has, however, handled this issue at the political and administrative levels well. A virtual consequence is that refugees have to be treated under the law applicable to aliens in India, unless it makes a specific provision as it did in the case of Ugandan refugees of Indian origin when it passed the Foreigners from Uganda Order 1973.[41]

The concept of 'Refugee Law' in the Indian judicial system has evolved over a period of time. Due to lack of a refugee specific statute, the judicial system is constrained to enforce upon refugees, laws which are applicable to foreigners in general thereby 'consciously or subconsciously ignoring the unique predicament peculiar to refugees'.[42] Continued developments through the courts, government and international fora will all contribute to the process of making additional space for the humanitarian and legal concerns of forced population movements which result in refugee flows.

From the above analysis it can be discerned that South Asia represents an important region in global politics facing the impact of refugee problem among its member states. Since this region is Indo-Centric in nature and India is also sharing borders with large number of states the problem of refugees has affected India the most. Despite this serious problem India has neither evolved a long term policy framework, nor it has adhered to institutional agreements at global level. India has yet to ratify the Refugee Convention of 1951 and its Protocol of 1967. Inter-state hostility and external intervention in the problem of South Asian countries have further complicated the discourse. It is a fact that by now India has not acceded to the 1951 Convention on Status of Refugees, but UNHCR has operated in India and is working among the refugees settled in India. Since 1969, it has been caring for the hordes of refugees coming to India, officially as well as unofficially. It has been involved with numerous categories of refugees: Tibetan, Bangladeshi, Afghan and Sri Lankan. Since 1995, India has also become a member of EXCOM of the Office of the UNHCR. Today UNHCR operates in India through its Office of Chief of Mission at Delhi and also has a sub-office at Chennai, which is basically meant for repatriation of refugees from Sri Lanka. However India is still not party to the Convention, nor it has any specific domestic laws on refugees, hence the latter are dealt with the Foreigner Act. 1946. UNHCR is also working in collaboration with the National Human Rights Commission (NHRC) of India, strengthening the protection of refugees, who are very often victim of human rights violations. It is consciously working towards building a legal framework to protect the rights of the refugees.

Evolving A New Framework

To protect the human rights of the refugees following suggestion seem to be in order: (i) There is urgency to make distinction between refugees and other kind of migrants. This can not be done without a clear cut and comprehensive definition of the term refugee. Without such definition ambiguity is likely to continue. (ii) India should endeavour to get a consensus among all the countries of South Asia to sign both the Convention and Protocol with immediate effect. (iii) India must evolve a very clear national policy on refugees. Besides it should have the backing by all regional states so that implementation of the same can be made very smoothly. (iv) India should bring this issue in the central agenda of SAARC, so that a consensual model among the states of South Asia be evolved. (v) India should make an effort in the direction of formation of a uniform refugees policy to be made at regional level regardless of their origin, cause of displacement cross border ethnic and political ties, etc. because it is essential to mitigate discriminations among both inter and intra refugee populations. (vi) It should also help in evolving a full proof mechanism for the evolution, interpretation and implementation made to define refugees, to accord status to them to finalize principle of non-refoulement inclusion and exclusion and to provide protection to them. (vii) It should also he convinced that all the states of South Asia should avoid using refugee population as pawns in the regional geo-politics or in the context of their bilateral ties. Thus, in the era of emerging regional co-operation, in the wake of the end of cold war and intensification of process of globalization, India, along with other states of South Asia, should take initiative to ponder over above suggestions. Development of a framework based on mutual consent to resolve such issue is likely to establish peace and tranquillity not only at the level of South Asia, but also at the global level.

Notes and References

1. A key element of the refugee definition as found in the 1951 Refugee Convention is fleeing one's country of origin 'owing to a well-founded fear of persecution.' Persecution is not defined in international refugee or human rights law. However, one commentator has offered the following description: '...persecution may be defined as the sustained or systematic violation of basic human rights demonstrative of a failure of state protection. A well-founded fear of persecution exists when one reasonably anticipates that the failure to leave the country may result in a form of serious harm which government cannot or will not prevent....' James Hathaway, "Fear of Persecution and the Law of Human Rights", *Bulletin of Human Right,* vol. 91, No. 1, United Nations, New York, 1992, p. 99.
2. Lok Raj Baral and S.D. Muni, "Untroduction: Refugees, South Asia and Security", S.D. Muni and Lok Raj Baral, ed., *Refugees and Regional Security in South Asia*, Konark, Delhi; 1996, p. 1.
3. J.M. Castro-Magluff, "Role of the UNHCR in Addressing the Problem of Forced Migration", ed., Om Parkash Mishra, *Forced Migration in the South Asian Region-Displacement, Human Rights and Conflict Resolution,* Manak, Delhi, 2004, pp. 97–98.
4. Joseph M. Kitagawa ed., *American Refugee Policy: Ethical and Religious Reflections*, Fund for World Relief, New York, 1983, p. 87.
5. UNHCR, *Convention and Protocol Relating to the Status of Refugees*, Geneva, 1996, p. 16.

6. UNHCR, *The State of the World's Refugees 1997–98*, n. 6, p. X.
7. *UNHCR by Numbers*, Public Information Section, UNHCR, Geneva, 1996.
8. Mel Gurtav, "Open Borders: A Global-Humanist Approach too the Refugee Crisis", *World Development*, Vol. 19, No. 5, 1991, p. 485.
9. Noilot, "The Era of Homeless Man", *Geography*, Vol. 72, No. 2, 1987, pp. 109–121.
10. S.D. Muni and Lok Raj Baral (ed.), Refugees and Regional Security in South Asia, Konark Publishers Pvt. Ltd., Delhi; 1996, pp. 9–18.
11. Rumki Basu, *The United Nations*, Sterling, New Delhi, 1992, p. 357.
12. Shrinivas Gupta, "Influx of refugees and international law", *Link*, November 22, 1992, p. 29.
13. Smrithi Talwar, "Building a Regional Consensus or Asylum: The Indian Perspective", *Regional Consultations on Refugee and migratory Movements in South Asia*, UNHCR, New Delhi, 1996, p. 45.
14. *Ibid*, pp. 6–7.
15. *The Constitution of India*, Central Law Publications, Allahabad, 1994, p. 21.
16. The word 'alien' is nowhere defined in Indian Legal corpus. However, it does appear in the Constitution of India (Article 22 para 3 and Entry 17, List I, Schedule 7), in section 83 of the Indian Civil Procedure code, and in section 3(2)(b) of the Indian Citizenship Act, 1995, as well as several other statutes.
17. The Constitution of India, n. 27, p. 191.
18. Foreigners Act 1946, Section 3, provides the power to make orders and is drafted very broadly – "The Central Government may by order make provision, either generally or with respect to all foreigners, or with respect to any particular foreigner or any prescribed class or description of foreigner for prohibiting, regulating or restricting the entry of foreigners into India or their departure therefore or their pressure."
19. Talwar, n. 13, p. 50.
20. *Ibid.*
21. *Ibid*, p. 51.
22. *Ibid.*
23 B.S. Chimni, "The Legal Conditions of Refugees in India", *Journal of Refugee Studies,* Vol. 7, No. 4, 1994, p. 380.
24. Talwar, n. 13, p. 52.
25. *Ibid,* p. 53.
26. B.S. Chimni, "Refugees in International Law", *Seminar,* No. 463, March 1998, New Delhi, p. 21.
27. Talwar, n. 13, p. 53.
28. A Leroy Bennet, *International Organisation: Principles and Issues,* Prentice Hall, New Jersey, 1998, p. 290.
29. B.S. Chimni, "The International Law", *Seminar*, No. 463, March 1998, New Delhi, p. 20.
30. Saumitra Mohan, "India, UNHCR and Refugees: An Analytical Study", *Journal of Peace Studies*, Vol. 10, No. 3, July-September, 2003, p. 44.
31. UNHCR, *India Fact Sheet*, No. 2, New Delhi, August 1998, p. 1.
32. UNHCR, *UNHCR in India: An Information Paper for Refugees and Asylum Seekers in India*, UNHCR, Delhi, 1998, p. 5.

35. B.S. Chimni, "The Legal Conditions of Refugees in India", *Journal of Refugees Studies*, Vol. 7, No. 4, 1994, p. 379.
36. Dr. Najma Heptulla, Special Address, *Refugees in the SAARC Region: Building a Legal framework*, a seminar jointly organized by SAARCLAW and UNHCR, 2–3 May 1993, New Delhi, p. 25.
37. Irene Khan, "Opening Remarks", *Ibid*, p. 29.
38. UNHCR, *Regional Consultations on Refugee and Migratory Movements in South Asia*, UNHCR, Delhi, 1996, p. 10.
39. "India may sign Convention on Refugees", *World Focus*, January 1999, p. 19.
40. V. Vijay Kumar, "Should India Ratify the Refugee Convention and Protocol?: A Policy Perspective", *Bulletin on IHL and Refugee Law*, Vol. 2 No. 2A, July-December, 1997, p. 326.
41. J.N. Saxena, "Refugee Rights", *Bulletin on IHL and Refugee Law*, Vol. 3, No. 2, July-December 1998, p. 245.
42. Sumbul Rizvi, "Response of the India Judicial System to the Refugee Problem", *Bulletin on IHL and Refugee Law*, Vol. 2, No. 1, January-June 1997, p. 65.

Bibliography

Books

Abhyankar, Rajendra M., ed., *West Asia and the Region: Defining India's Role,* Academic Foundation, New Delhi, 2008.

Ahmar, Moonis, *ed., The Arab-Israeli Peace Process: Lessons for India and Pakistan,* Oxford University Press, New Delhi, 2001,

Ahmar, Moonis, ed., *The Challenges of Confidence Building in South Asia*, New Delhi 2001.

Art., Robert J., *A Grand Strategy for America,* Manas, New Delhi, 2004.

Arya, Kedar S., *Perspectives on India's International Relations,* Akansha Pub., New Delhi, 2006.

Aziz, Jahangir et al., *China and India Learning From Each Other: Reforms and Policies for Sustained Growth,* International Monetary Fund, 2006.

Bajpai, Kanti P., et al., *Brsstacks and Beyond: Perception and Management of Crisis in South Asia*, New Delhi, 1995.

Bakshi, Jyotsna, *Russia and India: From Ideology to Geopolitics,* New Delhi, 1999.

Banerjee, Dipankar and Thakur, Ramesh, eds., *Emerging Challenges in UN Peacekeeping Operations: An Indo-Japanese Dialogue,* Samskriti, New Delhi, 2006.

Banerjee, Dipankar, ed., *Confidance Building Measures in South Aisa*, Regional Center for Strategic Studies, Colombo, 1999.

Benjamin, Joseph, ed., *Indo-Pak Relations,* 2004.

Bertsch, Gary K., et al., eds., *Engaging India*, New York, 1999.

Bezbaruah, Ranju, *America and India in Global and South Asian Settings,* 1999.

Bhola, P.L., *Foreign Policies of India, Pakistan and China,* RBSA Publishers, Jaipur, 2001.

Bhonsle, Rahul, et.al., eds., *Indo-U.S. Civil Nuclear Deal,* 2 Vols., Atlantic, New Delhi, 2007.

Bhutani, Sudarshan, *A Clash of Political Cultures: Sino-Indian Relations (1957-1962),* Roli, New Delhi, 2004.

Budania, Rajpal, *India's National Security Dilemma: Pakistan Factor and India's Policy Response*, New Delhi, 2001.

Chellaney, Brahma, *Asian Juggernaut: The Rise of China, India and Japan,* HarperCollins, New Delhi, 2006.

Chitkara, M.G., *Indo-Pak Relations Challenges Before New Millennium,* APH, New Delhi, 2001.

Chopra, V.D., ed., *Afghanistan and Asian Stability,* 1998,

Dahal, Dev Raj and Pandey, Nishchal Nath, eds., *Comprehensive Security in South Asia,* New Delhi, Manohar, 2006.

Das, Gurudas et.al., eds., *Indo-Myanmar Border Trade: Status, Problems and Potentials,* Akansha, New Delhi, 2005.

Dash, P.L. and Nazarkin, Andrei M., *India and Russia: Strategic Synergy Emerging,* Authorspress, New Delhi, 2007.

Dass, Tania, *Beyond Cold War: Security Council and International Politics,* Minerva Publications, Kolkata, 2004.

Dittmer, Lowell, ed., *South Asia's Nuclear Security Dilemma: India, Pakistan, and China,* Pentagon Press, New Delhi, 2005.

Dixit, J.N, *Makers of India's Foreign Policy: Raja Ram Mohun Roy to Yashwant Sinha,* HarperCollins, New Delhi, 2004.

________, *India's Foreign Policy and Its Neighbours,* Gyan Publishing, New Delhi, 2001.

________, *India's Foreign Policy Challenge of Terrorism: Fashioning New Interstate Equations,* Gyan, New Delhi, 2002.

Dwivedi, Dhirendra, *Collective Security Under United Nations: Retrospect and Prospects,* Kanishka, New Delhi, 2005.

Gaan, Narottam, *India and the United States: From Estrangement to Engagement,* Kalpaz Pub., Delhi, 2007.

Gaur, Mahendra, *Foreign Policy Annual, 2001: Events and Documents,* 2 Vols., Kalpaz, New Delhi, 2005.

Gaur, Mahendra, *Foreign Policy Annual, 2002: Events and Documents,* 2 Vols., Kalpaz, New Delhi, 2005.

Gopal, D. and Rumley, Dennis, eds., *India and Australia: Issues and Opportunities,* Authorspress, Delhi, 2004.

Gopal, D., ed., *Australia: In the Emerging Global Order: Evolving Australia-India Relations,* Shipra, Delhi, 2002.

Gopal, Krishan and Sharma, Sarbjit, *India and Israel: Towards Strategic Partnership,* Authorspress, Delhi, 2007.

Gujral, I.K., *Continuity and Change: India's Foreign Policy,* , Macmillan India, New Delhi, 2003.

Guruswamy, Mohan, *ed., Emerging Trends in India-China Relations,* Hope India Pub., Gurgaon, 2006.

Harshe, Rajen and Seethi, K.M., eds., *Engaging with the World: Critical Reflections on India's Foreign Policy,* Orient Longman, New Delhi, 2005.

Jahangir, B.K. and Ray, Jayant, eds., *India-Bangladesh Cooperation Broadening Measures*, KP Bagchi, Kolkata, 1997.

Jain, B.M., ed., *International System and the Great Power Relationship (U.S., China and India),* Reprint. INA Shree Pub., Jaipur, 2008.

Jain, Rajendra K. and Elsenhans, Hartmut, eds., *India, Europe and the Changing Dimensions of Security,* Radiant Pub., New Delhi, 2006.

__________, eds., *India, the European Union and the WTO,* Radiant Pub., New Delhi, 2006.

Jain, Rajendra K. ed., *India and the European Union: Building A Strategic Partnership,* Radiant, New Delhi, 2007.

_________, ed., *India, Europe and South Asia,* Radiant Pub., New Delhi, 2007.

Jain, Rajendra K., et.al., eds., *The European Union in World Politics,* Radiant, New Delhi, 2006.

Jayapalan, N., *Foreign Policy of India,* Atlantic, Delhi, 2001.

Jha, Nalini Kant, ed., *South Asia in Twenty-First Century: India, Her Neighbours, and the Great Powers,* South Asian Pub., New Delhi, 2003.

Jha, Shashikant and Sarkar, Bhaswati, *ed., Amidst Turbulence and Hope: Transition in Russia and Eastern Europe,* Lancer's Books, New Delhi, 2002,

Kapur, Ashok, et.al., *India and the United States in a Changing World,* Sage, New Delhi, 2002.

Kapur, S. Paul, *Dangerous Deterrent: Nuclear Weapons Proliferation and Conflict in South Asia,* Standford University Press, Standford, 2007.

Karim, Mohd Aminul, *Power Politics in the Asia-Pacific: The Case of Chinese Modernization,* Academic Press and Publishers Library, Dhaka, 2007.

__________, *Selected Papers on Security and Leadership,* Academic Press, New Delhi, 2008.

Kaur, Kulwnt and Mann, Baljit S., eds., *South Asia: Dynamics of Politics, Economy and Society,* New Delhi, Knowledge World, 2006.

Khan, Ahmad, *India and West Asia: Energy Market in the Liberalizing Era,* New Delhi, 1999.

Khan, Javed Ahmad, *India's Energy Security and the Arabian Gulf: Oil and Gas Market in Decontrolled Regimes,* Arise Pub., New Delhi, 2005.

Kiely, Ray, *Empire in the Age of Globalisation: US Hegemony and Neoliberal Disorder,* Orient Longman, Hyderabad, 2007.

Koshy, Ninan, *Under the Empire: India's New Foreign Policy,* Leftword Books, New Delhi, 2006.

Krepon, Michaal and Shivak, Amit, eds., *Crisis Prevention, Confidance Building and Reconciliation in South Aisa,* New Delhi, 1996.

Krishnamurthy, B., *Indo-French Relations: Prospects and Perspectives,* Shipra, Delhi, 2005.

Kumar, S., ed., *Foundations of International Relations: In Special Reference to India,* Anmol, New Delhi, 2006.

__________, ed., *India's International Relations: Issues in Asian Context,* Anmol, New Delhi, 2006.

Mahapatra, Chintamani, *Indo-US Relations into the 21 st century,* New Delhi, Knowledge World, 1998.

Maharaj, Sanjay Badri, *The Armageddon Factor: Nuclear Weapons in the India-Pakistan Context,* Lancer, New Delhi, 2000.

Malakar, S.N., ed., *India's Energy Security and the Gulf,* Academic Excellence, Delhi, 2006.

Malik, V.K. and Kapur, Ashok, eds., *India and United States in a Changing World,* New Delhi, 2002.

Malik, V.P. and Crome, Erhard, eds., *Europe and Asia: Perspectives on the Emerging International Order,* Lancer, New Delhi, 2006.

Mann, Poonam, *India's Foreign Policy in the Post Cold War Era,* Harman, Delhi, 2000.

Mansingh Lalit, et al., eds., *Indian Foreign Poliocy: Agenda for 21st Century*, Konark, New Delhi, 1998. (2 Vols)

Mathur, Anand and Meena Sohan Lal, eds., *India's Profile in Polycentric World Order,* RBSA, Jaipur, 2008.

Mathur, Vibha, *India: Foreign Trade Policy and WTO 1991-2003,* New Century, Delhi, 2003.

Mishra, S.K., ed., *India's Nuclear Policy, Disarmament and International Security,* Radha Pub., New Delhi, 2006.

Mohan, C. Raja, *Crossing the Rubicon: The Shaping of India's New Foreign Policy,* Palgrave Macmillan, New York, 2004.

__________, *Impossible Allies: Nuclear India, United States and the Global Order,* India Research Press, New Delhi, 2006.

Mohite, Dilip H. and Dholakia, Amit, eds., *India and the Emerging World Order: Foreign Policy and Security,* New Delhi, Kalinga, 2001.

Muni, S.D. and Pant, Girijesh, *India's Search for Energy Security: Prospects for Cooperation with Extended Neighbourhood,* Rupa, New Delhi, 2005.

Naaz, Farah, *West Asia and India: Changing Perspectives,* Shipra, New Delhi, 2005.

Nair, R. Sreekantan, *Dynamics of a Diplomacy Delayed: India and Israel,* Kalpaz Pub., Delhi, 2004.

Nanda, Ravi, *India and the Emerging Multipolar World,* Lancer's, New Delhi, 2001.

Narsimhan, Sushila and Kim, Do Young, eds., *Korea and India: A Forging Relationship,* Manak, New Delhi, 2006.

Nautiyal, Annpurna, ed., *Challenges to India's Foreign Policy in the New Era,* 2006.

Pagare, G.K., *International Politics in New World Order,* Cyber Tech, New Delhi, 2009.

Panagariya , Arvind , *India: The Emerging Giant*, Oxford University Press, 2008.

Panda, Rajaram and Fukazawa, Yoo, eds., *India and Japan in Search of Global Roles,* Promilla and Co., New Delhi, 2007.

Pasha, A.K. , *Arab-Israeli Peace Process: An Indian Perspective,* 2000,

Patil, V.T. and Jha.Nalini Kant, eds., *India in a Turbulent World: Perspectives on Foreign and Security Policies,* South Asian, New Delhi, 2003.

Pillai, K. Raman, ed., *Indian Foreign Policy in the 1990s,* 1997.

Prasad, Rajendra, ed., *India's Security in 21 Century: Challenges and Responses,* Dominant, New Delhi, 2002.

Raj, Christopher Sam and Nafey, Abdul, eds., *Canada's Global Engagements and Relations with India,* Manak, New Delhi, 2007.

Rajagopalan, Rajesh, *Second Strike: Arguments About Nuclear War in South Asia,* Penguin, New Delhi, 2005.

Rajain, Arpit, *Nuclear Deterrence in Southern Asia: China, India and Pakistan,* Sage, New Delhi, 2005.

Rajan, M.S., *India and International Affairs: A Collection of Essays,* 1999.

Rana, Kishan S., *Asian Diplomacy: The Foreign Ministries of China, India, Japan, Singapore, and Thailand,* Oxford University Press, New Delhi, 2007.

Rao, P.V., ed., *India and Australia: New Horizons,* Mittal Pub., New Delhi, 2003.

Rasgotra, M. and Chopra, V.D., eds., *India's Relations with Russia and China: A New Phase,* 1997.

Rumley, Dennis and Chaturvedi, Sanjay, eds., *Energy Security and the Indian Ocean Region,* South Asian Pub., New Delhi, 2005.

Sahadevan, P., ed., *Conflict and Peacemaking in South Asia,* New Delhi, 2001.

Saighal, Vinod, *Global Security Paradoxes 2000-2020,* Manas Publications, New Delhi, 2004.

Shams-Ud-Din. Ed., *India and Russia: Towards Strategic Partnership,* Lancer's Books, New Delhi, 2001.

Sharma, Anuraag and Trikha, Pradeep, eds., *Caring Cultures: Sharing Imaginations: Australia and India,* Sarup and Sons, New Delhi, 2006.

Sharma, Jagdish P., *Foreign Policy Challenges: India and the Afro-Arab World,* Anamika, New Delhi, 2003.

Sharma, R.R., ed., *India and Emerging Asia,* Sage, New Delhi, 2005.

Sharma, S.R., *Foundations of Indian Foreign Policy,* Omsons, New Delhi, 2002.

Sharma, Sita Ram, ed., *U.S. Nuclear Agreement for Cooperation with India 2006,* Alfa Pub., New Delhi, 2007.

Shirk, Susan L., *China Fragile Superpower,* Oxford University Press, New Delhi, 2007.

Shivam, Ravinder K., *India's Foreign Policy Nehru to Vajpayee,* Common wealth, New Delhi, 2001.

Singh, Jaswant, *Defending India,* Macmillan, Banglore, 1999.

Singh, M.K., *Diplomacy in India,* Navyug, New Delhi, 2008.

Singh, Mahavir, ed., *Building a New Asia,* Shipra, New Delhi, 2005.

Singh, Naunihal, *India and the United States,* Anmol, New Delhi, 2005.

Singh, Poonam, *Indo-American Relations,* Vista International, Delhi, 2006.

Singh, R.S.N., *Asian Strategic and Military Perspective,* Lancer, New Delhi, 2005.

Singh, S., ed., *India and China: Mutual Relations,* Anmol, New Delhi, 2006.

Sisodia, N.S. and Bhaskar, C. Uday, eds., *Emerging India: Security and Foreign Policy Perspective,* Promilla and Co., New Delhi, 2007.

Sondhi, M.L. and Kapur, Ashok, *US and India: Changing Strategic Parameters,* Manak, Delhi, 2002.

Sondhi, M.L. and Tyagi, K.G, eds., *India in the New Asia-Pacific,* Manas, New Delhi, 2001.

Sondhi, M.L. and Tyagi, K.G., eds., *Asia-Pacific: Security, Globalisation and Development,* Manas, New Delhi, 2001.

Sood, V.K. and Sawhney, *Operation Parakram: The War unfinished*, New Delhi, 2003.

Srivastava, Dhiraj, *India's Foreign Policy,* ABD Pub., Jaipur, 2007.

Sulaiman, Naushad Anwar, *India, Germany and European Union: Partners in Progress and Prosperity,* Kalinga, Delhi, 2002.

Swami Parveen, *The Kargil War*, New Delhi, 1999.

Talbott, Strobe, *Engaging India: Diplomacy, Democracy and the Bomb*, Brooking Institution Press, Washington 2004.

Tellis, Ashley J., *India's Emerging Nuclear Posture: Between Recessed Deterrent and Ready Arsenal,* RAND, Santa Monica, 2001.

Tiwari, Sanjeev Kumar, *Indian Ocean Rim-Association for Regional Cooperation (IOR-ARC): Problems and Prospects,* Abhijeet Pub., Delhi, 2004.

Upadhyay, S.S., *India and Sri Lanka: Economic and Political Relations,* ABD Pub., Jaipur, 2007.

Upadhyaya, Chandralekha, *India's Foreign Policy: A Study in South Asian Perspective,* Independent Pub., Delhi, 2003.

Varma, Shanta Nedungadi, *Foreign Policy Dynamics: Moscow and India's International Conflicts,* 1999.

Vivekanandan, B and Giri, D.K., eds., *Contemporary Europe and South Asia,* Concept, New Delhi, 2001.

Wadhva, Charan D. and Woo, Yuen Pau, eds., *Asian Regionalism: Canadian and Indian Perspectives,* A.P.H., New Delhi, 2005.

Winters, L. Alan and Yusuf Shahid, *Dancing with Giants: China, India and Global Economy*, World Bank, 2007.

Wulbers, Shazia Aziz, ed., *EU India Relations: A Critique,* Academic Foundations, New Delhi, 2008.

Yadav, R.S., ed., *India's Foreign Policy Towards 2000 A.D.*, New Delhi, Deep & Deep, 1993.

Yadav, R.S., *Bharat Ki Videsh Niti: Ek Vishleshan*, Kitab Mahal, Allahabad, 2005.

ARTICLES

Adhikari, Gautan, "India and America: Estranged No More," *Current History,* April 2004.

Alam, B. Mohammed, "Relations between Japan and India in the New Millennium," *World Affairs*, vol.8, no.1, 2007.

Bajpai, K.Shankar, "Untangling India and Pakistan," *Foreign Affairs,* May-June2003.

Bhagwat, Vishnu, "Global Oil Resources and India's Energy Strategy," *World Affairs*, vol.8, no.4, 2007.

Brar, Bhupender, "South Asia: A Region of States or Region of Regions," *South Asian Survey*, 6 (1), Jan-June 1999.

Broadman, Harry G., "China and India Go to Africa," *Foreign Affairs,* March-April 2008.

Burns, R. Nicholas, "America's Strategic Opportunity with India: The New US-India Partnership," *Foreign Affairs,* November-December 2006.

Buzan, Barry, "South Asia Moving Towards Transformation: Emergence of India as a Great Power," *International Studies,* vol.39, February 2002.

Carter, Ashton B., "America's New Strategic Partner?" *Foreign Affairs*, July-August 2006.

Das, Gurcharan, "The India Model," *Foreign Affairs,* July-August 2006.

Drezner, Daniel W., "The New New World Order," *Foreign Affairs*, March-April 2007.

Ganguly, Sumit, "Will Kashmir Stop India's Rise?" *Foreign Affairs,* July-August 2006.

Graver, John W., "Sino-Indian Rapprochement and the Sino-Pakistan Entente," *Political Science Quarterly,* vol.111, no.2, Summer 1996.

Guihong, Zhang, "US-India Strategic Partnership: Implications for China," *International Studies,* vol.42, October 2005.

Gujral, I.K., "Asia in the Contemporary World," *World Affairs*, vol.7, no.4, 2006.

Hoge, James F. Jr., "A Global Power Shift in the Making," *Foreign Affairs*, July-August 2004.

Imam, Zafar, "OIC and the Kashmir Issue: Options for India," *International Studies,* vol.39, May 2002.

"Indo-Russia Strategic Partnership for Enhanced Cooperation," *Strategic Digest*, 30 (11) November 2000.

Kaushik, Devendra, " The New Geopolitics of Central Asia: Russia, China and India," *Asia Annual 2000,* Shipra, New Delhi, 2000.

__________, "Commonwealth of Independent States and India," *International Studies,* 30 (2), April-June 1993.

__________, "India-Russia Relations: New Prospects," *World Focus*, 24 (1), January 2003.

Kirshnar, Jonathan, "Globalization, American Power and International Security," *Political Science Quarterly*, vol.123, no.3, Fall 2008.

Luthra, Girish, "Globalisation and Unipolarity: Walking the Tightrope," *World Affairs*, vol.7, no.3, 2007.

Mahapatra, Chintamani, "India, China and Russia: Strategic Triangle is Possible," *Strategic Analysis*, 22 (11), February 1999.

Milhollin, Gray, " The US-India Nuclear Pact: Bad for Security," *Current History*, November 2006.

Mistry, Dinshaw and Ganguly, Sumit, "The US-India Nuclear Pact: A Good Deal," *Current History*, November 2006.

Mohan, C. Raja, "India and the Balance of Power," *Foreign Affairs*, July-August 2006.

Muni, S.D. and Mohan, C. Raja, " Emerging Asia: India's Options," *International Studies*, vol.41, August 2004.

Ollapally, Deepa and Ramanna, Raja, "US-India Tensions: Misperceptions on Nuclear Proliferation," *Foreign Affairs*, January-February 1995.

Pant, Harsh V., "Feasibility of the Russia-China-India Strategic Triangle: Assessment of Theoretical and Empirical Issues," *International Studies*, vol.43, January 2006.

Pant, Harsh V., "The Demise of the Global Arms Control Regime: A role for India," *Asian Affairs*, Issue 24, 2004.

Percy, Charles H., "South Asia's Take-Off," *Foreign Affairs*, Winter 1992-93.

Potter, William C., "India and the New Look of US Nonproliferation Policy," *The Nonproliferation Review*, vol.12, Issue2, July 2005.

Pradhan, Bansidhar, "Changing Dynamics of India's West Asia Policy," *International Studies*, vol.41, February 2004.

Rana, A.P., "New Directions in the Study of SAARC: Evaluating the Basis of Regional Cooperation in South Asia," *South Asian Survey*, 10 (1), Jan-June 2003.

Rudnitsky, Artem, "Russia and India: In Search of New Strategy," *World Affairs*, 3 (2), Aprol-June 1999.

Ruisheng, Cheng, " Area of Possible Cooperation Between China, Russia and India," *China Report*, 38 (1), Jan-March 2002.

Scott, David, "Strategic Imperatives of India as an Emerging Player in Pacific Affairs," *International Studies*, vol.44, April 2007.

Singh, Jaswant, Against Nuclear Apartheid," *Foreign Affairs*, September-October 1998.

Sundararaman, Shankari, "Politics and Security in South-East Asia: Prospects for India-ASEAN Cooperation," *International Studies*, vol.41, October 2004.

Thakur, Ramesh, "India in the World: Neither rich, Powerful nor Principled," *Foreign Affairs*, July-August 1997.

Yadav, R.S., "Trends in the Studies of India's foreign Policy", *International Studies*, 30(1), January - March 1993.

__________, "NAM in the New World Order", *India Quarterly*, 49(3), July-September 1993.

__________," Indo-CIS Relations: Problems and Prospects", *Strategic Analysis*, 16(7), October 1993.

__________,"India's Role in the UN Peace -Keeping", *World Focus*, 18(214-215-216), October- December 1997(Annual number).

__________," India and the Central Asian Republics", *World Focus*, 20(238-239-240), October- December 1999 (Annual number).

__________,"Changing India-Japan Relations in the Post-Cold War Era", *India Quarterly*, 58(2), April- June, 2002.

__________,"Globalization and India's Foreign Policy", *Scolarie*, University of Kota, Kota, 2006.

__________, "Recent Changes in Asia and its Implications for India's Foreign Policy", in *Proceedings of the 14thInternational Symposium on Asian Studies, 1992,* Asian Research Centre, Hong Kong, 1994, Vol.5.

__________,"Contemporary Non-Proliferation Regime and South Asia: A Study of India's Response to CTBT" in Gopal Singh, ed., *South Asia: Democracy, Discontent and Societal Conflicts,* Anamika, New Delhi, 1998.

__________, "India and the Central Asian Republics: Challenges and Opportunities", in *B.G. Gafurov: Dialogue of Cultures and Civilizations,* Embassies of India and Tajikistan in the Russian Federation, Moscow, 2000.

__________," India-Australia Relations in the Post-Cold War Era" in Santosh Sareen, et al, eds., *Cultural Interfaces,* Indialog, New Delhi, 2004.

__________, "India-Russia Strategic Partners: Implications for Common Security of Asia" in Mahavir Singh, ed., *Building A New Asia,* Shipra, New Delhi, 2005.

__________,"Emerging India-China Relations and Bandung Spirit", *Political Science Review*, 36 (1&2), 2007.

__________, "Globalization and Foreign Economic Policy of India: A Study of Foreign Direct Investment" in Bhupinder Brar, et al, eds., *Globalization and the Politics of Identity in India*, Pearson, New Delhi, 2008.

__________, "India's Foreign Policy in the Changing World" in Anand Mathur and Sohan Lal Meena, eds., *India's Profile in Polycentric World Order,* R.B. S. A., Jaipur, 2008.

Yadav, R.S. and Dhanda, Suresh, "Oil Politics of Caspian Sea and Central Asia: Policy Options for India" *Contemporary Central Asia*, Vol. X, No.2, August 2006.

__________, "Nuclear Weapons and Security of States: A South Asian Dilemma" in S.K.Chaturvedi, et al., eds., *Human Development in South Asia in 21st Century*, Radha, New Delhi, 2008.

Contributors

Devendra Kaushik, Former Chairman, Executive Council, Maulana Abul Kalam Azad Institute of Asian Studies, Kolkata; and Former Professor, Centre for Russian and Central Asian Studies, School of International Studies, Jawaharlal Nehru University, New Delhi-110067.

R.S. Yadav, Professor & Chairman, Department of Political Science, Kurukshetra University. Director, Gandhian Study Centre in the Department and Director, Mahatima Gandhi All India Services Coaching Institute, Kurukshetra-136 119.

Chintamani Mahapatra, Professor and Chairman, Centre for US, Canada and Latin American Studics, School of International Studies, Jawaharlal Nehru University, New Delhi-110067.

Roop Singh Bareth, Professor and Chairman, Department of Political Science, University of Rajasthan, Jaipur-302004.

Savita Pande, Associate Professor, South Asian Studies Division, School of International Studies, Jawaharlal Nehru University, New Delhi-110067.

Udai Bhanu Singh, Research Officer, Institute for Defence Studies and Analyses, New Delhi-110010.

Baljit Singh, Reader, Department of Political Science, University of Jammu, Jammu Tawi-180006.

Rajendra K. Jain, Professor, Centre for West European Studies, School of International Studies, Jawaharlal Nehru University, New Delhi-110067.

Ashok Kumar, Lecturer, Post-Graduate Department of Political Science, RKSD (PG) College, Kaithal-132027, Haryana.

Suman Sharma, Department of Political Science, Moti Lal Nehru College, University of Delhi, Delhi-110021.

Kulwant Kaur, Professor and Chairman, Department of Political Science and Dean, Faculty of Social Sciences, University of Jammu, Jammu Tawi-180006.

Rajpal Budania, Reader, Department of Political Science, University of Allahabad, Allahabad-211002.

Suresh Dhanda, Head, Department of Political Science, S.A. Jain (P.G.) College, Ambala City-134003, Haryana.

Ajay Singh Manhas, Research Scholar, Department of Political Science, University of Jammu, Jammu Tawi-180006.

Anand P. Mavalankar, Professor, Department of Political Science, M.S. University, Vadodara-390001.

Anand Mathur, Professor and Chairperson, Department of Political Science, and Dean, Faculty of Arts, Education and Social Sciences, Jai Narain Vyas University, Jodhpur-342005, Rajasthan.

Ram Niwas Beniwal, Lecturer, Department of Political Science, Government College, Safidon-126112, Haryana.

Index